Lecture Notes in Computer Science   9688

Commenced Publication in 1973
Founding and Former Series Editors:
Gerhard Goos, Juris Hartmanis, and Jan van Leeuwen

Editorial Board

More information about this series at http://www.springer.com/series/7408

Elvira Albert · Ivan Lanese (Eds.)

Formal Techniques for Distributed Objects, Components, and Systems

36th IFIP WG 6.1 International Conference, FORTE 2016
Held as Part of the 11th International Federated Conference
on Distributed Computing Techniques, DisCoTec 2016
Heraklion, Crete, Greece, June 6–9, 2016
Proceedings

Springer

Editors
Elvira Albert
Complutense University of Madrid
Madrid
Spain

Ivan Lanese
University of Bologna/INRIA
Bologna
Italy

ISSN 0302-9743   ISSN 1611-3349   (electronic)
Lecture Notes in Computer Science
ISBN 978-3-319-39569-2   ISBN 978-3-319-39570-8   (eBook)
DOI 10.1007/978-3-319-39570-8

Library of Congress Control Number: 2016939908

LNCS Sublibrary: SL2 – Programming and Software Engineering

Printed on acid-free paper

This Springer imprint is published by Springer Nature
The registered company is Springer International Publishing AG Switzerland

Foreword

The 11th International Federated Conference on Distributed Computing Techniques (DisCoTec) took place at Aquila Atlantis Hotel in Heraklion, Greece, during June 6–9, 2016. It was organized by the Institute of Computer Science of the Foundation for Research and Technology – Hellas and the University of Ioannina, Greece. The DisCoTec series is one of the major events sponsored by the International Federation for Information Processing (IFIP). It comprises three conferences:

- COORDINATION, the IFIP WG 6.1 International Conference on Coordination Models and Languages
- DAIS, the IFIP WG 6.1 International Conference on Distributed Applications and Interoperable Systems
- FORTE, the IFIP WG 6.1 International Conference on Formal Techniques for Distributed Objects, Components and Systems

Together, these conferences cover a broad spectrum of distributed computing subjects, ranging from theoretical foundations and formal description techniques to systems research issues.

Each day of the federated event began with a plenary speaker nominated by one of the conferences. The three invited speakers were Tim Harris (Oracle Labs, UK), Catuscia Palamidessi (Inria, France), and Vijay Saraswat (IBM T.J. Watson Research Center, USA).

Associated with the federated event were also two satellite workshops, that took place during June 8–9, 2016:

- The 9th Workshop on Interaction and Concurrency Experience (ICE) with keynote lectures by Uwe Nestmann (Technische Universität Berlin, Germany) and Alexandra Silva (University College London, UK)
- The Final Public Workshop from the LeanBigData and CoherentPaaS projects

Sincere thanks go to the chairs and members of the Program and Steering Committees of the involved conferences and workshops for their highly appreciated efforts. Organizing DisCoTec 2016 was only possible thanks to the dedicated work of the Organizing Committee, including George Baryannis (Publicity Chair) and Vincenzo Gulisano (Workshops Chair), with excellent support from Nikos Antonopoulos and Alkis Polyrakis of PCO-Convin. Finally, many thanks go to IFIP WG 6.1 for sponsoring this event, to Springer *Lecture Notes in Computer Science* for their support and sponsorship, and to EasyChair for providing the refereeing infrastructure.

April 2016   Kostas Magoutis

Preface

This volume contains the papers presented at FORTE 2016, the 36th IFIP International Conference on Formal Techniques for Distributed Objects, Components and Systems. This conference was organized as part of the 11th International Federated Conference on Distributed Computing Techniques (DisCoTec) and was held during June 5–7, 2016 in Heraklion (Greece).

The FORTE conference series represents a forum for fundamental research on theory, models, tools, and applications for distributed systems. The conference encourages contributions that combine theory and practice, and that exploit formal methods and theoretical foundations to present novel solutions to problems arising from the development of distributed systems. FORTE covers distributed computing models and formal specification, testing, and verification methods. The application domains include all kinds of application-level distributed systems, telecommunication services, Internet, embedded, and real-time systems, as well as networking and communication security and reliability.

The conference received 44 submissions of authors from 21 countries. All full papers were reviewed by at least three members of the Program Committee. After careful deliberations, the Program Committee selected 18 papers for presentation. In addition to these papers, this volume contains an abstract of the invited talk by an outstanding researcher, Catuscia Palamidessi, on "Verifying Generalized Differential Privacy in Concurrent Systems."

The conference would not have been possible without the enthusiasm and dedication of the general chair, Kostas Magoutis (University of Ioannina, Greece), and the support of the Organizing Committee with George Baryannis (University of Huddersfield, UK) and Vincenzo Gulisano (Chalmers University of Technology, Sweden). For the work of the Program Committee and the compilation of the proceedings, the EasyChair system was employed; it freed us from many technical matters and allowed us to focus on the program, for which we are grateful. Conferences like FORTE rely on the willingness of experts to serve in the Program Committee; their professionalism and their helpfulness were exemplary. Finally, we would like to thank all the authors for their submissions, their willingness to continue improving their papers, and their presentations!

April 2016

Elvira Albert
Ivan Lanese

Organization

Program Committee

Erika Abraham	RWTH Aachen University, Germany
Gul Agha	University of Illinois at Urbana-Champaign, USA
Elvira Albert	Complutense University of Madrid, Spain
Ahmed Bouajjani	LIAFA, University Paris Diderot, France
Frank De Boer	CWI, The Netherlands
Lars-Ake Fredlund	Universidad Politécnica de Madrid, Spain
David Frutos Escrig	Universidad Complutense de Madrid, Spain
Stefania Gnesi	ISTI-CNR, Italy
Kim Guldstrand Larsen	Aalborg University, Denmark
Bart Jacobs	Katholieke Universiteit Leuven, Belgium
Einar Broch Johnsen	University of Oslo, Norway
Ivan Lanese	University of Bologna, Italy, and Inria, France
Antónia Lopes	University of Lisbon, Portugal
Hernan Melgratti	Universidad de Buenos Aires, Argentina
Massimo Merro	University of Verona, Italy
Peter Olveczky	University of Oslo, Norway
Luca Padovani	Università di Torino, Italy
Anna Philippou	University of Cyprus
Arnd Poetzsch-Heffter	University of Kaiserslautern, Germany
Kostis Sagonas	Uppsala University, Sweden
Alexandra Silva	University College London, UK
Jean-Bernard Stefani	Inria, France
Emilio Tuosto	University of Leicester, UK
Mahesh Viswanathan	University of Illinois, Urbana-Champaign, USA

Additional Reviewers

Abdoullah, Houssam	Brunnlieb, Malte
Akkoorath, Deepthi	Charalambides, Minas
Akshay, S.	Chatain, Thomas
Alborodo, Raul Nestor Neri	Cruz-Filipe, Luís
Aronis, Stavros	De Gouw, Stijn
Azadbakht, Keyvan	Fábregas, Ignacio
Basile, Davide	Jensen, Peter Gjøl
Benac Earle, Clara	Lang, Frederic
Bezirgiannis, Nikolaos	Lange, Julien
Bliudze, Simon	Lienhardt, Michael

Löscher, Andreas
Mariegaard, Anders
Mariño, Julio
Marti-Oliet, Narciso
Mathur, Umang
Mauro, Jacopo
Meyer, Roland
Mikučionis, Marius
Montenegro, Manuel
Nyman, Ulrik
Palmskog, Karl
Petri, Gustavo
Pichon, Jean
Rodriguez, Ismael

Roohi, Nima
Rubio, Albert
Sammartino, Matteo
Sandur, Atul
Semini, Laura
Stumpf, Johanna Beate
Suzuki, Tomoyuki
Taankvist, Jakob Haahr
Tamarit, Salvador
Tiezzi, Francesco
Toninho, Bernardo
Van Glabbeek, Rob
Weber, Mathias
Zeller, Peter

Verifying Generalized Differential Privacy in Concurrent Systems
(Abstract of Invited Talk)

Catuscia Palamidessi

INRIA Saclay and LIX, École Polytechnique

Privacy is a broad concept affecting a variety of modern-life activities. As a consequence, during the last decade there has been a vast amount of research on techniques to protect privacy, such as communication anonymisers [8], electronic voting systems [7], Radio-Frequency Identification (RFID) protocols [12] and private information retrieval schemes [6], to name a few.

In recent years, a new framework for privacy, called *differential privacy* (DP) has become increasingly popular in the area of statistical databases [9–11]. The idea is that, first, the access to the data should be allowed only through a query-based interface. Second, it should not be possible for the adversary to *distinguish*, from the answer to the query, whether a *certain individual is present or not* in the database. Formally, the *likelihood* of obtaining a certain answer should not change too much (i.e., more than a factor e^ϵ, where ϵ is a parameter) when the individual joins (or leaves) the database. This is achieved by adding *random noise* to the answer, resulting in a trade-off between the privacy of the mechanism and the utility of the answer: the stronger privacy we wish to achieve, the more the answer needs to be perturbed, thus the less useful it is. One of the important features of DP is that it does not depend on the side information available to the adversary. Related to this, another important advantage is that DP is robust with respect to composition attacks: by combining the results of several queries, the level of privacy of every mechanism necessarily decreases, but with DP it declines in a controlled way. This is a feature that can only be achieved with randomized mechanisms: With deterministic methods, such as *k-anonymity* [13, 14], composition attacks may be catastrophic.

DP has proved to be a solid foundation for privacy in statistical databases. Various people have also tried to extend it to other domains. The problem is that DP assumes that the disclosed information is produced by aggregating the data of multiple individuals. However, many privacy applications involve only a single individual, making differential privacy inapplicable.

In our team, we have addressed this issue by defining an extended DP framework in which the indistinguishability requirement is based on an arbitrary notion of distance (d_x-privacy, [3]). In this way we can naturally express (protection against) privacy threats that cannot be represented with the standard notion, leading to new applications of the differential privacy framework. In particular, we have explored applications in

---

This work is partially supported by the Large Scale Initiative CAPPRIS.

geolocation [1, 2] and smart metering [3]. In the context of geolocation, the problem of the correlated data becomes particularly relevant when we consider traces, which usually are composed of a large amount of highly related points. We addressed this issue using *prediction functions* [5], obtaining encouraging results.

Another shortcoming of the current approaches to privacy is that they are only applicable when the public information is well delimited and acquired in finite in time. Unfortunately, in most situation the source of public information is not necessarily bound, and some additional information can always be revealed in the future. At present, there are no techniques to verify privacy guarantees in situations in which the revelation of public information is not bound in time. This is a serious limitation, especially given that most of the systems which we use nowadays have an interactive nature, and usually are not under the control of the user.

In our team, we have started exploring a possible approach to this problem by defining a generalized version of the bisimulation distance based on the Kantorovich metric [4]. The standard Kantorovich lifting is based on an additive notion of distance, hence it is not suitable to capture d_x-privacy, that, like differential privacy, is inherently multiplicative. In contrast, our framework generalizes the Kantorovich lifting to arbitrary distances, and can therefore be applied also to d_x-privacy.

We show that the standard results extend smoothly to the generalized case, and that a bound on the generalized bisimulation distance is also a bound for the distance on traces, which guarantees the soundness of the method for proving DP. Furthermore, we provide an efficient method to compute it based on a dual form of the Kantorovich lifting. Finally, we explore an Hennessy-Milner-like logical characterization of our bisimulation distance, and we show how it can be use for reasoning about DP.

References

1. Andrés, M.E., Bordenabe, N.E., Chatzikokolakis, K., Palamidessi, C.: Geo-indistinguishability: differential privacy for location-based systems. In: Proceedings of the 20th ACM Conference on Computer and Communications Security (CCS 2013), pp. 901–914. ACM, New York (2013)
2. Bordenabe. N.E., Chatzikokolakis, N., Palamidessi, C.: Optimal geo-indistinguishable mechanisms for location privacy. In: Proceedings of the 21th ACM Conference on Computer and Communications Security (CCS 2014) (2014)
3. Chatzikokolakis, K., Andrés, M.E., Bordenabe, N.E., Palamidessi, C.: Broadening the scope of differential privacy using metrics. In: De Cristofaro, E., Wright, M. (eds.) PETS 2013, LNCS, vol. 7981, pp. 82–102. Springer, Heidelberg (2013)
4. Chatzikokolakis, K., Gebler, D., Palamidessi, C., Xu, L.: Generalized bisimulation metrics. In: Baldan, P., Gorla, D. (eds.) CONCUR 2014, LNCS, vol. 8704, pp. 32–46. Springer, Heidelberg (2014)
5. Chatzikokolakis, K., Palamidessi, C., Stronati, M.: A predictive differentially-private mechanism for mobility traces. In: De Cristofaro, E., Murdoch, S.J. (eds.) PETS 2014, LNCS, vol. 8555, pp. 21–41. Springer, Heidelberg (2014)

6. Chor, B., Goldreich, O., Kushilevitz, E., Sudan, M.: Private information retrieval. In: Proceedings of 36th Annual Symposium on Foundations of Computer Science, pp. 41–50. IEEE (1995)
7. Delaune, S., Kremer, S., Ryan, M.: Verifying privacy-type properties of electronic voting protocols. J. Comput. Secur. **17**(4), 435–487 (2009)
8. Dingledine, R., Mathewson, N., Syverson, P.F.: Tor: the second-generation onion router. In: Proceedings of the 13th USENIX Security Symposium, pp. 303–320. USENIX, (2004)
9. Dwork, C.: Differential privacy. In: Bugliesi, M., Preneel, B., Sassone, V., Wegener, I. (eds.) CALP 2006, Part II, LNCS, vol. 4052, pp. 1–12. Springer, Heidelberg (2006)
10. Dwork, C.: A firm foundation for private data analysis. Commun. ACM, **54**(1), 86–96 (2011)
11. Dwork, C., Lei, J.: Differential privacy and robust statistics. In: Mitzenmacher, M. (ed.) Proceedings of the 41st Annual ACM Symposium on Theory of Computing (STOC), Bethesda, MD, USA, May 31 – June 2, pp. 371–380. ACM (2009)
12. Juels, A.: Rfid security and privacy: a research survey. IEEE J. Sel. Areas Commun. **24**(2), 381–394 (2006)
13. Samarati, P.: Protecting respondents' identities in microdata release. IEEE Trans. Knowl. Data Eng. **13**(6), 1010–1027 (2001)
14. Samarati, P., Sweeney, L.: Generalizing data to provide anonymity when disclosing information (abstract). In: Proceedings of the ACM SIGACT–SIGMOD–SIGART Symposium on Principles of Database Systems, Seattle, Washington, June 1–3, 1998, p. 188. ACM Press (1998)

Contents

On the Power of Attribute-Based Communication

Yehia Abd Alrahman[1]([⊠]), Rocco De Nicola[1], and Michele Loreti[2]

[1] IMT School for Advanced Studies Lucca, Lucca, Italy
yehia.abdalrahman@imtlucca.it
[2] Università degli Studi di Firenze, Florence, Italy

Abstract. In open systems exhibiting adaptation, behaviors can arise as side effects of intensive components interaction. Finding ways to understand and design these systems, is a difficult but important endeavor. To tackle these issues, we present AbC, a calculus for attribute-based communication. An AbC system consists of a set of parallel agents each of which is equipped with a set of attributes. Communication takes place in an implicit multicast fashion, and interactions among agents are dynamically established by taking into account "connections" as determined by predicates over the attributes of agents. First, the syntax and the semantics of the calculus are presented, then expressiveness and effectiveness of AbC are demonstrated both in terms of modeling scenarios featuring collaboration, reconfiguration, and adaptation and of the possibility of encoding channel-based interactions and other interaction patterns. Behavioral equivalences for AbC are introduced for establishing formal relationships between different descriptions of the same system.

1 Introduction

In a world of *Internet of Things* (IoT), of *Systems of Systems* (SoS), and of *Collective Adaptive Systems* (CAS), most of the concurrent programming models still rely on communication primitives based on point-to-point, multicast with explicit addressing (i.e. IP multicast [13]), or on broadcast communication. In our view, it is important to consider alternative basic interaction primitives and in this paper we study the impact of a new paradigm that permits selecting groups of partners by considering the (predicates over the) attributes they expose.

The findings we report in this paper have been triggered by our interest in CAS, see e.g. [10], and the recent attempts to define appropriate linguistic primitives to deal with such systems, see e.g. TOTA [17], SCEL [7] and the calculi presented in [3,28]. CAS consists of large numbers of interacting components which exhibit complex behaviors depending on their attributes and objectives. Decision-making is complex and interaction between components may lead to

This research has been partially supported by the European projects IP 257414 ASCENS and STReP 600708 QUANTICOL, and by the Italian project PRIN 2010LHT4KM CINA.

E. Albert and I. Lanese (Eds.): FORTE 2016, LNCS 9688, pp. 1–18, 2016.
DOI: 10.1007/978-3-319-39570-8_1

unexpected behaviors. Components work in an open environment and may have different (potentially conflicting) objectives; so they need to dynamically adapt to their contextual conditions. New engineering techniques to address the challenges of developing, integrating, and deploying such systems are needed [26].

To move towards this goal, in our view, it is important to develop a theoretical foundation for this class of systems that would help in understanding their distinctive features. In this paper, we present AbC, a calculus comprising a minimal set of primitives that permit attribute-based communication. AbC systems are represented as sets of parallel components, each is equipped with a set of attributes whose values can be modified by internal actions. Communication actions (both send and receive) are decorated with predicates over attributes that partners have to satisfy to make the interaction possible. Thus, communication takes place in an implicit multicast fashion, and communication partners are selected by relying on predicates over the attributes in their interfaces. The semantics of output actions is non-blocking while input actions are blocking.

Many communication models addressing distributed systems have been introduced so far. Some of the well-known approaches include: channel-based models (e.g., CCS [18], CSP [12], π-calculus [20], etc.), group-based models [1,5,13], and publish/subscribe models [4,9]. The advantage of AbC over channel-based models is that interacting partners are anonymous to each other. Rather than agreeing on channels or names, they interact by relying on the satisfaction of predicates over their attributes. This makes AbC more suitable for modeling scalable distributed systems as anonymity is a key factor for scalability. Furthermore, the spaces (i.e., groups) in group-based models like Actorspace [1] are regarded as containers of actors and should be created and deleted with explicit constructs, while in AbC, there is no need for such constructs. The notion of *group* in AbC is quite abstract and can be specified by means of satisfying the sender's predicate at the time of interaction. On the other hand, the publish/subscribe model is a special case of AbC where publishers attach attributes to messages and send them with empty predicates (i.e., satisfied by all). Subscribers check the compatibility of the attached attributes with their subscriptions.

The concept of attribute-based communication can be exploited to provide a general unifying framework to encompass different communication models. Extended discussion for this paper can be found in the technical report in [2].

Contributions. (i) In Sects. 2 and 3, we present the AbC calculus, a refined and extended version of the one in [3]. The latter is a very basic calculus with a number of limitations, see Sect. 6 in [2]; (ii) we study the expressive power of AbC both in terms of the ability of modeling scenarios featuring collaboration, reconfiguration, and adaptation and of the possibility of modeling different interaction patterns, see Sect. 4; (iii) we define behavioral equivalences for AbC by first introducing a context based barbed congruence relation and then the corresponding extensional labelled bisimilarity, see Sect. 5; (iv) we show how to encode channel-based communication and prove the correctness of the encoding up to the introduced equivalence, see Sect. 6.

Table 1. The syntax of the AbC calculus

$$C ::= \Gamma{:}P \mid C_1\|C_2 \mid !C \mid \nu x C$$
$$P ::= 0 \mid \Pi(\tilde{x}).P \mid (\tilde{E})@\Pi.P \mid [\tilde{a} := \tilde{E}]P \mid \langle\Pi\rangle P \mid P_1 + P_2 \mid P_1|P_2 \mid K$$
$$\Pi ::= \text{tt} \mid \text{ff} \mid E_1 \bowtie E_2 \mid \Pi_1 \wedge \Pi_2 \mid \Pi_1 \vee \Pi_2 \mid \neg\Pi$$
$$E ::= v \mid x \mid a \mid this.a$$

2 The AbC Calculus

The syntax of the AbC calculus is reported in Table 1. The top-level entities of the calculus are *components* (C), a component consists of either a process P associated with an *attribute environment* Γ, denoted $\Gamma{:}P$, a parallel composition $C_1\|C_2$ of two components, a replication $!C$ which can always create a new copy of C. The *attribute environment* $\Gamma : \mathcal{A} \rightharpoonup \mathcal{V}$

Table 2. The predicate satisfaction

$\Gamma \models \text{tt}$	for all Γ
$\Gamma \models \text{ff}$	for no Γ
$\Gamma \models E_1 \bowtie E_2$	iff $\Gamma(E_1) \bowtie \Gamma(E_2)$
	where $\Gamma(v) = v$
$\Gamma \models \Pi_1 \wedge \Pi_2$	iff $\Gamma \models \Pi_1$ and $\Gamma \models \Pi_2$
$\Gamma \models \Pi_1 \vee \Pi_2$	iff $\Gamma \models \Pi_1$ or $\Gamma \models \Pi_2$
$\Gamma \models \neg\Pi$	iff not $\Gamma \models \Pi$

is a partial map from attribute identifiers $a \in \mathcal{A}$ to values $v \in \mathcal{V}$ where $\mathcal{A} \cap \mathcal{V} = \emptyset$. A value could be a number, a name (string), a tuple, etc. The scope of a name say n, can be restricted by using the restriction operator νn. For instance, the name n in $C_1 \| \nu n C_2$ is only visible within component C_2. Attribute values can be restricted while attribute identifiers[1] cannot, because they represent domain concepts. Each component in a system is aware of the set of attribute identifiers that represents the domain concepts.

A *process* is either the inactive process 0, an action-prefixed process $\bullet.P$ (where "$\bullet$" is replaced with an action), an attribute update process $[\tilde{a} := \tilde{E}]P$, an awareness process $\langle\Pi\rangle P$, a choice between two processes $P_1 + P_2$, a parallel composition between two processes $P_1|P_2$, or a recursive call K. We assume that each process has a unique process definition $K \triangleq P$. The attribute update construct in $[\tilde{a} := \tilde{E}]P$ sets the value of each attribute in the sequence $\tilde{a}$ to the evaluation of the corresponding expression in the sequence $\tilde{E}$.

The awareness construct in $\langle\Pi\rangle P$ is used to test awareness data about a component status or its environment by inspecting the local attribute environment where the process resides. This construct blocks the execution of process P until the predicate Π becomes true. The parallel operator "$|$" models the interleaving between processes. In what follows, we shall use the notation $[\![\Pi]\!]_\Gamma$ (resp. $[\![E]\!]_\Gamma$) to indicate the evaluation of a predicate Π (resp. an expression E) under the attribute environment Γ. The evaluation of a predicate consists of replacing variable references with their values and returns the result.

There are two kinds of *actions*: the attribute-based input $\Pi(\tilde{x})$ which binds to sequence $\tilde{x}$ the corresponding received values from components whose *communicated attributes* or values satisfy the predicate Π. The attribute-based output

---

[1] Occasionally, we will use "attribute" to denote "attribute identifier" in this paper.

$(\tilde{E})@\Pi$ which evaluates the sequence of expressions $\tilde{E}$ under the attribute environment Γ and then sends the result to the components whose attributes satisfy the predicate Π.

A *predicate* Π is either a binary operator $\bowtie$ between two values or a propositional combination of predicates. Predicate tt is satisfied by all components and is used when modeling broadcast while ff is not satisfied by any component and is used when modeling silent moves. The satisfaction relation $\models$ of predicates is presented in Table 2. In the rest of this paper, we shall use the relation $\simeq$ to denote a semantic equivalence for predicates as defined below.

Definition 1 (Predicate Equivalence). *Two predicates are semantically equivalent, written $\Pi_1 \simeq \Pi_2$, iff for every environment Γ, it holds that:*
$\Gamma \models \Pi_1$ *iff* $\Gamma \models \Pi_2$.

Clearly, the predicate equivalence, defined above, is decidable because we limit the expressive power of predicates by considering only standard boolean expressions and simple constraints on attribute values as shown in Table 2.

An *expression E* is either a constant value $v \in \mathcal{V}$, a variable x, an attribute identifier a, or a reference to a local attribute value this.a. The properties of *self-awareness* and *context-awareness* that are typical for CAS are guaranteed in AbC by referring to the values of local attributes via a special name this. (i.e., this.a). These values represent either the current status of a component (i.e., *self-awareness*) or the external environment (i.e., *context-awareness*). Expressions within predicates contain also variable names, so predicates can check whether the sent values satisfy specific conditions. This permits a sort of pattern-matching. For instance, component $\Gamma:(x > 2)(x, y)$ receives a sequence of values "x, y" from another component only if the value x is greater than 2.

We assume that processes are *closed*, and the constructs νx and $\Pi(\tilde{x})$ act as binders for names. We write $bn(P)$ to denote the set of bound names of P. The free names of P are those that do not occur in the scope of any binder and are denoted by $fn(P)$. The set of names of P is denoted by $n(P)$. The notions of bound and free names are applied in the same way to components, but free names also include attribute values that do not occur in the scope of any binder.

3   AbC Operational Semantics

The operational semantics of AbC is defined in two steps: first we define a component level semantics and then we define a system level semantics.

3.1   Operational Semantics of Component

We use the transition relation $\longmapsto \subseteq Comp \times CLAB \times Comp$ to define the local behavior of a component where $Comp$ denotes a component and $CLAB$ is the set of transition labels α generated by the following grammar:

$$\alpha ::= \lambda \ \mid \ \widetilde{\Pi(\tilde{v})} \qquad\qquad \lambda ::= \nu\tilde{x}\overline{\Pi}\tilde{v} \ \mid \ \Pi(\tilde{v})$$

Table 3. Component semantics

Brd $\dfrac{[\![\tilde{E}]\!]_\Gamma = \tilde{v} \quad [\![\Pi_1]\!]_\Gamma = \Pi}{\Gamma : (\tilde{E})@\Pi_1.P \xrightarrow{\overline{\Pi}\tilde{v}} \Gamma : P}$	**Rcv** $\dfrac{[\![\Pi[\tilde{v}/\tilde{x}]]\!]_\Gamma \simeq \mathsf{tt} \quad \Gamma \models \Pi'}{\Gamma : \Pi(\tilde{x}).P \xrightarrow{\Pi'(\tilde{v})} \Gamma : P[\tilde{v}/\tilde{x}]}$
Upd $\dfrac{[\![\tilde{E}]\!]_\Gamma = \tilde{v} \quad \Gamma[\tilde{a} \mapsto \tilde{v}] : P \xrightarrow{\lambda} \Gamma[\tilde{a} \mapsto \tilde{v}] : P'}{\Gamma : [\tilde{a} := \tilde{E}]P \xrightarrow{\lambda} \Gamma[\tilde{a} \mapsto \tilde{v}] : P'}$	**Aware** $\dfrac{[\![\Pi]\!]_\Gamma \simeq \mathsf{tt} \quad \Gamma : P \xrightarrow{\lambda} \Gamma' : P'}{\Gamma : \langle\Pi\rangle P \xrightarrow{\lambda} \Gamma' : P'}$
Sum $\dfrac{\Gamma : P_1 \xrightarrow{\lambda} \Gamma' : P_1'}{\Gamma : P_1 + P_2 \xrightarrow{\lambda} \Gamma' : P_1'}$	**Rec** $\dfrac{\Gamma : P \xrightarrow{\alpha} \Gamma' : P' \quad K \triangleq P}{\Gamma : K \xrightarrow{\alpha} \Gamma' : P'}$ **Int** $\dfrac{\Gamma : P_1 \xrightarrow{\lambda} \Gamma' : P_1'}{\Gamma : P_1\|P_2 \xrightarrow{\lambda} \Gamma' : P_1'\|P_2}$

The λ-labels are used to denote AbC output and input actions respectively. The output and input labels contain the sender's predicate Π, and the transmitted values $\tilde{v}$. An output is called "bound" if its label contains a bound name (i.e., if $\tilde{x} \neq \emptyset$). The α-labels include an additional label $\widetilde{\Pi(\tilde{v})}$ to denote the case where a process is not able to receive a message. This label is crucial to keep dynamic constructs (i.e., $+$) from dissolving after performing input refusal as it will be shown later in this section. Free names in α are specified as follows:

– $fn(\nu\tilde{x}\overline{\Pi}(\tilde{v})) = fn(\Pi(\tilde{v}))\backslash\tilde{x}$ and $fn(\Pi(\tilde{v})) = fn(\Pi) \cup \tilde{v}$
– $fn(\widetilde{\Pi(\tilde{v})}) = fn(\Pi) \cup \tilde{v}$.

The $fn(\Pi)$ denotes the set of names occurring in the predicate Π except for attribute identifiers. Notice that $\mathtt{this}.a$ is only a reference to the value of the attribute identifier a. Only the output label has bound names (i.e., $bn(\nu\tilde{x}\overline{\Pi}\tilde{v}) = \tilde{x}$).

Component Semantics. The set of rules in Table 3 describes the behavior of a single AbC component. We omitted the symmetric rules for **(Sum)** and **(Int)**.

Rule **(Brd)** evaluates the sequence of expressions $\tilde{E}$ to $\tilde{v}$ and the predicate Π_1 to Π by replacing any occurring reference (i.e., $\mathtt{this}.a$) to its value under Γ, sends this information in the message, and the process evolves to P.

Rule **(Rcv)** replaces the free occurrences of the input sequence variables $\tilde{x}$ in the receiving predicate Π with the corresponding message values $\tilde{v}$ and evaluates Π under Γ. If the evaluation semantically equals to tt and Γ satisfies the sender predicate Π', the input action is performed and the substitution $[\tilde{v}/\tilde{x}]$ is applied to the continuation process P. Rule **(Upd)** evaluates the sequence $\tilde{E}$ under Γ, apply attribute updates i.e., $\Gamma[\tilde{a} \mapsto \tilde{v}]$ where $\forall a \in \tilde{a}$ and $\forall v \in \tilde{v}$, $\Gamma[a \mapsto v](a') = \Gamma(a')$ if $a \neq a'$ and v otherwise, and then performs an action with a λ label if process P under the updated environment can do so.

Rule **(Aware)** evaluates the predicate Π under Γ. If the evaluation semantically equals to tt, process $\langle\Pi\rangle P$ proceeds by performing an action with a λ-label and continues as P' if process P can perform the same action.

Table 4. Discarding input

$$\textbf{FBrd} \quad \Gamma:(\tilde{E})@\Pi.P \xrightarrow{\widetilde{\Pi'(\tilde{v})}} \Gamma:(\tilde{E})@\Pi.P \qquad \textbf{FRcv} \quad \frac{[\![\Pi[\tilde{v}/\tilde{x}]]\!]_\Gamma \neq \text{tt} \ \lor \ (\Gamma \not\models \Pi')}{\Gamma:\Pi(\tilde{x}).P \xrightarrow{\widetilde{\Pi'(\tilde{v})}} \Gamma:\Pi(\tilde{x}).P}$$

$$\textbf{FUpd} \quad \frac{[\![\tilde{E}]\!]_\Gamma = \tilde{v} \quad \Gamma[\tilde{a} \mapsto \tilde{v}] : P \xrightarrow{\widetilde{\Pi(\tilde{w})}} \Gamma[\tilde{a} \mapsto \tilde{v}] : P}{\Gamma:[\tilde{a} := \tilde{E}]P \xrightarrow{\widetilde{\Pi(\tilde{w})}} \Gamma:[\tilde{a} := \tilde{E}]P} \qquad \textbf{FZero} \ \Gamma:0 \xrightarrow{\widetilde{\Pi(\tilde{v})}} \Gamma:0$$

$$\textbf{FAware1} \quad \frac{[\![\Pi]\!]_\Gamma \simeq \text{tt} \quad \Gamma:P \xrightarrow{\widetilde{\Pi'(\tilde{v})}} \Gamma:P}{\Gamma:\langle\Pi\rangle P \xrightarrow{\widetilde{\Pi'(\tilde{v})}} \Gamma:\langle\Pi\rangle P} \qquad \textbf{FAware2} \quad \frac{[\![\Pi]\!]_\Gamma \simeq \text{ff}}{\Gamma:\langle\Pi\rangle P \xrightarrow{\widetilde{\Pi'(\tilde{v})}} \Gamma:\langle\Pi\rangle P}$$

$$\textbf{FSum} \quad \frac{\Gamma:P_1 \xrightarrow{\widetilde{\Pi(\tilde{v})}} \Gamma:P_1 \quad \Gamma:P_2 \xrightarrow{\widetilde{\Pi(\tilde{v})}} \Gamma:P_2}{\Gamma:P_1 + P_2 \xrightarrow{\widetilde{\Pi(\tilde{v})}} \Gamma:P_1 + P_2} \qquad \textbf{FInt} \quad \frac{\Gamma:P_1 \xrightarrow{\widetilde{\Pi(\tilde{v})}} \Gamma:P_1 \quad \Gamma:P_2 \xrightarrow{\widetilde{\Pi(\tilde{v})}} \Gamma:P_2}{\Gamma:P_1|P_2 \xrightarrow{\widetilde{\Pi(\tilde{v})}} \Gamma:P_1|P_2}$$

Rule (**Sum**) and its symmetric version represent the non-deterministic choice between the subprocesses P_1 and P_2. Rule (**Rec**) is standard for process definition. Rule (**Int**) models the standard interleaving between two processes.

Discarding Input. The set of rules in Table 4 describes the meaning of the discarding label $\widetilde{\Pi(\tilde{v})}$. Rule (**FBrd**) states that any sending process discards messages from other processes and stays unchanged. Rule (**FRcv**) states that if one of the receiving requirements is not satisfied then the process will discard the message and stay unchanged.

Rule (**FUpd**) state that process $[\tilde{a} := \tilde{E}]P$ discards a message if process P is able to discard the same message after applying attribute updates. Rule (**FAware1**) states that process $\langle\Pi\rangle P$ discards a message even if Π evaluates to (tt) if process P is able to discard the same message. Rule (**FAware2**) states that if Π in process $\langle\Pi\rangle P$ evaluates to ff, process $\langle\Pi\rangle P$ discards any message from other processes.

Rule (**FZero**) states that process 0 always discards messages. Rule (**FSum**) states that process $P_1 + P_2$ discards a message if both its subprocesses P_1 and P_2 can do so. Notice that the choice and awareness constructs do not dissolve after input refusal. Rule (**FInt**) has a similar meaning of Rule (**FSum**).

3.2   Operational Semantics of System

AbC system describes the global behavior of a component and the underlying communication between different components. We use the transition relation $\longrightarrow \ \subseteq Comp \times SLAB \times Comp$ to define the behavior of a system where *Comp* denotes a component and *SLAB* is the set of transition labels γ which are generated by the following grammar:

$$\gamma ::= \nu\tilde{x}\overline{\Pi}\tilde{v} \ \mid \ \Pi(\tilde{v}) \ \mid \ \tau$$

The γ-labels extend λ with τ to denote silent moves. The τ-label has no free or bound names. The definition of the transition relation $\longrightarrow$ depends on

Table 5. System semantics

$$\text{Comp } \frac{\Gamma : P \xrightarrow{\lambda} \Gamma' : P'}{\Gamma : P \xrightarrow{\lambda} \Gamma' : P'} \qquad \text{C-Fail } \frac{\Gamma : P \xmapsto{\widetilde{\Pi(\tilde{v})}} \Gamma : P}{\Gamma : P \xrightarrow{\Pi(\tilde{v})} \Gamma : P} \qquad \text{Rep } \frac{C \xrightarrow{\gamma} C'}{!C \xrightarrow{\gamma} C' \| !C}$$

$$\tau\text{-Int } \frac{C_1 \xrightarrow{\nu \tilde{x}\overline{\Pi}\tilde{v}} C_1' \quad \Pi \simeq \text{ff}}{C_1 \| C_2 \xrightarrow{\tau} C_1' \| C_2} \qquad \text{Res } \frac{C[y/x] \xrightarrow{\gamma} C' \quad y \notin n(\gamma) \wedge y \notin fn(C)\backslash\{x\}}{\nu x C \xrightarrow{\gamma} \nu y C'}$$

$$\text{Sync } \frac{C_1 \xrightarrow{\Pi(\tilde{v})} C_1' \quad C_2 \xrightarrow{\Pi(\tilde{v})} C_2'}{C_1 \| C_2 \xrightarrow{\Pi(\tilde{v})} C_1' \| C_2'} \qquad \text{Com } \frac{C_1 \xrightarrow{\nu \tilde{x}\overline{\Pi}\tilde{v}} C_1' \quad C_2 \xrightarrow{\Pi(\tilde{v})} C_2' \quad \substack{\Pi \neq \text{ff} \\ \tilde{x} \cap fn(C_2) = \emptyset}}{C_1 \| C_2 \xrightarrow{\nu \tilde{x}\overline{\Pi}\tilde{v}} C_1' \| C_2'}$$

$$\text{Hide1 } \frac{C \xrightarrow{\nu \tilde{x}\overline{\Pi}\tilde{v}} C' \quad \substack{(\Pi \blacktriangleright y) \simeq \text{ff} \\ y \in n(\Pi)}}{\nu y C \xrightarrow{\nu \tilde{x}\overline{\text{ff}}\tilde{v}} \nu y \nu \tilde{x} C'} \qquad \text{Hide2 } \frac{C \xrightarrow{\nu \tilde{x}\overline{\Pi}\tilde{v}} C' \quad \substack{(\Pi \blacktriangleright y) \neq \text{ff} \\ y \in n(\Pi)}}{\nu y C \xrightarrow{\nu \tilde{x}\overline{\Pi \blacktriangleright y}\tilde{v}} \nu y C'}$$

$$\text{Open } \frac{C[y/x] \xrightarrow{\overline{\Pi}\tilde{v}} C' \quad \Pi \neq \text{ff} \quad y \in \tilde{v}\backslash n(\Pi) \wedge y \notin fn(C)\backslash\{x\}}{\nu x C \xrightarrow{\nu y \overline{\Pi}\tilde{v}} C'}$$

the definition of the relation $\longmapsto$ in the previous section in the sense that the effect of local behavior is lifted to the global one. The transition relation $\longrightarrow$ is formally defined in Table 5. We omitted the symmetric rules for τ-**Int** and **Com**.

Rule (**Comp**) states that the relations $\longmapsto$ and $\longrightarrow$ coincide when performing either an input or output action. Rule (**C-Fail**) states that any component $\Gamma : P$ can discard an input if its local process can do so. Rule (**Rep**) is standard for replication. Rule (τ-**Int**) models the interleaving between components C_1 and C_2 when performing a silent move (i.e., a send action $(\tilde{v})@\Pi$ with $\Pi \simeq \text{ff}$). In this paper, we will use ()@ff to denote a silent action/move.

Rule (**Res**) states that component $\nu x C$ with a restricted name x can still perform an action with a γ-label as long as x does not occur in the names of the label and component C can perform the same action. If necessary, we allow renaming with conditions to avoid name clashing.

Rule (**Sync**) states that two parallel components C_1 and C_2 can synchronize while performing an input action. This means that the same message is received by both C_1 and C_2. Rule (**Com**) states that two parallel components C_1 and C_2 can communicate if C_1 can send a message with a predicate that is different from ff and C_2 can possibly receive that message.

Rules (**Hide1**) and (**Hide2**) are peculiar to AbC and introduce a new concept that we call predicate restriction "$\bullet \blacktriangleright x$" as reported in Table 6. In process calculi with multiparty interaction like CSP [12] and $b\pi$-calculus [20], sending on a private channel is not observed. For example in $b\pi$-calculus, assume that $P = \nu a(P_1 \| P_2) \| P_3$ where $P_1 = \bar{a}v.Q$, $P_2 = a(x).R$, and $P_3 = b(x)$. Now if P_1 sends on a then only P_2 can observe it since P_2 is included in the scope of the restriction. P_3 and other processes only observe an internal action, so $P \xrightarrow{\tau} \nu a(Q \| R[v/x]) \| b(x)$.

This idea is generalized in AbC to what we call predicate restriction "$\bullet \blacktriangleright x$" in the sense that we either hide a part or the whole predicate using the predicate restriction operator "$\bullet \blacktriangleright x$" where x is a restricted name and the "$\bullet$" is replaced with a predicate. If the predicate restriction operator returns ff then we get the usual hiding operator like in CSP and $b\pi$-calculus because the resulting label is not exposed according to (τ-**Int**) rule (i.e., sending with a false predicate).

If the predicate restriction operator returns something different from ff then the message is exposed with a smaller predicate and the restricted name remains private. Note that any private name in the message values (i.e., $\tilde{x}$) remains private if $(\Pi \blacktriangleright y) \simeq$ ff as in rule (**Hide1**) otherwise it is not private anymore as in rule (**Hide2**). In other words, messages are sent on a channel that is partially exposed.

Table 6. Predicate restriction $\bullet \blacktriangleright x$

tt$\blacktriangleright x$	$=$	tt
ff$\blacktriangleright x$	$=$	ff
$(a = m)\blacktriangleright x$	$=$	$\begin{cases} \text{ff} & \text{if } x = m \\ a = m & \text{otherwise} \end{cases}$
$(\Pi_1 \wedge \Pi_2)\blacktriangleright x =$	$\Pi_1 \blacktriangleright x \ \wedge \ \Pi_2 \blacktriangleright x$	
$(\Pi_1 \vee \Pi_2)\blacktriangleright x =$	$\Pi_1 \blacktriangleright x \ \vee \ \Pi_2 \blacktriangleright x$	
$(\neg \Pi)\blacktriangleright x$	$=$	$\neg(\Pi \blacktriangleright x)$

For example, if a network sends a message with the predicate $(keyword = \text{this}.topic \vee capability = fwd)$ where the name "fwd" is restricted then the message is exposed to users at every node within the network with forwarding capability with this predicate $(keyword = \text{this}.topic)$. Network nodes observe the whole predicate but they receive the message only because they satisfy the other part of the predicate (i.e., $(capability = fwd)$). In the following Lemma, we prove that the satisfaction of a restricted predicate $\Pi \blacktriangleright x$ by an attribute environment Γ does not depend on the name x that is occurring in Γ.

Lemma 1. $\Gamma \models \Pi \blacktriangleright x$ iff $\forall v.\ \Gamma[v/x] \models \Pi \blacktriangleright x$ for any environment Γ, predicate Π, and name x.

Rule (**Open**) states that a component has the ability to communicate a private name to other components. The scope of the private name x only dissolves in the context where the rule is applied. Notice that, a component that is sending on a false predicate (i.e., $\Pi \simeq$ ff) cannot open the scope.

4   Expressiveness of AbC Calculus

In this section, we provide evidence of the expressive power of AbC by modeling systems featuring collaboration, adaptation, and reconfiguration and stress the possibility of using attribute-based communication as a unifying framework to encompass different communication models.

4.1   A Swarm Robotics Model in AbC

We consider a swarm of robots spreads in a given disaster area with the goal of locating and rescuing possible victims. All robots playing the same role execute the same code, defining their behavior, and a set of adaptation mechanisms, regulating the interactions among robots and their environments. Initially all robots are explorers and once a robot finds a victim, it changes its role to "rescuer" and sends victim's information to nearby explorers. if another robot receives this information, it changes its role to "helper" and moves to join the rescuers-swarm. Notice that some of the robot attributes are considered as the projection of the robot internal state that is monitored by sensors and actuators (i.e., *victimPerceived*, *position*, and *collision*).

We assume that each robot has a unique identity (*id*) and since the robot acquires information about its environment or its own status by means of reading the values provided by sensors, no additional assumptions about the initial state are needed. It is worth mentioning that sensors and actuators are not modeled here as they represent the robot internal infrastructure while AbC model represents the programmable behavior of the robot (i.e., its running code).

The robotics scenario is modeled as a set of parallel AbC components, each component represents a robot $(Robot_1 \| \ldots \| Robot_n)$ and each robot has the following form $(\Gamma_i : P_R)$. The behavior of a single robot is modeled in the following AbC process P_R:

$$P_R \triangleq (Rescuer + Explorer)| RandWalk$$

The robot follows a random walk in exploring the disaster arena. The robot can become a "Rescuer" when recognizing a victim by mean of locally reading the value of an attribute controlled by its sensors or stay as "explorer" and keep sending queries for information about the victim from nearby robots whose role is either "*rescuer*" or "*helper*".

If a victim is perceived (i.e., the value of "*victimPerceived* = tt", the robot updates its "*state*" to "*stop*" which triggers halting the movement, computes the victim position and the number of the required robots to rescue the victim and stores them in the attributes "*vPosition*" and "*count*" respectively, changes its role to "*rescuer*", and waits for queries from nearby explorers. Once a query is received, the robot sends back the victim information to the requesting robot addressing it by its identity "*id*" and the swarm starts forming.

$Rescuer \triangleq \langle \text{this}.victimPerceived = tt \rangle [\text{this}.state := stop, \text{this}.count := 3,$
$\qquad \text{this}.vPosition := <3, 4>, \text{this}.role := rescuer]()@\text{ff}.$
$\qquad (y = qry \land z = explorer)(x, y, z).$
$\qquad (\text{this}.vPosition, \text{this}.count, ack, \text{this}.role)@(id = x)$

If no victim is perceived, the robot keeps sending queries about victims to nearby robots whose role is either "rescuer" or "*helper*". This query contains the robot identity "*this.id*", a special name "*qry*" to indicate the request type, and the robot role "$\text{this}.role$". If an acknowledgement arrives containing victim's information, the robot changes its role to "*helper*" and start the helping procedure.

$Explorer \triangleq (\text{this}.id, qry, \text{this}.role)@(role = rescuer \lor role = helper).$
$\qquad (((z = rescuer \lor z = helper) \land x = ack)(vpos, c, x, z).$
$\qquad [\text{this}.role := helper]()@\text{ff}.Helper + Rescuer + Explorer)$

The helping robot stores the victim position in the attribute "*vPosition*" and updates its target to be the victim position. This triggers the actuators to move to the specified location. The robot waits until it reaches the victim and at the same time is willing to respond to other robots queries, if more than one robot is needed for the rescuing procedure. Once the robot reaches the victim, the robot changes its role to "*rescuer*" and joins the rescuer-swarm.

$$Helper \triangleq [\mathbf{this}.vPosition := vpos, \ \mathbf{this}.target := vpos]()@\mathsf{ff}.$$
$$(\langle \mathbf{this}.position = \mathbf{this}.target \rangle [\mathbf{this}.role := rescuer]()@\mathsf{ff}$$
$$| \ \langle c > 1 \rangle (y = qry \wedge z = explorer)(x, \ y, \ z).$$
$$(\mathbf{this}.vPosition, \ c - 1, \ ack, \ \mathbf{this}.role)@(id = x))$$

The "*RandWalk*" process is defined below. This process computes a random direction to be followed by the robot. Once a collision is detected by the proximity sensor, a new random direction is calculated.

$$RandWalk \triangleq [\mathbf{this}.direction := 2\pi rand()]()@\mathsf{ff}.$$
$$\langle \mathbf{this}.collision = \mathsf{tt} \rangle RandWalk$$

For more details, a runtime environment for the linguistic primitives of AbC can be found in the following website http://lazkany.github.io/AbC.

4.2   Encoding Interaction Patterns

In this section, we show how group-based [1,5,13] and publish/subscribe-based [4,9] interaction patterns can be naturally rendered in AbC. Since these interaction patterns do not have formal descriptions, we proceed by relying on examples.

We start with group-based interaction patterns and show that when modeling a group name as an attribute in AbC, the constructs for joining or leaving a given group can be modeled as attribute updates, see the following example:

$$\Gamma_1 : (msg, \ \mathbf{this}.group)@(group = a) \parallel \Gamma_2 : ((y = b)(x, \ y)) \parallel \dots$$
$$\parallel \ \Gamma_7 : ((y = b)(x, \ y) \ | \ [\mathbf{this}.group := a]()@\mathsf{ff})$$

initially $\Gamma_1(group) = b$, $\Gamma_2(group) = a$, and $\Gamma_7(group) = c$. Component 1 wants to send the message "*msg*" to group "*a*". Only Component 2 is allowed to receive it as it is the only member of group "*a*". If Component 7 leaves group "*c*" and joins group "*a*" before "*msg*" is emitted then both of Component 2 and Component 7 will receive the message.

A possible encoding of group interaction into $b\pi$-calculus has been introduced in [8]. The encoding is relatively complicated and does not guarantee the causal order of message reception. "Locality" is neither a first class construct in $b\pi$-calculus nor in AbC. However, "locality" (in this case, the group name) can be modeled as an attribute in AbC while in $b\pi$-calculus, it needs much more effort.

Publish/subscribe interaction patterns can be considered as special cases of the attribute-based ones. For instance, a natural modeling of the topic-based publish/subscribe model [9] into AbC can be accomplished by allowing publishers to broadcast messages with "tt" predicates (i.e., satisfied by all) and only subscribers can check the compatibility of the exposed publishers attributes with their subscriptions, see the following example:

$$\Gamma_1 : (msg,\ \text{this}.topic)@(\text{tt}) \parallel \Gamma_2 : (y = \text{this}.subscription)(x,\ y) \parallel$$
$$\dots \parallel \Gamma_n : (y = \text{this}.subscription)(x,\ y)$$

The publisher broadcasts the message "msg" tagged with a specific topic for all possible subscribers (the predicate "tt" is satisfied by all), subscribers receive the message if the topic matches their subscription.

5   Behavioral Theory for AbC

In this section, we define a behavioral theory for AbC. We start by introducing a barbed congruence, then we present an equivalent definition of bisimulation. In what follows, we shall use the following notations:

- $\Rightarrow$ denotes $\xrightarrow{\tau}^*$ where $\tau = \nu\tilde{x}\overline{\Pi}\tilde{v}$ with $\Pi \simeq \text{ff}$.
- $\xRightarrow{\gamma}$ denotes $\Rightarrow\xrightarrow{\gamma}\Rightarrow$ if $(\gamma \neq \tau)$.
- $\xRightarrow{\hat{\gamma}}$ denotes $\Rightarrow$ if $(\gamma = \tau)$ and $\xRightarrow{\gamma}$ otherwise.
- $\dashrightarrow$ denotes $\{\xrightarrow{\gamma} \mid \gamma$ is an output or $\gamma = \tau\}$ and $\dashrightarrow^*$ denotes $(\dashrightarrow)^*$.

A context $\mathcal{C}[\bullet]$ is a component term with a hole, denoted by $[\bullet]$ and AbC contexts are generated by the following grammar:

$$\mathcal{C}[\bullet] ::= [\bullet] \mid [\bullet]\|C \mid C\|[\bullet] \mid \nu x[\bullet] \mid ![\bullet]$$

Barbed Congruence. We define notions of strong and weak barbed congruence to reason about AbC components following the definition of maximum sound theory by Honda and Yoshida [14]. This definition is a slight variant of Milner and Sangiorgi's barbed congruence [21] and it is also known as open barbed bisimilarity [25].

Definition 2 (Barb). *A predicate Π^2 is observable (is a barb) in component C, denoted as $C{\downarrow}_\Pi$, if C can send a message with a predicate Π' (i.e., $C \xrightarrow{\nu\tilde{x}\overline{\Pi'}\tilde{v}}$ where $\Pi' \simeq \Pi$ and $\Pi' \neq \text{ff}$). We write $C{\Downarrow}_\Pi$ if $C \dashrightarrow^* C' {\downarrow}_\Pi$.*

Definition 3 (Barbed Congruence). *A symmetric relation $\mathcal{R}$ over the set of AbC components is a weak barbed congruence if whenever $(C_1, C_2) \in \mathcal{R}$,*

- *$C_1{\downarrow}_\Pi$ implies $C_2{\Downarrow}_\Pi$;*
- *$C_1 \dashrightarrow C_1'$ implies $C_2 \dashrightarrow^* C_2'$ and $(C_1', C_2') \in \mathcal{R}$;*
- *for all contexts $\mathcal{C}[\bullet]$, $(\mathcal{C}[c_1], \mathcal{C}[c_2]) \in \mathcal{R}$.*

---

[2] From now on, we use the predicate Π to denote only its meaning, not its syntax.

Two components are weak barbed congruent, written $C_1 \cong C_2$, if $(C_1, C_2) \in \mathcal{R}$ for some barbed congruent relation $\mathcal{R}$. The strong barbed congruence "$\simeq$" is obtained in a similar way by replacing $\Downarrow$ with $\downarrow$ and $\rightarrow^*$ with $\rightarrow$.

Bisimulation. We define an appropriate notion of bisimulation for AbC components and prove that bisimilarity coincides with barbed congruence, and thus represents a valid tool for proving that two components are barbed congruent.

Definition 4 (Weak Bisimulation). *A symmetric binary relation $\mathcal{R}$ over the set of* AbC *components is a weak bisimulation if for every action γ, whenever $(C_1, C_2) \in \mathcal{R}$ and γ is of the form $\tau, \Pi(\tilde{v})$, or $(\nu\tilde{x}\overline{\Pi}\tilde{v}$ with $\Pi \neq \mathrm{ff})$, it holds that:*

$$C_1 \xrightarrow{\gamma} C_1' \text{ implies } C_2 \xRightarrow{\hat{\gamma}} C_2' \text{ and } (C_1', C_2') \in \mathcal{R}$$

where every predicate Π occurring in γ is matched by its semantics meaning in $\hat{\gamma}$. Two components C_1 and C_2 are weak bisimilar, written $C_1 \approx C_2$ if there exists a weak bisimulation $\mathcal{R}$ relating them. Strong bisimilarity, "$\sim$", is defined in a similar way by replacing $\Rightarrow$ with $\rightarrow$.

Bisimilarity can be used as a reasoning tool and as a proof technique to compare systems at different levels of abstractions. For instance, the behavior of the robotic scenario in Sect. 4.1 can be compared with a centralized version where robots exchange information through a central node using an internet connection. Bisimilarity can also be used as a tool for state space reduction and minimization.

It is easy to prove that $\sim$ and $\approx$ are equivalence relations by relying on the classical arguments of [19]. However, our bisimilarity enjoys a much more interesting property: the closure under any context. So, in the next three lemmas, we prove that our bisimilarity is preserved by parallel composition, name restriction, and replication.

Lemma 2 ($\sim$ and $\approx$ are preserved by parallel composition). *Let C_1 and C_2 be two components, then*

- $C_1 \sim C_2$ *implies* $C_1 \| C \sim C_2 \| C$ *for all components C*
- $C_1 \approx C_2$ *implies* $C_1 \| C \approx C_2 \| C$ *for all components C.*

Lemma 3 ($\sim$ and $\approx$ are preserved by name restriction). *Let C_1 and C_2 be two components, then*

- $C_1 \sim C_2$ *implies* $\nu x C_1 \sim \nu x C_2$ *for all names x.*
- $C_1 \approx C_2$ *implies* $\nu x C_1 \approx \nu x C_2$ *for all names x.*

Lemma 4 ($\sim$ and $\approx$ are preserved by replication). *Let C_1 and C_2 be two components, then*

- $C_1 \sim C_2$ *implies* $!C_1 \sim !C_2$
- $C_1 \approx C_2$ *implies* $!C_1 \approx !C_2$.

As an immediate consequence of Lemmas 2, 3, and 4, we have that $\sim$ and $\approx$ are congruence relations (i.e., closed under any context). We are now ready to show that our bisimilarity represents a proof technique for establishing barbed congruence. The proofs follow in a standard way.

Theorem 1 (Soundness). *Let C_1 and C_2 be two components, then*

- $C_1 \sim C_2$ *implies* $C_1 \simeq C_2$
- $C_1 \approx C_2$ *implies* $C_1 \cong C_2$.

Lemma 5 (Completeness). *Let C_1 and C_2 be two components, then*

- $C_1 \simeq C_2$ *implies* $C_1 \sim C_2$
- $C_1 \cong C_2$ *implies* $C_1 \approx C_2$.

Theorem 2 (Characterization). *Bisimilarity and barbed congruence coincide.*

6   Encoding Channel-Based Interaction

The interaction primitives in AbC are purely based on attributes rather than explicit names or channels. Attribute values can be locally modified. Modifying attribute values introduces opportunistic interactions between components by means of changing the set of possible interaction partners. The reason is because selecting interaction partners depends on the predicates over attributes and this is why modeling adaptivity in AbC is quite natural. This possibility is missing in channel-based communication since internal actions and the opportunity of interaction are orthogonal in those models.

We argue that finding a compositional encoding for the following simple behavior is very difficult if not impossible in channel-based process calculi.

$$\Gamma_1 : (msg, \text{this}.b)@(\text{tt}) \parallel \Gamma_2 : ([\text{this}.a := 5]()@\text{ff}.P \mid (y \leq \text{this}.a)(x, y).Q)$$

Initially $\Gamma_1(b) = 3$ and $\Gamma_2(a) = 2$. Changing the value of the local attribute a to "5" by the left-hand side process in the second component provides an opportunity of receiving the message "msg" from the first component.

On the other hand, in channel-based communication, a channel instantly appears at the time of interaction and disappears afterwards. This feature is not present in AbC since attributes are persistent in the attribute environment and cannot disappear at any time. However, this is not

Table 7. Encoding bπ-calculus into AbC

(Component Level)

$(\!|G|\!)_c \triangleq \emptyset : (\!|G|\!)_p \qquad (\!|P\|Q|\!)_c \triangleq (\!|P|\!)_c \parallel (\!|Q|\!)_c$

$(\!|\nu x P|\!)_c \triangleq \nu x (\!|P|\!)_c$

(Process Level)

$(\!|\text{nil}|\!)_p \triangleq 0 \qquad (\!|\tau.G|\!)_p \triangleq ()@\text{ff}.(\!|G|\!)_p$

$(\!|a(\tilde{x}).G|\!)_p \triangleq \Pi(y, \tilde{x}).(\!|G|\!)_p$
  with $\Pi = (y = a)$ and $y \notin n((\!|G|\!)_p)$

$(\!|\bar{a}\tilde{x}.G|\!)_p \triangleq (a, \tilde{x})@(a = a).(\!|G|\!)_p$

$(\!|(rec\ A\langle \tilde{x} \rangle).G)\langle \tilde{y} \rangle|\!)_p \triangleq (A(\tilde{x}) \triangleq (\!|G|\!)_p)$
      where $fn((\!|G|\!)_p) \subseteq \{\tilde{x}\}$

$(\!|G_1 + G_2|\!)_p \triangleq (\!|G_1|\!)_p + (\!|G_2|\!)_p$

a problem in that we can exploit the fact that AbC predicates can check the received values. We simply add the channel name as a value in the message and the receiver checks its compatibility with its receiving channel.

To show the correctness of this encoding, we choose $b\pi$-calculus [8] as a representative for channel-based process calculi. The $b\pi$-calculus is a good choice because it is based on broadcast rather than binary communication which makes it a sort of variant of value-passing CBS [23]. Also, channels in $b\pi$-calculus can be communicated like in π-calculus [20]. We consider two level syntax for $b\pi$-calculus (i.e., only static contexts [19] are considered) as shown below.

$$P ::= G \mid P_1 \| P_2 \mid \nu x P$$
$$G ::= \mathtt{nil} \mid a(\tilde{x}).G \mid \bar{a}\tilde{x}.G \mid G_1 + G_2 \mid (rec\ A\langle \tilde{x}\rangle.G)\langle \tilde{y}\rangle$$

Dealing with one level $b\pi$-syntax would not add difficulties related to channel encoding, but only related to the encoding of parallel composition and name restriction when occurring under a prefix or a choice. As reported in Table 7, the encoding of a $b\pi$-calculus process P is rendered as an AbC component $(|P|)_c$ with $\Gamma = \emptyset$. The channel is rendered as the first element in the sequence of values. For instance, in the output action $(a, \tilde{x})@(a = a)$, a represents the interaction channel, so the input action $(y = a)(y, \tilde{x})$ will always check the first element of the received sequence to decide whether to accept or discard the message. Notice that the predicate $(a = a)$ is satisfied by any Γ, however including the channel name in the predicate is crucial to encode name restriction correctly.

Now, we prove that the encoding is faithful, i.e., preserves the semantics of the original process. More precisely, we will prove the following Theorem:

Theorem 3 (Operational Correspondence). *For any $b\pi$ process P,*

- **(Operational completeness)**: *if $P \rightarrow_{b\pi} P'$ then $(|P|)_c \rightarrow^* \simeq (|P'|)_c$.*
- **(Operational soundness)**: *if $(|P|)_c \rightarrow Q$ then $\exists P'$ such that $P \rightarrow^*_{b\pi} P'$ and $Q \rightarrow^* \simeq (|P'|)_c$.*
- **(Barb preservation)**: *both P and $(|P|)_c$ exhibit similar barbs i.e., $P \downarrow_{b\pi}$ and $(|P|)_c \downarrow_{AbC}$.*

The proof proceeds by induction on the shortest transition of $\rightarrow_{b\pi}$. It shows that we can mimic each transition of $b\pi$-calculus by exactly one transition in AbC. This implies that the completeness and the soundness of the operational correspondence can be even proved in a stronger way as in corollaries 1 and 2.

Corollary 1 (Strong Completeness). *if $P \rightarrow_{b\pi} P'$ then $\exists Q$ such that $Q \equiv (|P'|)_c$ and $(|P|)_c \rightarrow Q$.*

Corollary 2 (Strong Soundness). *if $(|P|)_c \rightarrow Q$ then $Q \equiv (|P'|)_c$ and $P \rightarrow_{b\pi} P'$*

As a result of Theorems 2 and 3 and of the strong formulations of Corollaries 1 and 2, this encoding is sound and complete with respect to bisimilarity as stated in the following corollaries.

Corollary 3 (Soundness w.r.t Bisimilarity).

- $(\!|P|\!)_c \sim (\!|Q|\!)_c$ *implies* $P \sim Q$
- $(\!|P|\!)_c \approx (\!|Q|\!)_c$ *implies* $P \approx Q$.

Corollary 4 (Completeness w.r.t Bisimilarity).

- $P \sim Q$ *implies* $(\!|P|\!)_c \sim (\!|Q|\!)_c$
- $P \approx Q$ *implies* $(\!|P|\!)_c \approx (\!|Q|\!)_c$.

7 Related Work

In this section, we report related works concerning languages and calculi with primitives that either model multiparty interaction or enjoy specific properties.

AbC is inspired by the SCEL language [6,7] that was designed to support programming of autonomic computing systems [24]. Compared with SCEL, the knowledge representation in AbC is abstract and is not designed for detailed reasoning during the model evolution. This reflects the different objectives of SCEL and AbC. While SCEL focuses on programming issues, AbC concentrates on a minimal set of primitives to study attribute-based communication.

Many calculi that aim at providing tools for specifying and reasoning about communicating systems have been proposed: CBS [22] captures the essential features of broadcast communication in a simple and natural way. Whenever a process transmits a value, all processes running in parallel and ready to input catch the broadcast. The CPC calculus [11] relies on pattern-matching. Input and output prefixes are generalized to patterns whose unification enables a two-way, or symmetric, flow of information and partners are selected by matching inputs with outputs and testing for equality. The attribute π-calculus [16] aims at constraining interaction by considering values of communication attributes. A λ-function is associated to each receiving action and communication takes place only if the result of the evaluation of the function with the provided input falls within a predefined set of values. The imperative π-calculus [15] is a recent extension of the attribute π-calculus with a global store and with imperative programs used to specify constraints. The broadcast Quality Calculus of [27] deals with the problem of denial-of-service by means of *selective* input actions. It inspects the structure of messages by associating specific contracts to inputs, but does not provide any mean to change the input contracts during execution.

AbC combines the learnt lessons from the above mentioned languages and calculi in the sense that AbC strives for expressivity while preserving minimality and simplicity. The dynamic settings of attributes and the possibility of inspecting/modifying the environment gives AbC greater flexibility and expressivity while keeping models as much natural as possible.

8 Concluding Remarks

We have introduced a foundational process calculus, named AbC, for attribute-based communication. We investigated the expressive power of AbC both in terms of its ability to model scenarios featuring collaboration, reconfiguration, and adaptation and of its ability to encode channel-based communication and other interaction paradigms. We defined behavioral equivalences for AbC and finally we proved the correctness of the proposed encoding up to some reasonable equivalence. We demonstrated that the general concept of attribute-based communication can be exploited to provide a unifying framework to encompass different communication models. We developed a centralized prototype implementation for AbC linguistic primitives to demonstrate their simplicity and flexibility to accommodate different interaction patterns.

We plan to investigate the impact of bisimulation in terms of axioms, proof techniques, etc. for working with the calculus and to consider alternative behavioral relations like testing preorders.

Another line of research is to investigate anonymity at the level of attribute identifiers. Clearly, AbC achieves dynamicity and openness in the distributed settings, which is an advantage compared to channel-based models. In our model, components are anonymous, however the "name-dependency" challenge arises at another level, that is, the attribute environments. In other words, the sender's predicate should be aware of the identifiers of receiver's attributes in order to explicitly use them. For instance, the sending predicate $(loc =< 1, 4 >)$ targets the components at location $< 1, 4 >$, however, different components might use different identifiers to denote their locations; this requires that there should be an agreement about the attribute identifiers used by the components. For this reason, appropriate mechanisms for handling *attribute directories* together with identifiers matching/correspondence will be considered. These mechanisms will be particularly useful when integrating heterogeneous applications.

Further attention will be also dedicated to provide an efficient distributed implementation for AbC linguistic primitives. We also plan to investigate the effectiveness of AbC not only as a tool for encoding calculi but also for dealing with case studies from different application domains.

References

1. Agha, G., Callsen, C.J.: ActorSpace: an open distributed programming paradigm, vol. 28. ACM (1993)
2. Alrahman, Y.A., De Nicola, R., Loreti, M.: On the power of attribute-based communication, extended report (2016)
3. Alrahman, Y.A., De Nicola, R., Loreti, M., Tiezzi, F., Vigo, R.: A calculus for attribute-based communication. In: Proceedings of the 30th Annual ACM Symposium on Applied Computing, SAC 2015, pp. 1840–1845. ACM (2015)
4. Bass, M.A., Nguyen, F.T.: Unified publish and subscribe paradigm for local and remote publishing destinations, US Patent 6,405,266, 11 June 2002
5. Chockler, G.V., Keidar, I., Vitenberg, R.: Group communication specifications: a comprehensive study. ACM Comput. Surv. **33**, 427–469. ACM (2001). doi:10.1145/503112.503113
6. De Nicola, R., Ferrari, G., Loreti, M., Pugliese, R.: A language-based approach to autonomic computing. In: Boer, F.S., Bonsangue, M.M., Beckert, B., Damiani, F. (eds.) FMCO 2011. LNCS, vol. 7542, pp. 25–48. Springer, Heidelberg (2012)

7. De Nicola, R., Loreti, M., Pugliese, R., Tiezzi, F.: A formal approach to autonomic systems programming: the scel language. ACM Trans. Auton. Adapt. Syst. **9**, 1–29 (2014)
8. Ene, C., Muntean, T.: A broadcast-based calculus for communicating systems. In: Parallel and Distributed Processing Symposium, International, vol. 3, p. 30149b. IEEE Computer Society (2001)
9. Eugster, P.T., Felber, P.A., Guerraoui, R., Kermarrec, A.-M.: The many faces of publish/subscribe. ACM Comput. (CSUR) **35**(2), 114–131 (2003)
10. Ferscha, A.: Collective adaptive systems. In: Proceedings of the 2015 ACM International Joint Conference on Pervasive and Ubiquitous Computing and Proceedings of the 2015 ACM International Symposium on Wearable Computers, pp. 893–895 (2015)
11. Given-Wilson, T., Gorla, D., Jay, B.: Concurrent pattern calculus. In: Calude, C.S., Sassone, V. (eds.) TCS 2010. IFIP AICT, vol. 323, pp. 244–258. Springer, Heidelberg (2010)
12. Antony Richard Hoare, C.: Communicating sequential processes. Commun. ACM **21**(8), 666–677 (1978)
13. Holbrook, H.W., Cheriton, D.R.: Ip multicast channels: express support for large-scale single-source applications. In: ACM SIGCOMM Computer Communication Review, vol. 29, pp. 65–78. ACM (1999)
14. Honda, K., Yoshida, N.: On reduction-based process semantics. Theor. Comput. Sci. **151**(2), 437–486 (1995)
15. John, M., Lhoussaine, C., Niehren, J.: Dynamic compartments in the imperative π-calculus. In: Degano, P., Gorrieri, R. (eds.) CMSB 2009. LNCS, vol. 5688, pp. 235–250. Springer, Heidelberg (2009)
16. John, M., Lhoussaine, C., Niehren, J., Uhrmacher, A.M.: The attributed Pi-calculus with priorities. In: Priami, C., Breitling, R., Gilbert, D., Heiner, M., Uhrmacher, A.M. (eds.) Transactions on Computational Systems Biology XII. LNCS, vol. 5945, pp. 13–76. Springer, Heidelberg (2010)
17. Mamei, M., Zambonelli, F.: Programming pervasive and mobile computing applications with the tota middleware. In: Proceedings of the Second IEEE Annual Conference on Pervasive Computing and Communications, 2004. PerCom 2004, pp. 263–273. IEEE (2004)
18. Milner, R. (ed.): A Calculus of Communication Systems. LNCS, vol. 92. Springer, Heidelberg (1980). doi:10.1007/3-540-10235-3
19. Milner, R.: Communication and Concurrency. Prentice-Hall Inc, Upper Saddle River (1989)
20. Milner, R., Parrow, J., Walker, D.: A calculus of mobile processes, ii. Inf. Comput. **100**(1), 41–77 (1992)
21. Milner, R., Sangiorgi, D.: Barbed bisimulation. In: Kuich, W. (ed.) ICALP 1992. LNCS, vol. 623, pp. 685–695. Springer, Heidelberg (1992)
22. Prasad, K.V.S.: A calculus of broadcasting systems. Sci. Comput. Program. **25**(2), 285–327 (1995)
23. Prasad, K.V.S.: A calculus of broadcasting systems. In: Abramsky, S. (ed.) CAAP 1991 and TAPSOFT 1991. LNCS, vol. 493, pp. 338–358. Springer, Heidelberg (1991)
24. Sanders, J.W., Smith, G.: Formal ensemble engineering. In: Wirsing, M., Banâtre, J.-P., Hölzl, M., Rauschmayer, A. (eds.) Software-Intensive Systems. LNCS, vol. 5380, pp. 132–138. Springer, Heidelberg (2008)
25. Sangiorgi, D., Walker, D.: The pi-calculus: A Theory of Mobile Processes. Cambridge University Press, Cambridge (2003)

26. Sommerville, I., Cliff, D., Calinescu, R., Keen, J., Kelly, T., Kwiatkowska, M., Mcdermid, J., Paige, R.: Large-scale complex it systems. Commun. ACM **55**(7), 71–77 (2012)
27. Vigo, R., Nielson, F., Nielson, H.R.: Broadcast, denial-of-service, and secure communication. In: Johnsen, E.B., Petre, L. (eds.) IFM 2013. LNCS, vol. 7940, pp. 412–427. Springer, Heidelberg (2013)
28. Viroli, M., Damiani, F., Beal, J.: A calculus of computational fields. In: Canal, C., Villari, M. (eds.) Advances in Service-Oriented and Cloud Computing, pp. 114–128. Springer, Heidelberg (2013)

Fencing Programs with Self-Invalidation and Self-Downgrade

Parosh Aziz Abdulla[1], Mohamed Faouzi Atig[1], Stefanos Kaxiras[1],
Carl Leonardsson[1], Alberto Ros[2], and Yunyun Zhu[1(✉)]

[1] Uppsala University, Uppsala, Sweden
{mohamed_faouzi.atig,Yunyun.Zhu}@it.uu.se
[2] Universidad de Murcia, Murcia, Spain

Abstract. Cache coherence protocols using self-invalidation and self-downgrade have recently seen increased popularity due to their simplicity, potential performance efficiency, and low energy consumption. However, such protocols result in memory instruction reordering, thus causing extra program behaviors that are often not intended by the programmer. We propose a novel formal model that captures the semantics of programs running under such protocols, and employs a set of fences that interact with the coherence layer. Using the model, we perfform a reachability analysis that can check whether a program satisfies a given safety property with the current set of fences. Based on an algorithm in [19], we describe a method for insertion of *optimal* sets of fences that ensure correctness of the program under such protocols. The method relies on a *counter-example* guided fence insertion procedure. One feature of our method is that it can handle a variety of fences (with different costs). This diversity makes optimization more difficult since one has to optimize the total cost of the inserted fences, rather than just their number. To demonstrate the strength of our approach, we have implemented a prototype and run it on a wide range of examples and benchmarks. We have also, using simulation, evaluated the performance of the resulting fenced programs.

1 Introduction

Background. Many traditional cache coherence protocols such as MESI or MOESI are *transparent* to the programmer in the sense that there is no effect on memory ordering due to the coherence protocol. On the other hand, there is an ever larger demand on hardware designers to increase *efficiency* both in performance and power consumption. The quest to increase performance while maintaining transparency has led to complex coherence protocols with many states and relying on directories, invalidations, broadcasts, etc., often at the price of high verification cost, area (hardware cost) and increased energy consumption. Therefore, many researchers have recently proposed ways to simplify coherence without compromising performance but at the price of relaxing the memory consistency model [7,8,12–15,18,23–25,31,32]. Principal techniques among these proposals are Self-Invalidation (SI) and Self-Downgrade (SD).

© IFIP International Federation for Information Processing 2016
E. Albert and I. Lanese (Eds.): FORTE 2016, LNCS 9688, pp. 19–35, 2016.
DOI: 10.1007/978-3-319-39570-8_2

In traditional cache coherence protocols, when a write is performed on a cache line, the copies in other cores are invalidated (discarded). Thus, the protocol needs to track sharers of a cache line in a directory structure. A protocol with Self-Invalidation allows old copies to be kept, without invalidation at each store by another core. This eliminates the need for tracking readers [18]. In an SI protocol, invalidation is caused by synchronization instructions which occur in the code of the same thread. For instance, when a core executes a fence, it informs its own L1 cache that it has to self-invalidate.

Correspondingly, in traditional protocols, when a read operation is performed on a cache line, the last writer of the line is downgraded (or copied to the shared cache). In a protocol with Self-Downgrade (SD), downgrades are not caused by read operations in other cores. SD eliminates the need to track the last writer of a cache line [24]. Like invalidations, in an SD protocol, downgrades can be caused by fence instructions.

A protocol with both self-invalidation and self-downgrade (SISD) does not need a directory, thus removing a main source of complexity and scalability constraints in traditional cache coherence protocols [24]. But this comes at a price: SISD protocols induce *weak memory semantics* that reorder memory instructions. The behavior of a program may now deviate from its behavior under the standard *Sequentially Consistent (SC)* semantics, leading to subtle errors that are hard to detect and correct.

In the context of weak memory, hardware designers provide memory *fence* instructions to help the programmer eliminate the undesired behaviors. A fence instruction, executed by a process, limits the allowed reorderings between instructions issued before and after the fence instruction. To enforce consistency under SISD, fences should also be made visible to caches, such that necessary invalidations or downgrades may be performed. In this paper, we consider different types of fences. The different types eliminate different kinds of non-SC behaviors, and may have different impact on the program performance. In fact, unnecessary fences may significantly downgrade program performance. This is particularly true for the fences considered here, since they both incur latency, and affect the performance of the cache coherence subsystem as a whole. These fences cause the invalidation of the contents of the cache. Hence the more fences the less caching and the higher traffic we have. Thus, it is desirable to find the *optimal* set of fences, which guarantee correctness at minimal performance cost.

Challenge. One possibility to make SISD transparent to the program is to require the programmer to ensure that the program does not contain any data races. In fact, data race freedom is often required by designers of SISD protocols in order to guarantee correct program behavior [7,13]. However, this approach would unnecessarily disqualify large sets of programs, since many data races are in reality not harmful. Examples of correct programs with races include lock-free data structures (e.g., the Chase-Lev Work-stealing queue algorithm [6]), transactional memories (e.g., the TL2 algorithm [9]), and synchronization library primitives (e.g. pthread_spin_lock in glibc). In this paper, we consider a different approach where fences are inserted to retrieve correctness. This means that we may

insert sufficiently many fences to achieve program correctness without needing
to eliminate all its races or non-SC behaviors. The challenge then is to find sets
of fences that guarantee program correctness without compromising efficiency.
Manual fence placement is time-consuming and error-prone due to the complex behaviors of multithreaded programs [11]. Thus, we would like to provide
the programmer with a tool for *automatic* fence placement. There are several
requirements to be met in the design of fence insertion algorithms. First, a set of
fences should be *sound*, i.e., it should have enough fences to enforce a sufficiently
ordered behavior for the program to be correct. Second, the set should be *optimal*, in the sense that it has a lowest total cost among all sound sets of fences.
In general, there may exist several different optimal sets of fences for the same
program. Our experiments (Sect. 4) show that different choices of sound fence
sets may impact performance and network traffic. To carry out fence insertion
we need to be able to perform *program verification*, i.e., to check correctness of
the program with a given set of fences. This is necessary in order to be able
to decide whether the set of fences is sound, or whether additional fences are
needed to ensure correctness. A critical task in the design of formal verification
algorithms, is to define the program semantics under the given memory model.

Our Approach. We present a method for automatic fence insertion in programs
running in the presence of SISD. The method is applicable to a large class of
self-invalidation and self-downgrade protocols such as the ones in [7,8,12–15,
18,23–25,31,32]. Our goal is to eliminate incorrect behaviors that occur due to
the memory model induced by SISD. We will not concern ourselves with other
sources of consistency relaxation, such as compiler optimizations. We formulate
the correctness of programs as *safety properties*. A safety property is an assertion
that some specified "erroneous", or "bad", program states can never occur during
execution. Such bad states may include e.g., states where a programmer specified
assert statement fails, or where uninitialized data is read. To check a safety
property, we check the reachability of the set of "bad" states.

We provide an algorithm for checking the reachability of a set of bad states
for a given program running under SISD. In the case that such states are reachable, our algorithm provides a counter-example (i.e., an execution of the program
that leads to one of the bad states). This counter-example is used by our fence
insertion procedure to add fences in order to remove the counter-examples introduced by SISD semantics. Thus, we get a counter-example guided procedure for
inferring the optimal sets of fences. The termination of the obtained procedure
is guaranteed under the assumption that each call to the reachability algorithm
terminates. As a special case, our tool detects when a program behaves incorrectly already under SC. Notice that in such a case, the program cannot be
corrected by inserting any set of fences.

Contributions. We make the following main contributions: (i) A novel formal
model that captures the semantics of programs running under SISD, and employs
a set of fences that interact with the coherence layer. The semantics support the
essential features of typical assembly code. (ii) A tool, MEMORAX, available at
https://github.com/memorax/memorax, that we have run successfully on a wide

range of examples under SiSd and under Si. Notably, our tool detects for the first time four bugs in programs in the Splash-2 benchmark suite [33], which have been fixed in a recent Splash-3 release [27]. Two of these are present even under SC, while the other two arise under SiSd. We employ the tool to infer fences of different kinds and evaluate the relative performance of the fence-augmented programs by simulation in GEMS.

We augment the semantics with a reachability analysis algorithm that can check whether a program satisfies a given safety property with the current set of fences. Inspired by an algorithm in [19] (which uses dynamic analysis instead of verification as backend), we describe a counter-example guided fence insertion procedure that automatically infers the optimal sets of fences necessary for the correctness of the program. The procedure relies on the counter-examples provided by the reachability algorithm in order to refine the set of fences. One feature of our method is that it can handle different types of fences with different costs. This diversity makes optimization more difficult since one has to optimize the total cost of the inserted fences, rather than just their number. Upon termination, the procedure will return all optimal sets of fences.

Related Work. Adve and Hill proposed SC-for-DRF as a contract between software and hardware: If the software is data race free, the hardware behaves as sequentially consistent [2]. Dynamic self-invalidation (for DRF programs) was first proposed by Lebeck and Wood [18]. Several recent works employ self-invalidation to simplify coherence, including SARC coherence [13], DeNovo [7,31,32], and VIPS-M [14,15,23–25].

A number of techniques for automatic fence insertion have been proposed, for different memory models and with different approaches. However, to our knowledge, we propose the first counter-example guided fence insertion procedure in the presence of a variety of fences (with different costs). In our previous work [1], we propose counter-example guided fence insertion for programs under TSO with respect to safety properties (also implemented in MEMORAX). Considering the SiSd model makes the problem significantly more difficult. TSO offers only one fence, whereas the SiSd model offers a variety of fences with different costs. This diversity makes the optimization more difficult since one has to minimize the total cost of the fences rather than just their number.

The work presented in [16] proposes an insertion procedure for different memory models w.r.t. safety properties. This procedure computes the set of needed fences in order to not reach each state in the transition graph. Furthermore, this procedure assigns a unique cost for all fences. The procedure is not counter-example based, and requires some modification to the reachability procedure.

In [4], the tool TRENCHER is introduced, which inserts fences under TSO to enforce robustness (formalised by Shasha and Snir in [30]), also using an exact, model-checking based technique. MUSKETEER [3] uses static analysis to efficiently overapproximate the fences necessary to enforce robustness under several different memory models. In contrast to our work, the fence insertion procedures in [3,4] first enumerate all solutions and then use linear programming to find the optimal set of fences.

The program semantics under SISD is different from those under other weak memory models (e.g. TSO and POWER). Hence existing techniques cannot be directly applied. To our knowledge, it is the first work that defines the SISD model, proposes a reachability analysis and describes a fence insertion procedure under SISD.

There exist works on the verification of cache coherence protocols. This paper is orthogonal to these works since we are concerned with verification of *programs* running on such architectures and not the protocols themselves.

2 Programs – Syntax and Semantics

In this section, we formalize SISD and SI protocols, by introducing a simple assembly-like programming language, and defining its syntax and semantics.

2.1 Syntax

The syntax of programs is given by the grammar in Fig. 1. A program has a finite set of processes which share a number of variables (memory locations) $\mathcal{M}$. A variable $x \in \mathcal{M}$ should be interpreted as one machine word at a particular memory address. For simplicity, we assume that all the variables and process registers assume their values from a common finite domain $\mathcal{V}$ of values. Each process contains a sequence of instructions, each consisting of a program label and a statement. To simplify the presentation, we assume that all instructions (in all processes) have unique labels. For a label λ, we apply three functions: Proc (λ) returns the process p in which the label occurs. Stmt (λ) returns the statement whose label id is λ. Next (λ) returns the label of the next statement in the process code, or **end** if there is no next statement.

$$
\begin{aligned}
\langle pgm \rangle &::= \textbf{data } \langle vdecl \rangle^{+} \langle proc \rangle^{+} \\
\langle vdecl \rangle &::= \langle var \rangle \texttt{ '='} (\texttt{'*'} \mid \langle val \rangle) \\
\langle proc \rangle &::= \textbf{process } \langle pid \rangle \textbf{ registers } \langle reg \rangle^{*} \langle stmts \rangle \\
\langle stmts \rangle &::= \textbf{begin } (\langle label \rangle \texttt{ ':' } \langle stmt \rangle \texttt{ ';' })^{+} \textbf{ end} \\
\langle stmt \rangle &::= \langle var \rangle \texttt{ ':=' } \langle expr \rangle \mid \langle reg \rangle \texttt{ ':=' } \langle var \rangle \mid \\
&\quad\; \langle reg \rangle \texttt{ ':=' } \langle expr \rangle \mid \texttt{llfence} \mid \texttt{fence} \mid \\
&\quad\; \texttt{cas '(' } \langle var \rangle \texttt{ ',' } \langle expr \rangle \texttt{ ',' } \langle expr \rangle \texttt{ ')'} \mid \\
&\quad\; \texttt{syncwr ':' } \langle var \rangle \texttt{ ':=' } \langle expr \rangle \mid \texttt{ssfence} \mid \\
&\quad\; \texttt{cbranch '(' } \langle bexpr \rangle \texttt{ ')' } \langle label \rangle
\end{aligned}
$$

Fig. 1. The grammar of concurrent programs.

2.2 Configurations

A *local configuration* of a process p is a triple $(\lambda, \mathsf{RVal}, \mathsf{L1})$, where λ is the label of the next statement to execute in p, RVal defines the values of the local registers, and $\mathsf{L1}$ defines the state of the L1 cache of p. In turn, $\mathsf{L1}$ is a triple $(\mathsf{Valid}, \mathsf{LStatus}, \mathsf{LVal})$. Here $\mathsf{Valid} \subseteq \mathcal{M}$ defines the set of shared variables that are currently in the valid state, and $\mathsf{LStatus}$ is a function from Valid to the set {dirty, clean} that defines, for each $x \in$ Valid, whether x is dirty or clean, and LVal is a function from Valid to $\mathcal{V}$ that defines for each $x \in$ Valid its current value in the L1 cache of p. The *shared part* of a configuration is given by a function LLC that defines for each variable $x \in \mathcal{M}$ its value $\mathsf{LLC}(x)$ in the LLC. A configuration c then is a pair $(\mathsf{LConf}, \mathsf{LLC})$ where LConf is a function that returns, for each process p, the local configuration of p.

2.3 Semantics

In the formal definition below, our semantics allows system events to occur non-deterministically. This means that we model not only instructions from the program code itself, but also events that are caused by unpredictable things as hardware prefetching, software prefetching, program preemption, false sharing, multiple threads of the same program being scheduled on the same core, etc. A transition t is either performed by a given process when it executes an instruction, or is a system event. In the former case, t will be of the form λ, i.e., t models the effect of a process p performing the statement labeled with λ. In the latter case, t will be equal to ω for some system event ω.

Instruction Semantics

$$\frac{\sigma = (\$r := x) \ , \ x \in \mathsf{Valid}}{c \xrightarrow{\lambda} (\mathsf{LConf}[p \leftarrow (\mathsf{Next}(\lambda), \mathsf{RVal}[\$r \leftarrow \mathsf{LVal}(x)], \mathsf{L1})], \mathsf{LLC})}$$

$$\frac{\sigma = (x := e) \ , \ x \in \mathsf{Valid} \ , \ S' = \mathsf{LStatus}[x \leftarrow \mathtt{dirty}]}{c \xrightarrow{\lambda} (\mathsf{LConf}[p \leftarrow (\mathsf{Next}(\lambda), \mathsf{RVal}, (\mathsf{Valid}, S', \mathsf{LVal}[x \leftarrow \mathsf{RVal}(e)]))], \mathsf{LLC})}$$

$$\frac{\sigma = \mathtt{fence} \ , \ \mathsf{Valid} = \varnothing}{c \xrightarrow{\lambda} (\mathsf{LConf}[p \leftarrow (\mathsf{Next}(\lambda), \mathsf{RVal}, \mathsf{L1})], \mathsf{LLC})}$$

$$\frac{\sigma = \mathtt{ssfence} \ , \ \forall x \in \mathcal{M}. \ (x \in \mathsf{Valid} \Rightarrow \mathsf{LStatus}(x) = \mathtt{clean})}{c \xrightarrow{\lambda} (\mathsf{LConf}[p \leftarrow (\mathsf{Next}(\lambda), \mathsf{RVal}, \mathsf{L1})], \mathsf{LLC})}$$

$$\frac{\sigma = \mathtt{llfence} \ , \ \forall x \in \mathcal{M}. \ (x \in \mathsf{Valid} \Rightarrow \mathsf{LStatus}(x) = \mathtt{dirty})}{c \xrightarrow{\lambda} (\mathsf{LConf}[p \leftarrow (\mathsf{Next}(\lambda), \mathsf{RVal}, \mathsf{L1})], \mathsf{LLC})}$$

$$\frac{\sigma = (\mathtt{syncwr} : x := e) \ , \ x \notin \mathsf{Valid}}{c \xrightarrow{\lambda} (\mathsf{LConf}[p \leftarrow (\mathsf{Next}(\lambda), \mathsf{RVal}, \mathsf{L1})], \mathsf{LLC}[x \leftarrow \mathsf{RVal}(e)])}$$

$$\frac{\sigma = \mathtt{cas}(x, e_0, e_1) \ , \ x \notin \mathsf{Valid} \ , \ \mathsf{LLC}(x) = \mathsf{RVal}(e_0)}{c \xrightarrow{\lambda} (\mathsf{LConf}[p \leftarrow (\mathsf{Next}(\lambda), \mathsf{RVal}, \mathsf{L1})], \mathsf{LLC}[x \leftarrow \mathsf{RVal}(e_1)])}$$

System Event Semantics

$$\frac{\omega = (\mathtt{fetch}(p, x)) \ , \ x \notin \mathsf{Valid} \ , \ S' = \mathsf{LStatus}[x \leftarrow \mathtt{clean}]}{c \xrightarrow{\omega} (\mathsf{LConf}[p \leftarrow (\lambda, \mathsf{RVal}, (\mathsf{Valid} \cup \{x\}, S', \mathsf{LVal}[x \leftarrow \mathsf{LLC}(x)]))], \mathsf{LLC})}$$

$$\frac{\omega = (\mathtt{wrllc}(p, x)) \ , \ x \in \mathsf{Valid} \ , \ \mathsf{LStatus}(x) = \mathtt{dirty} \ , \ S' = \mathsf{LStatus}[x \leftarrow \mathtt{clean}]}{c \xrightarrow{\omega} (\mathsf{LConf}[p \leftarrow (\lambda, \mathsf{RVal}, (\mathsf{Valid}, S', \mathsf{LVal}))], \mathsf{LLC}[x \leftarrow \mathsf{LVal}(x)])}$$

$$\frac{\omega = (\mathtt{evict}(p, x)) \ , \ x \in \mathsf{Valid} \ , \ \mathsf{LStatus}(x) = \mathtt{clean}}{c \xrightarrow{\omega} (\mathsf{LConf}[p \leftarrow (\lambda, \mathsf{RVal}, (\mathsf{Valid} \setminus \{x\}, \mathsf{LStatus}[x \leftarrow \bot], \mathsf{LVal}[x \leftarrow \bot]))], \mathsf{LLC})}$$

Fig. 2. Semantics of programs running under SISD.

For a function f, we use $f[a \leftarrow b]$, to denote the function f' such that $f'(a) = b$ and $f'(a') = f(a')$ if $a' \neq a$. We write $f(a) = \bot$ to denote that f is undefined for a.

Below, we give an intuitive explanation of each transition. The formal definition can be found in Fig. 2 where we assume $c = (\mathsf{LConf}, \mathsf{LLC})$, and

LConf(p) $=$ (λ, RVal, L1), and L1 $=$ (Valid, LStatus, LVal), Proc(λ) $=$ p, and Stmt(λ) $=$ σ. We leave out the definitions for local instructions, since they have standard semantics.

Instruction Semantics. Let p be one of the processes in the program, and let λ be the label of an instruction in p whose statement is σ. We will define a *transition relation* $\xrightarrow{\lambda}$, induced by λ, on the set of configurations. The relation is defined in terms of the type of operation performed by the given statement σ. In all the cases only the local state of p and LLC will be changed. The local states of the rest of the processes will not be affected. This mirrors the principle in SISD that L1 cache controllers will communicate with the LLC, but never directly with other L1 caches.

Read ($\$r := x$)**:** Process p reads the value of x from L1 into the register $\$r$. The L1 and the LLC will not change. The transition is only enabled if x is valid in the L1 cache of p. This means that if x is not in L1, then a system event `fetch` must occur before p is able to execute the read operation.

Write ($x := e$)**:** An expression e contains only registers and constants. The value of x in L1 is updated with the evaluation of e where registers have values as indicated by RVal, and x becomes dirty. The write is only enabled if x is valid for p.

Fence (`fence`)**:** A full fence transition is only enabled when the L1 of p is empty. This means that before the fence can be executed, all entries in its L1 must be evicted (and written to the LLC if dirty). So p must stall until the necessary system events (`wrllc` and `evict`) have occurred. Executing the fence has no further effect on the caches.

SS-Fence (`ssfence`)**:** Similarly, an `ssfence` transition is only enabled when there are no dirty entries in the L1 cache of p. So p must stall until all dirty entries have been written to the LLC by `wrllc` system events. In contrast to a full fence, an `ssfence` permits clean entries to remain in the L1.

LL-Fence (`llfence`)**:** This is the dual of an SS-Fence. An `llfence` transition is only enabled when there are no clean entries in the L1 cache of p. In other words, the read instructions before and after an `llfence` cannot be reordered.

Synchronized Write (`syncwr` : $x := e$)**:** A synchronized write is like an ordinary write, but acts directly on the LLC instead of the L1 cache. For a `syncwr` transition to be enabled, x may not be in the L1. (I.e., the cache must invalidate x before executing the `syncwr`.) When it is executed, the value of x in the LLC is updated with the evaluation of the expression e under the register valuation RVal of p. The L1 cache is not changed.

CAS (`cas`(x, e_0, e_1))**:** A compare and swap transition acts directly on the LLC. The `cas` is only enabled when x is not in the L1 cache of p, and the value of x in the LLC equals e_0 (under RVal). When the instruction is executed, it atomically writes the value of e_1 directly to the LLC in the same way as a synchronized write would.

System Event Semantics. The system may non-deterministically (i.e., at any time) perform a *system event*. A system event is not a program instruction, and so will not change the program counter (label) of a process. We will define a *transition relation* $\xrightarrow{\omega}$, induced by the system event ω. There are three types of system events as follows.

Eviction ($\texttt{evict}(p,x)$): An $\texttt{evict}(p,x)$ system event may occur when x is valid and clean in the L1 of process p. When the event occurs, x is removed from the L1 of p.

Write-LLC ($\texttt{wrllc}(p,x)$): If the entry of x is dirty in the L1 of p, then a $\texttt{wrllc}(p,x)$ event may occur. The value of x in the LLC is then updated with the value of x in the L1 of p. The entry of x in the L1 of p becomes clean.

Fetch ($\texttt{fetch}(p,x)$): If x does not have an entry in the L1 of p, then p may fetch the value of x from the LLC, and create a new, clean entry with that value for x in its L1.

2.4   Program Semantics Under an Si Protocol

In a self-invalidation protocol without self-downgrade, a writing process will be downgraded and forced to communicate its dirty data when another process accesses that location in the LLC. This behavior can be modelled by a semantics where writes take effect atomically with respect to the LLC. Hence, to modify the semantics given in Sect. 2.3 such that it models a program under an SI protocol, it suffices to interpret all write instructions as the corresponding $\texttt{syncwr}$ instructions.

2.5   Transition Graph and the Reachability Algorithm

Our semantics allows to construct, for a given program $\mathcal{P}$, a finite *transition graph*, where each node in the graph is a configuration in $\mathcal{P}$, and each edge is a transition. A *run* is a sequence $c_0 \xrightarrow{t_1} c_1 \xrightarrow{t_2} c_2 \cdots \xrightarrow{t_n} c_n$, which is a path in the transition graph, where $t_i (0 \leq i \leq n)$ is either a label λ or a system event ω.

Together with the program, the user provides a *safety property* ϕ that describes a set *Bad* of configurations that are considered to be errors. Checking ϕ for a program $\mathcal{P}$ amounts to checking whether there is a run leading from the initial configuration to a configuration in *Bad*. To do that, the input program under SISD is translated to the code recognized by the reachability analysis tool chosen by the user. The translated code simulates all the behaviors which are allowed in the SISD semantics. Also, there is instrumentation added to simulate the caches. Verifying the input program amounts to verifying the translated code which is analyzed under SC. If a bad configuration is encountered, a witness run is returned by the tool. Otherwise, the program is declared to be correct.

3   Fence Insertion

In this section we describe our fence insertion procedure, which is closely related to the algorithm described in [19]. Given a program $\mathcal{P}$, a cost function κ and a safety property ϕ, the procedure finds *all* the sets of fences that are optimal for $\mathcal{P}$ w.r.t. ϕ and κ.

In this section we take *fence constraint* (or *fence* for short) to mean a pair (λ, f) where λ is a statement label and f is a fence instruction. A fence constraint (λ, f) should be interpreted as the notion of inserting the fence instruction f into a program, between the statement labeled λ and the next statement (labeled by $\text{Next}(\lambda))$[1]. For a program $\mathcal{P}$ and a set F of fence constraints, we define $\mathcal{P} \oplus F$ to mean the program $\mathcal{P}$ where all fence constraints in F have been inserted. To avoid ambiguities in the case when F contains multiple fence constraints with the same statement label (e.g. $(\lambda, \texttt{llfence})$ and $(\lambda, \texttt{ssfence})$), we assume that fences are always inserted in some fixed order.

Definition 1 (Soundness of Fence Sets). *For a program $\mathcal{P}$, safety property ϕ, and set F of fence constraints, the set F is sound for $\mathcal{P}$ w.r.t. ϕ if $\mathcal{P} \oplus F$ satisfies ϕ under* SISD.

A *cost function* κ is a function from fence constraints to positive integer costs. We extend the notion of a cost function to sets of fence constraints in the natural way: For a cost function κ and a set F of fence constraints, we define $\kappa(F) = \sum_{c \in F} \kappa(c)$.

Definition 2 (Optimality of Fence Sets). *For a program $\mathcal{P}$, safety property ϕ, cost function κ, and set F of fence constraints, F is optimal for $\mathcal{P}$ w.r.t. ϕ and κ if F is sound for $\mathcal{P}$ w.r.t. ϕ, and there is no sound fence set G for $\mathcal{P}$ w.r.t. ϕ where $\kappa(G) < \kappa(F)$.*

In order to introduce our algorithm, we define the notion of a *hitting set*.

Definition 3 (Hitting Set). *For a set $S = \{S_0, \cdots, S_n\}$ of sets $S_0, \cdots, S_n$, and a set T, we say that T is a hitting set of S if $T \cap S_i \neq \varnothing$ for all $0 \leq i \leq n$.*

For example $\{a, d\}$ is a hitting set of $\{\{a, b, c\}, \{d\}, \{a, e\}\}$. For a set S of sets, hitting sets of S can be computed using various search techniques, such as e.g. constraint programming. We will assume that we are given a function $\textbf{hits}(S, \kappa)$ which computes all hitting sets for S which are cheapest w.r.t. κ. I.e., for a set S of finite sets, and a cost function κ, the call $\textbf{hits}(S, \kappa)$ returns the set of all sets T with $T \subseteq \bigcup_{S_i \in S} S_i$ such that (i) T is a hitting set of S, and (ii) there is no hitting set T' of S such that $\kappa(T') < \kappa(T)$.

We present our fence insertion algorithm in Fig. 3. The algorithm keeps two variables $\texttt{opt}$ and $\texttt{req}$. Both are sets of fence constraint sets, but are intuitively interpreted in different ways. The set $\texttt{opt}$ contains all the optimal fence constraint sets for $\mathcal{P}$ w.r.t. ϕ and κ that have been found thus far. The set $\texttt{req}$

---

[1] This definition can be generalized. Our prototype tool does indeed support a more general definition of fence positions, which is left out of the article for simplicity.

is used to keep track of the requirements that have been discovered for which fences are necessary for soundness of $\mathcal{P}$. We maintain the following invariant for req: Any fence constraint set F which is sound for $\mathcal{P}$ w.r.t. ϕ is a hitting set of req. As the algorithm learns more about $\mathcal{P}$, the requirements in req will grow, and hence give more information about what a sound fence set may look like. Notice that the invariant holds trivially in the beginning, when req $= \varnothing$.

In the loop on lines 3–14 we repeatedly compute a candidate fence set F (line 3), insert it into $\mathcal{P}$, and call the reachability analysis to check if F is sound (line 4). We assume that the call **reachable**($\mathcal{P} \oplus F, \phi$) returns $\bot$ if ϕ is unreachable in $\mathcal{P} \oplus F$, and a witness run otherwise. If $\mathcal{P} \oplus F$ satisfies the safety property ϕ, then F is sound. Furthermore, since F is chosen as one of the cheapest (w.r.t. κ) hitting sets of req, and all sound fence sets are hitting sets of req, it must also be the case that F is optimal. Therefore, we add F to opt on line 6.

If $\mathcal{P} \oplus F$ does not satisfy the safety property ϕ, then we proceed to analyze the witness run π. The witness analysis procedure is outlined in Sect. 3.1. The analysis will return a set C of fence constraints such that any fence set which is restrictive

```
Fencins(P,φ,κ)
1:  opt := ∅; // Optimal fence sets
2:  req := ∅; // Known requirements
3:  while(∃F ∈ hits(req, κ) \ opt){
4:      π := reachable(P ⊕ F, φ);
5:      if(π =⊥){
            // The fence set F is sound
            //  (and optimal)!
6:          opt := opt ∪ {F};
7:      }else{ // π is a witness run.
8:          C := analyze_witness(P ⊕ F, π);
            // C is the set of fences
            //  that can prevent π.
9:          if(C = ∅){ // error under SC!
10:             return ∅;
11:         }
12:         req := req ∪ {C};
13:     }
14: }
15: return opt;
```

Fig. 3. The fence insertion algorithm.

enough to prevent the erroneous run π must contain at least one fence constraint from C. Since every sound fence set must prevent π, this means that every sound fence set must have a non-empty intersection with C. Therefore we add C to req on line 12, so that req will better guide our choice of fence set candidates in the future.

Note that in the beginning, **hits**(req, κ) will return a singleton set of the empty set, namely $\{\varnothing\}$. Then F is chosen as the empty set $\varnothing$ and the algorithm continues. A special case occurs when the run π contains no memory access reorderings. This means that $\mathcal{P}$ can reach the bad states even under the SC memory model. Hence it is impossible to correct $\mathcal{P}$ by only inserting fences. The call **analyze_witness**($\mathcal{P} \oplus F, \pi$) will in this case return the empty set. The main algorithm then terminates, also returning the empty set, indicating that there are no optimal fence sets for the given problem.

3.1   Witness Analysis

The **analyze_witness** function takes as input a program $\mathcal{P}$ (which may already contain some fences inserted by the fence insertion algorithm), and a counter-example run π generated by the reachability analysis. The goal is to find a set G of fences such that (i) all sound fence sets have at least one fence in common with G and (ii) G contains no fence which is already in $\mathcal{P}$. It is desirable to keep G as small as possible, in order to quickly converge on sound fence sets.

There are several ways to implement **analyze_witness** to satisfy the above requirements. One simple way builds on the following insight: Any sound fence set must prevent the current witness run. The only way to do that, is to have fences preventing some access reordering that occurs in the witness. So a set G which contains all fences preventing some reordering in the current witness satisfies both requirements listed above.

Program fragment	Witness run
	. . .
	1.`fetch(P0,x)`
`process P0`	2.`L0: x := 1`
`. . .`	3.`fetch(P0,y)`
`L0: x := 1;`	4.`L1: $r_0 := y`
`L1: $r_0 := y;`	5.`fetch(P0,z)`
`L2: $r_1 := z;`	6.`L2: $r_1 := z`
`. . .`	
	7.`wrllc(P0,x)`
	. . .

Fig. 4. Left: Part of a program $\mathcal{P}$, containing three instructions of the thread P0. Right: A part of a counter-example run π of $\mathcal{P}$.

As an example, consider Fig. 4. On the left, we show part of a program $\mathcal{P}$ where the thread P0 performs three memory accesses L0, L1 and L2. On the right, we show the corresponding part of a counter-example run π. We see that the store L0 becomes globally visible at line 7, while the loads L1 and L2 access the LLC at respectively lines 3 and 5. Hence the order between the instructions L0 and L1 and the order between L0 and L2 in the program code, is opposite to the order in which they take effect w.r.t. the LLC in π. We say that L0 is *reordered* with L1 and L2. The loads are not reordered with each other. Let us assume that π does not contain any other memory access reordering. The reordering is caused by the late `wrllc` on line 7. Hence, this particular error run can be prevented by the following four fence constraints: $c_0 = (\text{L0}, \text{ssfence})$, $c_1 = (\text{L1}, \text{ssfence})$, $c_2 = (\text{L0}, \text{fence})$, and $c_3 = (\text{L1}, \text{fence})$. The fence set returned by **analyze_witness**$(\mathcal{P}, \pi)$ is $G = \{c_0, c_1, c_2, c_3\}$. Notice that G satisfies both of the requirements for **analyze_witness**.

4   Experimental Results

We have implemented our fence insertion algorithm together with a reachability analysis for SISD in the tool MEMORAX. It is publicly available at https://github.com/memorax/memorax. We apply the tool to a number of benchmarks (Sect. 4.1). Using simulation, we show the positive impact of using different types of fences, compared to using only the full fence, on performance and network traffic (Sect. 4.2).

4.1 Fence Insertion Results

We evaluate the automatic fence insertion procedure by running our tool on a number of different benchmarks containing racy code. For each example, the tool gives us all optimal sets of fences. We run our tool on the same benchmarks both for SiSd and for the Si protocol.[2] The results for SiSd are given in Table 1. We give the benchmark sizes in lines of code. All benchmarks have 2 or 3 processes. The fence insertion procedure was run single-threadedly on a 3.07 GHz Intel i7 CPU with 6 GB RAM.

The first set of benchmarks are classical examples from the context of lock-free synchronization. They contain mutual exclusion algorithms: a simple CAS lock *-cas-*, a test & TAS lock *-tatas-* [29], Lamport's bakery algorithm *-bakery-* [17], the MCS queue lock *-mcsqueue-* [22], the CLH queue lock *-clh-* [20], and Dekker's algorithm *-dekker-* [10]. They also contain a work scheduling algorithm *-postgresql-*[3], and an idiom for double-checked locking *-dclocking-* [28], as well as two process barriers *-srbarrier-* [29] and *-treebarrier-* [22]. The second set of benchmarks are based on the Splash-2 benchmark suite [33]. We use the race detection tool Fast & Furious [26] to detect racy parts in the Splash-2 code. We then manually extract models capturing the core of those parts.

In four cases the tool detects bugs in the original Splash-2 code. The *barnes* benchmark is an n-body simulation, where the bodies are kept in a shared tree structure. We detect two bugs under SiSd: When bodies are inserted (*barnes 2*), some bodies may be lost. When the center of mass is computed for each node (*barnes 1*), some nodes may neglect entirely the weight of some of their children. Our tool inserts fences that prevent these bugs. The *radiosity* model describes a work-stealing queue that appears in the Splash-2 *radiosity* benchmark. Our tool detects that it is possible for all workers but one to terminate prematurely, leaving one worker to do all remaining work. The *volrend* model is also a work-stealing queue. Our tool detects that it is possible for some tasks to be performed twice. The bugs in *radiosity* and *volrend* can occur even under SC. Hence the code cannot be fixed only by adding fences. Instead we manually correct it.

For each benchmark, we apply the fence insertion procedure in two different modes. In the first one ("Only full fence"), we use only full fences. In the table, we give the total time for computing all optimal sets, the number of such sets, and the number of fences to insert into each process. For treebarrier, one process (the root process) requires only one fence, while the others require two. Notice also that if a benchmark has one solution with zero fence, that means that the benchmark is correct without the need to insert any fences.

In the second set of experiments ("Mixed fences"), we allow all four types of fences, using a cost function assigning a cost of ten units for a full fence,

---

[2] Our methods could also run under a plain SD protocol. However, to our knowledge, no cache coherence protocol employs only SD without SI.

[3] http://archives.postgresql.org/pgsql-hackers/2011-08/msg00330.php

five units for an `ssfence` or an `llfence`, and one unit for a synchronized write. These cost assignments are reasonable in light of our empirical evaluation of synchronization cost in Sect. 4.2. We list the number of inserted fences of each kind. In `barnes 1`, the processes in the model run different codes. One process requires an `llfence`, the other an `ssfence`.

In addition to running our tool for SISD, we have also run the same benchmarks for SI. As expected, `ssfence` and `syncwr` are no longer necessary, and `fence` may be downgraded to `llfence`. Otherwise, the inferred fence sets are the same as for SISD. Since SI allows fewer behaviors than SISD, the inference for SI is mostly faster. Each benchmark is fenced under SI within 71 s.

Table 1. Automatic fence insertion for SISD.

Benchmark	Size	Only full fence			Mixed fences		
		Time	#solutions	#fences	Time	#solutions	Fences/proc
bakery	45 LOC	17.3 s	4	5	108.1 s	16	2×sw,4×11,1×ss
cas	32 LOC	<0.1 s	1	2	<0.1 s	1	1×11,1×ss
clh	37 LOC	4.4 s	4	4	3.7 s	1	3×sw,2×11,1×ss
dekker	48 LOC	2.0 s	16	3	2.9 s	16	1×sw,2×11,1×ss
mcslock	67 LOC	15.6 s	4	2	33.0 s	4	1×11,1×ss
testtas	38 LOC	<0.1 s	1	2	<0.1 s	1	1×11,1×ss
srbarrier	60 LOC	0.3 s	9	3	0.4 s	4	2×11,1×ss
treebarrier	56 LOC	33.2 s	12	1/2	769.9 s	132	1×11,1×ss
dclocking	44 LOC	0.8 s	16	4	0.9 s	16	1×sw,2×11,1×ss
postgresql	32 LOC	<0.1 s	4	2	0.1 s	4	1×11,1×ss
barnes 1	30 LOC	0.2 s	1	1	0.5 s	1	1×11/1×ss
barnes 2	96 LOC	16.3 s	16	1	16.1 s	16	1×ss
cholesky	98 LOC	1.6 s	1	0	1.6 s	1	0
radiosity	196 LOC	25.1 s	1	0	24.6 s	1	0
raytrace	101 LOC	69.3 s	1	0	70.1 s	1	0
volrend	87 LOC	376.2 s	1	0	376.9 s	1	0

4.2 Simulation Results

Here we show the impact of different choices of fences when executing programs. In particular we show that an optimal fence set w.r.t. the "Mixed fences" cost function yields a better performance and network traffic compared to an optimal fence set using the "Only full fence" cost function. We evaluate the micro-benchmarks analyzed in the previous section and the Splash-2 benchmarks suite [33]. All programs are fenced according to the optimal fence sets produced by our tool as described above.

Simulation Environment: We use the Wisconsin GEMS simulator [21]. We model an in-order processor that with the Ruby cycle-accurate memory simulator (provided by GEMS) offers a detailed timing model. The simulated system is a 64-core chip multiprocessor with a SISD architecture and 32 KB, 4-way private L1 caches and a logically shared but physically distributed L2, with 64 banks of 256 KB, 16-way each.

The DoI State: When an `llfence` is executed, eviction of all clean data in the L1 cache is forced. This should take a single cycle. However, when a cache line contains multiple words, with a per-word dirty bit, it may contain both dirty and clean words. To evict the clean words, we would have to write the dirty data to the LLC and evict the whole line. That would harm performance and enforce a stronger access ordering than is intended by an `llfence`. For this reason, when we implemented the SISD protocol in GEMS, we introduced a new L1 cache state: DoI (Dirty or Invalid). A cache line in this state contains words that are either dirty or invalid, as indicated by the dirty bit. This allows an efficient, one-cycle implementation of `llfence`, where cache lines in a mixed state transition to DoI, thus invalidating precisely the clean words. It also allows the `llfence` not to cause any downgrade of dirty blocks, thus improving its performance.

Cost of Fences: Our tool employs different weights in order to insert fences. Here, we calculate the weights based on an approximate cost of fences obtained by our simulations. The effect of fences on performance is twofold. First, there is a cost to execute the fence instructions (fence latency); the more fences and the more dirty blocks to self-downgrade the higher the penalty. Second, fences affect cache miss ratio (due to self-invalidation) and network traffic (due to extra fetches caused by self-invalidations and write-throughs caused by self-downgrades). The combined effect on cache misses and network traffic also affects performance. We calculate the cost of fences in time as follows: $time_{fence} = lat_{fence} + misses_{si} * lat_{miss}$ where lat_{fence} is the latency of the fence, $misses_{si}$ is the number of misses caused by self-invalidation, and lat_{miss} is the average latency of such misses. According to this equation, the average cost in time of each type of fence when running the Splash2 benchmarks, normalized with respect to a full fence is the following: the cost of an `llfence` is 0.68, the cost of an `ssfence` is 0.23, and the cost of a `syncwr` is 0.14. The cost of the fences in traffic is calculated as $traffic_{fence} = sd * traffic_{wt} + misses_{si} * traffic_{miss}$ where sd is the number of self-downgrades, $traffic_{wt}$ is the traffic caused by a write-through, and $traffic_{miss}$ is the traffic caused by a cache miss. Normalized to a full fence, the cost in traffic is 0.43 for an `llfence`, 0.51 for an `ssfence`, and 0.10 for a `syncwr`. Thus, the weights assigned to fences in our tool seem reasonable.

Execution Time: Figure 5 (top) shows simulated execution time for both the micro-benchmarks (top) and the Splash2 benchmarks (bottom). The use of mixed fences improves the execution time compared to using full fences by 10.4 % for the micro-benchmarks and by 1.0 % for the Splash2 benchmarks. The DoI-mixed column shows the execution time results for the same mixed fence sets as the mixed column. But in DoI case, `llfences` are implemented in GEMS using an extra L1 cache line state (the Dirty-or-Invalid state). This feature is an architectural optimization of the SISD protocol. Implementing the DoI state further improves the performance of the mixed fences, by 20.0 % for the micro-benchmarks and 2.1 % for the Splash2, on average, compared to using of full fences. Mixed fences are useful for applications with more synchronization.

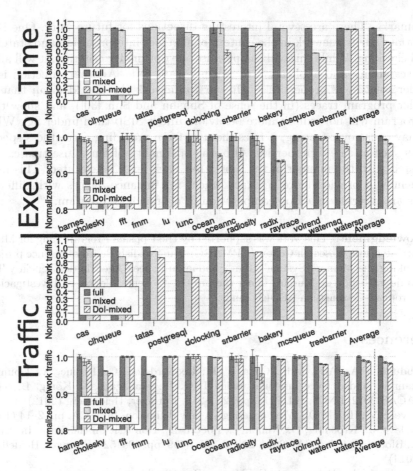

Fig. 5. Execution time and network traffic under different fence sets.

Traffic: Figure 5 (bottom) shows the traffic in the on-chip network generated by these applications. The use of `llfence`, `ssfence`, `syncwr` is able to reduce the traffic requirements by 11.1 % for the micro-benchmarks and 1.6 % for the Splash2 applications, on average, compared to using full fences. Additionally, when employing the DoI state, this reduction reaches 21.3 % and 1.9 %, on average, for the micro-benchmarks and the Splash2, respectively. Again, the more synchronization is required by the applications, the more traffic can be saved by employing mixed fences.

5 Conclusions and Future Work

We have presented a uniform framework for automatic fence insertion in programs that run on architectures that provide self-invalidation and self-downgrade. We have implemented a tool and applied it on a wide range of benchmarks. There are several interesting directions for future work. One is to instantiate our framework in the context of abstract interpretation and stateless model checking. While this will compromise the optimality criterion, it will allow more scalability and application to real program code. Another direction is to consider *robustness* properties [5]. In our framework this would mean that we consider program traces (in the sense of Shasha and Snir [30]), and show that the program will not exhibit more behaviors under SISD than under SC. While this may cause over-fencing, it frees the user from providing correctness specifications such as safety properties. Also, the optimality of fence insertion can be evaluated with the number of the times that each fence is executed. This measurement will provide more accuracy when, for instance, fences with different weighs are inserted in a loop computation in a branching program.

Acknowledgment. This work was supported by the Uppsala Programming for Multicore Architectures Research Center (UPMARC), the Swedish Board of Science project, "Rethinking the Memory System", the "Fundación Seneca-Agencia de Ciencia y Tecnología de la Región de Murcia" under the project "Jóvenes Líderes en Investigación" and European Commission FEDER funds.

References

1. Abdulla, P.A., Atig, M.F., Chen, Y.-F., Leonardsson, C., Rezine, A.: Counterexample guided fence insertion under TSO. In: Flanagan, C., König, B. (eds.) TACAS 2012. LNCS, vol. 7214, pp. 204–219. Springer, Heidelberg (2012)
2. Adve, S.V., Hill, M.D.: Weak ordering - a new definition. In: ISCA, pp. 2–14 (1990)
3. Alglave, J., Kroening, D., Nimal, V., Poetzl, D.: Don't sit on the fence. In: Biere, A., Bloem, R. (eds.) CAV 2014. LNCS, vol. 8559, pp. 508–524. Springer, Heidelberg (2014)
4. Bouajjani, A., Derevenetc, E., Meyer, R.: Checking and enforcing robustness against TSO. In: Felleisen, M., Gardner, P. (eds.) ESOP 2013. LNCS, vol. 7792, pp. 533–553. Springer, Heidelberg (2013)
5. Bouajjani, A., Meyer, R., Möhlmann, E.: Deciding robustness against total store ordering. In: Aceto, L., Henzinger, M., Sgall, J. (eds.) ICALP 2011, Part II. LNCS, vol. 6756, pp. 428–440. Springer, Heidelberg (2011)
6. Chase, D., Lev, Y.: Dynamic circular work-stealing deque. In: SPAA, pp. 21–28 (2005)
7. Choi, B., Komuravelli, R., Sung, H., Smolinski, R., Honarmand, N., Adve, S.V., Adve, V.S., Carter, N.P., Chou, C.T.: DeNovo: rethinking the memory hierarchy for disciplined parallelism. In: PACT, pp. 155–166 (2011)
8. Davari, M., Ros, A., Hagersten, E., Kaxiras, S.: An efficient, self-contained, on-chip, directory: DIR_1-SISD. In: PACT, pp. 317–330 (2015)
9. Dice, D., Shalev, O., Shavit, N.N.: Transactional locking II. In: Dolev, S. (ed.) DISC 2006. LNCS, vol. 4167, pp. 194–208. Springer, Heidelberg (2006)
10. Dijkstra, E.W.: Cooperating sequential processes (2002)
11. Herlihy, M., Shavit, N.: The Art of Multiprocessor Programming. Morgan Kaufmann Publishers Inc., San Francisco (2008)

12. Hower, D.R., Hechtman, B.A., Beckmann, B.M., Gaster, B.R., Hill, M.D., Reinhardt, S.K., Wood, D.A.: Heterogeneous-race-free memory models. In: ASPLOS, pp. 427–440 (2014)
13. Kaxiras, S., Keramidas, G.: SARC coherence: scaling directory cache coherence in performance and power. IEEE Micro **30**(5), 54–65 (2011)
14. Kaxiras, S., Ros, A.: A new perspective for efficient virtual-cache coherence. In: ISCA, pp. 535–547 (2013)
15. Koukos, K., Ros, A., Hagersten, E., Kaxiras, S.: Building heterogeneous unified virtual memories (UVMS) without the overhead. ACM TACO **13**(1), 1:1–1:22 (2016)
16. Kuperstein, M., Vechev, M., Yahav, E.: Automatic inference of memory fences. In: FMCAD, pp. 111–119. IEEE (2010)
17. Lamport, L.: A new solution of dijkstra's concurrent programming problem. Commun. ACM **17**(8), 453–455 (1974)
18. Lebeck, A.R., Wood, D.A.: Dynamic self-invalidation: reducing coherence overhead in shared-memory multiprocessors. In: ISCA, pp. 48–59 (1995)
19. Liu, F., Nedev, N., Prisadnikov, N., Vechev, M.T., Yahav, E.: Dynamic synthesis for relaxed memory models. In: PLDI, pp. 429–440 (2012)
20. Magnusson, P., Landin, A., Hagersten, E.: Queue locks on cache coherent multiprocessors. In: Proceedings of Eighth International Parallel Processing Symposium, pp. 165–171. IEEE (1994)
21. Martin, M.M., Sorin, D.J., Beckmann, B.M., Marty, M.R., Xu, M., Alameldeen, A.R., Moore, K.E., Hill, M.D., Wood, D.A.: Multifacet's general execution-driven multiprocessor simulator (GEMS) toolset. Comput. Archit. News **33**(4), 92–99 (2005)
22. Mellor-Crummey, J.M., Scott, M.L.: Algorithms for scalable synchronization on shared-memory multiprocessors. ACM Trans. Comput. Syst. (TOCS) **9**(1), 21–65 (1991)
23. Ros, A., Davari, M., Kaxiras, S.: Hierarchical private/shared classification: the key to simple and efficient coherence for clustered cache hierarchies. In: HPCA, pp. 186–197 (2015)
24. Ros, A., Kaxiras, S.: Complexity-effective multicore coherence. In: PACT, pp. 241–252 (2012)
25. Ros, A., Kaxiras, S.: Callback: efficient synchronization without invalidation with a directory just for spin-waiting. In: ISCA, pp. 427–438 (2015)
26. Ros, A., Kaxiras, S.: Fast & furious: a tool for detecting covert racing. In: PARMA and DITAM, pp. 1–6 (2015)
27. Sakalis, C., Leonardsson, C., Kaxiras, S., Ros, A.: Splash-3: a properly synchronized benchmark suite for contemporary research. In: ISPASS (2016)
28. Schmidt, D.C., Harrison, T.: Double-checked locking - an optimization pattern for efficiently initializing and accessing thread-safe objects. In: PLoP (1996)
29. Scott, M.L.: Shared-Memory Synchronization. Morgan & Claypool, San Rafael (2013)
30. Shasha, D., Snir, M.: Efficient and correct execution of parallel programs that share memory. ACM Trans. Program. Lang. Syst. (TOPLAS) **10**(2), 282–312 (1988)
31. Sung, H., Adve, S.V.: DeNovoSync: efficient support for arbitrary synchronization without writer-initiated invalidations. In: ASPLOS, pp. 545–559 (2015)
32. Sung, H., Komuravelli, R., Adve, S.V.: DeNovoND: efficient hardware support for disciplined non-determinism. In: ASPLOS, pp. 13–26 (2013)
33. Woo, S.C., Ohara, M., Torrie, E., Singh, J.P., Gupta, A.: The SPLASH-2 programs: characterization and methodological considerations. In: ISCA, pp. 24–36 (1995)

A Framework for Certified Self-Stabilization

Karine Altisen$^{(\boxtimes)}$, Pierre Corbineau, and Stéphane Devismes

VERIMAG UMR 5104, Université Grenoble Alpes, Grenoble, France
Karine.Altisen@imag.fr

Abstract. We propose a framework to build certified proofs of self-stabilizing algorithms using the proof assistant Coq. We first define in Coq the *locally shared memory model with composite atomicity*, the most commonly used model in the self-stabilizing area. We then validate our framework by certifying a non-trivial part of an existing self-stabilizing algorithm which builds a k-hop dominating set of the network. We also certify a quantitative property related to its output: we show that the size of the computed k-hop dominating set is at most $\lfloor \frac{n-1}{k+1} \rfloor + 1$, where n is the number of nodes. To obtain these results, we developed a library which contains general tools related to potential functions and cardinality of sets.

1 Introduction

In 1974, Dijkstra introduced the notion of *self-stabilizing* algorithm [12] as any distributed algorithm which resumes correct behavior within finite time, regardless of the initial configuration of the system. A self-stabilizing algorithm can withstand *any* finite number of transient faults. Indeed, after transient faults hit the system and place it in some arbitrary configuration — where, for example, the values of some variables have been arbitrarily modified — a self-stabilizing algorithm is guaranteed to resume correct behavior within finite time.

For more than 40 year, a vast literature on self-stabilizing algorithms has been developed. Self-stabilizing solutions have been proposed for many kinds of distributed problems, *e.g.*, token circulation [15], spanning tree construction [5], *etc.* Moreover, self-stabilizing algorithms have been designed to handle various environments, *e.g.*, wired networks [15], wireless sensor networks [1], peer-to-peer systems [3], *etc.* Progresses in self-stabilization led to researchers consider more and more adversarial environments. As an illustrative example, the three first algorithms proposed by Dijkstra in 1974 [12] were designed for oriented ring topologies and assuming sequential executions only, while nowadays most self-stabilizing algorithms are designed for fully asynchronous arbitrary connected networks, *e.g.*, [15]. Consequently, the design of self-stabilizing algorithms becomes more and more intricate, and accordingly, the proofs of their respective correctness and complexity are now often tricky to establish. However, proofs in distributed algorithmics, in particular in self-stabilization, are

This work has been partially supported by project PADEC (AGIR 2015 Pôle MSTIC).

E. Albert and I. Lanese (Eds.): FORTE 2016, LNCS 9688, pp. 36–51, 2016.
DOI: 10.1007/978-3-319-39570-8_3

commonly written by hand, based on informal reasoning. This potentially leads to errors when arguments are not perfectly clear, as explained by Lamport in its position paper [18]. So, in the current context, such methods are clearly pushed to their limits, justifying then the use of a *proof assistant*, a tool which allows to develop certified proofs interactively and check them mechanically.

Contribution. In this paper, we propose a general framework to build certified proofs of self-stabilizing algorithms for wired networks using the proof assistant Coq [19].

We first define in Coq the *locally shared memory model with composite atomicity* introduced by Dijkstra [12], the most common model in self-stabilization. Our modeling is versatile, *e.g.*, it supports any class of network topologies (including arbitrary ones), the diversity of anonymity levels (from fully anonymous to fully identified), and various levels of asynchrony (*e.g.*, sequential, synchronous, fully asynchronous).

We validate our framework by certifying a non-trivial part of an existing silent self-stabilizing algorithm which builds a k-hop dominating set of the network [8]. Starting from an arbitrary configuration, a silent algorithm [13] converges in finite time to a configuration from which all communication variables are fixed. This class of self-stabilizing algorithms is important, as self-stabilizing algorithms that build distributed data structures (*e.g.*, spanning tree or clustering) often achieve the silent property, and these silent self-stabilizing data structures are widely used as basic building blocks in more complex self-stabilizing solutions.

Using a classical scheme, the certified proof consists of two main parts, one relying on termination and the other on partial correctness. For the termination part, we developed tools on potential functions and termination at a fine-grained level. Precisely, we define a potential function as a multiset containing a local potential per node. We then exploit two criteria that are sufficient to meet the conditions for using the Dershowitz-Manna well-founded ordering on multisets. Note that the termination proof we propose assumes a distributed unfair daemon, the most general scheduling assumption of the model. By contrast, the proof given in [8] assumes a stronger daemon: a distributed weakly fair daemon. Finally, we certify a quantitative property, since we show that the size of the computed k-hop dominating set is at most $\lfloor \frac{n-1}{k+1} \rfloor + 1$, where n is the number of nodes in the network. To obtain this result, we had to write a library dealing with cardinality of sets in general and properties on cardinals of finite sets *w.r.t.* basic set operations, *e.g.*, Cartesian product, disjoint union, subset inclusion, *etc.* This work represents about 12,250 lines of code (as computed by coqwc: 4k lines of specifications, 7k lines of proofs) written in Coq 8.4pl4, compiled with OCaml 3.11.2.

Related Work. Several works have shown that proof assistants (in particular Coq) are well-suited to certification of distributed algorithms in various contexts [4,7,16]. Now, to the best of our knowledge, only three works deal with certification of self-stabilizing algorithms [6,10,17]. A formal correctness proof of Dijkstra's seminal self-stabilizing algorithm [12] is conducted with the proof assistant PVS [17], however only sequential executions are considered. In [6], Courtieu proposes a general setting for reasoning on self-stabilization in Coq. However, he restricts his study to very simple self-stabilizing algorithms, such as the 4-states algorithm of Ghosh [14], working on networks of very restrictive topologies *i.e.*, *lines* and *rings*. So, these two works address too simple cases to draw a general framework. Finally, Deng and Monin [10] propose to certify in Coq self-stabilizing population protocols. Population protocols are used as a theoretical model for a collection of tiny mobile agents that interact with one another to carry out a computation. In such a model, communication is implicit, as there is no notion of communication network: all pairs of agents interact infinitely often. Hence, this latter work is not relevant for wired networks, as considered here.

Roadmap. The rest of the paper is organized as follows. In Sect. 2, we describe how we define the locally shared memory model with composite atomicity in Coq. In Sect. 3, we express the definitions of self-stabilization and silence in Coq. In Sect. 4, we provide general results in Coq to certify termination of distributed algorithms. In Sect. 5, we present our case study. Section 6 is dedicated to the proof in Coq of our case study. We certify a bound on the size of the k-hop dominating set computed by our case-study algorithm in Sect. 7. We make concluding remarks in Sect. 8.

In this paper, we present our work together with a few pieces of Coq code that we simplify in order to make them readable. In particular, we intend to use notations, as defined in the model and algorithm, in those pieces of code. The Coq definitions, lemmas, theorems, and documentation related to the paper are available as an online browsing and a technical report available at http://www-verimag.imag.fr/~altisen/PADEC/. All source codes are also available at this address. We encourage the reader to visit this webpage for a deeper understanding of our work.

2   Locally Shared Memory Model with Composite Atomicity

Distributed Systems. A *distributed system* is a finite set of interconnected nodes. Each node has its own private memory, runs its own code, and can interact with other nodes *via* interconnections. Our model in Coq reflects this defining two independent classes: `Network` and `Algorithm`. A `Network` is equipped with a type `Node`, representing nodes, and defines functions and properties that depict its topology, *i.e.*, interconnections between nodes. Those interconnections are specified using the type `Channel`. The `Algorithm` of a node `p` is equipped with a type `State`, which describes memory state of `p`. Its main function, `run`, specifies how `p` executes and interacts with each other nodes through channels (type `Channel`).

Network and Topology. We view the communication network as a simple directed graph $G = (V, E)$, where V is a set of vertices representing nodes and $E \subseteq V \times V$ is a set of edges representing interconnections between distinct nodes. We note $n = |V|$ the numbers of nodes. Two distinct nodes p and q are said to be *neighbors* if $(p, q) \in E$. From a computational point of view, p uses a distinct channel $c_{p,q}$ to communicate with each of its neighbors q: it does not have direct access to q. In the type `Network`, the topology is defined using this narrow point of view, *i.e.*, interconnections are represented using channels only. In particular, the neighborhood of p is encoded with the set $\mathcal{N}_p$ which contains all channels $c_{p,q}$ outgoing from p. The sets $\mathcal{N}_p$, for all p, are modeled in Coq as lists. The function (`peer: Node` $\rightarrow$ `Channel` $\rightarrow$ `option Node`) returns the destination neighbor for a given channel name: (`peer` p $c_{p,q}$) returns (`Some` q), or $\perp^1$ if the name is unused.

Communications can be made bidirectional, assuming a property called `sym_net`, which states that for all nodes p_1 and p_2, the network defines a channel from p_1 to p_2 if and only if it also defines a channel from p_2 to p_1. In case of bidirectional links (p, q) and (q, p) in E, p can access its channel name at q using the function (ρ_p: `Channel` $\rightarrow$ `Channel`). Thus, we have: $\rho_p(c_{p,q})$ equals $c_{q,p} \in \mathcal{N}_q$ and $\rho_q(c_{q,p})$ equals $c_{p,q} \in \mathcal{N}_p$. Finally, we suppose that, since the number of nodes in the network is finite, we have a list `all_nodes` containing all the nodes.

Computational Model. In the *locally shared memory model with composite atomicity*, nodes communicate with their neighbors using finite sets of locally shared *variables*. A node can read its own variables and those of its neighbors, but can only write to its own variables. Each node operates according to its local *program*. A *distributed algorithm* $\mathcal{A}$ is defined as a collection of n programs, each operating on a single node. The *state* of a node in $\mathcal{A}$ is defined by the values of its local variables and is represented using an abstract Coq datatype `State`. This datatype is implemented as a record containing the values of the program variables. A node p can access the states of its neighbors using the corresponding channels: we call this the *local configuration* of p, and model it as a function typed (`Local_Env := Channel` $\rightarrow$ `option State`) which returns the current state of a neighbor, given the name of the corresponding channel (or $\perp$ for an invalid name). The program of each node p in $\mathcal{A}$ consists of a finite set of guarded actions: $\langle guard \rangle \hookrightarrow \langle statement \rangle$. The *guard* is a Boolean expression involving variables of p and its neighbors. The *statement* updates some variables of p. An action can be executed only if its guard evaluates to *true*; in this case, the action is said to be *enabled*. A node is said to be *enabled* if at least one of its actions is enabled. The local program at node p is modeled by a function `run` of type (`list Channel` $\rightarrow$ (`Channel` $\rightarrow$ `Channel`) $\rightarrow$ `State` $\rightarrow$ `Local_Env` $\rightarrow$ `option State`). This function accesses the local topology and states around p: it takes as first two arguments $\mathcal{N}_p$ and ρ_p; it then takes as inputs the current state of p and its current local configuration. The returned value is the next state of node p if p is enabled, $\perp$ otherwise. `run` provides a functional view of the algorithm: it includes the whole set of possible actions, but returns a single result; this model is thus restricted to *deterministic algorithms*.

A *configuration* is defined as an instance of the states of all nodes in the system, *i.e.*, a function with type (`Env := Node` $\rightarrow$ `State`). For a given node `p` and configuration `g`, the term (`g p`) represents the state of `p` in configuration `g`.

---

[1] Option type is used for partial functions which, by convention, return (`Some _`) when defined, and `None` otherwise (denoted by $\perp$ in this paper).

Thanks to this encoding, we easily obtain the local configuration (type Local_Env) of node p by composing g and peer as a function (local_env g p) which returns (g p') when (peer p c) returns Some p', and ⊥ otherwise. Hence, the execution of the algorithm on node p in current configuration g is obtained by: (run $\mathcal{N}_p$ ρ_p (g p) (local_env g p)). In configuration g, if there exist some enabled nodes, a *daemon* selects a non-empty set of them; every chosen node *atomically* executes its algorithm, leading to a new configuration g'. The transition from g to g' is called a *step*. To model steps in Coq, we use functions with type (Diff := Node → option State). We simply call *difference* a variable d of type Diff. A difference contains the updated states of the nodes that actually execute some action during the step, and maps any other node to ⊥. We define the predicate valid_diff that qualifies the current configuration and a difference expressing the result of a step by some enabled processes. It holds when at least one enabled node actually moves and all updates in the difference correspond to the execution of the algorithm by enabled processes, namely, run. The next configuration, g', is then obtained applying function (diff_eval d g) such that: ∀p, (g' p) = (d p) if (d p) ≠ ⊥, and (g' p) = (g p) otherwise.

Steps induce a binary relation ↦ over configurations defined in Coq by the relation Step: (Step g2 g1) expresses that g1 ↦ g2 (meaning that g1 ↦ g2 is actually a valid step), *i.e.*, there exists some valid difference d for g1 (valid_diff g1 d) and g2 is equal to (diff_eval d g1). An *execution* of $\mathcal{A}$ is a sequence of configurations g_0 g_1 ... g_i ... such that g_{i-1} ↦ g_i for all $i > 0$. Executions may be finite or infinite and are modeled in Coq with a type and a predicate:

```
CoInductive Exec: Type :=
| e_one:  Env → Exec        | e_cons: Env → Exec → Exec.
CoInductive valid_exec: Exec → Prop :=
| v_one: ∀g, valid_exec (e_one g)
| v_cons: ∀e g, valid_exec e → Step (Fst e) g →
                 valid_exec (e_cons g e).
```

where (Fst e) returns the first configuration of e. The keyword **CoInductive** generates a greatest fixed point capturing potentially infinite constructions.[2] Thus, variable e of type Exec actually represents an (valid) execution of $\mathcal{A}$ if (valid_exec e) holds, *i.e.*, if each pair of consecutive configurations g1, g2 in e satisfies (Step g2 g1).

Maximal executions are either infinite, or end at a *terminal* configuration in which no action of $\mathcal{A}$ is enabled at any node. Terminal configurations are detected in Coq using the proposition (terminal g), for a configuration g, which holds when *every node* computes run from g and returns ⊥. This predicate is decidable since we assume that the set of nodes is finite. A maximal execution is described by the coinductive proposition:

```
CoInductive max_exec: Exec → Prop :=
| max_one: ∀g, terminal g → max_exec (e_one g)
| max_cons: ∀g e, max_exec e → max_exec (e_cons g e).
```

---

[2] As opposed to this, the keyword **Inductive** only captures finite constructions.

As explained before, each step from a configuration to another is driven by a *daemon*. In our case study, we assume that the daemon is *distributed* and *unfair*. *Distributed* means that while the configuration is not terminal, the daemon should select at least one enabled node, maybe more. *Unfair* means that there is no fairness constraint, *i.e.*, the daemon might never select an enabled node unless it is the only one enabled. The propositions `valid_diff`, `Step` and henceforth `valid_exec` are sufficient to handle the distributed unfair daemon.

We allow a part of a node state to be read-only: this is modeled with type `ROState` and by the projection function (`RO_part: State → ROState`) which typically represents a subset of the variables handled in the `State` of the node. We add the property `RO_stable` to express the fact that those variables are actually read-only, namely no execution of `run` can change their values. From the assumption `RO_stable`, we show that any property defined on the read-only variables of a configuration is indeed preserved during steps. The introduction of Read-Only variables has been motivated by the fact that we want to encompass the diversity of anonymity levels from the distributed computing literature, *e.g.*, fully anonymous, semi-anonymous, rooted, fully identified networks, *etc.* By default (with empty `RO_part`), our Coq model defines fully anonymous network thanks to the distinction between nodes (type `Node`) and channels (type `Channel`). We enriched our model to reflect other assumptions, *e.g.*, fully identified networks. We define predicate `Assume` which constrains read-only variables of a configuration (in the case of the fully identified nodes assumption, it expresses uniqueness of identifiers). It will be assumed at each initial configuration and, by `RO_stable` it will remain true all along any execution.

Setoids. When using Coq function types to represent configurations and differences, we need to state pointwise function equality, which equates functions having equal values (extensional equality). The Coq default equality is inadequate for functions since it asserts equality of implementations (intensional equality). So, instead we chose to use the setoid paradigm: we endow every base type with an *equivalence relation*. Consequently, every function type is endowed with a *partial equivalence relation* (*i.e.*, symmetric and transitive) which states that, given equivalent inputs, the outputs of two equivalent functions are equivalent. However, we also need reflexivity to reason, *i.e.*, functions equivalent to themselves. Such functions are called *compatible*: they return equivalent results when executed with equivalent parameters. In all the framework, we assume *compatible configurations only*. We also prove compatibility for every function and predicate defined in the sequel. Additionally, we assume that equivalence relations on base types are decidable.

3   Self-Stabilization and Silence

We now express self-stabilization [12] in the locally shared memory model with composite atomicity using Coq properties. Let $\mathcal{A}$ be a distributed algorithm. Let $\mathbb{S}$ be a predicate on executions (type (`Exec → Prop`)). $\mathcal{A}$ is *self-stabilizing w.r.t. specification* $ (predicate (`self_stab` $)) if there exists a predicate ℙ on configurations (type (`Env` → **Prop**)) such that:

- *A converges* to ℙ, *i.e.*, every maximal execution contains a configuration which satisfies ℙ:

  ```
  ∀e, Assume (Fst e) → valid_exec e → max_exec e →
    safe_suffix (fun suf => ℙ (Fst suf)) e
  ```

  (`safe_suffix` S e) inductively checks that e contains a suffix that satisfies S;
- ℙ is *closed* under *A*, *i.e.*, for each possible step g ↦ g', (ℙ g) implies (ℙ g'):
  ∀g1 g2, Assume g1 → ℙ g1 → Step g2 g1 → ℙ g2; and
- *A meets* $ from ℙ, *i.e.*, every maximal execution, starting from configurations which satisfy ℙ, satisfies $:

  ```
  ∀e, Assume (Fst e) → valid_exec e → max_exec e →
    ℙ (Fst e) → S e.
  ```

The configurations which satisfy the predicate ℙ are said to be *legitimate*.

An algorithm is *silent* if the communication between the nodes is fixed from some point of the execution [13]. This latter definition can be transposed in the locally shared memory model by *A* is *silent* if all its executions are finite:

```
Inductive finite_exec: Exec → Prop :=
  | f_one: ∀g, finite_exec (e_one g)
  | f_cons: ∀e g, finite_exec e → finite_exec (e_cons g e).
silence := ∀e, Assume (Fst e) → valid_exec e → finite_exec e.
```

By definition, maximal executions of a *silent and self-stabilizing* algorithm *w.r.t* some specification $ end in configurations which are usually used as legitimate configurations, *i.e.*, satisfying ℙ. In this case, $ only allows executions made of a single configuration which must be legitimate; $ is then noted $ℙ. To prove that *A* is both silent and self-stabilizing *w.r.t.* $ℙ, we use a common sufficient condition which requires to prove that:

- all executions of *A* are finite:

  ```
  termination := ∀g, Assume g → Acc Step g
  ```

- and all terminal configurations of *A* satisfy ℙ:

  ```
  P_correctness ℙ := ∀g, Assume g → terminal g → SPEC g.
  ```

The inductive proposition `Acc` is taken from Library `Coq.Init.Wf` which provides tools on well-founded inductions. Predicate (`Acc Step g`) means that any descending chain from g is finite. The sufficient condition, used to prove that an algorithm is both silent and self-stabilizing, is then:

```
Lemma silent_self_stab ℙ:
    termination ∧ P_correctness ℙ → silence ∧ self_stab $ℙ.
```

4 General Tools for Proving Termination

Usual termination proofs are based on some global potential built from local ones. For example, local potentials can be integers and the global potential can be the sum of them. In this case, the argument for termination may be, for example, the fact that the global potential is lower bounded and strictly decreases at each step of the algorithm. Global potential decrease is due to the modification of local states at some nodes, however studying aggregators such as sums may hide scenarios, making the proof more complex. Instead, we build here a global potential as the multiset containing the local potential of each node and provide a sufficient condition for termination on this multiset. Our method is based on two criteria that are sufficient to meet the conditions for using the Dershowitz-Manna well-founded ordering on multisets [11]. Given those criteria, we can show that the multiset of (local) potentials globally decreases at each step. For multisets and Dershowitz-Manna order, we used results from Library CoLoR [2].

Steps. One difficulty we faced, when trying to apply this technique straightly, is that we cannot always define the local potential function at a node without assuming some properties on its local state, and so on the associated configuration. Thus, we had to assume the existence of some stable set of configurations in which the local potential function can be defined. When necessary, we use our technique to prove termination of a subrelation of the relation Step, provided that the algorithm has been initialized in the required stable set of configurations. This point is modeled by a predicate on configurations, (safe: Env → Prop), and a type safeEnv := { g | safe g } which represents the set of *safe configurations* into which we restrict the termination proof. Precisely, safeEnv is a type whose values are ordered pairs containing a term g and a proof of (safe g). Safe configurations should be stable, *i.e.*, it is assumed that no step can exit from the set. The relation for which termination will be proven is then defined by safeStep sg2 sg1 := Step (getEnv sg2) (getEnv sg1) where getEnv accesses the actual configuration (of type Env).

Potential. We assume that within safe configurations, each node can be endowed with a potential value obtained using function pot: safeEnv → Node → Mnat. Notice that Mnat simply represents natural numbers[3] encoded using the type from Library CoLoR.MultisetNat [2]; it is equipped with the usual equivalence relation, noted $=_P$, and the usual well-founded order on natural numbers, noted $<_P$.

Multiset Ordering. We recall that a multiset of elements in the setoid P endowed with its equivalence relation $=_P$, is defined as a set containing *finite numbers of occurrences (w.r.t. $=_P$) of elements of P*. Such a multiset is usually formally defined as a multiplicity function $m : P \to \mathbb{N}_{\geq 1}$ which maps any element to its number of occurrences in the multiset. We focus here on *finite multisets*, namely, multisets whose multiplicity function has finite support.

---

[3] Natural numbers cover many cases and we expect the same results when further extending to other types of potential.

Now, we assume that P is also ordered using relation $<_P$, compatible with $=_P$. We use the Dershowitz-Manna order on finite multisets [11] defined as follows: the multiset N is smaller than the multiset M, noted $N \prec M$, if and only if there are three multisets X, Y and Z such that $X \neq \emptyset \wedge M = Z + X \wedge N = Z + Y \wedge \forall y \in Y, \exists x \in X, y <_P x$, where '+' between multisets means adding multiplicities. Informally, to obtain a multiset N smaller than M, we may remove from M all elements of X and then add all elements of Y. Elements in Z are the ones that are present in both M and N. It is required that at least one element is removed ($X \neq \emptyset$) and each element that is added must be smaller ($w.r.t.$ $<_P$) than some removed element. It has been shown that if $<_P$ is a well-founded order, then so is the corresponding order $\prec$.

In our context, we consider finite multisets over Pot, ($i.e.$, $=_P$ is $=_p$ and $<_P$ stands for $<_p$). We have chosen to model them as lists of elements of Pot and we build the potential of a configuration as the multiset of the potentials of all nodes, namely a multiset of (local) potentials of a configuration sg is defined by

```
Pot sg := List.map (pot sg) all_nodes
```

where all_nodes is the list of all nodes in the network (see Sect. 2) and (List.map f l) is the standard operation that returns the list made of each elements of l on which f has been applied. The corresponding Dershowitz-Manna order is defined using the library CoLoR [2]. The library also contains the proof that (well_founded $<_P$) $\rightarrow$ (well_founded $\prec$) ((well_founded R := $\forall$a, Acc R a) is taken from standard Coq Library Coq.Init.Wf, as Acc). Using this latter result and the standard result which proves (well_founded $<_P$), we easily deduce (well_founded $\prec$).

Termination Theorem. Proving the termination of an algorithm then consists in showing that for any safe step of the algorithm, the corresponding global potential decreases $w.r.t.$ the Dershowitz-Manna order $\prec$, namely:

```
safe_incl := ∀sg1 sg2, safeStep sg2 sg1 → (Pot sg2) ≺ (Pot sg1)
```

We establish a sufficient condition made of two criteria on node potentials which validates safe_incl. The *Local criterion* finds for any node p whose potential has increased, a witness node p' whose potential has decreased from a value that is even higher than the new potential of p:

Hypothesis local_crit: $\forall$sg1 sg2, safeStep sg2 sg1 $\rightarrow$
  $\forall$p, (pot sg1 p)$<_P$(pot sg2 p) $\rightarrow$
  $\exists$p',(pot sg1 p')$\neq_P$(pot sg2 p') $\wedge$ (pot sg2 p)$<_P$(pot sg1 p').

Global criterion exhibits, at any step, a node whose potential has changed:

Hypothesis global_crit: $\forall$sg1 sg2, safeStep sg2 sg1 $\rightarrow$
  $\exists$p, (pot sg2 p)$\neq_P$(pot sg1 p).

Assuming both hypothesis, we are able to prove safe_incl as follows: we define Z as the multiset of local potentials which did not change, and X (resp. Y) as the complement of Z in the multiset of local potentials (Pot sg1) (resp. (Pot sg2)). Global criterion is used to show that $X \neq \emptyset$, and local criterion is used to

---

Algorithm 1. $\mathcal{D}(k)$, code for each process p

Constant Input: $Par(p) \in \mathcal{N}_p \cup \{\bot\}$

Variable: $p.\alpha \in \{0, ..., 2k\}$

Predicates: $IsRoot(p) \equiv Par(p) = \bot$; $IsShort(p) \equiv p.\alpha < k$; $IsTall(p) \equiv p.\alpha \geq k$;
$kDominator(p) \equiv (p.\alpha = k) \vee (IsShort(p) \wedge IsRoot(p))$

Macros:

$Children(p)\quad = \{q \in \mathcal{N}_p \mid Par(q) = \rho_p(q)\}$

$ShortChildren(p) = \{q \in Children(p) \mid IsShort(q)\}$

$TallChildren(p)\ = \{q \in Children(p) \mid IsTall(q)\}$

$MaxAShort(p)\quad = \textbf{if } ShortChildren(p) = \emptyset \textbf{ then } -1 \textbf{ else } \max\{q.\alpha \mid q \in ShortChildren(p)\}$

$MinATall(p)\quad = \textbf{if } TallChildren(p) = \emptyset \textbf{ then } 2k+1 \textbf{ else } \min\{q.\alpha \mid q \in TallChildren(p)\}$

$Alpha(p)\quad = \textbf{if } MaxAShort(p) + MinATall(p) \leq 2k - 2$
$\qquad\qquad\textbf{then } MinATall(p) + 1 \textbf{ else } MaxAShort(p) + 1$

Action: $\qquad\qquad\qquad\qquad p.\alpha \neq Alpha(p) \hookrightarrow p.\alpha \leftarrow Alpha(p)$

---

show that $\forall y \in Y, \exists x \in X, y <_P x$. Since any relation included in a well-founded order is also well-founded, we get that relation `safeStep` is well-founded. Finally, since we know that property `safe` is stable (from `stable_safe`), we get $(\forall g,$ `safe g` $\rightarrow$ `Acc Step g`) which proves that the algorithm terminates from any safe configuration.

5 Case Study

We have certified a non trivial part of the silent self-stabilizing algorithm proposed in [8]. Given a non-negative integer k, this algorithm builds a k-clustering of a bidirectional connected network $G = (V, E)$ containing at most $\lfloor \frac{n-1}{k+1} \rfloor + 1$ k-clusters, where n is the number of nodes. A k-cluster of G is a set $C \subseteq V$, together with a designated node $Clusterhead(C) \in C$, such that each member of C is within distance k of $Clusterhead(C)$.[4] A k-clustering is then a partition of V into distinct k-clusters. The k-clustering problem is related to the notion of k-hop dominating set since the set of clusterheads of any k-clustering is a k-hop dominating set, i.e., a subset D of V such that every node is within distance k from at least one node of D.

The algorithm proposed in [8] is actually a hierarchical collateral composition [9] of two silent self-stabilizing sub-algorithms: the former builds a rooted spanning tree, the latter is a k-clustering construction which stabilizes once a rooted spanning tree is available in the network. The crucial part of the second sub-algorithm consists in computing, in a self-stabilizing and silent way, a k-hop dominating set D of size at most $\lfloor \frac{n-1}{k+1} \rfloor + 1$ in an arbitrary rooted spanning tree. D will designate the set of clusterheads in the computed k-clustering. This task is performed using the 1-rule Algorithm $\mathcal{D}(k)$, whose code is given in Algorithm 1.

---

[4] the distance $\|p, q\|$ between two nodes p and q is the length of a shortest path from p to q in G.

We have used our framework to encode $\mathcal{D}(k)$, its assumptions, its specification, and to build a certified proof which shows that $\mathcal{D}(k)$ is silent and self-stabilizing for building a k-hop dominating set of at most $\lfloor \frac{n-1}{k+1} \rfloor + 1$ nodes in any bidirectional network equipped with a rooted spanning tree.

Local States. We denote the spanning tree and its root by T and r, respectively. In $\mathcal{D}(k)$, the knowledge of T is locally distributed at each node p using the constant input $\text{Par}(p) \in \mathcal{N}_p \cup \{\bot\}$. When $p \neq r$, $\text{Par}(p) \in \mathcal{N}_p$ and designates its parent in the tree. Otherwise, p is the root and $\text{Par}(p) = \bot$. Then, each node p maintains a single variable: $p.\alpha$, an integer in range $\{0, ..., 2k\}$. We have instantiated the Coq `State` of a node as a record containing fields (`Par`: `option` `Channel`) and (α: Z). (`Par p`) stands for $\text{Par}(p)$ and is the unique *read-only* variable for `p`. Moreover, (α `p`) stands for $p.\alpha$ and is taken in Z (integers). We chose to encode every number in the algorithm as integer in Z, since some of them may be negative (see *MaxAShort*) and computations use minus (see *Alpha*). Furthermore, we have proven $p.\alpha$ is in range $\{0, ..., 2k\}$ after p participates in any step and also when the system is in a terminal configuration.

Spanning Tree. We express the assumption about the spanning tree using predicate (`span_tree r Par`). This predicate checks that the graph T induced by `Par` is a subgraph of G which actually encodes a spanning tree rooted at r by the conjunction of

- r is the unique node such that $\text{Par}(r) = \bot$,
- $\text{Par}(p)$, for every non-root node p, is an existing channel outgoing from p,
- T contains no loop.

From the last point, we show that, since the number of nodes is finite, the relation extracted from `Par` between nodes and their parents (resp. children) in T is well-founded. We call this result `WF_par` (resp. `WF_child`) and express it using `well_founded`.

We expressed the assumptions on the network G, *i.e.*, in any configuration `g`, G is bidirectional and a rooted spanning tree is available in G (*n.b.*, this latter also implies that G is connected), in the predicate `Assume`:

$$\text{Assume}_{\text{kdom}} \ \mathbf{g} \ := \ \texttt{sym\_net} \ \wedge \ \exists r, \ \texttt{span\_tree} \ r \ \texttt{Par}$$

Specification. The goal of $\mathcal{D}(k)$ is to compute an output predicate $kDominator(p)$ for every node p (see Algorithm 1 for its definition) in such way that the system converges to a terminal configuration in which the set $Dom = \{p \in V \mid kDominator(p)\}$ defines a k-hop dominating set of T (and so of G). We consider any positive parameter k, *i.e.*, k is taken in Z (as for other numbers) and is assumed to be positive. We define the expected specification using the predicate $\mathbb{P}_{\text{kDom}}$ on configurations, where $\mathbb{P}_{\text{kDom}}$ holds in configuration `g` if and only if the set $Dom = \{p \in V \mid kDominator(p)\}$ is a k-hop dominating set of T:

$$\mathbb{P}_{\text{kDom}} \ \mathbf{g} \ := \ \forall \mathbf{p}, \ \exists \mathbf{kdom}, \ (kDominator \ \mathbf{g} \ \mathbf{kdom}) \ \wedge$$
$$\exists \texttt{path}, \ (\texttt{is\_path} \ \mathbf{g} \ \texttt{path} \ \mathbf{kdom} \ \mathbf{p}) \ \wedge \ (\texttt{length} \ \texttt{path}) \ \leq \ k.$$

where predicate is_path detects if the list of nodes path actually represents a path in the tree T between the nodes kdom and p, and length computes the length of the path.

$\mathcal{D}(k)$ **in Coq.** We translate the unique rule of $\mathcal{D}(k)$ into the type Algorithm. Every predicate and macro of Algorithm 1 is directly encoded in Coq: the translation is quasi-syntactic (see Library KDomSet_algo in the online browsing) and provides a definition of run. The definition of $\mathcal{D}(k)$, of type Algorithm, comes with a proof that run is compatible, as a composition of compatible functions, and also with a straightforward proof of RO_stable which asserts that the read-only part of the state, Par, is constant during steps, when applying run.

Overview of $\mathcal{D}(k)$. Algorithm $\mathcal{D}(k)$, whose code is given in Algorithm 1, computes a k-hop dominating set of T (and so of G), noted Dom, using the variable α at each node. Precisely, Dom is defined as the set of nodes p such that $kDominator(p)$ holds, i.e., where $p.\alpha = k$, or $p.\alpha < k$ and $p = r$. Dom is constructed in a bottom-up fashion starting from the leaves of T. The goal of variable $p.\alpha$ at each node p is twofold. First, it allows to determine a path of length at most k from p to a particular node q of Dom which acts as a *witness* for guaranteeing the k-hop domination of Dom. Consequently, q will be denoted as $Witness(p)$ in the following. Second, once correctly evaluated, the value $p.\alpha$ is equal to $\|p, x\|$, where x is the furthest node in $T(p)$, the subtree of T rooted at p, that has the same witness as p.

We divide processes into *short* and *tall* according to the value of their α-variable: If p satisfies $IsShort(p)$, i.e., $p.\alpha < k$, then p is said to be *short*; otherwise, p satisfies $IsTall(p)$ and is said to be *tall*. In a terminal configuration, the meaning of $p.\alpha$ depends on whether p is *short* or *tall*.

If p is short, we have two cases: $p \neq r$ or $p = r$. In the former case, $Witness(p) \in Dom$ is outside of $T(p)$, that is, the path from p to $Witness(p)$ goes through the parent link of p in the tree, and the distance from p to $Witness(p)$ is at most $k - p.\alpha$. See, for example, in Configuration (I) of Fig. 1, $k = 2$ and $j.\alpha = 0$ mean that $Witness(j)$ is at most at distance $k - 0 = 2$, now its witness e is at distance 2. In the latter case, $p\ (= r)$ may not be k-hop dominated by any process of Dom inside its subtree and, by definition, there is no process outside its subtree, indeed $T(p) = T$, see the root a in Configuration (I) of Fig. 1. Thus, p must be placed in Dom.

If p is tall, there is a process q at $p.\alpha - k$ hops below p such that $q.\alpha = k$. So, $q \in Dom$ and p is k-hop dominated by q. Hence, $Witness(p) = q$. The path from p to $Witness(p)$ goes through a tall child with minimum α-value. See, for example, in Configuration (I) of Fig. 1, $k = 2$ and $c.\alpha = 4$ mean that $Witness(c)$, here e, is $4 - k = 2$ hops below c. Note that, if $p.\alpha = k$, then $p.\alpha - k = 0$, that is, $p = q = Witness(p)$ and p belongs to Dom.

Two examples of 2-clustering computed by $\mathcal{D}(2)$ are given in Fig. 1. In Fig. 1.(I), the root is a *short* process, consequently it belongs to Dom. In Fig. 1.(II), the root is a *tall* process, consequently it does not belong to Dom.

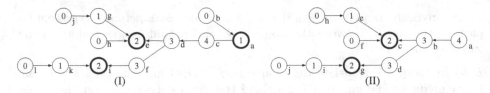

Fig. 1. Two examples of 2-hop dominating sets computed by $\mathcal{D}(2)$. We only draw the spanning tree, other edges are omitted. The root of each tree is the rightmost node. α-values are given inside the nodes. Bold circles represent members of *Dom*. Arrows represent the path from nodes to their associated witnesses.

6   Self-Stabilization of $\mathcal{D}(k)$

According to the sufficient condition (Lemma `silent_self_stab`) given in Sect. 3, we prove the self-stabilization of $\mathcal{D}(k)$ in two steps: termination in Subsect. 6.1 and partial correctness in Subsect. 6.2.

6.1   Termination of $\mathcal{D}(k)$.

We use the general result from Sect. 4 to prove termination of $\mathcal{D}(k)$, expressed as follows:

Theorem `k_dom_set_terminates`: $\forall g$, `Assume`$_{\text{kdom}}$ $g \rightarrow$ `Acc Step` g.

First, we assume `sym_net` and that the root node r exists. We instantiate `safe` as every configuration in which read-only variables `Par` satisfy (`span_tree` r `Par`). Notice that the assumption on the existence of the spanning tree T rooted at r is mandatory, since, as we will see below, the local potentials we use in our proof are based on the depth of nodes in T. Finally, note that it is easy to prove that `safe` is stable since it only depends on read-only variables.

Potential. We define the *depth* of a node as the distance between the node and the root r in the spanning tree T. Let `sg` be a safe configuration and `p` be a node. (`depth sg p`) is 1 (natural number, type `nat`) if `p` is the root r, and (1 + (`depth sg q`)) where `q` the parent of `p` in T otherwise. This definition relies on structural induction on (`WF_par n`). We define the potential (`pot sg p`) of node `p` in safe configuration `sg` as 0 if `p` is not enabled in `sg`, and (`depth sg p`) otherwise.

Local Criterion. Let `sg1` and `sg2` be two safe configurations such that (`safeStep sg2 sg1`). Consider a node `p` whose potential increases during the step, *i.e.*, such that (`pot sg1 p`) $<_{\text{P}}$ (`pot sg2 p`). This means, from definition of `pot`, that `p` is disabled at `sg1` (potential is 0) and becomes enabled at `sg2` (potential equals (`depth sg2 p`)>0). To show the local criterion, we exhibit a down-path in the tree T from `p` to some leaf that contains a node `q` enabled in `sg1` which becomes disabled in the next configuration, `sg2`. We prove the result in two steps. First, we necessarily exhibit a child of node `p`, `child`, which executes its algorithm during the step. As second step, we prove Lemma `moving_node_has_disabled_desc`, which states that when the node `child` moves, it is down-linked in T to a node (maybe the node itself) which was enabled and becomes disabled during the step. This result is proven by induction on (WF_child child), *i.e.*, on the down-paths from child in T.

Global Criterion. Global criterion requires to find a node whose potential differs between sg1 and sg2. We show that there is a node p with potential (depth sg1 p) in sg1 (>0, by definition), and potential 0 in sg2. Namely, p is enabled in sg1, but disabled in sg2. The proof uses the fact that at least one node has moved during the step. Then, we reuse Lemma moving_node_has_disabled_desc to show that any node that participates to the step has a descendant (on a given down-path of T) which is enabled in sg1, but disabled in sg2.

Termination. Theorem k_dom_set_terminates follows directly from local and global criteria.

6.2   Partial Correctness of $\mathcal{D}(k)$

The proof of partial correctness consists in showing that predicate $\mathbb{P}_{kDom}$ holds in any terminal configuration satisfying Assume$_{kdom}$:

Theorem kdom_set_at_terminal :
   $\forall$g, Assume$_{kdom}$ g $\rightarrow$ terminal g $\rightarrow$ $\mathbb{P}_{kDom}$ g .

From definition of $\mathbb{P}_{kDom}$, we need to check the existence of a path in G between any node p and any node kdom $\in Dom$, such that this path is of length at most k. To achieve this property, the algorithm builds tree paths of particular shape: those paths use edges of T in both direct sense (from a node to its parent) and reverse sense (from a node to one of its children). Precisely, these edges are defined using relation is_kDom_edge, which depends on α-values: for any short node s, we select the edge linking s to its parent in T (using Par); while for any tall node t which is not in Dom, we select an edge linking t to a child c such that $c.\alpha = t.\alpha - 1$. The relation is_kDom_edge defines a subgraph of G called kdom-graph. So, to show Theorem kdom_at_terminal, it is sufficient prove that for any configuration g such that (Assume$_{kdom}$ g) and (terminal g), we have:

   $\forall$p, $\exists$kdom, (*kDominator* g kdom) $\wedge$
      $\exists$path, (is_kDom_path g path kdom p) $\wedge$ (length path) $\leq$ k.

where is_kDom_path checks that its parameter path is a path on the kdom-graph between kdom and p.

   The rest of the analysis is conducted assuming a terminal configuration g such that (Assume$_{kdom}$ g) holds. We first prove that any node p satisfying $p.\alpha > 0$ has a child q such that $p.\alpha = q.\alpha + 1$ (the proof is simply a case analysis on $MaxAShort(q) + MinATall(q) \leq 2k - 2$). Then, the proof is split into two cases, depending on whether the node is tall or short. We prove, for every tall (resp. short) node p and every $i \in \mathbb{N}$, that when $p.\alpha = k + i$ (resp. $k - i$), there exists a witness node q for which *kDominator* holds and a path, of length at most i, from p to q in kdom-graph. In both cases, the proof is conducted by induction on i.

Conclusion. Using Lemma silent_self_stab, we obtain that $\mathcal{D}(k)$ is a silent self-stabilizing algorithm for $\mathbb{P}_{kDom}$:

Theorem `kdom_set_silent_self_stab`:
   silence Assume$_\text{kdom}$ $\wedge$ self_stab Assume$_\text{kdom}$ $\mathbb{S}_{\mathbb{P}_\text{kDom}}$.

7 Quantitative Properties

In addition to partial correctness, we have shown that the k-hop dominating Dom set built by $\mathcal{D}(k)$ satisfies $|Dom| \leq \lfloor \frac{n-1}{k+1} \rfloor + 1$, where n is the number of nodes. Precisely, we have formally proven the equivalent property which states that $(n-1) \geq (k+1)(|Dom| - 1)$. Intuitively, this means that at least all but one element of Dom have been chosen as witness by at least $k+1$ distinct nodes each.

Counting Elements in Sets. We have set up a library dealing with cardinality of sets in general, and then finite sets. The library contains basic properties about set operations such as cardinality of Cartesian product, disjoint union, subset inclusion, *etc.* We also proved in Coq the existence of finite cardinality for finite sets using lists. Those proofs have been conducted using standard techniques.

Proving Counting for $\mathcal{D}(k)$. First, we assume a terminal configuration g. Using above results about the number of elements in the list `all_nodes`, we show the existence of the natural number n, *i.e.*, the number of nodes. Similarly, the existence of the natural number $|Dom|$ is obtained using the list `all_nodes` restricted to nodes p such that ($kDominator$ (g p) = true).

Then, we define as *regular head* each node of Dom such that $\alpha = k$. By definition the set of regular heads is included in Dom. Again, we prove the existence of the natural number rh which represents the number of regular heads in g.

Next, we define a *regular node* as a node which designates a regular head as witness. We prove the existence of the natural number rn which is the number of regular nodes in g. We prove that for each regular head h, for any $0 \leq i \leq k$, there is a regular node p_i such that $\alpha = i$ which designates h as witness in g. This implies that there is a path of length $k+1$ in the `kdom`-graph linking p_0 to h. We then group each regular head together with the regular nodes that designate it as witness: each group contains at least $k+1$ regular nodes. Thus, $rn \geq (k+1)rh$.

Now, we have two cases. If the root is tall in g (*i.e.*, $r.\alpha \geq k$), then $rh = |Dom|$ and $rn = n$. Otherwise, the root is short in g, and Dom contains both the regular heads and the root (which is not regular in this case). Thus, $|Dom| = rh + 1$ and, similarly, the set of nodes contains at least regular nodes plus the root, so $rn \leq n - 1$. Hence, in either case, $(n-1) \geq (k+1)(|Dom| - 1)$ holds in g.

8 Conclusion

We proposed a general framework to build certified proofs of self-stabilizing algorithms. To achieve our goals, we developed, in particular, general tools about potential functions, which are commonly used in termination proofs of self-stabilizing algorithms. We also proposed a library dealing with cardinality of sets. We use this latter to show a quantitative property on the output of our case-study algorithm.

In future works, we expect to certify more complex self-stabilizing algorithms. Such algorithms are usually designed by composing more basic blocks. In this line of thought, we envision to certify general theorems related to classic composition techniques such as collateral or fair compositions.

Finally, we expect to use our experience on quantitative properties to tackle the certification of time complexity of stabilizing algorithms, *a.k.a.* the stabilization time.

References

1. Ben-Othman, J., Bessaoud, K., Bui, A., Pilard, L.: Self-stabilizing algorithm for efficient topology control in wireless sensor networks. J. Comput. Sci. **4**(4), 199–208 (2013)
2. Blanqui, F., Koprowski, A.: CoLoR: a coq library on well-founded rewrite relations and its application to the automated verification of termination certificates. Math. Struct. Comput. Sci. **21**(4), 827–859 (2011)
3. Caron, E., Chuffart, F., Tedeschi, C.: When self-stabilization meets real platforms: an experimental study of a peer-to-peer service discovery system. future gener. comput. syst. **29**(6), 1533–1543 (2013)
4. Chen, M., Monin, J.F.: Formal verification of netlog protocols. In: TASE (2012)
5. Chen, N., Yu, H., Huang, S.: A self-stabilizing algorithm for constructing spanning trees. Inf. Process. Lett. **39**, 147–151 (1991)
6. Courtieu, P.: Proving self-stabilization with a proof assistant. In: IPDPS (2002)
7. Courtieu, P., Rieg, L., Tixeuil, S., Urbain, X.: Impossibility of gathering, a certification. Inf. Process. Lett. **115**(3), 447–452 (2015)
8. Datta, A.K., Larmore, L.L., Devismes, S., Heurtefeux, K., Rivierre, Y.: Competitive self-stabilizing k-clustering. In: ICDCS (2012)
9. Datta, A.K., Larmore, L.L., Devismes, S., Heurtefeux, K., Rivierre, Y.: Self-stabilizing small k-dominating sets. IJNC **3**(1), 116–136 (2013)
10. Deng, Y., Monin, J.F.: Verifying self-stabilizing population protocols with Coq. In: TASE (2009)
11. Dershowitz, N., Manna, Z.: Proving termination with multiset orderings. Commun. ACM **22**(8), 465–476 (1979)
12. Dijkstra, E.W.: Self-stabilizing systems in spite of distributed control. Commun. ACM **17**, 643–644 (1974)
13. Dolev, S., Gouda, M.G., Schneider, M.: Memory requirements for silent stabilization. In: PODC, pp. 27–34 (1996)
14. Ghosh, S.: An alternative solution to a problem on self-stabilization. ACM Trans. Program. Lang. Syst. **15**(4), 735–742 (1993)
15. Huang, S., Chen, N.: Self-stabilizing depth-first token circulation on networks. Distrib. Comput. **7**(1), 61–66 (1993)
16. Küfner, P., Nestmann, U., Rickmann, C.: Formal verification of distributed algorithms. In: Baeten, J.C.M., Ball, T., de Boer, F.S. (eds.) TCS 2012. LNCS, vol. 7604, pp. 209–224. Springer, Heidelberg (2012)
17. Kulkarni, S.S., Rushby, J.M., Shankar, N.: A case-study in component-based mechanical verification of fault-tolerant programs. In: WSS, pp. 33–40 (1999)
18. Lamport, L.: How to write a 21st century proof. J. fixed point theory appl. **11**(1), 43–63 (2012)
19. The Coq Development Team: The Coq Proof Assistant, Reference Manual. http://coq.inria.fr/refman/

Developing Honest Java Programs with Diogenes

Nicola Atzei and Massimo Bartoletti(✉)

Università Degli Studi di Cagliari, Cagliari, Italy
{atzeinicola,bart}@unica.it

Abstract. Modern distributed applications are typically obtained by integrating new code with legacy (and possibly untrusted) third-party services. Some recent works have proposed to discipline the interaction among these services through *behavioural contracts*. The idea is a dynamic discovery and composition of services, where only those with compliant contracts can interact, and their execution is monitored to detect and sanction contract breaches. In this setting, a service is said *honest* if it always respects the contracts it advertises. Being honest is crucial, because it guarantees a service not to be sanctioned; further, compositions of honest services are deadlock-free. However, developing honest programs is not an easy task, because contracts must be respected even in the presence of failures (whether accidental or malicious) of the context. In this paper we present Diogenes, a suite of tools which supports programmers in writing honest Java programs. Through an Eclipse plugin, programmers can write a specification of the service, verify its honesty, and translate it into a skeletal Java program. Then, they can refine this skeleton into proper Java code, and use the tool to verify that its honesty has not been compromised by the refinement.

1 Introduction

Developing modern distributed applications is a challenging task: programmers have to reliably compose loosely-coupled services which can dynamically discover and invoke other services through open networks, and may be subject to failures and attacks. Unless these services are implemented in a decentralized manner (e.g., as smart contracts in Ethereum or Contractvm [11,13]), they will be under the governance of mutually distrusting providers, possibly competing among each other. Typically, these providers offer little or no guarantees about the services they control, and in particular they reserve the right to change the service code (if not the Service Level Agreement *tout court*) at their discretion.

Therefore, to guarantee the reliability and security of distributed applications, one cannot directly apply standard analysis techniques for programming languages (like e.g., type systems or model checking). Indeed, these analysis techniques usually need to inspect the code of the *whole* application, while under the given assumptions one can only reason about the services under their control. In particular, compositional verification based on choreographies [1,16] is not suitable in this setting, because to ensure the correctness of the whole application, all its components have to be verified.

© IFIP International Federation for Information Processing 2016
E. Albert and I. Lanese (Eds.): FORTE 2016, LNCS 9688, pp. 52–61, 2016.
DOI: 10.1007/978-3-319-39570-8_4

From Service-Oriented to Contract-Oriented Computing. A possible counter-measure to these issues is to use *contracts* to regulate the interaction between services. By advertising a contract, a service commits itself to respect a given behaviour when, after stipulation, it will interact with others. In this setting, a service infrastructure acts as a trusted third party, which collects all the advertised contracts, and establishes sessions between participants with compliant ones. Participants can then interact through sessions, by sending and receiving messages as required by their contracts (or even choosing to violate them, if they find this choice more convenient). An actual implementation of this paradigm is the middleware in [5], which offers a set of APIs through which services can advertise, stipulate, and execute contracts (based on binary session types [14]).

To incentivize honest behaviour, contract-oriented infrastructures monitor all the messages exchanged among services, to sanction those which do not respect their contracts. Sanctions can be of different nature: e.g., pecuniary compensations, adaptations of the service binding [19], or they can decrease the reputation of a service whenever it violates a contract, in order to marginalize dishonest services in the selection phase [5].

Experimental evidence about the programming paradigm and incentive mechanisms of [5] shows that contract-orientation can mitigate the effort of handling potential misbehaviour of external services, at the cost of a tolerable loss in efficiency due to the contract-based service selection and monitoring.

Honesty Attacks. The sanction mechanism of contract-oriented services allows a new kind of attacks: adversaries can try to exploit possible discrepancies between the promised and the actual behaviour of a service, in order to make it sanctioned. For instance, consider a naïve online store with the following behaviour:

1. advertise a contract to "receive an **order** from a client, and then either **ship** the ordered item or **abort** the transaction";
2. wait to receive an **order**;
3. advertise a contract to "receive a **quote** from a package delivery service, and then either **confirm** or **abort**";
4. wait to receive a quote from the delivery service;
5. if the quote is below a certain threshold, then **confirm** the delivery and **ship** to the client; otherwise, **abort** both transactions.

Now, assume an adversary which plays the role of a delivery service, and never sends the **quote**. This makes the store violate its contract with the client: indeed, the store should either **ship** or **abort**, but these actions can only be performed after the delivery service has sent a **quote**. Therefore, the store can be sanctioned.

Since these *honesty attacks* may compromise the service and cause economic damage to its provider, it is important to detect the underlying vulnerabilities *before* deployment. Intuitively, a service is vulnerable if, in *some* execution context, it does *not* respect some of the contracts it advertises. This may happen either unintentionally (because of errors in the service specification, or in its implementation), or even because of malicious behaviour. Therefore, to avoid sanctions a service must be able to respect *all* the contracts it advertises, in *all* possible contexts — even those populated by adversaries. We call this property *honesty*. Whenever compliance between contracts ensures their deadlock-freedom (as for the relations in [2,3,17,20]), the honesty property can be lifted from contracts to services: systems of honest services are deadlock-free (Theorem 6 in [9]).

Some recent works have studied honesty at the specification level, using the process calculus CO_2 for modelling contract-oriented services [6,8,9]. Practical experience with CO_2 has shown that writing honest specifications is not an easy task, especially when a service has to juggle with multiple sessions. The reason of this difficulty lies in the fact that, to devise an honest specification, a designer has to anticipate all the possible moves of the context, but at design time he does not yet know in which context his service will be run. Hence, tools to automate the verification of honesty in CO_2 may be of great help.

A further obstacle to the development of honest services is that, even if we start from an honest CO_2 specification, it is still possible that honesty is not preserved when refining the specification into an actual implementation. Analysis techniques for checking honesty at the level of the implementation are therefore needed in order to develop reliable contract-oriented applications.

Contributions. To support programmers in the development of contract-oriented applications, we provide a suite of tools (named *Diogenes*) with the following features: (i) writing CO_2 specifications of services within an Eclipse plugin; (ii) verifying honesty of these specifications; (iii) generating from them skeletal Java programs which use the contract-oriented APIs of the middleware in [5]; (iv) verifying the honesty of Java programs upon refinement. We validate our tools by applying them to all the case studies in [6]: in particular, we specify each of these case studies in CO_2, and we successfully verify the honesty of both the specifications and their Java refinements. Overall, we can execute these verified services using the middleware in [5], being guaranteed that they will not incur in sanctions, and that interactions with other honest services will be deadlock-free. Our tools, the case studies, and a tutorial are available at co2.unica.it/diogenes.

2 Diogenes in a Nutshell

In this section we show the main features of our tools with the help of a small example. Suppose we want to implement an online store which receives orders from customers, and relies upon external distributors to retrieve items.

Contracts. The store has two contracts: C specifies the interaction with customers, and D with distributors. In C, the store declares that it will wait for an **order**, and then send either the corresponding **amount** or an **abort** message (e.g., in case the ordered item is not available). The answer may depend on an external distributor service, which waits for a **request**, and then answers **ok** or **no**. We specify these two contracts as the following binary session types [15]:

```
contract C { order? string . ( amount! int (+) abort! ) }
contract D { req! string . ( ok? + no? ) }
```

Receive actions are marked with the symbol ? and grouped by +; instead, send actions are marked with ! and grouped by (+). The symbol . denotes sequential composition. We specify the sort of a message (int, string, or unit) after the action label; sort unit is used for pure synchronization, and it can be omitted.

Specification. A naïve CO_2 specification of our store is the following:

```
1   specification StoreDishonest {
2       tellAndWait x C .
3       receive x order? v:string . (
4           tellAndWait y D . (
5               send y req! *:string .
6               receive [
7                   y <- ok? . send x amount! *:int
8                   y <- no? . send x abort!
9               ] + t . send x abort!))
10  }
```

At line 2, the store advertises the contract C, and then waits until a session is established with some customer; when this happens, the variable x is bound to the session name. At line 3 the store waits to receive an **order**, binding it to the variable v. At line 4 the store advertises the contract D to establish a session y with a distributor; at line 5, it sends a **request** with the value v. Finally, the store waits to receive a response **ok** or **no** from the distributor, and accordingly responds **amount** or **abort** to the customer (lines 6 − 8). The sent amount *:int is placeholder, to be replaced upon refinement. The internal action t at line 9 models a timeout, fired in case no response is received from the distributor.

Our tool correctly detects that this specification is *dishonest*, outputting:

```
result: ("y",$ 0)(
    StoreDishonest[tell "y" D . ask "y" True . (...)]
    | $ 0["abort" ! unit . 0 (+) "amount" ! int . 0])
result: ($ 0,$ 1)(
    StoreDishonest[do $ 0 "abort" ! unit . (0).Sum]
    | $ 0["abort" ! unit . 0 (+) "amount" ! int . 0]
    | $ 1[ready "no" ? unit . 0])
honesty: false
```

There are two causes for dishonesty. First, if the session y is never established (e.g., because no distributor is available), the store is stuck at line 4 and cannot fulfil C at session x ($0 in the output message). Second, if the distributor response arrives after the timeout (line 9), the store does not consume its input, and so it does not respect the contract D at session y ($1 in the output message).

A possible way to fix the previous specification is the following:

```
1   specification StoreHonest {
2       tellAndWait x C .
3       receive x order? v:string . (
4           tellRetract y D . (
5               send y req! *:string .
6               receive [
7                   y <- ok? . send x amount! *:int
8                   y <- no? . send x abort!
9               ] + t . (send x abort! | receive y ok? no?))
10              : send x abort!)
11  }
```

The primitive `tellRetract` at line 4 ensures that if the session `x` is not established within a given deadline (immaterial in the specification) the contract `D` is retracted, and the control passes to line 10. Further, in the timeout branch we have added a parallel execution of a `receive` to consume orphan inputs (line 9). Now the tool correctly detects that the revised specification is honest.

An Execution Context. We now show a possible context wherein to execute our online store. Although the context is not needed for checking the honesty of the store, we use it to complete the presentation of the primitives of CO_2.

```
1   specification Buyer {
2       tellAndReturn x { order! string . ( amount? int + abort? ) } .
3       send x order! *:string .
4       receive [
5           x <- amount? n:int
6           x <- abort?
7       ]
8   }
9
10  specification Distributor {
11      tellRetract x { req? string . ( ok! (+) no! ) } .
12      receive x req? msg:string .
13      if *:boolean then send x ok! else send x no!
14  }
```

The contracts of the `Buyer` (lines 2) and that of the `Distributor` (line 11) are compliant with the contracts `C` and `D` advertised by the store. The `Buyer` uses the statement `tellAndReturn` to advertise its contract: it does not wait the session is established, but postpone the waiting phase until it is strictly required (line 3 in this case), although the session could be already started in the meantime. The `Distributor` uses a conditional statement (with a dummy guard `*:boolean`) to choose whether accepting or not the store request.

Code Generation and Refinement. Diogenes translates CO_2 specifications into Java skeletons, using the APIs of the middleware in [5]. For instance, from the `StoreHonest` specification given above, it generates the following skeleton[1]:

```
1   public class StoreHonest extends Participant {
2     public void run() {
3       Session<TST> x = tellAndWait(C);                    // (line 2)
4
5       Message msg = x.waitForReceive("order");            // (line 3)
6       String v = msg.getStringValue();
7
8       try {
9         Session<TST> y = tellAndWait(D, 10000);           // (line 4)
10        y.sendIfAllowed("req", stringP);                  // (line 5)
11
12        try {
13          Message msg_1 = y.waitForReceive(10000,"ok","no"); // (line 6)
14          switch (msg_1.getLabel()) {
15          case "ok": x.sendIfAllowed("amount", intP); break; // (line 7)
16          case "no": x.sendIfAllowed("abort"); break;        // (line 8)
17          }
18        }
19        catch (TimeExpiredException e) {                  // (line 9)
```

---
[1] Minor cosmetic changes are applied to improve readability.

```
20              parallel(()->{x.sendIfAllowed("abort");});
21              parallel(()->{y.waitForReceive("ok","no");});
22          }
23      }
24      catch(ContractExpiredException e) {
25          //contract D retracted
26          x.sendIfAllowed("abort");                    // (line 10)
27      }
28    }
29  }
```

We use Java exceptions to deal with both the tellRetract and receive primitives: the ContractExpiredException is thrown by line 9 if the session y is not established within a given timeout (10 s), while the TimeExpiredException is thrown by line 13 if a message is not received within the timeout. The parallel method at lines 20-21 starts a new thread which executes the given Runnable instance. The timeout values, as well as the order amount at line 15 , are just placeholders; in an actual implementation of the store service, we may want to delegate the computation of amount to a separated method, e.g.:

```
30      public int getOrderAmount(String order) throws MyException {...}
```

and change the placeholder intP at line 15 with getOrderAmount(v). The method could read the order amount from a file or a database, and suppose that each possible exception is caught and hidden behind MyException. The failure of this method can be considered non-deterministic, so we need to "instruct" our verification tool in order to consider all the possible ways the method can terminate. To this purpose, we provide the annotation @SkipMethod(value="<value>"), interpreted by the checker as follows: (i) assumes that the method does not perform any action directed to the middleware; (ii) considers <value> as the returning value on success; (iii) considers the declared exceptions as possible exit points on failure. Diogenes can symbolically consider both the case of a normal method termination and all the possible exceptional terminations.

Verification. We can check the honesty of a Java program through the static method HonestyChecker.isHonest(StoreHonest.class), which returns one of the following values:

- HONEST: the tool has inferred a CO_2 specification and verified its honesty;
- DISHONEST: as above, but the inferred CO_2 specification is inferred, but it is dishonest;
- UNKNOWN: the tool has been unable to infer a CO_2 specification, e.g. because of unhandled exceptions within the class under test.

For our refined store, the Java honesty checker returns UNKNOWN and outputs:

```
1   error details: MyException:
2       This exception is thrown by the honesty checker. Please catch it!
3       at i.u.c.store.StoreHonest.getOrderAmount(Store.java:30)
4       at i.u.c.store.StoreHonest.run(Store.java:15)
5       at i.u.c.honesty.HonestyChecker.runProcess(HonestyChecker.java:182)
```

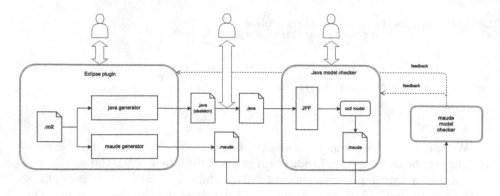

Fig. 1. Data flow schema

This means that if the method `getOrderAmount` fails, then the program will terminate abruptly, and so the store may violate the contract. We can recover honesty by catching `MyException` with `x.sendIfAllowed("abort")`. With this modification, the Java honesty checker correctly outputs `HONEST`.

3 Architecture

Diogenes has three main components: an honesty checker for CO_2, an honesty checker for Java, and an Eclipse plugin which integrates the two checkers with an editor of CO_2 specifications. We sketch the architecture of our tools in Fig. 1.

The CO_2 honesty checker implements the verification technique introduced in [6]. This technique is built upon an abstract semantics of CO_2 which approximates both values (sent, received, and in conditional expressions) and the actual *context* wherein a process is executed. This abstraction is a *sound* over-approximation of honesty: namely, if the abstraction of a process is honest, then also the concrete one is honest. Further, in the fragment of CO_2 without conditional statements the analysis is also *complete*, i.e. if a concrete process is honest, then also its abstraction is honest. For processes without delimitation/parallel under process definitions, the associated abstractions are finite-state, hence we can verify their honesty by model checking a (finite) state space. For processes outside this class the analysis is still correct, but it may not terminate; indeed, a negative result in [9] excludes the existence of algorithms for honesty that are at the same time sound, complete, and terminating in full CO_2. Our implementation first translates a CO_2 process into a Maude term [10], and then uses the Maude LTL model checker [12] to decide honesty of its abstract semantics.

The Java honesty checker is built on top of *Java PathFinder* (JPF, [18,21]). The JPF core is a virtual machine for Java bytecode that can be configured to act as a model checker. We define suitable *listeners* to catch the requests to the contract-oriented middleware [5], and to simulate *all* the possible responses that the application can receive from it. Through JPF we symbolically execute and backtrack the program, and eventually we infer a CO_2 specification that over-approximates its behaviour. Then, we apply the CO_2 honesty checker to establish the honesty of the Java program. The accuracy of the inferred CO_2 specification partially relies on the programmer: the methods involved in the application logic have to be correctly annotated, and in particular they have to declare all possible exceptions that can be thrown at runtime.

The Eclipse plugin supports writing CO_2 specifications, providing syntax highlighting, code auto-completion, syntactic/semantic checks, and static type checking on sort usage. It relies on Xtext (www.eclipse.org/Xtext), a framework for developing programming languages, and on Xsemantics (xsemantics.sourceforge.net), a domain-specific language for writing type systems.

4   Conclusions

Diogenes fills a gap between foundational research on honesty [6,8,9] and more practical research on contract-oriented programming [5]. Its effectiveness can be improved in several ways, ranging from the precision of the analysis, to the informative quality of output messages provided by the honesty checkers.

The accuracy of the honesty analysis could be improved e.g., by implementing the type checking technique of [7], which can correctly classify the honesty of some forms of infinite-state of processes (while the current honesty checker is only guaranteed to terminate for processes without delimitation/parallel within recursion). Another form of improvement would be to extend the analysis to deal with timing constraints. This could be done e.g. by exploiting the timed version of CO_2 proposed in [5] and the timed session types of [4]. Although the current analysis for honesty does not consider timing constraints, it may give useful feedback also when applied to timed specifications. For instance, it could detect that some prescribed actions cannot be performed because the actions they depend on may be blocked by an unresponsive context.

The error reporting facilities could be improved in several directions: e.g., it would be helpful for programmers to know which parts of the program make it dishonest, what are the contract obligations that are not fulfilled, and in what session. Further, it would be useful to suggest possible corrections to the designer.

Another direction for future work concerns relating the original CO_2 specification with the refined Java code. In fact, our tools only guarantee that the Java skeleton generated from an (honest) CO_2 specification is (honest and) coherent with the specification. If the programmer further refines the Java code, e.g. by removing some contract advertisements, then the Java honesty checker can still check that the resulting code is honest, but the coherence with the original specification may be lost. An additional static analysis could establish that the CO_2 process inferred from the refined Java code by JPF is a (sort of) *subtype* of the original specification, and so that it can be safely used in the same contexts.

Acknowledgments. This work has been partially supported by Aut. Reg. of Sardinia P.I.A. 2013 "NOMAD", and by EU COST Action IC1201 "Behavioural Types for Reliable Large-Scale Software Systems" (BETTY).

References

1. van der Aalst, W.M.P., Lohmann, N., Massuthe, P., Stahl, C., Wolf, K.: Multiparty contracts: agreeing and implementing interorganizational processes. Comput. J. **53**(1), 90–106 (2010)
2. Acciai, L., Boreale, M., Zavattaro, G.: Behavioural contracts with request-response operations. In: Clarke, D., Agha, G. (eds.) COORDINATION 2010. LNCS, vol. 6116, pp. 16–30. Springer, Heidelberg (2010)
3. Barbanera, F., de'Liguoro, U.: Two notions of sub-behaviour for session-based client/server systems. In: PPDP, pp. 155–164. ACM (2010)
4. Bartoletti, M., Cimoli, T., Murgia, M., Podda, A.S., Pompianu, L.: Compliance and subtyping in timed session types. In: Graf, S., Viswanathan, M. (eds.) Formal Techniques for Distributed Objects, Components, and Systems. LNCS, vol. 9039, pp. 161–177. Springer, Heidelberg (2015)
5. Bartoletti, M., Cimoli, T., Murgia, M., Podda, A.S., Pompianu, L.: A contract-oriented middleware. In: Braga, C., et al. (eds.) FACS 2015. LNCS, vol. 9539, pp. 86–104. Springer, Heidelberg (2016). doi:10.1007/978-3-319-28934-2_5. http://co2.unica.it
6. Bartoletti, M., Murgia, M., Scalas, A., Zunino, R.: Verifiable abstractions for contract-oriented systems. JLAMP (2015, to appear)
7. Bartoletti, M., Scalas, A., Tuosto, E., Zunino, R.: Honesty by typing. In: Beyer, D., Boreale, M. (eds.) FORTE 2013 and FMOODS 2013. LNCS, vol. 7892, pp. 305–320. Springer, Heidelberg (2013). http://tcs.unica.it/papers/HbT.pdf
8. Bartoletti, M., Tuosto, E., Zunino, R.: Contract-oriented computing in CO_2. Sci. Ann. Comp. Sci. **22**(1), 5–60 (2012)
9. Bartoletti, M., Zunino, R.: On the decidability of honesty and of its variants. In: Hildebrandt, T., Ravara, A., van der Werf, J.M., Weidlich, M. (eds.) WS-FM 2014 + WS-FM 2015. LNCS, vol. 9421, pp. 143–166. Springer, Heidelberg (2016). doi:10.1007/978-3-319-33612-1_9
10. Clavel, M., Durán, F., Eker, S., Lincoln, P., Martí-Oliet, N., Meseguer, J., Quesada, J.F.: Maude: specification and programming in rewriting logic. In: TCS (2001)
11. Contractvm. https://github.com/contractvm
12. Eker, S., Meseguer, J., Sridharanarayanan, A.: The maude LTL model checker. Electr. Notes Theor. Comput. Sci. **71**, 162–187 (2002)
13. Ethereum. https://github.com/ethereum/
14. Honda, K.: Types for dyadic interaction. In: Best, E. (ed.) CONCUR 1993. LNCS, vol. 715, pp. 509–523. Springer, Heidelberg (1993)
15. Honda, K., Vasconcelos, V.T., Kubo, M.: Language primitives and type discipline for structured communication-based programming. In: Hankin, C. (ed.) ESOP 1998. LNCS, vol. 1381, pp. 122–138. Springer, Heidelberg (1998)
16. Honda, K., Yoshida, N., Carbone, M.: Multiparty asynchronous session types. J. ACM **63**(1), 9:1–9:67 (2016)
17. Laneve, C., Padovani, L.: The *must* preorder revisited. In: Caires, L., Vasconcelos, V.T. (eds.) CONCUR 2007. LNCS, vol. 4703, pp. 212–225. Springer, Heidelberg (2007)
18. Lerda, F., Visser, W.: Addressing dynamic issues of program model checking. In: Dwyer, M.B. (ed.) SPIN 2001. LNCS, vol. 2057, pp. 80–102. Springer, Heidelberg (2001)

19. Mukhija, A., Dingwall-Smith, A., Rosenblum, D.: QoS-aware service composition in Dino. In: ECOWS, LNCS, vol. 5900, pp. 3–12. Springer (2007)
20. Rensink, A., Vogler, W.: Fair testing. Inf. Comput. **205**(2), 125–198 (2007)
21. Visser, W., Havelund, K., Brat, G., Park, S., Lerda, F.: Model checking programs. Autom. Softw. Eng. **10**(2), 203–232 (2003)

Playing with Our CAT
and Communication-Centric Applications

Davide Basile[1,2](✉), Pierpaolo Degano[2], Gian-Luigi Ferrari[2],
and Emilio Tuosto[3]

[1] I.S.T.I "A.Faedo" CNR Pisa, Pisa, Italy
dbasile@isti.cnr.it
[2] Department of Computer Science, University of Pisa, Pisa, Italy
{degano,giangi}@di.unipi.it
[3] Department of Computer Science, University of Leicester, Leicester, UK
emilio@le.ac.uk

Abstract. We describe CAT, a toolkit supporting the analysis of communication-centric applications, i.e., applications consisting of ensembles of interacting services. Services are modelled in CAT as *contract automata* and communication safety is defined in terms of *agreement properties*. With the help of a simple (albeit non trivial) example, we demonstrate how CAT can (*i*) verify agreement properties, (*ii*) synthesise an orchestrator enforcing communication safety, (*iii*) detect misbehaving services, and (*iv*) check when the services form a choreography. The use of mixed-integer linear programming is a distinguished characteristic of CAT that allows us to verify context-sensitive properties of agreement.

1 Introduction

Communication is increasingly important in modern applications, especially for the distributed ones. Remote procedure/method invocations are loosing their prominence at the application level due to their poor scalability, crucial in modern distributed applications. Communication-based modelling is also appealing for non-distributed software. For instance, application-level protocols can be devised to specify the behavioural constraints ensuring the correct use of a library or of an off-the-shelf component. This trend is also witnessed by the growth that service-oriented or cloud computing had in the software industry. In this context, composition of software becomes paramount and requires proper theoretical foundations as well as tool support. In fact, although scalable, communication-centric applications may pose non trivial obstacles to validation.

We showcase CAT, a prototype toolkit supporting the validation of communication-centric applications. This toolkit (available at [3]) is based on *contract automata* [4–6], a recently proposed formal model of service composition. Contract automata abstractly describe (the communication pattern of)

The first three authors have been partially supported by project PRA_2016_64 "Through the fog" funded by the University of Pisa.

© IFIP International Federation for Information Processing 2016
E. Albert and I. Lanese (Eds.): FORTE 2016, LNCS 9688, pp. 62–73, 2016.
DOI: 10.1007/978-3-319-39570-8_5

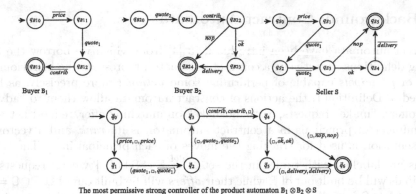

The most permissive strong controller of the product automaton $B_1 \otimes B_2 \otimes S$

Fig. 1. The contract automata for 2BP

services as automata whose transitions represent *requests* and *offers*. An interaction between two services occurs when a *match* action is possible, that is when one service's offer matches a partner's request. Intuitively, contract automata capture the behaviour of services by tracking the interactions they are keen to execute with each other. Service composition is naturally described in terms of product automata. The matching between offers and requests has to guarantee *agreement* properties that amount to *safe* communications. Intuitively, an automaton admits *strong agreement* if it has at least one trace made only by match transitions; and it is *strongly safe* if all the traces are in strong agreement. Basically, strong agreement guarantees that the composition of services has a sound execution, while strong safety guarantees that *all* executions of the composition are sound. Likewise for *agreement* but for the fact that traces also admit (unmatched) offers to model interactions with an external environment.

By means of an example we describe how the analysis of communication-centric applications can be supported by CAT. To this purpose we borrow here the two-buyers protocol (2BP) from [10] which we now briefly recall. Two buyers, say B_1 and B_2, collaborate in purchasing an item from a seller S. Buyer B_1 starts the protocol by asking S the price of the desired item (*price*); the seller S makes an offer by sending the message $quote_1$ to B_1 and the message $quote_2$ to B_2. Once received its quote, buyer B_1 sends to B_2 its contribution for purchasing the item (message *contrib*). Buyer B_2 waits for the quote from S and the contribution from B_1. Then, it decides whether to terminate by issuing the *nop* message to S, or to proceed by sending an acknowledgement to S. In the latter case, S sends the item to B_2 (*delivery*), while if it receives *nop* it terminates with no further action. Figure 1 shows the contract automata of B_1, B_2, and S where each interaction is split in offers (over-lined labels) and requests (non over-lined labels).

We will apply CAT to the above protocol and show how, when the agreement property of interest is violated, we identify and fix defects.

2 Background: Contract Automata

Contract automata have been introduced in [4] from which we borrow the following definitions. Intuitively, a contract automaton represents the behaviour of a set of *principals* capable of performing some *actions*; more precisely, as formalised in Definition 1, the actions of contract automata allow them to "advertise" offers, "make" requests, or "handshake" on matching offer/request actions. The number of principals in a contract automaton is its *rank*, and a vectorial representation is used for tracking the moves of each principal in it. The transitions are labelled with tuples in the set $\mathbb{L} \overset{\text{def}}{=} \mathbb{R} \cup \mathbb{O} \cup \{\square\}$ where: requests of principals will be built out of $\mathbb{R}$ while their *offers* will be built out of $\mathbb{O}$, $\mathbb{R} \cap \mathbb{O} = \emptyset$, and $\square \notin \mathbb{R} \cup \mathbb{O}$ is a distinguished label to represent components that stay idle. We let $a, b, c, \dots$ range over $\mathbb{L}$ and fix an involution $\bar{\cdot} : \mathbb{L} \to \mathbb{L}$ such that

$$\overline{\mathbb{R}} \subseteq \mathbb{O}, \qquad \overline{\mathbb{O}} \subseteq \mathbb{R}, \qquad \forall a \in \mathbb{R} \cup \mathbb{O} : \overline{\overline{a}} = a, \quad \text{and} \quad \overline{\square} = \square$$

Offer actions are overlined, e.g. $\bar{a}$. Let $\vec{v} = (a_1, \dots, a_n)$ be a vector of *rank* r_v, then $\vec{v}_{(i)}$ denotes the i-th element. We write $\vec{v}_1 \vec{v}_2 \dots \vec{v}_m$ for the concatenation of m vectors $\vec{v}_i$; $|\vec{v}| = n$ is the rank of $\vec{v}$; and $\vec{v}^n$ for the vector obtained by n concatenations of $\vec{v}$.

Definition 1. *A tuple $\square^* b \square^*$ on $\mathbb{L}$ is a* request (resp. offer) *action on b iff $b \in \mathbb{R}$ (resp. $b \in \mathbb{O}$). A* match (action) *on b is a tuple $\square^* b \square^* \bar{b} \square^*$ on $\mathbb{L}$ ($b \in \mathbb{R} \cup \mathbb{O}$). Let $\bowtie \subseteq \mathbb{L}^* \times \mathbb{L}^*$ be the symmetric closure of $\bowtie \subseteq \mathbb{L}^* \times \mathbb{L}^*$ where $\vec{a}_1 \bowtie \vec{a}_2$ iff $|\vec{a}_1| = |\vec{a}_2|$ and both the following conditions hold*

- $\exists b \in \mathbb{R} \cup \mathbb{O}$: $\vec{a}$ *is either a request or an offer on b;*
- $\exists b \in \mathbb{R} \cup \mathbb{O}$: $\vec{a}_1$ *is an offer on b $\implies$ $\vec{a}_2$ is a request on b*
- $\exists b \in \mathbb{R} \cup \mathbb{O}$: $\vec{a}_1$ *is a request on b $\implies$ $\vec{a}_2$ is a offer on b.*

Definition 2. *Assume as given a finite set of states $\mathfrak{Q} = \{q_1, q_2, \dots\}$. Then a contract automaton $\mathcal{A}$ of rank n is a tuple $\langle Q, \vec{q_0}, A^r, A^o, T, F \rangle$, where*

- $Q = Q_1 \times \dots \times Q_n \subseteq \mathfrak{Q}^n$
- $\vec{q_0} \in Q$ *is the initial state*
- $A^r \subseteq \mathbb{R}, A^o \subseteq \mathbb{O}$ *are finite sets (of requests and offers, respectively)*
- $F \subseteq Q$ *is the set of final states*
- $T \subseteq Q \times A \times Q$ *is the set of transitions, where $A \subseteq (A^r \cup A^o \cup \{\square\})^n$ and if $(\vec{q}, \vec{a}, \vec{q'}) \in T$ then both the following conditions hold:*
  - $\vec{a}$ *is either a request or an offer or a match*
  - *if $\vec{a}_{(i)} = \square$ then it must be $\vec{q}_{(i)} = \vec{q'}_{(i)}$.*

A principal *is a contract automaton of rank 1 such that $A^r \cap co(A^o) = \emptyset$.*

A principal is not allowed to make a request on actions that it offers. We have two different operators for composing contract automata, that interleave or match the transitions of their operands. We only force a synchronisation to happen when two contract automata are ready on their respective request/offer action.

These operators represent two different policies of orchestration. The first operator, called *product*, considers the case when a service S joins a group of services already clustered as a single orchestrated service S'. In the product of S and S', the first can only accept the still available offers (requests, respectively) of S' and vice versa. In other words, S cannot interact with the principals of the orchestration S', but only with it as a whole component.

The second operation of composition, called *a-product*, puts instead all the principals of S at the same level of those of S'. Any matching request-offer of either contracts are split, and the offers and requests become available again, and are re-combined with complementary actions of S, and viceversa. The a-product turns out to satisfactorily model coordination policies in dynamically changing environments, because the a-product is a form of *dynamic orchestration*, that adjusts the workflow of messages when new principals join the contract.

We now introduce our first operation of composition; recall that we implicitly assume the alphabet of a contract automaton of rank m to be $A \subseteq (A^r \cup A^o \cup \{\square\})^m$.

Definition 3 (Product). *Let* $\mathcal{A}_i = \langle Q_i, \vec{q}_{0i}, A_i^r, A_i^o, T_i, F_i \rangle, i \in 1 \ldots n$ *be contract automata of rank* r_i. *The product* $\bigotimes_{i \in 1 \ldots n} \mathcal{A}_i$ *is the contract automaton* $\langle Q, \vec{q}_0, A^r, A^o, T, F \rangle$ *of rank* $m = \sum_{i \in 1 \ldots n} r_i$, *where:*

- $Q = Q_1 \times \ldots \times Q_n$, *where* $\vec{q}_0 = \vec{q}_{01} \ldots \vec{q}_{0n}$
- $A^r = \bigcup_{i \in 1 \cdots n} A_i^r$, $A^o = \bigcup_{i \in 1 \cdots n} A_i^o$
- $F = \{\vec{q}_1 \ldots \vec{q}_n \mid \vec{q}_1 \ldots \vec{q}_n \in Q, \vec{q}_i \in F_i, i \in 1 \ldots n\}$
- T *is the least subset of* $Q \times A \times Q$ *s.t.* $(\vec{q}, \vec{c}, \vec{q}') \in T$ *iff, when* $\vec{q} = \vec{q}_1 \ldots \vec{q}_n \in Q$, **either** *there are* $1 \le i < j \le n$ *s.t.* $(\vec{q}_i, \vec{a}_i, \vec{q}_i') \in T_i$, $(\vec{q}_j, \vec{a}_j, \vec{q}_j') \in T_j$, $\vec{a}_i \bowtie \vec{a}_j$
  and

$$\begin{cases} \vec{c} = \square^u \vec{a}_i \square^v \vec{a}_j \square^z \text{ with } u = r_1 + \ldots + r_{i-1}, \ v = r_{i+1} + \ldots + r_{j-1}, |\vec{c}| = m \\ and \\ \vec{q}' = \vec{q}_1 \ldots \vec{q}_{i-1} \ \vec{q}_i' \ \vec{q}_{i+1} \cdots \ \vec{q}_{j-1} \ \vec{q}_j' \ \vec{q}_{j+1} \ldots \vec{q}_n \end{cases}$$

  or *there is* $1 \le i \le n$ *s.t.* $(\vec{q}_i, \vec{a}_i, \vec{q}_i') \in T_i$ *and*
  $\vec{c} = \square^u \vec{a}_i \square^v$ *with* $u = r_1 + \ldots + r_{i-1}, \ v = r_{i+1} + \ldots + r_n$, *and*
  $\vec{q}' = \vec{q}_1 \ldots \vec{q}_{i-1} \ \vec{q}_i' \ \vec{q}_{i+1} \ldots \vec{q}_n$ *and*
  $\forall j \ne i, 1 \le j \le n, (\vec{q}_j, \vec{a}_j, \vec{q}_j') \in T_j$ *it does not hold that* $\vec{a}_i \bowtie \vec{a}_j$.

To retrieve the principals involved in a contract automaton obtained through the product introduced above, we introduce the following:

Definition 4 (Projection). *Let* $\mathcal{A} = \langle Q, \vec{q}_0, A^r, A^o, T, F \rangle$ *be a contract automaton of rank* n, *then the* projection *on the* i-*th principal is* $\prod^i(\mathcal{A}) = \langle \prod^i(Q), \vec{q}_{0(i)}, \prod^i(A^r), \prod^i(A^o), \prod^i(T), \prod^i(F) \rangle$ *where* $i \in 1 \ldots n$ *and:*

$$\prod^i(Q) = \{\vec{q}_{(i)} \mid \vec{q} \in Q\} \quad \prod^i(F) = \{\vec{q}_{(i)} \mid \vec{q} \in F\} \quad \prod^i(A^r) = \{a \mid a \in A^r, (q, a, q') \in \prod^i(T)\}$$

$$\prod^i(A^o) = \{\overline{a} \mid \overline{a} \in A^o, (q, \overline{a}, q') \in \prod^i(T)\} \quad \prod^i(T) = \{(\vec{q}_{(i)}, \vec{a}_{(i)}, \vec{q}'_{(i)}) \mid (\vec{q}, \vec{a}, \vec{q}') \in T \wedge \vec{a}_{(i)} \ne \square\}$$

We now define the associative product.

Definition 5 (a-Product). *Let $\mathcal{A}_1, \mathcal{A}_2$ be two contract automata of rank n and m, respectively, and let $I = \{\prod^i(\mathcal{A}_1) \mid 0 < i \leq n\} \cup \{\prod^j(\mathcal{A}_2) \mid 0 < j \leq m\}$. Then the a-product of $\mathcal{A}_1$ and $\mathcal{A}_2$ is $\mathcal{A}_1 \boxtimes \mathcal{A}_2 = \bigotimes_{\mathcal{A}_i \in I} \mathcal{A}_i$.*

3   CAT at Work

We have implemented CAT in Java according to the simple architecture of Fig. 2. The main class of CAT extends JAMATA [3], a framework for manipulating automata yielding methods for loading, storing, printing, and representing finite state automata. In other words, CAT originally specializes JAMATA on contract automata, offering to the developers an API for creating and verifying contract automata. Also, CAT interfaces with a separate module for solving linear optimization problems, called AMPL [8], described in Sect. 5. This is an original facet of CAT; in fact, it maps the (check of) agreement properties of interest on a linear optimization problem.

Fig. 2. The architecture of CAT

The user of CAT has access to its API, that can be conceptually classified as follows:

Automata operations consist of the methods CA proj(int i), that returns the automaton specifying the ith service of the composition, CA product (CA[] aut) and CA aproduct(CA[] aut) that compute respectively the product and the *associative* product of contract automata. Interestingly, product has to filter out the offers and request transitions when the source state has a corresponding outgoing match transition. Method aproduct is built on top of product by invoking product on the services obtained as projections of the automaton in input.

Safety check consists of the instance methods safe, agreement, strong Agreement, and strongSafe returning true if the corresponding agreement property holds on the contract automaton. Section 5 discusses the property of *weak agreement*.

Controllers consist of the methods CA mpc() and CA smpc() that return the *most permissive controller* (MPC), for respectively agreement and strong agreement. A controller basically represents the largest (strongly) safe sub-automaton and is obtained through a standard construction of Control Theory [7].

Liable detection consists of the methods CATransition[] liable() - returning transitions from a state s to a state t such that s is in the MPC but t

is not - and `CATransition[]` `strongLiable()` that similarly returns such transitions for the MPC of the strong agreement property. In particular, liable services are those responsible for leading a contract composition into a failure.

Decentralization includes `int[][]` `branchingCondition()`, that returns two states and an action for which the branching condition is violated. Basically, the branching condition holds if the actions of a service are not affected by the states of the other services in the composition. Another similar method that deals with open-ended interactions is `int[][]` `extendedBranchingCondition()`. The last method in this category is `int[]` `mixedChoice()` that returns a mixed-choice state (a state where a principal has enabled both offers and requests inside matches). All such methods return `null` when the conditions they check do not hold.

We describe how to interact with the API of CAT through a simple command line interface (we plan to develop a GUI as well). The API is displayed and the user can choose one of the options (this is not shown here). Each displayed option corresponds to one of the methods described above. For instance, after choosing to compute a product, the user is asked to set the contract automata on which to take the product.

```
─────────────────────────── Output 1 ───────────────────────────
Do you want to create/load other contract automata? yes                          1
Insert the name of the automaton  to load or leave empty for create a new one: B1  2
                                                                                   3
Contract automaton:                                                                4
Rank: 1, Number of states: [4], Initial state: [0], Final states: [[3]]            5
Transitions: ([0],[1],[1]), ([1],[-2],[2]), ([2],[3],[3])                          6
                                                                                   7
Do you want to create/load other contract automata? yes                          8
─────────────────────────────────────────────────────────────────
```

The user inputs the automata in CAT by providing their file names (line 2 of Output 1) and `yes` on line 8 until there are no more automata to load (in which case the user enters `no` to obtain the result of the product). For each entered automaton, CAT prints a textual description on the screen (lines 4–6 in Output 1) reporting the rank, initial and final states, and the list of transitions. The transitions are triples $(s, 1, t)$ where s is the source state, 1 is the label, and t is the target state. These elements are lists of length r (the rank of the automaton), for instance, in Output 1 $r = 1$ (cf. on line 5). The i-th element of each list corresponds to the i-th service. In particular, the i-th action in the list of labels identifies the action performed by the i-th service; such action is strictly positive (if the action is an offer), strictly negative (if it is a request), and 0 if the service is idle in the transition. For B1, actions $price$, $quote_1$, and $contrib$ are represented with the integers 1, −2, and 3, respectively.

First CAT computes the product automaton, and then it displays the result (`B1xB2xS` in our example and stores it in a file named `B1xB2xS.data`). From the main menu, the user can now choose to compute the MPC of the product automaton (shown in Fig. 1); the result is displayed in Output 2 below. Once the product automaton is loaded, CAT will compute the MPC:

```
──────────────────────────────── Output 2 ────────────────────────────────
The most permissive controller for strong agreement is:                      1
Rank: 3                                                                       2
Number of states: [4, 5, 6], Initial state: [0, 0, 0], Final states: [[3][4][5]]   3
Transitions:                                                                  4
([0, 0, 0],[1, 0, -1],[1, 0, 1])  ([1, 0, 1],[-2, 0, 2],[2, 0, 2])            5
([2, 1, 3],[3, -3, 0],[3, 2, 3])  ([2, 0, 2],[0, -7, 7],[2, 1, 3])            6
([3, 2, 3],[0, 4, -4],[3, 3, 4])  ([3, 2, 3],[0, 5, -5],[3, 4, 5])            7
([3, 3, 4],[0, -6, 6],[3, 4, 5])                                              8
Do you want to save this automaton? (write yes or no) yes  KS_B1xB2xS         9
```

The resulting automaton is of rank 3 and corresponds to the MPC of Fig. 1. The final states are represented as a list where the i-th element is the list of the final states of the i-th service. This representation allows to check if a state of the MPC is final or not without needing to explicitly enumerate all the final states of the MPC.

The transitions on lines 5–8 in Output 2 represent the transitions of the MPC; note that in each transition there is always an idle service. For instance, consider the transition ([0, 0, 0], [1, 0, –1], [1, 0, 1]): it corresponds to the transition $(\vec{q_0}, (\overline{price}, \square, price), \vec{q_1})$ of the MPC in Fig. 1 (the second component of the label is 0 because B2 is idle). The MPC can now be saved in a file as per line 9 in Output 2.

The underlying coordination mechanism of contract automata is orchestration. More precisely, services are oblivious of their partners and exchange messages through a "hidden" orchestrator (formalised by the MPC, if any). Whenever possible, one would like to have services interacting without the "supervision" of an orchestrator, using FIFO buffers. Mild conditions [6] ensure that choreographies are sound, in other words that all the interactions among services are successful. We briefly discuss this issue below. For synchronous interactions (where buffers have size 1 and a single buffer may be non empty), services have to enjoy the *branching condition* that is necessary and sufficient for services to form a sound choreography. As said, a branching condition guarantees "unsupervised" communications soundness when the communication are synchronous [5,6]. However, such branching condition does not suffice for asynchronous interactions (namely when buffers are unbounded and more than one buffer is possibly non empty). In this case, an additional sufficient and commonly required condition is the absence of *mixed choice states*, i.e., states where more than one service can perform an offer (see [6]). Consider now Fig. 1, where in Output 3 the state $\vec{q_2}$ corresponds to [2,0,2], the state $\vec{q_3}$ to [2,1,3], and the transition $(\overline{contrib}, contrib, \square)$ to the label [3,--3,0]. The MPC does not enjoy the branching condition, as CAT reports:

```
──────────────────────────────── Output 3 ────────────────────────────────
State [2,0,2] violates the branching condition because it has no transition labelled   1
 [3,-3,0] which is instead enabled in state [2,1,3]                           2
```

It is important to observe that the message in Output 3 also flags states and transitions for which the condition is violated. We discuss the problem by considering the automata in Fig. 1. The local state of buyer B1 in $\vec{q_2}$ and $\vec{q_3}$ is q_{B12}, while the locale state of B2 in $\vec{q_2}$ is q_{B20}, and in $\vec{q_3}$ is q_{B21}. Therefore, in the case that B_2 is in local state q_{B20} where it is waiting for $\overline{quote_2}$, without an orchestrator the offer $\overline{contrib}$ from B_1 could fill up the 1-buffer of B_2, leading to a deadlock. A simple fix consists in swapping the order in which the quotes are sent by the seller; CAT reports that the amended protocol (not shown here) enjoys the branching condition. The contract automaton has no mixed choice states, as detected by CAT. A mixed choice state could be introduced in 2BP if, e.g., B_2 could send the acknowledgement to S or receive $\overline{contrib}$ from B_1 in any order. For this variant of 2BP, CAT finds the mixed choice state, so showing that these services do not form a sound choreography.

4   Detailing the Implementation of CAT

CAT consists of a class CAUtil and of other classes CA and CATransition, extending two corresponding super-classes of JAMATA. The class CA provides the main functionalities of CAT; its instance variables capture the basic structure of our automata:

- int rank is the rank of the automaton;
- int[] initial is the initial state of the automaton (the array is of size rank);
- int[] states the vector of the number of local states of each principal in the contract automaton (the array is of size rank);
- int[][] finalstates the final states of each principal in the contract automaton;
- CATransition[] tra the transitions of the contract automaton.

The n local states of a principal are represented as integers in the range $0, \ldots, n-1$; in this case, states.length = 1 and states[0] = n. The state of an automaton of rank $m > 1$ is an m-vector states such that states[i] yields the number of states of the ith principal. This low-level representation (together with the encoding of actions and labels as integers) enabled us to optimize space.

The class CATransition, describes a transition of a contract automaton. The instance variables of a CATransition object are:

- int[] source (the starting state of the transition);
- int[] label (the label of the transition);
- int[] target (the arriving state of the transition).

The class CATransition provides methods to extract its instance variables, to check if the transition is an offer, a request or a match, and to extract the (index of the) principal performing the offer, if any.

5   Linear Programming and Contract Automata

The properties of weak agreement were introduced for solving circularity issues, in which all services are stuck waiting the fulfilment of their requests before providing the corresponding offers [4]. For example, consider the services (rendered as regular expressions) $A = a.\overline{b}$ and $B = b.\overline{a}$; their product does not admit agreement. Circularity is solved by allowing matches between requests and offers even though they are not simultaneous; intuitively, offers may be fired "on credit" provided that the corresponding requests are honoured later on. A trace of an automaton is a weak agreement if for each request there is a corresponding offer, no matter in which order they occur in the trace. The notions of *admitting* weak agreement and of *weakly* safety are then similar to the ones of (strong) agreement reviewed earlier. For example, $A \otimes B$ admits weak agreement. The underlying theory and the decision procedures for the properties of weak agreement are developed in [4], and are formalised as mixed linear integer programming. This is because the properties of weak agreement are context-sensitive, and thus no controller can exist, i.e., a contract automaton for enforcing them. Below, we briefly review a component for solving the optimization problems related to contract automata, that complements the functionalities offered by CAT.

The decision procedures are implemented in *A Mathematical Programming Language* (AMPL) [8], a widely used language for describing and solving optimization problems. In this way, the automatic verification of contract automata under properties of weak agreement exploits efficient techniques and algorithms developed in the area of operational research. We now briefly describe the implementation of the techniques for verifying weak agreement. The script flow.run, to be launched with the command ampl, is described below:

```
————————————————————— flow.run —————————————————————
#reset;                                                                    1
option solver cplex;          // use the simplex algorithm in C            2
model weakagreement.mod;      // select model for weak agreement           3
data flow.dat;                // load                                      4
solve;                        // apply the simplex algorithm               5
display gamma;                // display the result: if gamma >= 0 then property holds   6
```

The script firstly loads the automaton from the file flow.dat (line 4). The description of the automata consists of the number of nodes, the cardinality of the alphabet of actions, and a matrix of transitions for each action a, where there is value 0 at position (s, t) if there is no transition from state s to state t labelled by a, and respectively 1 or -1 if there is an offer or request transition on a. In this case, the contract automaton described in flow.dat is representative.

The AMPL linear program to load is given as input parameter to the script (line 3). The two optimization problems available are: weakagreement.mod, the file contains the formalization of the optimization problem for deciding whether a contract automaton admits weak agreement, and weaksafety.mod that contains the formalization of the optimization problem for deciding whether a contract automaton is weakly safe.

Both formal descriptions are then solved using the solver cplex, that is the simplex method implemented in C. However it is possible to select other available solvers in the script flow.run (line 2). The execution of the script will prompt to the user the value of variables. As proved in [4], if the variable gamma is non negative then the contract automaton satisfies the given property. Bi-level optimization problems can not be defined directly in AMPL. Therefore, we cannot

```
―――――――――――――――――――― weakagreement.mod ――――――――――――――――――――
# n number of nodes # m number of actions                                        2
param n; param m; param K; param final; #final node                             3
set N := {1..n}; set M := {1..m}; param t{N,N}; param a{N,N,M};                  4
var x_t{N,N} >=0 integer;  var z_t{N,N,N} >=0;                                   5
var gamma; var p{N} binary; var wagreement;                                      6
                                                                                 7
#flow constraints                                                                8
subject to Flow_Constraints {node in N}:                                         9
        sum{i in N}( x_t[i,node]*t[i,node] ) - sum{i in N}(x_t[node,i]*t[node,i]) = 10
        if (node == 1) then   -1                                                 11
        else if (node == final) then 1                                           12
        else 0;                                                                  13
;                                                                                14
                                                                                 15
subject to p1{node in N}: p[node] <= sum{i in N}( x_t[node,i]*t[node,i]);        16
subject to p2{node in N}: sum{i in N}( x_t[node,i]*t[node,i]) <= p[node]*K;      17
                                                                                 18
subject to Auxiliary_Flow_Constraints {snode in N diff {1},node in N}:           19
        sum{i in N}( z_t[snode,i,node]*t[i,node] ) - sum{i in N}(z_t[snode,node,i]*t[node,i]) = 20
        if (node == 1) then    - p[snode]                                        21
        else if (node == snode)  then p[snode]                                   22
        else 0;                                                                  23
                                                                                 24
subject to Auxiliary_Flow_Constraints2{i in N, j in N,snode in N}:               25
        z_t[snode,i,j]*t[i,j] <= x_t[i,j]*t[i,j];                                26
                                                                                 27
subject to threshold_constraint {act in M}:                                      28
  sum{i in N,j in N} x_t[i,j]*t[i,j]*a[i,j,act] >= gamma;                        29
                                                                                 30
#objective function                                                              31
maximize cost: gamma;                                                            32
```

```
―――――――――――――――――――― weaksafety.mod ――――――――――――――――――――
# n number of nodes # m number of actions                                        2
param n; param m;  param K; param final; #final node                             3
set N := {1..n}; set M := {1..m}; param t{N,N}; param a{N,N,M};                  4
var x_t{N,N} >=0 integer; var z_t{N,N,N} >=0;                                    5
var gamma; var p{N} binary; var v{M} binary; var wagreement;                     6
                                                                                 7
#flow constraints                                                                8
subject to Flow_Constraints {node in N}:                                         9
        sum{i in N}( x_t[i,node]*t[i,node] ) - sum{i in N}(x_t[node,i]*t[node,i]) = 10
        if (node == 1) then   -1                                                 11
        else if (node == final)  then 1                                          12
        else 0;                                                                  13
;                                                                                14
                                                                                 15
subject to p1{node in N}: p[node] <= sum{i in N}( x_t[node,i]*t[node,i]);        16
subject to p2{node in N}: sum{i in N}( x_t[node,i]*t[node,i]) <= p[node]*K;      17
                                                                                 18
subject to Auxiliary_Flow_Constraints {snode in N diff {1},node in N}:           19
        sum{i in N}( z_t[snode,i,node]*t[i,node] ) - sum{i in N}(z_t[snode,node,i]*t[node,i]) = 20
        if (node == 1) then    - p[snode]                                        21
        else if (node == snode)  then p[snode]                                   22
        else 0;                                                                  23
                                                                                 24
subject to Auxiliary_Flow_Constraints2{i in N, j in N,snode in N}:               25
        z_t[snode,i,j]*t[i,j] <= x_t[i,j]*t[i,j];                                26
                                                                                 27
subject to v1: sum{i in M} v[i] = 1;                                             28
                                                                                 29
subject to threshold_constraint :                                                30
sum{act in M,i in N,j in N} (v[act]*x_t[i,j]*t[i,j]*a[i,j,act]) <= gamma;        31
                                                                                 32
#objective function                                                              33
minimize cost: gamma;                                                            34
```

Fig. 3. The implementation in AMPL of the optimization problem for deciding weakagreement and weak safety.

plainly apply formalisation of [4] for representing weakly liable transitions as an optimization problem. However, different techniques of relaxation of the bi-level problem for over approximating the set of weakly liable transitions can be used, as for example lagrangian relaxation. As future work, we are planning to develop a toolchain for fully integrating the above techniques in CAT, in order to reuse them for the functionalities described in Sect. 3. In particular, CAT will automatically generate a contract automaton description `flow.dat`, execute the script `flow.run` and collect the results. The code of `weakagreement.mod` and `weaksafety.mod` is depicted in Fig. 3. For further details about CAT, we refer the interested reader to the full documentation, available online at [3].

6   Concluding Remarks

We described CAT, a tool supporting the analysis of communication-centric applications attained with novel techniques based on combinatorial optimization. A non trivial example was used to show main features of CAT.

An interesting application domain for CAT are service-oriented applications. In this context, model-driven approaches have been advocated for the analysis of service composition. In particular, automata have been used as target models to translate BPEL processes [11] in [9,13]; for instance, constraint automata semantics of REO [1,2] is used in [12] to analyse web-services. Relations of contract automata with service composition are studied in [4–6]. The properties verified by CAT have not been considered by other approaches. For example, the identification - even in presence of circular dependencies of services (see Sect. 5) - of liable transitions that may spoil a composition complement the verification done in [12]. We conjecture that it would be possible to define model transformations from contract automata to BPEL which preserve the analysis discussed here.

A model-driven approach would also ease the integration of CAT with e.g., the tools discussed above. This would provide developers with a wide variety of tools for guaranteeing the quality of the composition of services according to different criteria.

The tool is still a prototype; we plan to improve its efficiency, extend it with new functionalities (e.g., relaxation), and improve its usability (e.g., adding a user-friendly GUI and pretty-printing automata). We note that CAT provides a valid support to the analysis of applications. In fact, CAT is able to detect possible violations of the properties of interest (for example branching condition, mixed choice). A drawback of CAT is that it does not support modelling and design of applications. An interesting evolution of CAT would be to add functionalities for amending applications violating properties of interest. For instance, once liable transitions are identified, CAT could suggest how to modify services to guarantee the property. This may also be coupled with the model-driven approach by featuring functionalities tracing transitions in the actual source-code of services.

References

1. Arbab, F.: Reo: a channel-based coordination model for component composition. Math. Struct. Comput. Sci. **14**(3), 329–366 (2004). http://dblp.uni-trier.de/db/journals/mscs/mscs14.html#Arbab04
2. Baier, C., Sirjani, M., Arbab, F., Rutten, J.: Modeling component connectors in Reo by constraint automata. Sci. Comput. Program. **61**(2), 75–113 (2006). http://dx.doi.org/10.1016/j.scico.2005.10.008
3. Basile, D.: JAMATA and CAT. https://github.com/davidebasile/workspace
4. Basile, D., Degano, P., Ferrari, G.-L.: Automata for analysing service contracts. In: Maffei, M., Tuosto, E. (eds.) TGC 2014. LNCS, vol. 8902, pp. 34–50. Springer, Heidelberg (2014)
5. Basile, D., Degano, P., Ferrari, G.L., Tuosto, E.: From orchestration to choreography through contract automata. In: ICE 2014, pp. 67–85 (2014)
6. Basile, D., Degano, P., Ferrari, G.L., Tuosto, E.: Relating two automata-based models of orchestration and choreography. J. Logical Algebr. Methods Programm. **85**(3), 425–446 (2016). http://www.sciencedirect.com/science/article/pii/S2352220815000930
7. Cassandras, C.G., Lafortune, S.: Introduction to Discrete Event Systems. Springer, Secaucus (2006)
8. Fourer, R., Gay, D.M., Kernighan, B.W.: AMPL: A Mathematical Programming Language. AT & T Bell Laboratories Murray Hill, NJ 07974 (1987)
9. Fu, X., Bultan, T., Su, J.: Analysis of interacting BPEL web services. In: WWW 2004, pp. 621–630. ACM (2004). http://doi.acm.org/10.1145/988672.988756
10. Honda, K., Yoshida, N., Carbone, M.: Multiparty asynchronous session types. In: Necula, G.C., Wadler, P. (eds.) POPL, pp. 273–284. ACM (2008)
11. Juric, M.B.: Business Process Execution Language for Web Services BPEL and BPEL4WS, 2nd edn. Packt Publishing, Birmingham (2006)
12. Tasharofi, S., Vakilian, M., Moghaddam, R.Z., Sirjani, M.: Modeling web service interactions using the coordination language reo. In: Dumas, M., Heckel, R. (eds.) WS-FM 2007. LNCS, vol. 4937, pp. 108–123. Springer, Heidelberg (2008). http://dblp.uni-trier.de/db/conf/wsfm/wsfm2007.html#TasharofiVMS07
13. Wombacher, A., Fankhauser, P., Neuhold, E.: Transforming BPEL into annotated deterministic finite state automata for service discovery. In: Web Services (2004)

Multiparty Session Types Within a Canonical Binary Theory, and Beyond

Luís Caires[1] and Jorge A. Pérez[2(✉)]

[1] NOVA LINCS, Universidade NOVA de Lisboa, Lisbon, Portugal
[2] University of Groningen, Groningen, The Netherlands
j.a.perez@rug.nl

Abstract. A widespread approach to software service analysis uses *session types*. Very different type theories for *binary* and *multiparty* protocols have been developed; establishing precise connections between them remains an open problem. We present the first formal relation between two existing theories of binary and multiparty session types: a binary system rooted in linear logic, and a multiparty system based on automata theory. Our results enable the analysis of multiparty protocols using a (much simpler) type theory for binary protocols, ensuring protocol fidelity and deadlock-freedom. As an application, we offer the first theory of multiparty session types with *behavioral genericity*. This theory is natural and powerful; its analysis techniques reuse results for binary session types.

1 Introduction

The purpose of this paper is to demonstrate, in a precise technical sense, how an expressive and extensible theory of multiparty systems can be extracted from a basic theory for binary sessions, thus developing the first formal connection between multiparty and binary session types. Our approach relies on a theory of binary session types rooted in linear logic and on *medium processes* that capture the behavior of global types.

Relating the global behavior of a distributed system and the components that implement it is a challenging problem in many scenarios. This problem is also important in the analysis of software services, where the focus is on message-passing programs with advanced forms of concurrency and distribution. Within language-based techniques, notable approaches include *interface contracts* (cf. [8]) and *behavioral types* [15]. Our interest is in the latter: by classifying behaviors (rather than values), behavioral types abstract structured protocols and enforce disciplined communication exchanges.

Session types [13,14] are a much-studied class of behavioral types. They organize multiparty protocols as *sessions*, basic units of structured conversations. Several session typed frameworks have been developed (see [15] for an overview). This diversity makes it hard to compare their associated techniques, and hinders the much desirable transfer of techniques between different typed models.

© IFIP International Federation for Information Processing 2016
E. Albert and I. Lanese (Eds.): FORTE 2016, LNCS 9688, pp. 74–95, 2016.
DOI: 10.1007/978-3-319-39570-8_6

In this paper, we formally relate two distinct typed models for structured communications. By relying on a type theory of binary sessions rooted in linear logic [5], we establish natural bridges between typed models for *binary* and *multiparty* sessions [13,14]. Our results reveal logically motivated justifications for key concepts in typed models of global/local behaviors, and enable the transfer of reasoning techniques from binary to multiparty sessions. In fact, our approach naturally enables us to define the first model of multiparty session types with *parametric polymorphism*, which in our setting means *behavioral genericity* (i.e., passing first-class behavioral interfaces in messages), not just datatype genericity. This new model is very powerful; we equip it with analysis techniques for behavioral genericity by reusing results for binary session types [4].

Binary protocols [13] involve two partners, each abstracted by a behavioral type; correct interactions rely on *compatibility*, i.e., when one partner performs an action, the other performs a complementary one. Multiparty protocols may involve more than two partners: there is a global specification to which all of them, from their local perspectives, should adhere. In multiparty session types [12,14], these visions are described by a *global type* and *local types*, respectively; a *projection function* relates the two. Previous research shows that type systems for multiparty protocols have a more involved theory than binary ones. For instance, the analysis of deadlock-freedom in multiparty protocols is challenging [10], and certainly harder than for binary protocols.

The question is then: *could multiparty session types be reduced into binary ones?* Defining such a reduction is far from trivial, as it should satisfy at least two requirements. First, the resulting collection of binary interactions must preserve crucial *sequencing information* among multiparty exchanges. Second, it should avoid *undesirable behaviors*: synchronization errors, deadlocks, non-terminating reductions.

This paper answers the above question in the affirmative. We tightly relate: (i) a standard theory of multiparty session types [12,14], and (ii) the theory of deadlock-free binary session types proposed in [5]. The key device in our approach is the *medium process* of a multiparty protocol.

Given a global type G, its medium process $\mathsf{M}[\![G]\!]$ is an entity that mediates in all communications. Therefore, $\mathsf{M}[\![G]\!]$ extracts the semantics of G, uniformly capturing its sequencing information. Process $\mathsf{M}[\![G]\!]$ is meant to interact with well-typed implementations for all participants declared in G. This way, for instance, given the global type $G = \mathsf{p} \twoheadrightarrow \mathsf{q}:\{l_i\langle U_i\rangle.G_i\}_{i\in I}$ (i.e., a labeled, directed exchange from p to q, indexed by I, which precedes execution of a protocol G_i), its medium $\mathsf{M}[\![G]\!]$ first receives a label l_j and message of type U_j sent by p's implementation (with $j \in I$); then, it forwards these two objects to q's implementation; lastly, it executes process $\mathsf{M}[\![G_j]\!]$.

Interestingly, our medium-based approach applies to global types with name passing, delegation, and parallel composition. To fully characterize a global type G, we determine the conditions under which $\mathsf{M}[\![G]\!]$ may be well-typed using binary session types, with respect to its local types. A key ingredient here is the theory for binary session types introduced in [5]. Due to their logical foundations, typability in [5] entails: *fidelity* (protocols are respected), *safety* (absence of communication errors), *deadlock-freedom* (processes do not get stuck), and *termination* (infinite internal behavior is ruled out). Most relevant for our approach is deadlock-freedom, not directly ensured by alternative type systems.

Here we present an analysis of multiparty session types using a theory of binary session types, ensuring fidelity and deadlock-freedom. Our *technical contributions* are:

- *Characterization results* relating (a) a global type that is well-formed (correct projectability) and (b) typability of its medium using binary session types (Theorems 4 and 5).
- *Operational correspondence results* relating (a) the behavior of a global type and (b) the behavior of its medium (instrumented in a natural way) composed with well-typed implementations for each local type (Theorem 7). These results confirm that our analysis does not introduce extra sequentiality in protocols.
- A proof that *behavioral transformations* of global types [6] can be justified by typed equalities for binary sessions [19] expressed at the level of mediums (Theorem 6). This result offers a deep semantic justification of structural identities on global types, such as those capturing parallelism via interleaving of causally independent exchanges.
- *Transfer of techniques* from binary to multiparty protocols. We define the first theory of multiparty session types with *behavioral genericity*; its analysis techniques reuse the binary session type theory with parametric polymorphism given in [4].

Our results define the first formal relation between multiparty and binary session types. They highlight the fundamental character of the notions involved, since they can be independently explained by communicating automata (cf. [12]) and linear logic (cf. [5]).

Next, we collect definitions on multiparty sessions [12,14] and binary sessions [5]. Our technical contributions are reported in Sect. 3. In Sect. 4 we illustrate these contributions by means of an example that features non-trivial forms of replication and sharing. In Sect. 5 we introduce multiparty session types with behavioral genericity, and in Sect. 6 we illustrate our approach in the analysis of a multiparty protocol. Section 7 concludes and discusses related works.

2   Preliminaries: Binary and Multiparty Session Types

Binary Session Types. We build upon the theory of binary session types of [5,21], based on an interpretation of session types as linear logic propositions. We assume no background on linear logic from the reader; we refer to [5] for further details.

The Process Model. We define a synchronous π-calculus [20] with forwarding and n-ary labeled choice. We use $l_1, l_2, \ldots$ to range over *labels*. Given an infinite set (id) $(\boldsymbol{\nu}x)([x \leftrightarrow y] \mid P) \xrightarrow{\tau} P\{y/x\}$ (n.out) $\overline{x}\,y.P \xrightarrow{\overline{x}\,y} P$ (n.in) $x(y).P \xrightarrow{x(z)} P\{z/y\}$

(s.out) $x \triangleleft l; P \xrightarrow{x\triangleleft l} P$ (s.in) $x \triangleright \{l_i : P_i\}_{i \in I} \xrightarrow{x\triangleleft l_j} P_j$ $(j \in I)$

Fig. 1. LTS for processes (Excerpt).

Λ of *names* (x, y, z, u, v), the set of *processes* (P, Q, R) is defined by

$$P ::= \mathbf{0} \quad \mid \quad P \mid Q \quad \mid \quad (\boldsymbol{\nu}y)P \mid \overline{x}\,y.P \mid x(y).P \mid\, !x(y).P \mid$$
$$x \triangleleft l_i; P \mid x \triangleright \{l_i : P_i\}_{i \in I} \mid [x \leftrightarrow y]$$

Operators $\mathbf{0}$ (inaction), $P \mid Q$ (parallel composition), and $(\boldsymbol{\nu}y)P$ (restriction) are standard. We have $\overline{x}\,y.P$ (send y on x, proceed as P), $x(y).P$ (receive a z on x, proceed as P with y replaced by z), and the replicated input $!x(y).P$. Operators $x \triangleleft l; P$ and $x \triangleright \{l_i:P_i\}_{i \in I}$ define labeled choice [13]. Forwarding $[x \leftrightarrow y]$ equates x and y; it is a copycat process, similar to *wires* in [20]. Also, $\overline{x}(y)$ denotes the bound output $(\boldsymbol{\nu}y)\overline{x}\,y$.

In restriction $(\boldsymbol{\nu}y)P$ and input $x(y).P$ the occurrence of name y is binding, with scope P. The set of *free names* of a process P is denoted $fn(P)$. In a statement, a name is *fresh* if it is not among the names of the objects (processes, actions, etc.) of the statement. A process is *closed* if it does not contain free occurrences of names. We identify processes up to consistent renaming of bound names. The capture-avoiding substitution of x for y in P is denoted $P\{x/y\}$. Notation $\widetilde{k}$ denotes a finite sequence of pairwise distinct names $k_1, k_2, \cdots$. We sometimes treat sequences of names as sets.

Reduction expresses the internal behavior of processes. Closed under structural congruence (noted $\equiv$, see [5]), it is the binary relation on processes defined by the rules:

$$\overline{x}\,y.Q \mid x(z).P \to Q \mid P\{y/z\} \qquad \overline{x}\,y.Q \mid !x(z).P \to Q \mid P\{y/z\} \mid !x(z).P$$
$$(\boldsymbol{\nu}x)([x \leftrightarrow y] \mid P) \to P\{y/x\} \qquad Q \to Q' \Rightarrow P \mid Q \to P \mid Q'$$
$$P \to Q \Rightarrow (\boldsymbol{\nu}y)P \to (\boldsymbol{\nu}y)Q \quad x \triangleleft l_j; P \mid x \triangleright \{l_i : Q_i\}_{i \in I} \to P \mid Q_j \ (j \in I)$$

The interaction of a process with its environment is defined by an early labeled transition system (LTS) for the π-calculus [20], extended with labels and transition rules for choice and forwarding. Transition $P \xrightarrow{\lambda} Q$ says that P may evolve to Q by performing the action represented by label λ, defined as: $\lambda ::= \tau \mid x(y) \mid x \triangleleft l \mid \overline{x}\,y \mid \overline{x}(y) \mid \overline{x \triangleleft l}$. Actions are the input $x(y)$, the offer $x \triangleleft l$, and their co-actions: the output $\overline{x}\,y$ and bound output $\overline{x}(y)$ actions, and the selection $\overline{x \triangleleft l}$, resp. The bound output $\overline{x}(y)$ denotes extrusion of y along x. Internal action is denoted τ. Figure 1 gives a selection of the rules that define $P \xrightarrow{\lambda} Q$. Weak transitions are as usual: $\Longrightarrow$ is the reflexive, transitive closure of $\xrightarrow{\tau}$. Notation $\xRightarrow{\lambda}$ stands for $\Longrightarrow \xrightarrow{\lambda} \Longrightarrow$ (given $\lambda \neq \tau$) and $\xRightarrow{\hat{\tau}}$ stands for $\Longrightarrow$.

Session Types as Linear Logic Propositions. The type theory of [5] connects session types as linear logic propositions. Main properties derived from typing,

$$(\text{Tid}) \qquad\qquad\qquad (\text{T1R})$$

$$\frac{}{\Gamma; x{:}A \vdash [x \leftrightarrow z] :: z{:}A} \qquad \frac{}{\Gamma; \cdot \vdash \mathbf{0} :: x{:}\mathbf{1}}$$

$$(\text{Tcut}) \quad \frac{\Gamma; \Delta \vdash P :: x{:}A \quad \Gamma; \Delta', x{:}A \vdash Q :: z{:}C}{\Gamma; \Delta, \Delta' \vdash (\boldsymbol{\nu}x)(P \mid Q) :: z{:}C}$$

$$(\text{T}{\multimap}\text{L}) \; \frac{\Gamma; \Delta \vdash P :: y{:}A \quad \Gamma; \Delta', x{:}B \vdash Q :: z{:}C}{\Gamma; \Delta, \Delta', x{:}A{\multimap}B \vdash \overline{x}(y).(P \mid Q) :: z{:}C} \qquad (\text{T}{\otimes}\text{L}) \; \frac{\Gamma; \Delta, y{:}A, x{:}B \vdash P :: z{:}C}{\Gamma; \Delta, x{:}A \otimes B \vdash x(y).P :: z{:}C}$$

$$(\text{T}{\oplus}\text{L}) \; \frac{\Gamma; \Delta, x{:}A_1 \vdash P_1 :: z{:}C \quad \cdots \quad \Gamma; \Delta, x{:}A_k \vdash P_k :: z{:}C \quad I = \{1, \ldots, k\}}{\Gamma; \Delta, x{:} \oplus\{l_i : A_i\}_{i \in I} \vdash x \triangleright \{l_i : P_i\}_{i \in I} :: z{:}C}$$

$$(\text{T}\&\text{R}) \; \frac{\Gamma; \Delta \vdash P_1 :: x{:}A_1 \quad \cdots \quad \Gamma; \Delta \vdash P_k :: x{:}A_k \quad I = \{1, \ldots, k\}}{\Gamma; \Delta \vdash x \triangleright \{l_i : P_i\}_{i \in I} :: x{:} \&\{l_i : A_i\}_{i \in I}}$$

$$(\text{T}\&\text{L}_1) \qquad\qquad\qquad\qquad (\text{T}\&\text{L}_2)$$

$$\frac{\Gamma; \Delta, x{:}A \vdash P :: z{:}C}{\Gamma; \Delta, x{:} \&\{l_i{:}A\}_{\{i\}} \vdash x \triangleleft l_i; P :: z{:}C} \qquad \frac{\Gamma; \Delta, x{:} \&\{l_i{:}A_i\}_{i \in I} \vdash P :: z{:}C \quad k \notin I}{\Gamma; \Delta, x{:} \&\{l_j{:}A_j\}_{j \in I \cup \{k\}} \vdash P :: z{:}C}$$

Fig. 2. The type system for binary sessions (Excerpt).

absent from other binary session type theories, are *global progress* (deadlock-freedom) and *termination* [19]. The syntax of binary types is as follows:

Definition 1 (Binary Types). *Types* (A, B, C) *are given by*

$$A, B ::= \mathbf{1} \mid !A \mid A \otimes B \mid A{\multimap}B \mid \&\{l_i : A_i\}_{i \in I} \mid \oplus\{l_i : A_i\}_{i \in I}$$

We use $A \otimes B$ (resp. $A{\multimap}B$) to type a name that performs an output (resp. an input) to its partner, sending (resp. receiving) a name of type A, and then behaves as type B. Thus, $A \otimes B$ and $A{\multimap}B$ represent the session types $!A; B$ and $?A; B$ introduced in [13]. We generalize [5] by considering n-ary offer & and choice $\oplus$. Given a finite index set I, $\&\{l_i{:}A_i\}_{i \in I}$ types a name that offers a choice between an l_i. Dually, $\oplus\{l_i{:}A_i\}_{i \in I}$ types the selection of one of the l_i. Type $!A$ types a shared channel, used by a server to spawn an arbitrary number of new sessions (possibly none), each one conforming to A. Type $\mathbf{1}$ is the terminated session; names of type $\mathbf{1}$ may be passed around as opaque values.

A *type environment* collects type assignments of the form $x{:}A$, where x is a name and A is a type, the names being pairwise disjoint. We consider two typing environments, subject to different structural properties: a *linear* part Δ and an *unrestricted* part Γ, where weakening and contraction principles hold for Γ but not for Δ.

A *type judgment* $\Gamma; \Delta \vdash P :: z{:}C$ asserts that P provides behavior C at channel z, building on "services" declared in $\Gamma; \Delta$. This way, e.g., a client Q that relies on external services and does not provide any is typed as $\Gamma; \Delta \vdash Q :: z{:}\mathbf{1}$. The domains of Γ, Δ and $z{:}C$ are required to be pairwise disjoint. We write $dom(\Gamma)$ (resp. $dom(\Delta)$) to denote the domain of Γ (resp. Δ), a sequence of names. Empty environments are denoted '$\cdot$'. As π-calculus terms are considered up to structural congruence, typability is closed under $\equiv$ by definition. We sometimes abbreviate $\Gamma; \Delta \vdash P :: z{:}\mathbf{1}$ as $\Gamma; \Delta \vdash P$.

Figure 2 presents selected typing rules; see [5] for a full account. We have right and left rules: they say how to *implement* and *use* a session of a given type, respectively. We briefly comment on some of the rules. Rule (Tid) defines identity in terms of forwarding. Rule (Tcut) define typed composition via parallel composition and restriction. Implementing a session type $\&\{l_i:A_i\}_{i\in I}$ amounts to offering a choice between n sessions with type A_i (Rule (T&R)); its use on name x entails selecting an alternative, using prefix $x \triangleleft l_j$ (Rules T&L$_1$ and (T&L$_2$)). Type $\oplus\{l_i : A_i\}_{i\in I}$ has a dual interpretation.

We now recall some main results for well-typed processes. For any P, define $live(P)$ iff $P \equiv (\boldsymbol{\nu}\tilde{n})(\pi.Q \mid R)$, for some names $\tilde{n}$, a process R, and a *non-replicated* guarded process $\pi.Q$. Also, we write $P \Downarrow$, if there is no infinite reduction path from process P.

Theorem 1 (Properties of Well-Typed Processes).

1. *Subject Reduction [5]: If $\Gamma; \Delta \vdash P :: x{:}A$ and $P \to Q$ then $\Gamma; \Delta \vdash Q{::}x{:}A$.*
2. *Global Progress [5]: If $\cdot; \cdot \vdash P{::}z{:}\mathbf{1}$ and $live(P)$ then exists a Q such that $P \to Q$.*
3. *Termination/Strong Normalization [19]: If $\Gamma; \Delta \vdash P :: x{:}A$ then $P \Downarrow$.*

Theorem 1 (2), key in our work, implies that our type discipline ensures deadlock freedom. Further properties of well-typed processes concern *proof conversions* and *typed behavioral equivalences*. The correspondence in [5] is realized by relating *proof conversions* in linear logic with appropriate process equivalences. There is a group of *commuting conversions* that induces a behavioral congruence on typed processes, noted $\simeq_c$. Process equalities justified by $\simeq_c$ include, e.g., (see [19] for details):

$$\Gamma; \Delta, y{:}A \otimes B \vdash (\boldsymbol{\nu}x)(P \mid y(z).Q) \simeq_c y(z).(\boldsymbol{\nu}x)(P \mid Q){::}z{:}C$$
$$\Gamma; \Delta, y{:}A \multimap B \vdash (\boldsymbol{\nu}x)(P \mid \overline{y}(z).(Q \mid R)) \simeq_c \overline{y}(z).(Q \mid (\boldsymbol{\nu}x)(P \mid R)){::}T$$
$$\Gamma; \Delta, y{:} \&\{l_i{:}A_i\}_{i\in I} \vdash (\boldsymbol{\nu}x)(P \mid y \triangleleft l_i; Q) \simeq_c y \triangleleft l_i; (\boldsymbol{\nu}x)(P \mid Q){::}T$$

These equalities reflect a behavioral equivalence over session-typed processes, called *context bisimilarity* (noted $\approx$) [19]. Roughly, typed processes $\Gamma; \Delta \vdash P :: x{:}A$ and $\Gamma; \Delta \vdash Q{::}x{:}A$ are context bisimilar if, once composed with their requirements (described by Γ, Δ), they perform the same actions on x (as described by A). Context bisimilarity is a congruence relation on well-typed processes. We have:

Theorem 2 ([19]). *If $\Gamma; \Delta \vdash P \simeq_c Q :: z{:}C$ then $\Gamma; \Delta \vdash P \approx Q :: z{:}C$.*

Multiparty Session Types. Our syntax of global types includes constructs from [12,14]. With respect to [12], we consider value passing in branching (cf. U below), fully supporting delegation and add parallel composition. Below, *participants* are ranged over by $\mathsf{p}, \mathsf{q}, \mathsf{r}, \ldots$; *labels* are ranged over by $l_1, l_2, \ldots$. To streamline the presentation, we consider standard global types without recursion. Our approach extends to global types with recursion, exploiting the extension of [5] with co-recursion [21]. Results for global types with recursion can be found in an online technical report [3].

Definition 2 (Global/Local Types). *Define global types (G) and local types (T) as*

$$G ::= \mathsf{end} \mid \mathsf{p} \twoheadrightarrow \mathsf{q} : \{l_i \langle U_i \rangle . G_i\}_{i \in I} \mid G_1 \mid G_2 \qquad U ::= \mathsf{bool} \mid \mathsf{nat} \mid \mathsf{str} \mid \ldots \mid T$$
$$T ::= \mathsf{end} \mid \mathsf{p}?\{l_i \langle U_i \rangle . T_i\}_{i \in I} \mid \mathsf{p}!\{l_i \langle U_i \rangle . T_i\}_{i \in I}$$

$\mathcal{G}$ denotes the above set of global types. Given a finite I and pairwise different labels, $\mathsf{p} \twoheadrightarrow \mathsf{q} : \{l_i \langle U_i \rangle . G_i\}_{i \in I}$ specifies that by choosing label l_i, participant p may send a message of type U_i to participant q, and then continue as G_i. We decree $\mathsf{p} \neq \mathsf{q}$, so reflexive interactions are disallowed. The global type $G_1 \mid G_2$ allows the concurrent execution of G_1 and G_2. We write end to denote the completed global type. The local type $\mathsf{p}?\{l_i \langle U_i \rangle . T_i\}_{i \in I}$ denotes an offer of a set of labeled alternatives; the local type $\mathsf{p}!\{l_i \langle U_i \rangle . T_i\}_{i \in I}$ denotes a behavior that chooses one of such alternatives. The terminated local type is end. Following [14], there is no local type for parallel.

Example 1. Consider a global type G_{BS}, a variant of the the two-buyer protocol in [14], in which two buyers (B_1 and B_2) coordinate to buy an item from a seller (S):

$$G_{\mathsf{BS}} = \mathsf{B}_1 \twoheadrightarrow \mathsf{S} : \{\mathit{send}\langle \mathsf{str}\rangle . \mathsf{S} \twoheadrightarrow \mathsf{B}_1 : \{\mathit{rep}\langle \mathsf{int}\rangle . \mathsf{S} \twoheadrightarrow \mathsf{B}_2 : \{\mathit{rep}\langle \mathsf{int}\rangle .$$
$$\mathsf{B}_1 \twoheadrightarrow \mathsf{B}_2 : \{\mathit{shr}\langle \mathsf{int}\rangle . \mathsf{B}_2 \twoheadrightarrow \mathsf{S} : \{\mathit{ok}\langle 1 \rangle . \mathsf{end}, \ \mathit{quit}\langle 1 \rangle . \mathsf{end}\}\}\}\}\}$$

Intuitively, B_1 requests the price of an item to S, who replies to B_1 and B_2. Then B_1 communicates to B_2 her contribution in the transaction; finally, B_2 either confirms the purchase to S or closes the transaction.

We now define *projection* for global types. Following [12], projection relies on a *merge* operator on local types, which in our case considers messages U.

Definition 3 (Merge). *We define $\sqcup$ as the commutative partial operator on base and local types such that: 1. $\mathsf{bool} \sqcup \mathsf{bool} = \mathsf{bool}$ (and similarly for other base types); 2. $\mathsf{end} \sqcup \mathsf{end} = \mathsf{end}$; 3. $\mathsf{p}!\{l_i \langle U_i \rangle . T_i\}_{i \in I} \sqcup \mathsf{p}!\{l_i \langle U_i \rangle . T_i\}_{i \in I} = \mathsf{p}!\{l_i \langle U_i \rangle . T_i\}_{i \in I}$; and*

4. $\mathsf{p}?\{l_k \langle U_k \rangle . T_k\}_{k \in K} \sqcup \mathsf{p}?\{l'_j \langle U'_j \rangle . T'_j\}_{j \in J} =$
$\quad \mathsf{p}?\big(\{l_k \langle U_k \rangle . T_k\}_{k \in K \setminus J} \cup \{l'_j \langle U'_j \rangle . T'_j\}_{j \in J \setminus K} \cup \{l_l \langle U_l \sqcup U'_l \rangle . (T_l \sqcup T'_l)\}_{l \in K \cap J}\big)$

and is undefined otherwise.

Therefore, for $U_1 \sqcup U_2$ to be defined there are two options: (a) U_1 and U_2 are identical base, terminated or selection types; (b) U_1 and U_2 are branching types, but not necessarily identical: they may offer different options but with the condition that the behavior in labels occurring in both U_1 and U_2 must be mergeable. The set of participants of G ($\mathsf{part}(G)$) is defined as: $\mathsf{part}(\mathsf{end}) = \emptyset$, $\mathsf{part}(G_1 \mid G_2) = \mathsf{part}(G_1) \cup \mathsf{part}(G_2)$, $\mathsf{part}(\mathsf{p} \twoheadrightarrow \mathsf{q} : \{l_i \langle U_i \rangle . G_i\}_{i \in I}) = \{\mathsf{p}, \mathsf{q}\} \cup \bigcup_{i \in I} \mathsf{part}(G_i)$.

Definition 4 (Projection [12]). *Let G be a global type. The projection of G under participant r, denoted $G{\restriction}\mathsf{r}$, is defined as: $\mathsf{end}{\restriction}\mathsf{r} = \mathsf{end}$ and*

$$(\text{SW1})$$

$$\dfrac{\{p_1,q_1\}\#\{p_2,q_2\}}{p_1 \rightarrow\!\!\!\rightarrow q_1\colon\big\{l_i\langle U_i\rangle.p_2 \rightarrow\!\!\!\rightarrow q_2\colon\{l'_j\langle U'_j\rangle.G_{ij}\}_{j\in J}\big\}_{i\in I}}$$

$$\simeq_{\text{sw}}$$

$$p_2 \rightarrow\!\!\!\rightarrow q_2\colon\big\{l'_j\langle U'_j\rangle.p_1 \rightarrow\!\!\!\rightarrow q_1\colon\{l_i\langle U_i\rangle.G_{ij}\}_{i\in I}\big\}_{j\in J}$$

$$(\text{SW2})$$

$$\dfrac{\{p,q\}\#\text{part}(G_1) \qquad \forall i,j \in I.G_i^1 = G_j^1}{p \rightarrow\!\!\!\rightarrow q\colon\{l_i\langle U_i\rangle.(G_i^1 \mid G_i^2)\}_{i\in I}}$$

$$\simeq_{\text{sw}}$$

$$G_1^1 \mid p \rightarrow\!\!\!\rightarrow q\colon\{l_i\langle U_i\rangle.G_i^2\}_{i\in I}$$

Fig. 3. Swapping relation on global types (Definition 6). $A\#B$ denotes that sets A,B are disjoint.

- $p \rightarrow\!\!\!\rightarrow q\colon\{l_i\langle U_i\rangle.G_i\}_{i\in I}\!\restriction\! r = \begin{cases} p!\{l_i\langle U_i\rangle.G_i\!\restriction\! r\}_{i\in I} & \text{if } r = p \\ p?\{l_i\langle U_i\rangle.G_i\!\restriction\! r\}_{i\in I} & \text{if } r = q \\ \bigsqcup_{i\in I} G_i\!\restriction\! r & \text{otherwise } (\sqcup \text{ as in Definition 3}) \end{cases}$

- $(G_1 \mid G_2)\!\restriction\! r = \begin{cases} G_i\!\restriction\! r & \text{if } r \in \text{part}(G_i) \text{ and } r \notin \text{part}(G_j), i \neq j \in \{1,2\} \\ \text{end} & \text{if } r \notin \text{part}(G_1) \text{ and } r \notin \text{part}(G_2) \end{cases}$

When a side condition does not hold, the map is undefined.

Definition 5 (Well-Formed Global Types [12]**).** *Global type $G \in \mathcal{G}$ is well-formed (WF) if for all $r \in \text{part}(G)$, the projection $G\!\restriction\! r$ is defined.*

The last notion required in our characterization of multiparty session types as binary sessions is a *swapping relation* over global types [6], which enables transformations among causally independent communications. Such transformations may represent optimizations that increase parallelism while preserving the intended global behavior.

Definition 6 (Global Swapping). *The swapping relation $\simeq_{\text{sw}}$ is the smallest congruence on $\mathcal{G}$ which satisfies the rules in Fig. 3. (The symmetric of (SW2) is omitted.)*

3 Relating Multiparty and Binary Session Type Theories

Our analysis of multiparty protocols as binary sessions relies on the *medium process* of a global type. Mediums offer a simple device for analyzing global types using the binary session types of [5]. Mediums uniformly capture the sequencing behavior in a global type, for they take part in all message exchanges between local participants.

After defining mediums (Definition 7), we establish their characterization results (Theorems 4 and 5). We then present a process characterization of global swapping (Definition 6) in terms of context bisimilarity (Theorem 6). Subsequently, we state operational correspondence results (Theorem 7), exploiting the auxiliary notions of *instrumented* mediums (Definition 10) and *multiparty systems* (Definition 11). We use the following conventions.

Convention 3 (Indexed/Annotated Names). *We consider names indexed by participants* $p, q, \ldots$, *noted* $c_p, c_q, \ldots$ *and names annotated by participants, noted* $k^p, k^q, \ldots$. *Given* $p \neq q$, *indexed names* c_p *and* c_q *denote two different objects; in contrast, annotated names* k^p *and* k^q *denote the same name* k *with different annotations. Given a* G *with* $\mathsf{part}(G) = \{p_1, \ldots, p_n\}$, *we will write* $\mathsf{npart}(G)$ *to denote the set that contains a unique name* c_{p_j} *for every participant* p_j *of* G. *We will occasionally use* $\mathsf{npart}(G)$ *as an unordered sequence of names.*

Definition 7 (Mediums). *The* medium *of* $G \in \mathcal{G}$, *denoted* $\mathsf{M}[\![G]\!]$, *is defined as follows:*

- $\mathsf{M}[\![\mathsf{end}]\!] = \mathbf{0}$
- $\mathsf{M}[\![G_1 \mid G_2]\!] = \mathsf{M}[\![G_1]\!] \mid \mathsf{M}[\![G_2]\!]$
- $\mathsf{M}[\![p \twoheadrightarrow q{:}\{l_i \langle U_i \rangle . G_i\}_{i \in I}]\!] = c_p \triangleright \{l_i : c_p(u).c_q \triangleleft l_i; \overline{c_q}(v).([u \leftrightarrow v] \mid \mathsf{M}[\![G_i]\!])\}_{i \in I}$

The key case is $\mathsf{M}[\![p \twoheadrightarrow q{:}\{l_i \langle U_i \rangle . G_i\}_{i \in I}]\!]$: note how the medium uses two prefixes (on name c_p) to mediate with p, followed by two prefixes (on name c_q) to mediate with q. We illustrate mediums by means of an example:

Example 2. The medium process for global type G_{BS} in Example 1 is:

$$\mathsf{M}[\![G_{\mathsf{BS}}]\!] = c_{\mathsf{B1}} \triangleright \{ send : c_{\mathsf{B1}}(v).c_{\mathsf{S}} \triangleleft send; \overline{c_{\mathsf{S}}}(w).([w \leftrightarrow v] \mid$$
$$c_{\mathsf{S}} \triangleright \{ rep : c_{\mathsf{S}}(v).c_{\mathsf{B1}} \triangleleft rep; \overline{c_{\mathsf{B1}}}(w).([w \leftrightarrow v] \mid$$
$$c_{\mathsf{S}} \triangleright \{ rep : c_{\mathsf{S}}(v).c_{\mathsf{B2}} \triangleleft rep; \overline{c_{\mathsf{B2}}}(w).([w \leftrightarrow v] \mid$$
$$c_{\mathsf{B1}} \triangleright \{ shr : c_{\mathsf{B1}}(v).c_{\mathsf{B2}} \triangleleft shr; \overline{c_{\mathsf{B2}}}(w).([w \leftrightarrow v] \mid$$
$$c_{\mathsf{B2}} \triangleright \{ ok : c_{\mathsf{B2}}(v).c_{\mathsf{S}} \triangleleft ok; \overline{c_{\mathsf{S}}}(w).([w \leftrightarrow v] \mid \mathbf{0}),$$
$$quit : c_{\mathsf{B2}}(v).c_{\mathsf{S}} \triangleleft quit; \overline{c_{\mathsf{S}}}(w).([w \leftrightarrow v] \mid \mathbf{0})\})\})\})\})\}$$

Intuitively, we expect that (well-typed) process implementations for B_1, B_2, and S should interact with $\mathsf{M}[\![G_{\mathsf{BS}}]\!]$ through channels c_{B1}, c_{B2}, and c_{S}, respectively. □

We now move on to state our characterization results. We require two auxiliary notions, given next. Below, we sometimes write $\Gamma; \Delta \vdash \mathsf{M}[\![G]\!]$ instead of $\Gamma; \Delta \vdash \mathsf{M}[\![G]\!] :: z{:}\mathbf{1}$, when $z \notin fn(\mathsf{M}[\![G]\!])$.

Definition 8 (Compositional Typing). *We say* $\Gamma; \Delta \vdash \mathsf{M}[\![G]\!]{::}z{:}C$ *is a compositional typing if: (i) it is a valid typing derivation; (ii)* $\mathsf{npart}(G) \subseteq dom(\Delta)$; *and (iii)* $C = \mathbf{1}$.

A compositional typing says that $\mathsf{M}[\![G]\!]$ depends on behaviors associated to each participant of G; it also specifies that $\mathsf{M}[\![G]\!]$ does not offer any behaviors of its own. We relate binary session types and local types: the main difference is that the former do not mention participants. Below, B ranges over base types ($\mathsf{bool}, \mathsf{nat}, \ldots$) in Definition 2.

Definition 9 (Local Types $\to$ Binary Types). *Mapping* $\langle\!\langle \cdot \rangle\!\rangle$ *from local types* T *(Definition 2) into binary types* A *(Definition 1) is inductively defined as* $\langle\!\langle \mathsf{end} \rangle\!\rangle = \langle\!\langle B \rangle\!\rangle = \mathbf{1}$ *and*

$$\langle\!\langle p!\{l_i \langle U_i \rangle . T_i\}_{i \in I} \rangle\!\rangle = \oplus\{l_i : \langle\!\langle U_i \rangle\!\rangle \otimes \langle\!\langle T_i \rangle\!\rangle\}_{i \in I}$$
$$\langle\!\langle p?\{l_i \langle U_i \rangle . T_i\}_{i \in I} \rangle\!\rangle = \&\{l_i : \langle\!\langle U_i \rangle\!\rangle \multimap \langle\!\langle T_i \rangle\!\rangle\}_{i \in I}.$$

3.1   Characterization Results

Our characterization results relate process $\mathsf{M}[\![G]\!]$ (well-typed with a compositional typing) and $\langle\!\langle G{\restriction}\mathsf{p}_1\rangle\!\rangle, \ldots, \langle\!\langle G{\restriction}\mathsf{p}_n\rangle\!\rangle$ (i.e., the local types of G transformed into binary session types via Definition 9). Our characterization results are in two directions, given by Theorems 4 and 5. The first direction says that well-formedness of global types (Definition 5) ensures compositional typings for mediums with (logic based) binary session types:

Theorem 4 (Global Types $\rightarrow$ Typed Mediums). *Let $G \in \mathcal{G}$. If G is WF with* $\mathsf{part}(G) = \{\mathsf{p}_1, \ldots, \mathsf{p}_n\}$ *then* $\Gamma; c_{\mathsf{p}_1}{:}\langle\!\langle G{\restriction}\mathsf{p}_1\rangle\!\rangle, \ldots, c_{\mathsf{p}_n}{:}\langle\!\langle G{\restriction}\mathsf{p}_n\rangle\!\rangle \vdash \mathsf{M}[\![G]\!]$ *is a compositional typing, for some Γ.*

The second direction of the characterization is the converse of Theorem 4: compositional typings for mediums induce global types which are WF. Given local types T_1, T_2, below we write $T_1 \preceq^{\sqcup} T_2$ if there exists a local type T' such that $T_1 \sqcup T' = T_2$ (cf. Definition 3). This notation allows us to handle the labeled alternatives silently introduced by rule (T&L$_2$).

Theorem 5 (Well-Typed Mediums $\rightarrow$ Global Types). *Let $G \in \mathcal{G}$. If* $\Gamma; c_{\mathsf{p}_1}{:}A_1, \ldots, c_{\mathsf{p}_n}{:}A_n \vdash \mathsf{M}[\![G]\!]$ *is a compositional typing then* $\exists T_1, \ldots, T_n$ *such that* $G{\restriction}\mathsf{p}_j \preceq^{\sqcup} T_j$ *and* $\langle\!\langle T_j\rangle\!\rangle = A_j$, *for all* $\mathsf{p}_j \in \mathsf{part}(G)$.

Theorems 4 and 5 tightly connect (i) global types, local types and projection, and (ii) medium processes, and logic-based binary session types. They also provide an independent deep justification, through purely logical arguments, to the notion of projection.

3.2   A Behavioral Characterization of Global Swapping

Global swapping (Definition 6, Fig. 3) can be directly justified from more primitive notions, based on the characterizations given by Theorems 4 and 5. By abstracting a global type's behavior in terms of its medium we may reduce transformations on global types to type-preserving transformations on processes. This is the content of Theorem 6 below, which connects global swapping ($\simeq_{\mathsf{sw}}$) and context bisimilarity ($\approx$). Hence, sequentiality of mediums can be relaxed in the case of causally independent exchanges captured by $\simeq_{\mathsf{sw}}$.

Theorem 6. *Let $G_1 \in \mathcal{G}$ such that $\mathsf{M}[\![G_1]\!]$ has a compositional typing $\Gamma; \Delta \vdash \mathsf{M}[\![G_1]\!]$, for some Γ, Δ. If $G_1 \simeq_{\mathsf{sw}} G_2$ then $\Gamma; \Delta \vdash \mathsf{M}[\![G_1]\!] \approx \mathsf{M}[\![G_2]\!]$.*

Since $\mathsf{M}[\![G]\!]$ is a low-level representation of G, the converse of Theorem 6 is less interesting, for type-preserving transformations at the (low) level of mediums do not always correspond to behavior-preserving transformations at the (high) level of global types. That is, since $\mathsf{M}[\![G]\!]$ implements each communication in G using several prefixes, swapping in G occurs only when *all* relevant prefixes in $\mathsf{M}[\![G]\!]$ can be commuted via $\simeq_c$.

3.3 Operational Correspondence Results

The results given so far focus on the static semantics of multiparty and binary systems, and are already key to justify essential properties such as absence of global deadlock. We now move on to dynamic semantics, and establish operational correspondence results between a global type and its medium process (Theorem 7).

We define the *instrumented medium* of a global type G, denoted $\mathbf{M}_{\widetilde{k}}[\![G]\!]$, as a natural extension of Definition 7. Process $\mathbf{M}_{\widetilde{k}}[\![G]\!]$ exploits fresh sessions (denoted $\widetilde{k}$), to emit a visible signal for each action of G. We use $\widetilde{k}$ as annotated names (cf. Convention 3): each action on a k_i contains the identity of the participant of G which performs it. Then, using $\mathbf{M}_{\widetilde{k}}[\![G]\!]$ we define the set of *systems* associated to G (Definition 11), which collects process implementations for G mediated by $\mathbf{M}_{\widetilde{k}}[\![G]\!]$. Since interactions between local implementations and $\mathbf{M}_{\widetilde{k}}[\![G]\!]$ are unobservable actions, Theorem 7 connects (i) the visible behavior of a system along annotated names $\widetilde{k}$, and (ii) the visible behavior of G, defined by an LTS on global types (a variant of that in [12]). Below, $k^{\mathrm{p}}.P$ stands for $k^{\mathrm{p}}(x).P$ when x is not relevant in P. Also, $\widehat{k^{\mathrm{p}}}.P$ stands for $\overline{k^{\mathrm{p}}}(v).(\mathbf{0} \mid P)$ for some v.

Definition 10 (Instrumented Mediums). *Let $\widetilde{k}$ be fresh, annotated names. The* instrumented medium *of $G \in \mathcal{G}$ with respect to $\widetilde{k}$, denoted $\mathbf{M}_{\widetilde{k}}[\![G]\!]$, is defined as follows:*

- $\mathbf{M}_k[\![\mathrm{end}]\!] = \mathbf{0}$
- $\mathbf{M}_{k_1,k_2}[\![G_1 \mid G_2]\!] = \mathbf{M}_{k_1}[\![G_1]\!] \mid \mathbf{M}_{k_2}[\![G_2]\!]$
- $\mathbf{M}_k[\![\mathrm{p} \rightarrow \mathrm{q} : \{l_i\langle U_i\rangle.G_i\}_{i \in I}]\!] =$
  $c_{\mathrm{p}} \triangleright \big\{ l_i :\ k^{\mathrm{p}} \triangleleft l_i; c_{\mathrm{p}}(u).\widehat{k^{\mathrm{p}}}.\big(c_{\mathrm{q}} \triangleleft l_i; k^{\mathrm{q}} \triangleright \{l_i : \overline{c_{\mathrm{q}}}(v).([u \leftrightarrow v] \mid k^{\mathrm{q}}.\mathbf{M}_k[\![G_i]\!])\}_{\{i\}} \big) \big\}_{i \in I}$

The key case is $\mathbf{M}_k[\![\mathrm{p} \rightarrow \mathrm{q} : \{l_i\langle U_i\rangle.G_i\}_{i \in I}]\!]$. Each action of the multiparty exchange is "echoed" by an action on annotated name k: the selection of label l_i by p is followed by prefix $k^{\mathrm{p}} \triangleleft l_i$; the output from p (captured by the medium by the input $c_{\mathrm{p}}(u)$) is echoed by prefix k^{p}. This way, the instrumented process $\mathbf{M}_{\widetilde{k}}[\![G]\!]$ induces a fine-grained correspondence with G, exploiting process actions with explicit participant identities.

To state our operational correspondence result, we introduce *extended* global types and a labeled transition system (LTS) for (extended) global types. The syntax of extended global types is defined as $G ::= \mathbf{G} \mid \mathbf{G}_1 \mid \mathbf{G}_2$ with

$$\mathbf{G} ::= \mathrm{end} \mid \mathrm{p} \rightarrow \mathrm{q} : \{l_i\langle U_i\rangle.\mathbf{G}_i\}_{i \in I} \mid \mathrm{p} \rightsquigarrow \mathrm{q} : l\langle U\rangle.\mathbf{G} \mid \mathrm{p} \rightsquigarrow \mathrm{q} : l((U)).\mathbf{G} \mid \mathrm{p} \rightsquigarrow \mathrm{q} : ((U)).\mathbf{G}$$

We consider parallel composition of sequential global types. We also have three auxiliary forms for global types, denoted with $\rightsquigarrow$: they represent intermediate steps. Types $\mathrm{p} \rightsquigarrow \mathrm{q} : l\langle U\rangle.G$ and $\mathrm{p} \rightsquigarrow \mathrm{q} : l((U)).G$ denote the commitment of p to *output* and input along label l, resp. Type $\mathrm{p} \rightsquigarrow \mathrm{q} : ((U)).G$ represents the state just before the actual input action by q. We need the expected extension of Definition 10 for these types.

$$p \twoheadrightarrow q: \{l_i \langle U_i \rangle . G_i\}_{i \in I} \xrightarrow{\overline{p \triangleleft l_j}} p \rightsquigarrow q: l_j \langle U_j \rangle . G_j \quad (j \in I) \qquad p \rightsquigarrow q: l \langle U \rangle . G \xrightarrow{\overline{p}} p \rightsquigarrow q: l(\!(U)\!) . G$$

$$p \rightsquigarrow q: l(\!(U)\!) . G \xrightarrow{q \triangleleft l} p \rightsquigarrow q: (\!(U)\!) . G \qquad\qquad p \rightsquigarrow q: (\!(U)\!) . G \xrightarrow{q} G$$

Fig. 4. LTS over finite, extended global types (Excerpt).

We adapt the LTS in [12] to the case of (extended) global types. The set of observables is $\sigma ::= p \mid p \triangleleft l \mid \overline{p} \mid \overline{p \triangleleft l}$. Below, $psubj(\sigma)$ denotes the participant in σ. This way, e.g., $psubj(p \triangleleft l) = p$. The LTS over global types, noted $G \xrightarrow{\sigma} G'$, is defined by rules including those in Fig. 4. Since Definition 10 annotates prefixes on k with participant identities, their associated actions will be annotated too; given a participant p, we may define the set of annotated visible actions as: $\lambda^p ::= k^p(y) \mid k^p \triangleleft l \mid \overline{k^p} \, y \mid \overline{k^p}(y) \mid \overline{k^p \triangleleft l}$. We write k^p and $\widehat{k^p}$ to denote actions $k^p(y)$ and $\overline{k^p}(y)$, resp., whenever object y is unimportant. Also, $psubj(\lambda^p)$ denotes the participant p which annotates λ. This way, e.g., $psubj(k^p) = p$ and $psubj(\overline{k^q \triangleleft l}) = q$. To relate labels for global types and process labels, given an annotated name k, we define mappings $\{\!\!\{ \cdot \}\!\!\}^k$ and $\| \cdot \|$ as follows:

$$\{\!\!\{ p \}\!\!\}^k = k^p \qquad \{\!\!\{ p \triangleleft l \}\!\!\}^k = k^p \triangleleft l \qquad \{\!\!\{ \overline{p} \}\!\!\}^k = \widehat{k^p} \qquad \{\!\!\{ \overline{p \triangleleft l} \}\!\!\}^k = \overline{k^p \triangleleft l}$$

$$\| k^p \| = p \qquad \| k^p \triangleleft l \| = p \triangleleft l \qquad \| \widehat{k^p} \| = \overline{p} \qquad \| \overline{k^p \triangleleft l} \| = \overline{p \triangleleft l}$$

Operational correspondence is stated in terms of the *multiparty systems* of a global type. Following Definition 8, we say that $\Gamma; \Delta, \Delta' \vdash \mathbf{M}_{\widetilde{k}}[\![G]\!] :: z{:}C$ is an *instrumented* compositional typing if (i) it is a valid typing derivation; (ii) $\mathsf{npart}(G) \subseteq dom(\Delta)$; (iii) $C = \mathbf{1}$; (iv) $dom(\Delta') = \widetilde{k}$:

Definition 11 (Systems). *Let $G \in \mathcal{G}$ be a WF global type, with $\mathsf{part}(G) = \{p_1, \ldots, p_n\}$. Also, let $\Gamma; \Delta, \Delta' \vdash \mathbf{M}_{\widetilde{k}}[\![G]\!]$ be an instrumented compositional typing, with $\Delta = c_{p_1} {:} \langle\!\langle G \upharpoonright p_1 \rangle\!\rangle, \ldots, c_{p_n} {:} \langle\!\langle G \upharpoonright p_n \rangle\!\rangle$, for some Γ. Let $\widetilde{z} = \mathsf{npart}(G)$. The set of systems of G is defined as:*

$$\mathcal{S}_{\widetilde{k}}(G) = \left\{ (\boldsymbol{\nu} \widetilde{z})(Q_1 \mid \cdots \mid Q_n \mid \mathbf{M}_{\widetilde{k}}[\![G]\!]) \ \mid \ \cdot; \cdot \vdash Q_j :: c_{p_j} {:} \langle\!\langle G \upharpoonright p_j \rangle\!\rangle, j \in 1 \ldots n \right\}$$

Thus, given G, a multiparty system is obtained by composing $\mathbf{M}_{\widetilde{k}}[\![G]\!]$ with well-typed implementations for each of the local projections of G. An $R \in \mathcal{S}_{\widetilde{k}}(G)$ is an implementation of the multiparty protocol G. By construction, its only visible actions are on annotated names: interactions between all the Q_j and $\mathbf{M}_{\widetilde{k}}[\![G]\!]$ will be unobservable.

Theorem 7 below connects global types and systems: it confirms that (instrumented) medium processes faithfully mirror the communicating behavior of extended global types. Below, we write $G \xrightarrow{\sigma[p]} G'$ if $G \xrightarrow{\sigma} G'$ and $psubj(\sigma) = p$. Also, we write $P \xrightarrow{\lambda[p]} P'$ (resp. $P \xRightarrow{\lambda[p]} P'$) if $P \xrightarrow{\lambda} P'$ (resp. $P \xRightarrow{\lambda} P'$) holds and $psubj(\lambda) = p$.

Theorem 7 (Operational Correspondence). *Let G be an extended WF global type and $R \in \mathcal{S}_{\widetilde{k}}(G)$. We have: If $G \xrightarrow{\sigma[\mathrm{p}]} G'$ then $R \xRightarrow{\lambda[\mathrm{p}]} R'$, for some $\lambda, R', k \in \widetilde{k}$ such that $\lambda = \{\!|\sigma|\!\}^k$ and $R' \in \mathcal{S}_{\widetilde{k}}(G')$. Moreover, if there is some R_0 s.t. $R \Longrightarrow R_0 \xrightarrow{\lambda[\mathrm{p}]} R'$ then $G \xrightarrow{\sigma[\mathrm{p}]} G'$, for some σ, G' such that $\sigma = \|\lambda\|$ and $R' \in \mathcal{S}_{\widetilde{k}}(G')$.*

4   Example: Sharing in Multiparty Conversations

Here we further illustrate reasoning about global types in $\mathcal{G}$ by exploiting the properties given in Sect. 3. In particular, we illustrate non-trivial forms of replication and sharing.

Let us consider the global type G_{BS}, given in Example 1. The medium processes of G_{BS}, denoted $\mathsf{M}[\![G_{\mathrm{BS}}]\!]$, has been detailed in Example 2; we proceed to examine its properties. Relying on Theorems 4 and 5, we have the compositional typing:

$$\Gamma; c_1{:}\mathsf{B1}, c_2{:}\mathsf{S}, c_3{:}\mathsf{B2} \vdash \mathsf{M}[\![G_{\mathrm{BS}}]\!] :: -{:}\mathbf{1} \tag{1}$$

for some Γ and with $\mathsf{B1} = \langle\!\langle G_{\mathrm{BS}}{\restriction}\mathsf{B_1} \rangle\!\rangle$, $\mathsf{S} = \langle\!\langle G_{\mathrm{BS}}{\restriction}\mathsf{S} \rangle\!\rangle$, and $\mathsf{B2} = \langle\!\langle G_{\mathrm{BS}}{\restriction}\mathsf{B_2} \rangle\!\rangle$. To implement the protocol, one may simply compose $\mathsf{M}[\![G_{\mathrm{BS}}]\!]$ with type compatible processes $\cdot;\cdot \vdash Buy1 :: c_1{:}\mathsf{B1}$, $\cdot;\cdot \vdash Sel :: c_2{:}\mathsf{S}$, and $\cdot;\cdot \vdash Buy2 :: c_3{:}\mathsf{B2}$:

$$\Gamma;\cdot \vdash (\boldsymbol{\nu}c_1)(Buy1 \mid (\boldsymbol{\nu}c_2)(Sel \mid (\boldsymbol{\nu}c_3)(Buy2 \mid \mathsf{M}[\![G_{\mathrm{BS}}]\!]))) \tag{2}$$

The binary session types in Sect. 2 allows us to infer that the multiparty system defined by (2) adheres to the declared projected types, is deadlock-free, and terminating.

Just as we inherit strong properties for $Buy1$, Sel, and $Buy2$ above, we may inherit the same properties for more interesting system configurations. In particular, local implementations which appeal to replication and sharing, admit also precise analyses thanks to the characterizations in Sect. 3. Let us consider a setting in which the processes to be composed with the medium must be invoked from a replicated service (a source of generic process definitions). We may have $\cdot;\cdot \vdash !u_1(w).Buy1_w :: u_1{:}!\mathsf{B1}$ and

$$\cdot;\cdot \vdash !u_2(w).Sel_w :: u_2{:}!\mathsf{S} \qquad \cdot;\cdot \vdash !u_3(w).Buy2_w :: u_3{:}!\mathsf{B2}$$

and the following "initiator processes" would spawn a copy of the medium's requirements, instantiated at appropriate names:

$$\cdot;u_1{:}!\mathsf{B1} \vdash \overline{u_1}(x).[x \leftrightarrow c_1] :: c_1{:}\mathsf{B1} \qquad \cdot;u_2{:}!\mathsf{S} \vdash \overline{u_2}(x).[x \leftrightarrow c_2] :: c_2{:}\mathsf{S}$$
$$\cdot;u_3{:}!\mathsf{B2} \vdash \overline{u_3}(x).[x \leftrightarrow c_3] :: c_3{:}\mathsf{B2}$$

Let us write $RBuy1$, $RBuy2$, and $RSel$ to denote the composition of replicated definitions and initiators above. Intuitively, they represent the "remote" variants of $Buy1$, $Buy2$, and $RSel$, respectively. We may then define the multiparty system:

$$\Gamma;\cdot \vdash (\boldsymbol{\nu}c_1)(RBuy1 \mid (\boldsymbol{\nu}c_2)(RSel \mid (\boldsymbol{\nu}c_3)(RBuy2 \mid \mathsf{M}[\![G_{\mathrm{BS}}]\!])))$$

which, with a concise specification, improves (2) with concurrent invocation/instantiation of replicated service definitions. As (2), the revised composition above is correct, deadlock-free, and terminating.

Rather than appealing to initiators, a scheme in which the medium invokes and instantiates services directly is also expressible in our framework, in a type consistent way. Using (1), and assuming $\Gamma = u_1{:}B1, u_2{:}S, u_3{:}B2$, we may derive:

$$\Gamma; \cdot \vdash \overline{u_1}(c_1).\overline{u_2}(c_2).\overline{u_3}(c_3).\mathsf{M}[\![G_{\mathrm{BS}}]\!] \tag{3}$$

Hence, prior to engaging in the mediation behavior for G_{BS}, the medium first spawns a copy of the required services. We may relate the guarded process in (3) with the multicast session request construct in multiparty session processes [14]. Observe that (3) cleanly distinguishes between session initiation and actual communication behavior: the distinction is given at the level of processes (cf. output prefixes on u_1, u_2, and u_3) but also at the level of typed interfaces.

The service invocation (3) may be regarded as "eager": all required services must be sequentially invoked prior to executing the protocol. We may also obtain, in a type-consistent manner, a medium process implementing a "lazy" invocation strategy that spawns services only when necessary. For the sake of example, consider process

$$Eager_{\mathrm{BS}} \triangleq \overline{u_3}(c_3).\mathsf{M}[\![G_{\mathrm{BS}}]\!]$$

in which only the invocation on u_3 is blocking the protocol, with "open" dependencies on c_1, c_2. That is, we have $\Gamma; c_1{:}B1, c_2{:}S \vdash Eager_{\mathrm{BS}} :: z{:}1$. It could be desirable to postpone the invocation on u_3 as much as possible. By combining the commutations on process prefixes realized by $\simeq_c$ [19] and Theorem 2, we may obtain:

$$\Gamma; c_1{:}B1, c_2{:}S \vdash Eager_{\mathrm{BS}} \approx Lazy_{\mathrm{BS}} :: -{:}1$$

where $Lazy_{\mathrm{BS}}$ is obtained from $Eager_{\mathrm{BS}}$ by "pushing inside" prefix $\overline{u_3}(c_3)$.

5   Multiparty Session Types with Behavioral Genericity

To illustrate the modularity of our approach, we conservatively extend, for the first time, multiparty session types with *parametric polymorphism*, developed for binary sessions in [4,22]. Although expressed by second-order quantifiers on (session) types—in the style of the polymorphic λ-calculus—parametric polymorphism in our setting means *behavioural genericity* in multiparty conversations (i.e., passing first-class behavioral interfaces in messages), not just datatype genericity. In this section we describe how to extend the approach and results in Sect. 3 to polymorphic, multiparty session types.

In [4] we have extended the framework of [5] with impredicative universal and existential quantification over session types, denoted with $\forall X.A$ and $\exists X.A$, respectively. These two types are interpreted as the input and output of a session type, respectively. More precisely, $\forall X.A$ is the type of a process that inputs some session type S (which we may as a kind of interface passing) and then behaves as prescribed by $A\{S/X\}$. $\exists X.A$ is the type of a process that sends some session type S and then behaves as prescribed by $A\{S/X\}$. From the point of view of the receiver of such S, the protocol S is in a sense opaque; therefore, after inputting S the receiver behaves parametrically (in the sense of behavioral polymorphism) for any such S. In any case, any usage of S by the sender will necessarily be matched by some appropriate parties in the system. A relevant example of the phenomenon can be recovered from [4]. Consider the type

$$\mathsf{CloudServer} : \forall X.(\mathsf{api} \multimap X) \multimap X$$

A session with this type will first input some session type X, say GMail, and then will input a session with type $\mathsf{api} \multimap \mathsf{GMail}$ (that may be realized by a piece of code that will first receive a channel implementing the api behavior and will after—building on it—behave as specified by GMail) and then offers the behavior GMail. A system implementing the CloudServer type must somehow provide the api service internally and pass it to the channel of type $\mathsf{api} \multimap \mathsf{GMail}$ (e.g., representing a piece of mobile code). Notice that after that the GMail service may be produced by copy-cating the resulting behavior to the cloud server client. The crucial point here is that the cloud server behaves uniformly for whatever session type X is requested for it to execute; its role in this case is to provide the suitable api. Of course, at runtime, all interactions at X will take place as prescribed by the concrete session type involved (in this example, GMail), which may be an arbitrarily complex (behaviorally generic) session type.

5.1 Binary Session Types with Parametric Polymorphism

We now recall key definitions from [4]. The process model in Sect. 2 is extended with processes $\overline{x}\,A.P$ (output type A, proceed as P) and $x(X).P$ (receive a type A, proceed as $P\{A/X\}$) and the reduction rule: $\overline{x}\,A.Q \mid x(X).P \to Q \mid P\{A/X\}$, where $\{A/X\}$ is the substitution of type variable X with session type A. Thus, our process syntax allows terms such as, e.g., $\overline{x}\,A.Q \mid x(X).\overline{y}\,X.P$, where A is a session typed protocol.

We extend binary types (cf. Definition 1) with existential and universal quantification:

$$A, B ::= \mathbf{1} \mid\, !A \mid A \otimes B \mid A \multimap B \mid \&\{l_i{:}A_i\}_{i \in I} \mid \oplus\{l_i{:}A_i\}_{i \in I} \mid X \mid \exists X.A \mid \forall X.A$$

Besides Δ and Γ, the polymorphic type system uses environment Ω to record type variables. We have two judgments. Judgment $\Omega \vdash A\ \mathsf{type}$ denotes that A is a well-formed type with free variables registered in Ω (see [4] for well-formedness rules). Also, judgement $\Omega; \Gamma; \Delta \vdash P :: x{:}A$ states that P implements a session of type A along channel x, provided it is composed with processes providing sessions linearly in Δ and persistently in Γ, such that the types occurring in Ω are well-formed.

The required typing rules result by adding Ω in Fig. 2 and by considering rules in Fig. 5, which explain how to *provide* and *use* sessions of a polymorphic type. Rule (T∀R) types the offering of a session of universal type $\forall X.A$ by inputing an arbitrary type, bound to X, and proceeding as A, which may bind the type

$$\dfrac{(\text{T}\forall\text{L})}{\varOmega \vdash B\ \text{type}\quad \varOmega;\varGamma;\varDelta,x:A\{B/X\} \vdash P :: T}{\varOmega;\varGamma;\varDelta,x:\forall X.A \vdash \overline{x}\,B.P :: T} \qquad \dfrac{(\text{T}\forall\text{R})}{\varOmega,X;\varGamma;\varDelta \vdash P :: z:A}{\varOmega;\varGamma;\varDelta \vdash z(X).P :: z:\forall X.A}$$

$$\dfrac{(\text{T}\exists\text{L})}{\varOmega,X;\varGamma;\varDelta,x:A \vdash P :: T}{\varOmega;\varGamma;\varDelta,x:\exists X.A \vdash x(X).P :: T} \qquad \dfrac{(\text{T}\exists\text{R})}{\varOmega \vdash B\ \text{type}\quad \varOmega;\varGamma;\varDelta \vdash P :: x:A\{B/X\}}{\varOmega;\varGamma;\varDelta \vdash \overline{x}\,B.P :: x:\exists X.A}$$

Fig. 5. Typing rules for polymorphic, binary session types.

variable X, regardless of what the received type is. Rule (T$\forall$L) says that the use of type $\forall X.A$ consists of the output of a type B (well-formed under $\varOmega$) which then warrants the use of the session as $A\{B/X\}$. The existential type is dual: providing an existentially typed session $\exists X.A$ is accomplished by outputting a type B and then providing a session of type $A\{B/X\}$ (Rule (T$\exists$R)). Using an existential session $\exists X.A$ implies inputing a type and then using the session as A, regardless of the received session type (Rule (T$\exists$L)).

Well-typed polymorphic processes satisfy Theorem 1 and *relational parametricity* [4], a reasoning principle stated next. We require some notation, fully detailed in [4]: $\omega{:}\varOmega$ denotes a type substitution that assigns a closed type to variables in $\varOmega$. Notation $\widehat{\omega}(P)$ denotes the application of ω to type variables in P. Also, $\eta{:}\omega_1 \Leftrightarrow \omega_2$ is an equivalence candidate assignment (a typed relation on processes) between ω_1 and ω_2. Moreover, $\approx_{\text{L}}$ denotes a *logical equivalence* relation that coincides with barbed congruence.

Theorem 8 (Relational Parametricity [4]**).** *If* $\varOmega;\varGamma;\varDelta \vdash P :: z:A$ *then, for all* $\omega_1{:}\varOmega$, $\omega_2{:}\varOmega$, *and* $\eta{:}\omega_1 \Leftrightarrow \omega_2$: $\varGamma;\varDelta \vdash \widehat{\omega_1}(P) \approx_{\text{L}} \widehat{\omega_2}(P) :: z:A[\eta{:}\omega_1 \Leftrightarrow \omega_2]$.

Theorem 8 entails *behavioral genericity*, a form of representation independence: it says that process P behaves the same independently from instantiations of its free type variables.

5.2 Multiparty Session Types with Polymorphism

We extend global types in $\mathcal{G}$ (Definition 2) with variables $X, X', \ldots$ and with a construct $\text{p} \rightarrow \text{q}{:}\{l[X].G'\}$, which introduces parametric polymorphism (X is meant to occur in G'). To our knowledge, this is the first theory of its kind:

Definition 12 (Polymorphic Session Types). *Define global types and local types as*

$$G ::= \text{end} \mid G_1 \mid G_2 \mid \text{p} \rightarrow \text{q}{:}\{l_i\langle U_i\rangle.G_i\}_{i\in I} \mid \text{p} \rightarrow \text{q}{:}\{l[X].G\} \mid X$$

$$U ::= \text{bool} \mid \text{nat} \mid \text{str} \mid \ldots \mid T \mid (T)^{\dagger}$$

$$T ::= \text{end} \mid \text{p}?\{l_i\langle U_i\rangle.T_i\}_{i\in I} \mid \text{p}!\{l_i\langle U_i\rangle.T_i\}_{i\in I} \mid \text{p}!\{l[X].T\} \mid \text{p}?\{l[X].T\} \mid X$$

Above $(\cdot)^{\dagger}$ *denotes a function on local types that discards participant identities. E.g.,* $(\text{p}?\{l[X].T\})^{\dagger} = ?\{l[X].(T)^{\dagger}\}$ *and* $(\text{p}?\{l_i\langle U_i\rangle.T_i\}_{i\in I})^{\dagger} = ?\{l_i\langle U_i\rangle.(T_i)^{\dagger}\}_{i\in I}$.

We write $\mathcal{G}^{\forall\exists}$ to denote the above global types. The global type $\mathsf{p} \twoheadrightarrow \mathsf{q}:\{l[X].G\}$ signals that p sends to q an arbitrary local type (protocol), thus specifying q as a generic partner. Also, G is a *generic* global specification: its behavior will be depend on the type sent by p to q, which should be explicit in p's implementation. This new global type is related to local types $\mathsf{p}!\{l[X].T\}$ and $\mathsf{p}?\{l[X].T\}$, which are to be understood as existential and universal quantification on local types, respectively—see below. The global type X should be intuitively understood as a behavior that remains "globally abstract", in the sense that it is determined by a concrete local type exchanged between two participants, namely, as a result of a (previous) communication of the form $\mathsf{p} \twoheadrightarrow \mathsf{q}:\{l[X].G\}$. As a result, the (global) communication behavior associated to local type exchanged between p and q should remain abstract (opaque) to other participants of the protocol.

The *projection* of $G \in \mathcal{G}^{\forall\exists}$ onto participant r, denoted $G \upharpoonright \mathsf{r}$, extends Definition 4 by adding $X \upharpoonright \mathsf{r} = X$ and by letting:

$$(\mathsf{p} \twoheadrightarrow \mathsf{q}:\{l[X].G\}) \upharpoonright \mathsf{r} = \begin{cases} \mathsf{p}!\{l[X].(G \upharpoonright \mathsf{r})\} & \text{if } \mathsf{r} = \mathsf{p} \\ \mathsf{p}?\{l[X].(G \upharpoonright \mathsf{r})\} & \text{if } \mathsf{r} = \mathsf{q} \\ G \upharpoonright \mathsf{r} & \text{otherwise} \end{cases}$$

Well-formedness of global types in $\mathcal{G}^{\forall\exists}$ is based on projectability but also on consistent uses of type variables: a participant can only communicate the types it knows. (This condition is similar to *history-sensitivity*, as in [1].) This way, e.g., an ill-formed type is $\mathsf{p} \twoheadrightarrow \mathsf{q}:\{l_1[X].\mathsf{r} \twoheadrightarrow \mathsf{s}:\{l_2\langle?\{l\langle\mathsf{int}\rangle.X\}\rangle.\mathsf{end}\}\}$, since r, s do not know the type sent by p.

5.3 Mediums for Multiparty Session Types with Polymorphism

Mediums for global types in $\mathcal{G}^{\forall\exists}$ are defined by extending Definition 7 as follows:

$$\mathsf{M}[\![\mathsf{p} \twoheadrightarrow \mathsf{q}:\{l[X].G\}]\!] = c_\mathsf{p} \triangleright \{l : c_\mathsf{p}(X).c_\mathsf{q} \triangleleft l; \overline{c_\mathsf{q}} X.\mathsf{M}[\![G]\!]\} \qquad\qquad \mathsf{M}[\![X]\!] = 0$$

Observe that type variable X should not generate a mediator behavior, as we want to remain generic. The relation between local types and binary types extends Definition 9 with:

$$\langle\!\langle \mathsf{p}!\{l[X].T\}\rangle\!\rangle = \oplus\{l : \exists X.\langle\!\langle T\rangle\!\rangle\} \qquad \langle\!\langle \mathsf{p}?\{l[X].T\}\rangle\!\rangle = \&\{l : \forall X.\langle\!\langle T\rangle\!\rangle\}$$

and by letting $\langle\!\langle X\rangle\!\rangle = X$ and $\langle\!\langle (T)^\dagger\rangle\!\rangle = \langle\!\langle T\rangle\!\rangle$. The characterization results in Sect. 3.1 hold also for global types in $\mathcal{G}^{\forall\exists}$.

6 Mediums at Work: A Behaviorally Generic Multiparty Protocol

We illustrate our approach and results via a simple example. Consider the global type G_p, inspired by the CloudServer from [4] already hinted to above. It features behavioral genericity (as enabled by parametric polymorphism); below, str, bool, denote basic data types, and api is a session type describing the cloud infrastructure API.

$$G_p = p \rightarrow q{:}\{l_1 \langle \text{bool} \rangle . q \rightarrow r{:}\{l[X].q \rightarrow r{:}\{l_2 \langle ?\{l_3 \langle \text{api} \rangle . X\} \rangle . X\}\}\}$$

We have participants p, q, and r. The intent is that r is a behaviorally generic participant, that provides a behavior of type api required by q. Crucially, r may interact with q independently of the local type sent by q. Such a local type is explicit in q's implementation (see below), rather than in the global type G_p.

In G_p, participant p first sends a boolean value to q; then, q sends an unspecified protocol to r, say M, which is to be used subsequently in an exchange from q to r. Notice that M occurs in the value that r receives from q and influences the behavior after that exchange. Indeed, the value $?\{l_3 \langle \text{api} \rangle . X\}$ denotes an unspecified session type that relies on the reception of a session of type api. The local projections for G_p are $G_p {\restriction} p = p!\{l_1 \langle \text{bool} \rangle . \text{end}\}$ and

$$G_p {\restriction} q = p?\{l_1 \langle \text{bool} \rangle . q!\{l[X].q!\{l_2 \langle ?\{l_3 \langle \text{api} \rangle . X\} \rangle . X\}\}\}$$
$$G_p {\restriction} r = q?\{l[X].q?\{l_2 \langle ?\{l_3 \langle \text{api} \rangle . X\} \rangle . X\}\}$$

Above, the occurrences of X at the end of both $G_p {\restriction} q$ and $G_p {\restriction} r$ may appear surprising, as they should represent dual behaviors. Notice that in each case, X should be interpreted according to the local type that "bounds" X (i.e., the output $q!\{l[X]\ldots\}$ in $G_p {\restriction} q$ and the input $q?\{l[X]\ldots\}$ in $G_p {\restriction} r$). This dual perspective should become evident when looking at the binary session types associated to these projections. First, notice that we have that $\langle\!\langle ?\{l_3 \langle \text{api} \rangle . X\} \rangle\!\rangle = \&\{l_3{:}(\text{api}{\multimap}X)\}$. Writing $(\text{api}{\multimap}X)$ to stand for $\&\{l_3{:}(\text{api}{\multimap}X)\}$), we have the binary session types $\langle\!\langle G_p {\restriction} p \rangle\!\rangle = \oplus\{l_1 : \mathbf{1} \otimes \mathbf{1}\}$ and

$$\langle\!\langle G_p {\restriction} q \rangle\!\rangle = \&\{l_1 : \mathbf{1} \multimap \oplus\{l : \exists X. \oplus\{l_2 : (\text{api}{\multimap}X) \otimes X\}$$
$$\langle\!\langle G_p {\restriction} r \rangle\!\rangle = \&\{l : \forall X. \&\{l_2 : (\text{api}{\multimap}X){\multimap}X\}\}\}\}$$

The medium process for G_p is then:

$$\mathsf{M}[\![G_p]\!] = c_p \triangleright \{l_1 : c_p(u).c_q \triangleleft l_1; \overline{c_q}(v).([u \leftrightarrow v] \mid$$
$$c_q \triangleright \{l : c_q(X).c_r \triangleleft l; \overline{c_r} X.$$
$$c_q \triangleright \{l_2 : c_q(u).c_r \triangleleft l_2; \overline{c_r}(v).([u \leftrightarrow v] \mid \mathbf{0})\}\})\}$$

Using our extended characterization results, we may show that $\mathsf{M}[\![G_p]\!]$ can safely interact with implementations for p, q, and r whose types correspond to the projections of G_p onto p, q, and r. Indeed, $\mathsf{M}[\![G_p]\!]$ can safely interact with any P, Q_i, and R such that $\Omega; \Gamma; \Delta_1 \vdash P :: c_p{:}\langle\!\langle G_p {\restriction} p \rangle\!\rangle$ and

$$\Omega; \Gamma; \Delta_3 \vdash R :: c_r{:}\langle\!\langle G_p {\restriction} r \rangle\!\rangle \qquad \Omega; \Gamma; \Delta_2 \vdash Q_i :: c_q{:}\langle\!\langle G_p {\restriction} q \rangle\!\rangle$$

Process $(\nu c_p, c_q, c_r)(\mathsf{M}[\![G_p]\!] \mid P \mid R \mid Q_i)$ is a system for G_p (cf. Definition 11). It is well-typed; we have $\Omega; \Gamma; \Delta_1, \Delta_2, \Delta_3 \vdash (\nu c_p, c_q, c_r)(\mathsf{M}[\![G_p]\!] \mid P \mid R \mid Q_i) :: - :$
1. Process $c_p \triangleleft l_1; \overline{c_p}(f).(B_f \mid \mathbf{0})$ is a concrete implementation for P, where name f stands for a boolean implemented by B_f. As for R and Q_i, we may have:

$$R = c_r \vartriangleright \{l : c_r(Y).c_r \vartriangleright \{l_2 : c_r(y).\overline{y}(a).(A_a \mid [c_r \leftrightarrow a])\}\}$$
$$Q_1 = c_q \vartriangleright \{l_1 : c_q(b).c_q \vartriangleleft l; \overline{c_q}\, S.c_q \vartriangleleft l_2; \overline{c_q}(w).(w(a).\mathrm{SMTP}^b_{w,a} \mid [m \leftrightarrow c_q])\}$$

Crucially, following the type $\langle\!\langle G_p \restriction r \rangle\!\rangle$, process R is *behaviorally generic*: independently of the type received from Q_i via the medium $\mathrm{M}[\![G_p]\!]$ (cf. the type input prefix $c_r(Y)$), R enables process A_a to provide the API along name a. Process Q_1 is just one possible implementation for q: it provides an implementation of a service $\mathrm{SMTP}^b_{w,a}$ that relies on behavior api along name a and a boolean along b to implement protocol S along w. A different implementation for q is process Q_2 below, which concerns session protocol I:

$$Q_2 = c_q \vartriangleright \{l_1 : c_q(b).c_q \vartriangleleft l; \overline{c_q}\, I.c_q \vartriangleleft l_2; \overline{c_q}(w).(w(a).\mathrm{IMAP}^b_{w,a} \mid [m \leftrightarrow c_q])\}$$

where $\mathrm{IMAP}^b_{w,a}$ uses api along a and boolean b to implement protocol I along w. Note that R and any Q_i have limited interactions with $\mathrm{M}[\![G_p]\!]$: to respect the genericity stipulated by G_p, the polymorphic process $\mathrm{M}[\![G_p]\!]$ only mediates the exchange of the local type (S or I) and plugs the necessary connections; other exchanges are direct between R and Q_1 or Q_2, and known to comply with the (dynamically passed protocol) specified by the session type S or I.

Both $(\nu c_p, c_q, c_r)(\mathrm{M}[\![G_p]\!] \mid P \mid R \mid Q_1)$ and $(\nu c_p, c_q, c_r)(\mathrm{M}[\![G_p]\!] \mid P \mid R \mid Q_2)$ are well-typed systems; hence, they satisfy fidelity and deadlock-freedom (Theorem 1). Using properties of well-typed processes together with relational parametricity (Theorem 8), we may further show that they are *observationally equivalent*, provided a typed relation between session types S and I. That is, Theorem 8 allows us to state the behavioral independence of the sub-system formed by $\mathrm{M}[\![G_p]\!]$, P, and R with respect to any implementation Q_i for participant q.

7   Concluding Remarks and Related Works

We developed the first analysis of multiparty protocols using binary session types. Our *medium processes* capture the semantics of multiparty session types and connect global types to well-typed implementations; this allows us to exploit properties for typed processes to reason about multiparty systems. Since mediums have a uniform definition, we may analyze global types with features such as delegation, which go beyond the scope of recent automata-based analyses of global types [12, 16]. Our work thus complements such recent works. Our approach naturally supports the analysis of multiparty session types with *behavioral genericity*. This model, the first of its kind, is very powerful; it reuses techniques from binary sessions [4], notably *relational parametricity*. These features suggest that extensions of known multiparty sessions with behavioral genericity would be hard to obtain without following linear logic foundations, as done here.

Given a global type, our *characterization results* relate its medium and its local projections; these relations allow us to transfer properties of [5] (e.g., deadlock-freedom) to multiparty protocols. Our results stress the fundamental character of key notions in multiparty sessions (e.g., projections), and build on connections between two distinct session type theories based on linear logic [5] and on automata [12]. Our developments do not depend on the interpretation of session types in [5] being intuitionistic; clearly, its reasoning techniques (e.g., behavioral equivalences [19]) are important in our results. Our approach should extend also to interpretations based on classical linear logic [22].

Related Work. One challenge in decomposing a multiparty session type is preserving its sequencing information. The work [9] shows how to decompose a global type into simpler, independent pieces: global types use an additional `calls` construct to invoke these pieces in the appropriate order, but connections with binary sessions are not established. *Correspondence assertions* [2] track data dependencies and detect unintended operations; they may allow to relate independent binary sessions. Using standard binary/multiparty session types, we capture sequencing information using a process extracted from a global type. Our approach relies on deadlock-freedom (not available in [2]) and offers a principled way of transferring it to multiparty systems.

To our knowledge, ours is the first formal characterization of multiparty session types using binary session types. Previous works have, e.g., compared different multiparty session types but without connecting to binary types [11]. The work [18] (extended version) identifies a class of multiparty systems for which deadlock-freedom analysis can be reduced to the analysis of linear π-calculus processes. This reduction, however, does not connect with binary session types, nor exploits other properties of processes to analyze global types. The work [7] relates global types and a variant of classical linear logic; as in our work, a challenge in [7] is capturing sequencing information in global types. While [7] captures sequencing information in global types via role annotations in propositions/types (using an extra proof system, called coherence), our medium-based approach enables process reasoning on global types, uses standard linear logic propositions, and allows for conservative extensions with powerful reasoning techniques, notably behavioral genericity as enabled by parametric polymorphism.

Medium processes are loosely related to the concept of *orchestrators* in service-oriented computing. The work [17] shows how to synthesize an orchestrator from a service choreography, using finite state machines. In contrast, we consider choreographies given as behavioral types; mediums are obtained directly from those types.

Acknowledgments. Thanks to Bernardo Toninho for useful discussions. We are also grateful to the anonymous reviewers for their improvement suggestions. This work was partially supported by NOVA LINCS (Ref. UID/CEC/04516/2013) and COST Action IC1201 (Behavioural Types for Reliable Large-Scale Software Systems).

References

1. Bocchi, L., Honda, K., Tuosto, E., Yoshida, N.: A theory of design-by-contract for distributed multiparty interactions. In: Gastin, P., Laroussinie, F. (eds.) CONCUR 2010. LNCS, vol. 6269, pp. 162–176. Springer, Heidelberg (2010)

2. Bonelli, E., Compagnoni, A., Gunter, E.: Correspondence assertions for process synchronization in concurrent communications. J. Funct. Program. **15**, 219–247 (2005)
3. Caires, L., Pérez, J.A.: A typeful characterization of multiparty structured conversations based on binary sessions. CoRR, abs/1407.4242 (2014)
4. Caires, L., Pérez, J.A., Pfenning, F., Toninho, B.: Behavioral polymorphism and parametricity in session-based communication. In: Felleisen, M., Gardner, P. (eds.) ESOP 2013. LNCS, vol. 7792, pp. 330–349. Springer, Heidelberg (2013). See also Technical Report CMU-CS-12-108, April 2012
5. Caires, L., Pfenning, F.: Session types as intuitionistic linear propositions. In: Gastin, P., Laroussinie, F. (eds.) CONCUR 2010. LNCS, vol. 6269, pp. 222–236. Springer, Heidelberg (2010)
6. Carbone, M., Montesi, F.: Deadlock-freedom-by-design: multiparty asynchronous global programming. In: POPL, pp. 263–274. ACM (2013)
7. Carbone, M., Montesi, F., Schürmann, C., Yoshida, N.: Multiparty session types as coherence proofs. In: CONCUR 2015. LIPIcs, vol. 42, pp. 412–426. Dagstuhl (2015)
8. Castagna, G., Gesbert, N., Padovani, L.: A theory of contracts for web services. In: POPL, ACM SIGPLAN Notices 43, pp. 261–272. ACM (2008)
9. Chen, T.: Lightening global types. J. Logic Algebraic Meth. Program. **84**(5), 708–729 (2015)
10. Coppo, M., Dezani-Ciancaglini, M., Yoshida, N., Padovani, L.: Global progress for dynamically interleaved multiparty sessions. Math. Struct. Comput. Sci. **26**(2), 238–302 (2016)
11. Demangeon, R., Yoshida, N.: On the expressiveness of multiparty session types. In: FSTTCS 2015. LIPIcs. Dagstuhl (2015)
12. Deniélou, P.-M., Yoshida, N.: Multiparty compatibility in communicating automata: characterisation and synthesis of global session types. In: Fomin, F.V., Freivalds, R., Kwiatkowska, M., Peleg, D. (eds.) ICALP 2013, Part II. LNCS, vol. 7966, pp. 174–186. Springer, Heidelberg (2013)
13. Honda, K., Vasconcelos, V.T., Kubo, M.: Language primitives and type discipline for structured communication-based programming. In: Hankin, C. (ed.) ESOP 1998. LNCS, vol. 1381, pp. 122–138. Springer, Heidelberg (1998)
14. Honda, K., Yoshida, N., Carbone, M.: Multiparty asynchronous session types. In: POPL, pp. 273–284. ACM (2008)
15. Huttel, H., et al.: Foundations of session types and behavioural contracts. ACM Comput. Surv. **49**(1), 3:1–3:36 (2016). doi:10.1145/2873052
16. Lange, J., Tuosto, E., Yoshida, N.: From communicating machines to graphical choreographies. In: Proceedings of POPL 2015, pp. 221–232. ACM (2015)
17. McIlvenna, S., Dumas, M., Wynn, M.T.: Synthesis of orchestrators from service choreographies. In: APCCM. CRPIT, vol. 96. Australian Computer Society (2009)
18. Padovani, L.: Deadlock and lock freedom in the linear π-calculus. In: Proceedings of CSL-LICS 2014, pp. 72:1–72:10. ACM (2014). http://hal.archives-ouvertes.fr/hal-00932356v2/document
19. Pérez, J.A., Caires, L., Pfenning, F., Toninho, B.: Linear logical relations and observational equivalences for session-based concurrency. Inf. Comput. **239**, 254–302 (2014)
20. Sangiorgi, D., Walker, D.: The π-calculus: A Theory of Mobile Processes. CUP, Cambridge (2001)

21. Toninho, B., Caires, L., Pfenning, F.: Corecursion and non-divergence in session-typed processes. In: Maffei, M., Tuosto, E. (eds.) TGC 2014. LNCS, vol. 8902, pp. 159–175. Springer, Heidelberg (2014)
22. Wadler, P.: Propositions as sessions. J. Funct. Program. 24(2–3), 384–418 (2014)

A Type Theory for Robust Failure Handling in Distributed Systems

Tzu-Chun Chen[1]($\boxtimes$), Malte Viering[1], Andi Bejleri[1], Lukasz Ziarek[2],
and Patrick Eugster[1,3]

[1] Department of Computer Science, TU Darmstadt, Darmstadt, Germany
{tc.chen,viering,bejleri,peugster}@dsp.tu-darmstadt.de
[2] Department of Computer Science and Engineering, SUNY Buffalo, New York, USA
lziarek@buffalo.edu
[3] Department of Computer Science, Purdue University, West Lafayette, USA

Abstract. This paper presents a formal framework for programming distributed applications capable of handling partial failures, motivated by the non-trivial interplay between failure handling and messaging in asynchronous distributed environments. Multiple failures can affect protocols at the level of individual interactions (**alignment**). At the same time, only participants affected by a failure or involved in its handling should be informed of it, and its handling should not be mixed with that of other failures (**precision**). This is particularly challenging, as through the structure of protocols, failures may be linked to others in subsequent or concomitant interactions (**causality**). Last but not least, no central authority should be required for handling failures (**decentralisation**). Our goal is to give developers a description language, called protocol types, to specify robust failure handling that accounts for alignment, precision, causality, and decentralisation. A type discipline is built to statically ensure that asynchronous failure handling among multiple endpoints is free from orphan messages, deadlocks, starvation, and interactions are never stuck.

Keywords: Session types · Partial failure handling · Distributed systems

1 Introduction

For distributed systems where application components interact asynchronously and concurrently, the design and verification of communication protocols is critical. These systems are prone to *partial failures*, where some components or interactions may fail, while others must continue while respecting certain invariants. Since not all failures can be simply *masked* [10], programmers must *explicitly* deal with failures.

Financially supported by ERC grant FP7-617805 "LiVeSoft – Lightweight Verification of Software".

To ease the burden on programmers for constructing resilient communication protocols in the presence of partial failures, we propose a framework for *robust failure handling*. Our framework ensures safety during normal execution and in case of failures. In particular our framework provides the following properties:

1. **P1 (alignment)**: The occurrences of failures are specified at the level of individual interactions, which they be raised.
2. **P2 (precision)**: If a failure occurs, an endpoint is informed iff it is affected by the failure or involved in handling it, and its handling is not mixed with that of other failures.
3. **P3 (causality)**: Dependencies between failures are considered, i.e., a failure can affect (enable, disable) others which may occur in subsequent or concomitant interactions.
4. **P4 (decentralisation)**: No central authority or component controls the decisions or actions of the participants to handle a failure.

Inspired by session types [12,19], we introduce *protocol types* to achieve these properties. The basic design is shown in Eq. (1):

$$T[p_1 \to p_2 : \widetilde{S} \vee f_1, ..., f_n; \mathbf{G}]\mathbf{H}[f_1 : \mathbf{G}_1, ..., f_n : \mathbf{G}_n, ...] \tag{1}$$

where the first term expresses that a participant p_1 either sends a message of type $\widetilde{S}$ to another participant p_2, or raises one of several failures (i.e., $f_1, ..., f_n$). $\mathbf{G}$ specifies the subsequent interactions and $\mathbf{G}_i$ specifies the handling protocols for f_i, $i = 1..n$ in $\mathbf{H}$. In short, failures are thus associated with elementary interactions (**P1**), only participants affected by such a failure in $\mathbf{G}$ (e.g., they are expecting communication from p_2) or those involved in the corresponding failure handling activity are informed (**P2**). There is at most one f appearing in $\mathbf{H}$ that will be handled/raised (**P3**). Our semantics ensure that there is no central authority (**P4**), meaning, notifications of failures (and absence thereof) are delivered asynchronously from failure sources and processes are typed by local (i.e., endpoint) types achieved by the projection of participants over protocol types.

This design results in a distinguishable type system from the design of Eq. (2):

$$T[p_1 \to p_2 : \widetilde{S}; \mathbf{G}]\mathbf{H}[\mathbf{G}'] \tag{2}$$

In Eq. (2), only one failure may occur in a try-block and where/when it will occur is not specified; once a failure — no matter which one — occurs somewhere in $p_1 \to p_2 : \widetilde{S}$ or $\mathbf{G}$, the handling activity $\mathbf{G}'$ simply takes over. Previous works on dealing with failures [2–4,6] are based on Eq. (2) and/or centralised authorities, and hence do not satisfy all of **P1** to **P4** (see Sect. 7 for details).

Just as multiparty session types aim to specify the interactions among participants and verify implementations of these participants, protocol types specify the global interplay of failures in interactions among participants and verify the failure-handling activities of these participants. To the best of our knowledge, this is the first work that presents a type system for statically checking fine-grained failure handling activities across asynchronous/concurrent processes for partial failures in practical distributed systems. We define a calculus of processes with the ability to not only raise ("throw") and handle ("catch") failures, but to also automatically notify processes of failures or absence thereof at runtime.

Our framework also gives protocol designers and endpoint application developers simple and intuitive description/programming abstractions, and ensures safe interactions among endpoint applications in concurrent environments.

Paper Structure. Section 2 gives motivating examples to introduce the design of protocol types, which capture the properties **P1** to **P4**; then we introduce an operation called *transformation* to transform a protocol type to local (i.e., endpoint) types while preserving the desired properties. Section 3 gives a process calculus with de-centralised multiple-failure-handling capability, including the syntax for programs and networks, and the operational semantics for runtime. Section 5 gives a type system for local processes and Sect. 4 gives a type system for networks to maintain communication coherent. Section 6 states the property of safety, including subject reduction and communication safety, and the property of progress. Section 7 discusses related works. Finally Sect. 8 concludes our work.

Detailed formal and auxiliary definitions, lemmas, and proofs are presented in the extended version of this paper [9].

2 Protocol Types, Local Types, and Transformation

This section uses examples to show the design behind protocol types and uses Fig. 1 to illustrate an operation called *transformation*, which generates local types from protocol types. All formal definitions can be found in the extended version of this paper [9].

The first example, visualised by Fig. 1, shows the properties **P1** and **P2**. Assume that in a network all outgoing traffic passes through a proxy (Proxy), monitoring the traffic and logging general information, e.g., consumed bandwidth. The proxy sends this information to a log server (Log). If the proxy detects suspicious behaviour in the traffic, it raises a SuspiciousB failure and notifies Log and a supervision server (SupServer) to handle the failure by having Log send the traffic logs to SupServer; if the proxy detects that the quota of Client is low, it raises a QuotaWarn failure and notifies Log and Client to handle the failure by having Log send quota information to Client. Then Proxy forwards the traffic from Client to an external server (EServer). We propose the following type to formalise the above scenario:

$$\mathbf{G}_{proxy} = \mathrm{T}[\mathsf{Client} \rightarrow \mathsf{Proxy} : \mathsf{str};$$
$$\mathsf{Proxy} \rightarrow \mathsf{Log} : \mathsf{str} \vee \mathsf{SuspiciousB}, \mathsf{QuotaWarn}; \mathsf{Proxy} \rightarrow \mathsf{EServer} : \mathsf{str}]$$
$$\mathrm{H}[\mathsf{SuspiciousB} : \mathsf{Log} \rightarrow \mathsf{SupServer} : \mathsf{str}, \quad \mathsf{QuotaWarn} : \mathsf{Log} \rightarrow \mathsf{Client} : \mathsf{str}]; \mathsf{end}$$

It specifies that either SuspiciousB or QuotaWarn may occur at interaction Proxy → Log (**P1**). Proxy can raise the failure and correspondingly sends

$\mathbf{G}_{proxy}$ = T[Client → Proxy : str; Proxy → Log : str ∨ SuspiciousB, QuotaWarn; Proxy → EServer : str]
H[SuspiciousB : Log → SupServer : str, QuotaWarn : Log → Client : str]; end

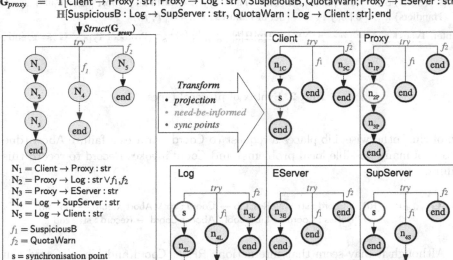

N_1 = Client → Proxy : str
N_2 = Proxy → Log : str ∨ f_1, f_2
N_3 = Proxy → EServer : str
N_4 = Log → SupServer : str
N_5 = Log → Client : str

f_1 = SuspiciousB
f_2 = QuotaWarn

s = synchronisation point

n_{p_i} = ⌈(N_i, p)
e.g.
n_{1C} = ⌈(N_1, Client) = sn⟨Proxy! str⟩

Fig. 1. Overview of *transformation* to obtain local types from a protocol type. The left-hand-side figure visualises a protocol type, $\mathbf{G}_{proxy}$, as a global structure by function *Struct*. The right-hand-side figures are local types for participants in $\mathbf{G}_{proxy}$. They are gained by an operation called *transformation*, which firstly *projects* the global structure onto participants to get *simple* local types, then adds the information of *need-be-informed* participants to the positions with green rings, and finally adds *synchronisation points* to the positions with blue rings. After *transformation*, local types for robust failure handling are reached. (Color figure online)

failure/non-failure notifications to all relevant parties. SuspiciousB affects Log and SupServer since they both handle that failure; it also affects Client because the occurrence of SuspiciousB implies that QuotaWarn will never occur, and thus Client will not yield to the handling activity for QuotaWarn. When QuotaWarn occurs, the situation is similar to SuspiciousB's. Once one of them occurs, Proxy sends failure notifications carrying the occurred failure to Log, SupServer, and Client; when no failures occur, Proxy sends non-failure notifications carrying both failures to the same participants to inform them not to yield to handling activity. No failures will affect Proxy and EServer (**P2**) because Proxy and EServer are not involved in any failure handling activities: Proxy continues sending to EServer after it raises a failure and EServer still receives a message from Proxy as expected.

The next example shows **P2** and **P3**. Assume a resource provider (RP) informs a coordinator (Coord) of which resources it can provide. The library (Lib) can get the resource by requesting Coord only if RP sends a list of resources to Coord. If failure NoRes occurs, meaning absence of resource, Coord informs

(Sorts) $S ::=$ bool | unit | int | str   (Failure) $f ::=$ AuthFail | Abort | ExecFail | ...
(Handlers) $h ::= \emptyset \mid h, f : g$ (Set of Failures) $F ::= \emptyset \mid F, f$
(Inter. Types) $g ::= \varepsilon \mid p \to p : \widetilde{S} \vee F \mid \mathbf{T}[g]\mathbf{H}[h] \mid g;g \mid t \mid \mu t.g$ (Protocol Types) $\mathbf{G} ::= g;$ end

Fig. 2. Syntax of protocol types.

Lib of this; otherwise, Lib places a request to Coord or raises a failure Abort (due to one of many possible local problems) and Coord invokes Record to record this failure:

$$\mathbf{G}_{coord} = \mathrm{T}[\mathsf{RP} \to \mathsf{Coord} : \mathsf{str} \vee \mathsf{NoRes}; \mathsf{Lib} \to \mathsf{Coord} : \mathsf{str} \vee \mathsf{Abort}; \mathsf{Coord} \to \mathsf{Lib} : \mathsf{int}]$$
$$\mathrm{H}[\mathsf{NoRes} : \mathsf{Coord} \to \mathsf{Lib} : \mathsf{bool}, \ \mathsf{Abort} : \mathsf{Coord} \to \mathsf{Record} : \mathsf{str}]; \mathsf{end}$$

Although it may seem that interactions $\mathsf{RP} \to \mathsf{Coord}$ and $\mathsf{Lib} \to \mathsf{Coord}$ can run concurrently, this is not the case because, Lib can only get the resource if RP gives Coord a resource list, which implies failures NoRes and Abort are dependent (**P3**). Additionally, we constrain that failure handling should be not be mixed (**P2**). *Synchronisation* of Lib to yield to the completion of $\mathsf{RP} \to \mathsf{Coord}$ is thus needed. This helps programmers tremendously in reasoning about the states that participants are in after failures. Note that, if $\mathsf{RP} \to \mathsf{Coord}$ and $\mathsf{Lib} \to \mathsf{Coord}$ have no failures specified, then $\mathsf{RP} \to \mathsf{Coord}$ and $\mathsf{Lib} \to \mathsf{Coord}$ can run concurrently because there is no failure dependency.

2.1 Protocol Types

To handle *partial failures* in interactions which exhibit the properties **P1** to **P4**, Fig. 2 defines protocol types based on the definition of session types given in the work by Bettini *et al.* [1]. Protocol types, denoted by $\mathbf{G}$, are composed of interaction types g and terminated by end. We use $(p, ...)$ to range over identifiers, $(S, ...)$ to range over basic types like bool, unit, int, and str, and $(F, ...)$ to range over sets of failures. We highlight the key concepts:

(A) $p_1 \to p_2 : \widetilde{S} \vee F$ is a *failure-raising interaction tagged with F*, or *F-raising interaction* for short. When $\widetilde{S} \neq \emptyset$ and $F \neq \emptyset$, either p_1 sends a content of type $\widetilde{S}$ or raises *one* failure in F to p_2. When one of S and F is empty, p_1 only makes an output based on the non-empty one. We do not allow both F and $\widetilde{S}$ to be empty.

(B) $\mathbf{T}[g]\mathbf{H}[h]$ defines default interaction in g, which is an interaction type, and a *handling environment*, $h = \{f_i : g_i\}_{i \in I}$, which maps failures to handling activities defined in global types. Our design allows h to deal with different failures, with exactly one handler taking over once failures occur.

(C) In (A), if F is empty, we do not require the interaction to be enclosed in a try-handle term; otherwise, the interaction *must* appear within a try-handle term.

In the remaining syntax, we use ε for idle, and $g_1; g_2$ for sequential composition. A type variable is denoted by t, and a recursive type under an equi-recursive approach [18] is denoted by $\mu t.g$, assuming every t appearing in g is guarded by prefixes.

For brevity, our protocol types presentation omits parallel composition, thus we do not allow session interleaving or multi-threading at a local participant. Note that we can still implement two individual interactions running in parallel by implementing two disjoint groups of interacting participants who execute two respective protocols. We omit branching with multiple options of ongoing interactions, since the term $\mathrm{T}[p_1 \to p_2 : l_1, ..., l_n; g]\mathrm{H}[l_1 : g_1, ..., l_n : g_n]$ is able to encode the branching in multiparty session types [1,12] by using failures $l_1, ..., l_n$ as labels for branches. We leave unaffected participants to continue default actions regardless of the occurrence of failures; we do not inform them of the failure. Moreover, we do not have well-formedness constraints on the shape of interactions in branches (i.e. failure handlers in our syntax) as most multiparty session types and choreographic programming related works require [1, 3–5, 8, 12, 13, 16, 17, 21].

2.2 Local Types and Transformation

In order to achieve our desired properties we use an operation, called *transformation*, to synthesize a guidance to locally guide which participants need to coordinate with others once a failure occurs, or inversely to assert that none has occurred, before proceeding with the next action. The operation *transformation* includes the following steps:

1. **Generating a global structure** from a given protocol type and alpha renaming it.
2. **Projecting** the above structure to every participants to obtain *simple* local types, which are not yet sufficient for robust failure handling. The projection algorithm is similar to the mechanism in multiparty session types [1,12].
3. **Adding** the information of *need-(to)-be-informed* participants, who are those affected by or involved in handling failures, and synchronisation points to local types.

After these 3 steps, we obtain local types which are sufficient for our type system to ensure *robust failure handling*.

Figure 1 uses the example of $\mathbf{G}_{proxy}$ to demonstrate the operation of *transforming* a protocol type to each participants' local types, which are defined below:

Definition 1 (Local Types T).

(Local Types) $\mathbf{T} ::= \mathbf{n} \mid try\{\mathbf{T}, \mathbf{H}\} \mid \mathbf{n} \dashrightarrow \mathbf{T} \mid t \mid \mu t.\mathbf{T}$ (Handlers) $\mathbf{H} ::= \emptyset \mid \mathbf{H}, f : \mathbf{T}$

(Action) $\mathbf{n} ::= \varepsilon \mid \text{end} \mid sn\langle p! \ \widetilde{S} \vee F, \widetilde{p}, \widetilde{p}\rangle \mid rn\langle p? \ \widetilde{S} \vee F\rangle \mid yield\langle F\rangle$

A local type is either an action ($\mathbf{n}$), a try-handle type ($try\{\mathbf{T}, \mathbf{H}\}$), a sequencing type ($\mathbf{n} \dashrightarrow \mathbf{T}$), a local type variable (t), or a recursive type ($\mu t.\mathbf{T}$). We use

ε to type an idle action, while end types termination. A sending action, typed by $sn\langle p!\ \widetilde{S} \vee F, \widetilde{p}', \widetilde{p}''\rangle$, specifies a sending of normal content of type $\widetilde{S}$ to p or raising a failure in F. When a failure is raised, the sender also sends failure notifications to participants $\widetilde{p}'$. When normal content is sent, the sender also sends non-failure notifications to participants $\widetilde{p}''$. A receiving action, typed by $rn\langle p?\ \widetilde{S} \vee F\rangle$, specifies the reception of content of type $\widetilde{S}$ from p, who may raise a failure in F instead. An action yielding to the arrival of a non-failure notification informing that no failures in F occurred, is typed by $yield\langle F\rangle$. A handling environment in local types, denoted by $\mathbf{H} = \{f_i : \mathbf{T}_i\}_{i \in I}$, maps failures to corresponding local handling actions defined in local types.

In Fig. 1, we firstly create a **global structure** for $\mathbf{G}_{proxy}$ by $Struct(\mathbf{G}_{proxy})$. Global structures, denoted by T, consist of either a single interaction (N), a try-handle structure ($try\{\mathtt{T},\mathtt{H}\}$) where H has a similar shape to handling environments in local types, a sequence ($\mathtt{N} \dashrightarrow \mathtt{T}$), or a recursive structure ($\mu t.\mathtt{T}$). We define N as either $p \rightarrow p : \widetilde{S} \vee F$ or ε or end. By defining $Struct$(single interaction) $= \mathtt{N}$, a try-handle structure is obtained by $Struct(\mathbf{T}[g]\mathbf{H}[\,f_1 : g_1, ..., f_n : g_n]; \mathbf{G}) = try\{Struct(g; \mathbf{G}),\ f_1 : Struct(g_1; \mathbf{G}), ...,\ f_n : Struct(g_n; \mathbf{G})\}$, while a recursive structure is obtained by $Struct(\mu t.\mathbf{G}) = \mu t.Struct(\mathbf{G})$.

The *simple* local types are gained by *projecting* T, created by $Struct(\mathbf{G})$, on each participants. The projection rules are defined below:

Definition 2 (Projecting T onto Endpoint p). Assume $\mathtt{T} = Struct(\mathbf{G})$ and T is alpha-renamed so that all failures in T are unique. Define $\upharpoonright(\mathtt{T}, p)$ as generating a local type on p:

(1) $\upharpoonright(\mathsf{end}, p) = \mathsf{end}$ (2) $\upharpoonright(p_1 \rightarrow p_2 : \widetilde{S} \vee F, p) = \begin{cases} sn\langle p_2!\ \widetilde{S} \vee F, \_, \_\rangle & \text{if } p = p_1 \neq p_2 \\ rn\langle p_1?\ \widetilde{S} \vee F\rangle & \text{if } p = p_2 \neq p_1 \\ \varepsilon_F & \text{otherwise} \end{cases}$

(3) $\upharpoonright(try\{\mathtt{T},\ f_1 : \mathtt{T}_1, ...,\ f_n : \mathtt{T}_n\}, p) = try\{\upharpoonright(\mathtt{T}, p),\ f_1 : \upharpoonright(\mathtt{T}_1, p), ...,\ f_n : \upharpoonright(\mathtt{T}_n, p)\}$

(4) $\upharpoonright(\mathtt{N} \dashrightarrow \mathtt{T}, p) = \upharpoonright(\mathtt{N}, p) \dashrightarrow \upharpoonright(\mathtt{T}, p)$ (5) $\upharpoonright(t, p) = t$ (6) $\upharpoonright(\mu t.\mathtt{T}, p) = \mu t.\ \upharpoonright(\mathtt{T}, p)$

Others are undefined.

Rule (2) is for dually interacting participants. It introduces ε_F, which has equivalent meaning to ε (i.e. idle action) but is only used in *transformation* for adding synchronisation points. As we project an interaction $p_1 \rightarrow p_2 : \widetilde{S} \vee F$ with $p_1 \neq p_2$ onto p_1 (resp. p_2), we get an action $sn\langle p_2!\ \widetilde{S} \vee F, , \_, \_\rangle$ (resp. $rn\langle p_1?\ \widetilde{S} \vee F\rangle$). Note that the two slots $\_$ in the sending action are preserved for adding the need-be-informed participants as a failure occurs (the first slot), and those as no failures occur (the second slot). As we project the interaction to some participant who is *not* in the interaction, we get ε_F (idle action). The subscript F indicates that if p is affected by some failures in F a synchronisation point will be added at this position. Rule (3) simply projects every sub-structure in the try block and handlers onto the participant. Rule (4) sequences two local types projected from a global structure. Other rules are straightforward.

After projection, we add *need-be-informed participants* into the failure-raiser's sending actions (e.g., the one marked in green ring in Fig. 1). We use

$C(\mathtt{T}, F)$ to get the set of need-be-informed participants regarding a unique F in a global structure T. It is the least fixed point of $c(\mathtt{T}, \mathtt{T}, F, r)$, which recursively collects the need-be-informed participants regarding F based on T. Since for every protocol the number of participants is finite, function c will converge to a fixed set of participants. The key calculation is done by the rule below

$$c(\mathtt{T}, \mathtt{N}, F, r) = \begin{cases} r \cup pid(\mathtt{N}) \cup C(\mathtt{T}, FSet(\mathtt{N})) & \text{if } (F \text{ appears before N in T}) \wedge \\ & ((pid(\mathtt{N}) \cap r \neq \emptyset) \vee (FSet(\mathtt{N}) \neq \emptyset)) \\ r & \text{otherwise} \end{cases}$$

where we require the *initial* r to be the set containing the receiver of F-raising interaction and the participants involved in handling F in T; later r acts as an accumulator collecting the participants causally related to the initial r. N is an interaction, $pid(\mathtt{N})$ is the set of participants in N, and $FSet(\mathtt{N})$ returns the failures tagged on N. This rule says that if the interaction we are checking appears after the F-raising interaction, and some of its interacting participants are related to r or the interaction itself can raise another failure set (e.g. the interaction Lib $\rightarrow$ Coord : str $\vee$ Abort in RP $\rightarrow$ Coord : str $\vee$ NoRes; Lib $\rightarrow$ Coord : str $\vee$ Abort is related to $F = \{\mathsf{NoRes}\}$), then we collect its participants (i.e. $pid(\mathtt{N})$) and the need-be-informed participants with respect to the failures that can be raised by N.

After adding those participants, we add synchronisation points $yield\langle F \rangle$ to the positions where a participant yields to the arrival of non-failure notifications (e.g. those marked in blue rings in Fig. 1). The key rule is:

$$Sync(\mathtt{T}, \mathbf{n}, p) = \begin{cases} yield\langle FSet(\mathtt{N}) \rangle \dashrightarrow \mathbf{n} & \text{if } (\mathbf{n} = \lceil(\mathtt{N}, p)) \wedge (p \in C(\mathtt{T}, FSet(\mathtt{N})) \wedge p \neq snd(\mathtt{N}) \\ \mathbf{n} \dashrightarrow yield\langle FSet(\mathtt{N}) \rangle & \text{if } (\mathbf{n} = \lceil(\mathtt{N}, p)) \wedge (p \in C(\mathtt{T}, FSet(\mathtt{N})) \wedge p = snd(\mathtt{N}) \\ \mathbf{n} & \text{otherwise} \end{cases}$$

where $snd(\mathtt{N})$ is the sender for interaction N. This rule says the followings: If p needs to be informed of $F = FSet(\mathtt{N})$ (i.e. $p \in C(\mathtt{T}, FSet(\mathtt{N}))$) then it must add a synchronisation point. If p's action (i.e., $\mathbf{n}$) regarding F is ε_F (e.g. in $\mathbf{G}_{coord}$ the participant Lib has $\varepsilon_{\mathsf{NoRes}}$ by Definition 2), $yield\langle F \rangle$ is positioned ahead of p's action (e.g. a sending action of Lib to Coord specified in $\mathbf{G}_{coord}$), because p needs to wait for the notification regarding F before taking any action. If p is the receiver, we have $yield\langle F \rangle$ positioned before the receiving action because $yield\langle F \rangle$ is the point deciding whether the process will handle a failure regarding F or proceed. If p is the sender, we should have $yield\langle F \rangle$ positioned after the sending action, because as p is involved for some failure handling activity regarding F, it needs to first send out failure notifications then go back to execute the handling activity; otherwise the process will get stuck.

In Fig. 1, green ring appears at Proxy's second action because, if a failure occurs, Proxy has to inform Log, SupServer, and Client about that failure. Blue rings appear at Client, Log, and SupServer's try blocks because they are involved in handling activity, and they can terminate only after getting the notifications that no failures occurred.

Overall, we define the operation of transformation as $Transform(\mathbf{G}, p)$, which transforms $\mathbf{G}$ to a local type for p.

3 Processes for Decentralised Multiple-Failure-Handling

We abstract distributed systems as a finite set of processes communicating by outputting (resp. inputting) messages into (resp. from) the shared global queue asynchronously and concurrently. The semantics of the calculus is in the same style as that of the π-calculus and does not involve any centralised authority for specifying how messages are exchanged (**P4**). The shared queue is only *conceptually* global for convenience, and could be split into individual participant queues.

Syntax. In Fig. 3, we define x as value variables, y as channel variables, a as shared names (e.g., names for services or protocol managers), and s as session names (i.e., session IDs), p as participant identifiers, and X as process variables. We use u for names and c for channels, which are either variables or a combination of s and p. The definition for expressions e is standard. We define the syntax of processes $(P, ...)$ and that of networks $(N, ...)$, which represent interactions of processes at runtime. Process $\mathbf{0}$ is inactive. Process $c!(p, \langle \tilde{e} \rangle^F)$ denotes an output, which may alternatively raise a failure f in F, sends a message with content $\tilde{e}$ to p via channel c; while $c?(p, (\tilde{x})^F).P$ denotes an input using c to receive a content from p, which may alternatively raise a failure from F. Every $\tilde{x}$ appearing in P is bound by the input prefix. When $F = \emptyset$, we omit F since the process will not raise/receive a failure. Process c raise(f) to p raises f to p via channel c. Process $c \otimes F$ is guarded by $\otimes F$, a synchronisation point, yielding to non-failure notification for F. A try-handle process try$\{P\}$h$\{H\}$ executes P until a handler $f \in dom(H)$ is triggered, then the triggered handler takes over. A handling environment, denoted by H, maps failure names to handling processes. We write $P_1; P_2$ to represent a sequential composition where P_2 follows P_1. Process def D in P defines a recursion, where declaration $D = (X(\tilde{x} \, c) = P)$ is a recursive call. The term if e then P else P is standard. We define evaluation context $\mathcal{E}$ over processes. It is either a hole, a context in a try-handle term, or a context sequencing next processes.

(Variables) x, y (Shared Names) a (Session Names) s (Process IDs) p (Process Variables) X

(Values) $v ::=$ unit $\mid$ false $\mid$ true $\mid 1 \mid 2 \mid ...$ (Names) $u ::= a \mid s$

(Expressions) $e ::= x \mid y \mid v \mid u \mid e + e \mid -e \mid e \vee e \mid ...$ (Channels) $c ::= y \mid s[p]$

(Processes) $P ::= \mathbf{0} \mid c!(p, \langle \tilde{e} \rangle^F) \mid c?(p, (\tilde{x})^F).P \mid c$ raise(f) to $p \mid c \otimes F$
$\qquad\qquad \mid$ try$\{P\}$h$\{H\} \mid P; P \mid X\langle \tilde{e} \, c \rangle \mid$ def D in $P \mid$ if e then P else P

(Handlers) $H ::= \emptyset \mid H, f : P$ (Declaration) $D ::= X(\tilde{x} \, c) = P$

(Messages) $m ::= \varepsilon \mid \langle p, p, \langle \tilde{v} \rangle \rangle^F \mid \langle p, f \rangle \mid \langle\langle p, F \rangle\rangle$ (Context) $\mathcal{E} ::= [\,] \mid$ try$\{\mathcal{E}\}$h$\{H\} \mid \mathcal{E}; P$

(Network) $N ::= a[p](y).P \mid [P]_{\mathbf{T}} \mid s : q \mid N \| N \mid$ (new s)N (Queues) $q ::= m \mid q \cdot m$

Fig. 3. Syntax for processes and networks.

A network N is composed by linking points, denoted by $a[p](y).P$, and runtime processes, denoted by $[P]_{\mathbf{T}}$ with global transports (i.e., $s : q$) for proceeding communications in a private session (i.e., (new $s)N$). Our framework asks a process to join one session at a time. A linking point $a[p](y).P$ is guarded by $a[p](y)$ for session initiation, where shared name a associates a service to a protocol type. $[P]_{\mathbf{T}}$ represents a runtime process which is guided by $\mathbf{T}$ for notifying need-be-informed participants.

A session queue, denoted by $s : q$, is a queue for messages floating in session s. Message $\langle p_1, p_2, \langle \tilde{v} \rangle \rangle^F$ carries content $\tilde{v}$, sent from p_1 to p_2 prone to failure $f \in F$. Message $\langle p, f \rangle$ (resp. $\langle\langle p, F \rangle\rangle$) carries a failure name f to indicate that *failure f occurred* (resp. a set of failures F to indicate that *no failures in F occurred*) to p. Conventionally we say $\langle\langle p, \emptyset \rangle\rangle = \varepsilon$. When session s is initiated for a network, a private (i.e., hidden) session is created, in which activities cannot be witnessed from the outside. We use structural congruence rules, defined by $\equiv$, which are standard according to the works of multiparty session types [1,12].

Operational Semantics. Figure 4 gives the operational semantics for networks (i.e., runtime processes) through the reduction relation $N \rightarrow N$. We have added boxes to those rules which differ from standard session type definitions. In rule [link], a session is generated with a fresh name s through shared name a obeying protocol type $\mathbf{G}$. This indicates that all processes in the new session s will obey to the behaviours defined in $\mathbf{G}$. At the same time, a global queue $s : \varepsilon$ is generated, and the local process associated with p replaces y_p with $s[p]$; a local type $\mathbf{T}_p$ is generated by *Transform*$(\mathbf{G}, p)$ to guide the local process associated with p for propagating notifications. Note that, as we enclose a local process with $\mathbf{T}$, together they become an element of a network. $\mathbf{T}$ is merely a local type and the reduction of the network does not change $\mathbf{T}$.

Rule [rcv] states that, in s, a process associated with p_1 is able to receive a value $\tilde{v}$ from participant associated with p_2 and message $\langle p_2, p_1, \langle \tilde{v} \rangle \rangle^F$ is on the top of q. Then $\tilde{v}$ will replace the free occurrences of $\tilde{x}$ in P. The shape of $s[p_1]?(p_2, (\tilde{x})^F)$ indicates that its dual action may send it a failure from F; in other words, if $F \neq \emptyset$, a process should be structured by a try-handle term for possible failure handling. Rule [snd] is dual to [rcv]. We define $node(\mathbf{T}, F)$ as a function returning an action tagged with F in a local type $\mathbf{T}$. Rule [sndF] states that, if there is an action in $\mathbf{T}$ matching $s[p_1]!(p_2, \langle \tilde{e} \rangle^F)$ and $\tilde{e} \Downarrow \tilde{v}$, then the process associated with p_1 in s is allowed to send a message with content $\tilde{v}$ to p_2 and non-failure notifications $\langle\langle p_1', F \rangle\rangle...\langle\langle p_n', F \rangle\rangle$. Note that, non failure notifications are automatically generated at runtime. If a process follows the guidance of the attached $\mathbf{T}$, since $\mathbf{T}$ is alpha-renamed, every failure raised by the process is unique. Similarly, [thwf] states for a process associated with p_1 in s, to raise f to p_2 and other affected ones, $p_1', .., p_n'$. Very importantly, in [sndF] and [thwf], q has no failure notification to trigger H because, as a failure-raising interaction is ready to fire (i.e. its sender is about to send), it implies that, globally, either this interaction is the first failure-raising interaction in s (thus no failure yet occurs in s), or its previous interactions did not raise a failure in $dom(H)$ (thus by $\mathbf{P2}$, this interaction is able to raise a failure in $dom(H)$, and

$$\frac{a : \langle \mathbf{G} \rangle \quad \forall p \in \{1..n\}.\mathbf{T}_p = Transform(\mathbf{G}, p) \quad s \text{ fresh}}{a[1](y_1).P_1 \parallel ... \parallel a[n](y_n).P_n \to (\text{new } s)([P_1[s[1]/y_1]]_{\mathbf{T}_1} \parallel ... \parallel [P_n[s[n]/y_n]]_{\mathbf{T}_n} \parallel s : \varepsilon)} \quad \textbf{[link]}$$

$$[s[p_1]?(p_2, (\tilde{x})^F).P]_{\mathbf{T}} \parallel s : \langle p_2, p_1, \langle \tilde{v} \rangle \rangle^F \cdot q \to [P[\tilde{v}/\tilde{x}]]_{\mathbf{T}} \parallel s : q \quad \textbf{[rcv]}$$

$$[s[p_1]!(p_2, \langle \tilde{e} \rangle); P]_{\mathbf{T}} \parallel s : q \to [P]_{\mathbf{T}} \parallel s : q \cdot \langle p_1, p_2, \langle \tilde{v} \rangle \rangle \quad \tilde{e} \Downarrow \tilde{v} \quad \textbf{[snd]}$$

$$\frac{\tilde{e} \Downarrow \tilde{v} \quad node(\mathbf{T}, F) = sn\langle p_2! \, \tilde{S} \vee F, \tilde{p}, \{p_1', ..., p_n'\} \rangle \quad F \neq \emptyset}{\begin{array}{l}[\text{try}\{s[p_1]!(p_2, \langle \tilde{e} \rangle^F); P\}\text{h}\{H\}]_{\mathbf{T}} \parallel s : q \\ \quad \to [\text{try}\{P\}\text{h}\{H\}]_{\mathbf{T}} \parallel s : q \cdot \langle p_1, p_2, \langle \tilde{v} \rangle \rangle^F \cdot \langle\langle p_1', F \rangle\rangle ... \langle\langle p_n', F \rangle\rangle\end{array}} \quad \textbf{[sndF]}$$

$$\frac{node(\mathbf{T}, F) = sn\langle p_2! \, \tilde{S} \vee F, \{p_2, p_1', ..., p_n'\}, \tilde{p} \rangle \quad f \in F}{\begin{array}{l}[\text{try}\{s[p_1] \text{ raise}(f) \text{ to } p_2; P\}\text{h}\{H\}]_{\mathbf{T}} \parallel s : q \\ \quad \to [\text{try}\{P\}\text{h}\{H\}]_{\mathbf{T}} \parallel s : q \cdot \langle p_2, f \rangle \cdot \langle p_1', f \rangle ... \langle p_n', f \rangle\end{array}} \quad \textbf{[thwf]}$$

$$\frac{act(P) = s[p] \quad [P]_{\mathbf{T}} \parallel s : q \to [P']_{\mathbf{T}} \parallel s : q' \quad q = \langle p', f' \rangle \cdot q' \Rightarrow (p' \neq p) \vee (f' \notin dom(H))}{[\text{try}\{P\}\text{h}\{H\}; P'']_{\mathbf{T}} \parallel s : q \to [\text{try}\{P'\}\text{h}\{H\}; P'']_{\mathbf{T}} \parallel s : q'} \quad \textbf{[try]}$$

$$\frac{f \in dom(H) \cap F}{[\text{try}\{\mathscr{E}[s[p] \otimes F]\}\text{h}\{H\}; P']_{\mathbf{T}} \parallel s : \langle p, f \rangle \cdot q \to [H(f); P']_{\mathbf{T}} \parallel s : q} \quad \textbf{[hdl]}$$

$$\frac{F' \subseteq F}{[s[p] \otimes F'; P]_{\mathbf{T}} \parallel s : \langle\langle p, F \rangle\rangle \cdot q \to [P]_{\mathbf{T}} \parallel s : q} \quad \textbf{[sync-done]}$$

$$\frac{F'' = F' \setminus F \neq \emptyset}{[s[p] \otimes F'; P]_{\mathbf{T}} \parallel s : \langle\langle p, F \rangle\rangle \cdot q \to [s[p] \otimes F''; P]_{\mathbf{T}} \parallel s : q} \quad \textbf{[sync]}$$

$$[\text{try}\{v\}\text{h}\{H\}]_{\mathbf{T}} \to [0]_{\mathbf{T}} \quad \textbf{[try-end]}$$

$$[\text{if true then } P_1 \text{ else } P_2]_{\mathbf{T}} \to [P_1]_{\mathbf{T}} \quad [\text{if false then } P_1 \text{ else } P_2]_{\mathbf{T}} \to [P_2]_{\mathbf{T}} \quad \textbf{[if]}$$

$$\frac{[P_1]_{\mathbf{T}} \parallel s : q \to [P_2]_{\mathbf{T}} \parallel s : q'}{[P_1; P]_{\mathbf{T}} \parallel s : q \to [P_2; P]_{\mathbf{T}} \parallel s : q'} \quad \textbf{[seq]} \qquad \frac{\tilde{e} \Downarrow \tilde{v} \quad X(\tilde{x}\,c) = P \in D}{[\text{def } D \text{ in } X\langle \tilde{e}\,c \rangle]_{\mathbf{T}} \to [\text{def } D \text{ in } (P[\tilde{v}/\tilde{x}])]_{\mathbf{T}}} \quad \textbf{[call]}$$

$$\frac{N_1 \to N_2}{N_1 \parallel N \to N_2 \parallel N} \quad \textbf{[net]} \qquad \frac{[P_1]_{\mathbf{T}} \parallel s : q \to [P_2]_{\mathbf{T}} \parallel s : q'}{[\text{def } D \text{ in } P_1]_{\mathbf{T}} \parallel s : q \to [\text{def } D \text{ in } P_2]_{\mathbf{T}} \parallel s : q'} \quad \textbf{[defin]}$$

$$\frac{N_1 \equiv N_2 \to N_3 \equiv N_4}{N_1 \to N_4} \quad \textbf{[str]} \qquad \frac{N_1 \to N_2}{(\text{new } s)N_1 \to (\text{new } s)N_2} \quad \textbf{[new]}$$

Fig. 4. Reduction rules for networks (i.e., runtime processes).

no failures in $dom(H)$ yet occurs in s). For convenience, we use act to extract the channel that a process or the set of handlers is acting on, i.e. $act(P) = s[p]$ says P is acting on channel $s[p]$, and $act(H) = act(H(f))$ for every $f \in dom(H)$.

In **[try]**, if the H in a try-handle process associated with p in s will not be triggered by the top message in $s : q$, then the process in the try block will take action according to the process's interaction with the queue. In **[hdl]**, as f arrives to a try-handle process associated with p in s whose try block is yielding to non-failure notification for F and H is able to handle f, the handling process $H(f)$ takes over. Due to asynchrony, other processes' handlers for f may become active before this process. Thus some messages in q may be sent from other processes' handlers of f for P. Note that none of the messages in q are for $\mathcal{E}$ because, all default sending actions in other processes are also guarded by synchronisation points.

Synchronisation either proceeds with [sync-done], where F is sufficient to remove F', or with [sync], where F is included in F' carried in the notification. For the former, some processes in the failure-handling activity only take care of partial failures in F, i.e. F', when they receive F, to ensure that no failures in F occurred. For the latter, further synchronisation is required by $F'' = (F' \setminus F) \neq \emptyset$. In [try-end], since we have added sufficient synchronisation points to guard processes who must yield to non-failure notifications, when a network reaches $[\text{try}\{v\}\text{h}\{H\}]_{\mathbf{T}}$, it is safe to be inactive because no more failure notifications will occur. In other rules, the operations enclosed in $\mathbf{T}$ are standard according to the works of multiparty session types [1, 12].

4   Typing Local Processes

This section introduces rules to type user-defined processes. Based on the multiparty session types [1, 12], type environments and typing rules for processes are given in Fig. 5. A shared environment Γ is a finite mapping from variables to sorts and from process variables to local types; a session environment Δ is a finite mapping from session channels to local types. $\Gamma, x : S$ means that x does not occur in Γ, so does $\Gamma, X : (\tilde{x}\ \mathbf{T})$ and $\Delta, c : \mathbf{T}$. We assume that expressions are typed by sorts. $\Gamma \vdash e : S$ is the typing judgment for expressions, whose typing rules are standard. The typing judgment $\Gamma \vdash P \rhd \Delta$ for local processes reads as "Γ proves that P complies with abstract specification Δ".

Rule [T-0] states that an idle process is typed by end-only Δ, which means $\forall c \in dom(\Delta), \Delta(c) = \text{end}$. Rule [T-seq] types sequential composition by sequencing P_2's action in Δ_2 after P_1's action in Δ_1 as long as P_1 and P_2 are acting on the same channel. We define $\Delta_1 \circ \Delta_2$ as the one defined in the multiparty session types extended with failure-handling ability [3]. Rule [T-rcv] specifies that $s[p_1]?(p_2, (\tilde{x})^F).P$ is valid as it corresponds to local type $rn\langle p_2 ?\ \widetilde{S} \vee F\rangle \dashrightarrow \mathbf{T}$ as long as P, associated with p_1 in session s, is well-typed by $\mathbf{T}$ under an environment which knows $\tilde{x} : \widetilde{S}$. In [T-snd] and [T-thwf], since the slots are not related to typing, their contents are omitted. Rules [T-snd] and [T-thwf] share the same action for typing because $sn\langle p_2 !\ \widetilde{S} \vee F, \_, \_\rangle$ specifies two possible actions: a sending action $s[p_1]!(p_2, \langle \tilde{e}\rangle^F)$ in which $\tilde{e}$ must have type $\widetilde{S}$, and action $s[p_1]\ \text{raise}(f)$ to p_2 in which f must be in F. Then the continuing process P is typed by the following $\mathbf{T}$.

For typing handling activities, rule [T-try] types a try-handle term if its default action (i.e., P) with its following process is well-typed, and those in handlers with their follow-up processes are all well-typed. We require the following process P' should not contain any failure appearing in H. Since P and any processes in H are acting on the same channel and $act(H)$ represents the channel that every processes in H is acting on, we use $act(H)$ to get the channel in order to type $\text{try}\{0\}\text{h}\{H\}$. Recall Fig. 1 and projection rules defined in Definition 2, for local

Γ (Shared Environments) $::= \emptyset \mid \Gamma, x : S \mid \Gamma, X : (\tilde{x}\,\mathbf{T})$ Δ (Session Environments) $::= \emptyset \mid \Delta, c : \mathbf{T}$

$$\dfrac{\Delta \text{ end only}}{\Gamma \vdash \mathbf{0} \rhd \Delta} \;\text{[T-0]}\qquad \dfrac{\forall i \in \{1,2\}.\Gamma \vdash P_i \rhd \Delta_i}{\Gamma \vdash P_1 ; P_2 \rhd \Delta_1 \circ \Delta_2} \;\text{[T-seq]}$$

$$\dfrac{\Gamma, \tilde{x} : \tilde{S} \vdash P \rhd s[p_1] : \mathbf{T}}{\Gamma \vdash s[p_1]?(p_2, (\tilde{x})^F).P \rhd s[p_1] : rn\langle p_2?\,\tilde{S} \vee F\rangle \dashrightarrow \mathbf{T}} \;\text{[T-rcv]}$$

$$\dfrac{\tilde{S} \neq / \;0\;\Gamma \vdash \tilde{e} : \tilde{S}\quad \Gamma \vdash P \rhd s[p_1] : \mathbf{T}}{\Gamma \vdash s[p_1]!(p_2, \langle \tilde{e}\rangle^F); P \rhd s[p_1] : sn\langle p_2!\,\tilde{S} \vee F, \_, \_\rangle \dashrightarrow \mathbf{T}} \;\boxed{\text{[T-snd]}}$$

$$\dfrac{f \in F \quad \Gamma \vdash P \rhd s[p_1] : \mathbf{T}}{\Gamma \vdash s[p_1]\;\mathsf{raise}(f)\;\mathsf{to}\;p_2; P \rhd s[p_1] : sn\langle p_2!\,\tilde{S} \vee F, \_, \_\rangle \dashrightarrow \mathbf{T}} \;\boxed{\text{[T-thwf]}}$$

$$\dfrac{\begin{array}{c}dom(H) = dom(\mathbf{H})\quad \forall f \in dom(H).f \notin P' \\ \Gamma \vdash P; P' \rhd act(H) : \mathbf{T}\quad \forall f \in dom(H).\Gamma \vdash H(f); P' \rhd act(H) : H(f)\end{array}}{\Gamma \vdash \mathsf{try}\{P\}\mathsf{h}\{H\}; P' \rhd act(H) : try\{\mathbf{T}, \mathbf{H}\}} \;\boxed{\text{[T-try]}}$$

$$\dfrac{\Gamma \vdash P \rhd c : \mathbf{T}}{\Gamma \vdash c \otimes F; P \rhd c : yield\langle F\rangle \dashrightarrow \mathbf{T}} \;\text{[T-sync]}\qquad \dfrac{\Gamma \vdash e : \mathsf{bool}\quad i = 1, 2.\;\Gamma \vdash P_i; P \rhd \Delta}{\Gamma \vdash \mathsf{if}\; e\; \mathsf{then}\; P_1\; \mathsf{else}\; P_2; P \rhd \Delta} \;\text{[T-if]}$$

$$\Gamma, X : (\tilde{S}\,\mathbf{T}) \vdash X\langle \tilde{e}\,c\rangle \rhd c : \mathbf{T}\;\text{[T-var]}\qquad \dfrac{\Gamma, \tilde{x} : \tilde{S}, X : (\tilde{S}\,\mathbf{T}) \vdash P \rhd c : \mathbf{T}\quad \Gamma, X : (\tilde{S}\,\mathbf{T}) \vdash P' \rhd \Delta}{\Gamma \vdash \mathsf{def}\; X(\tilde{x}\,c) = P\;\mathsf{in}\;P' \rhd \Delta} \;\text{[T-rec]}$$

Fig. 5. Typing rules for processes.

types the sequencing action is linked at every leaf in a try-handle term; in other words, the type of P' is attached to the type of P and also to every handler in $\mathbf{H}$. Therefore, as we type a try-handle term, we also consider its following process.

Rule [T-sync] specifies that process $c \otimes F; P$ is well-typed if the local type for c has synchronisation point $yield\langle F\rangle$ and P is well-typed w.r.t. $\mathbf{T}$. The algorithm for adding synchronisation points (introduced in Sect. 2) automatically places the synchronisation points in local types and ensures that once a failure is raised, other possible failure-raising actions must not fire. Since the operational semantics defined in Fig. 4 only deliver notifications regarding F to need-be-informed participants and only one failure in F can be raised, our type system ensures only one failure in a try-handle term is handled and all participants affected by F have consistent failure handling activities.

Rule [T-var] types a local process variable, and rule [T-rec] types a recursion with Δ, where the recursive call $X(\tilde{x}, c) = P$ is typed by $c : \mathbf{T}$, indicating that P follows behaviour $\mathbf{T}$ at c. Others are standard according to the works of multiparty session types [1,12].

5   Typing the Network

Ultimately our framework needs to ensure that the network is coherent. *Coherence*, according to the works of multiparty session types [1,12], describes an environment where all *interactions* are complying with the guidance of some $\mathbf{G}$, such that the behaviour of every participant in Δ, say $s[p]$, obeys to $Transform(\mathbf{G}, p)$,

$$\mathbf{M} \text{ (Message Types) } ::= \varepsilon \mid \langle p_1, p_2, \langle \widetilde{S} \rangle \rangle^F \mid \langle p, f \rangle \mid \langle\!\langle p, F \rangle\!\rangle$$
$$\mathbf{q} \text{ (Queue Type) } ::= \mathbf{M} \mid \mathbf{q} \cdot \mathbf{M}$$
$$\Delta \text{ (Extended Session Environments) } ::= \dots \mid \Delta, s : \mathbf{q}$$

$$\Gamma \vdash s : \varepsilon \rhd \{s : \varepsilon\} \quad \text{[T-m}\varepsilon\text{]} \qquad \frac{\Gamma \vdash \widetilde{v} : \widetilde{S} \quad \Gamma \vdash s : q \rhd \{s : \mathbf{q}\}}{\Gamma \vdash s : q \cdot \langle p_1, p_2, \langle \widetilde{v} \rangle \rangle^F \rhd \{s : \mathbf{q} \cdot \langle p_1, p_2, \langle \widetilde{S} \rangle \rangle^F\}} \quad \text{[T-m]}$$

$$\frac{\Gamma \vdash s : q \rhd \{s : \mathbf{q}\}}{\Gamma \vdash s : q \cdot \langle p, f \rangle \rhd \{s : \mathbf{q} \cdot \langle p, f \rangle\}} \quad \text{[T-mf]} \qquad \frac{\Gamma \vdash s : q \rhd \{s : \mathbf{q}\}}{\Gamma \vdash s : q \cdot \langle\!\langle p, F \rangle\!\rangle \rhd \{s : \mathbf{q} \cdot \langle\!\langle p, F \rangle\!\rangle\}} \quad \text{[T-mF]}$$

$$\frac{\Gamma \vdash a : \langle \mathbf{G} \rangle \quad \Gamma \vdash P \rhd y : Transform(\mathbf{G}, p)}{\Gamma \vdash a[p](y).P \rhd \emptyset} \quad \boxed{\text{[T-link]}}$$

$$\frac{\Gamma \vdash P \rhd \Delta \quad act(P) = s[p] \quad \exists \mathbf{G}. \text{ s.t. } \mathbf{T} = Transform(\mathbf{G}, p) \quad \mathbf{T} \text{ contains } \Delta(s[p])}{\Gamma \vdash [P]_{\mathbf{T}} \rhd \Delta} \quad \boxed{\text{[T-guide]}}$$

$$\frac{\forall i \in 1, 2. \Gamma \vdash N_i \rhd \Delta_i \quad dom(\Delta_1) \cap dom(\Delta_2) = \emptyset}{\Gamma \vdash N_1 \parallel N_2 \rhd \Delta_1, \Delta_2} \quad \text{[T-net]} \qquad \frac{\Gamma \vdash N \rhd \Delta \quad \Delta \langle s \rangle \text{ coherent}}{\Gamma \vdash (\text{new } s) N \rhd \Delta \setminus \Delta \langle s \rangle} \quad \text{[T-new]}$$

Fig. 6. Typing rules for networks.

which denotes a local type. To reason about coherence of default and handling interactions in a session, we statically type check the interactions by modeling the outputs and inputs among local processes and the shared global queue.

The typing rules for networks are defined in Fig. 6 by extending the session environments such as to map queues to queue types. A queue type, denoted by $\mathbf{q}$, is composed by message types, which are typed by their contents or shapes: Rule [T-mε] types an empty queue, while rule [T-m] types a message carrying a value under the assumption that $\Gamma \vdash \widetilde{v} : \widetilde{S}$ and the following queue is well-typed; rule [T-mf] types $\langle p, f \rangle$ by message type $\langle p, f \rangle$, while rule [T-mF] types $\langle\!\langle p, F \rangle\!\rangle$ by message type $\langle\!\langle p, F \rangle\!\rangle$. Rule [T-link] types a linking point $a[p](y).P$ by assuming that a provides a behaviour pattern defined in $\mathbf{G}$. For guiding P associated with p, [T-link] uses local type $\mathbf{T}$ generated by $Transform(\mathbf{G}, p)$ to type P acting on channel y. Rule [T-guide] states that $[P]_{\mathbf{T}}$ is well-typed by Δ if P is well-typed by Δ, and $\mathbf{T}$, gained by some $\mathbf{G}$, contains the type which types P acting on channel $s[p]$. Note that, by rule [link] (see Fig. 4), $[P]_{\mathbf{T}}$ is created after linking and $\mathbf{T}$ is not changed after any reduction; thus $\mathbf{G}$ in rule [T-guide] comes from rule [T-link]. Rule [T-net] ensures the parallel composition of two networks if each of them is well-typed and they do not share a common channel (i.e., $dom(\Delta_1) \cap dom(\Delta_2) = \emptyset$). The composed network exhibits the union of the session environments. Rule [T-new] types hiding (i.e., $(\text{new } s) N$) when the session environment of networks under s, denoted by

$$\Delta \langle s \rangle \overset{\text{def}}{=} \{s'[p] : \mathbf{T} \mid s'[p] \in dom(\Delta), s' = s\} \cup \{s : \mathbf{q}\},$$

is coherent:

Definition 3 (Coherence). We say $\Delta \langle s \rangle$ is coherent if there exists $\mathbf{G}$ such that $pid(\mathbf{G}) = \{p \mid s'[p] \in dom(\Delta), s' = s\}$ and either (1) $\forall s[p] \in dom(\Delta \langle s \rangle)$ we have

$Transform(\mathbf{G}, p)$ is equal to the type of $\Delta(s[p])$ after $s[p]$ absorbs all messages heading to it; or (2) there exists $\Delta' \subset \Delta$ such that $\forall s[p] \in dom(\Delta\langle s\rangle \setminus \Delta'\langle s\rangle)$ we have that $Transform(\mathbf{G}, p)$ is equal to the type of $\Delta(s[p])$ after $s[p]$ absorbs all messages heading to it, and $\Delta'\langle s\rangle$ is coherent.

Note that due to asynchrony, after a sender takes action, the type of the sender and its receiver may be temporarily incoherent if the sender has moved forward and the output is still in the global queue. Therefore, coherence holds only after a receiver has absorbed all messages heading to it.

As we aim to handle partial failure(s), either (1) no failures occurred such that there exists $\mathbf{G}$ defining interactions for every $s[p]$ in $\Delta\langle s\rangle$, or (2) a failure occurs such that the need-be-informed participants, who are in $\Delta'\langle s\rangle$, are handling that failure in a coherent way, and other unaffected ones, who are in $\Delta\langle s\rangle \setminus \Delta'\langle s\rangle$, still follow the behaviour defined in $\mathbf{G}$.

6   Properties

We prove that our typing discipline ensures the properties of *safety* and *progress*. The property of safety is defined by *subject reduction* and *communication safety*. Firstly we define $\Delta \rightharpoonup \Delta'$ as reductions of session environments. Intuitively, the reductions correspond closely to the operational semantics defined in Fig. 4. Subject reduction states that a well-typed network (resp. coherent session environment) is always well-typed (resp. coherent) after reduction:

Theorem 1 (Subject Congruence and Reduction).

1. (subject congruence) $\Gamma \vdash N \triangleright \Delta$ and $N \equiv N'$ imply that $\Gamma \vdash N' \triangleright \Delta$.
2. (subject reduction) $\Gamma \vdash N \triangleright \Delta$ with Δ coherent and $N \rightarrow N'$ imply that $\Gamma \vdash N' \triangleright \Delta'$ such that $\Delta \rightharpoonup \Delta'$ or $\Delta \equiv \Delta'$ and Δ' is coherent.

According to the definition of communication safety in the works of multiparty session types [1,12], it is a corollary of Theorem 1. Note that, since our calculus is based on the work of Bettini *et al.* [1], global linearity-check is not needed. For convenience, we define here contexts on networks:

$$\mathscr{C} ::= [\,] \mid \mathscr{C} \parallel N \mid N \parallel \mathscr{C} \mid (\text{new } s)\mathscr{C}$$

Corollary 1 (Communication Safety). Suppose $\Gamma \vdash N \triangleright \Delta$ and Δ is coherent. Let $N_1 = \mathscr{C}_1[s : q \cdot \langle p_2, p_1, \langle \tilde{v}\rangle\rangle^F \cdot q']$ and $N_2 = \mathscr{C}_2[s : q \cdot \langle p_1, f\rangle \cdot q']$ and $N_3 = \mathscr{C}_3[s : q \cdot \langle\!\langle p_1, F\rangle\!\rangle \cdot q']$ and no messages in q is sending to p_1.

1. If $N = \mathscr{C}[\mathscr{E}[s[p_1]?(p_2, (\tilde{x})^F).P]_{\mathbf{T}}]$, then $N \equiv N_1$ or $N \rightarrow^* N_1$.
2. If $N = \mathscr{C}[\mathscr{E}[\text{try}\{s[p_1]\} \otimes F'; P\}\mathsf{h}\{H\}]_{\mathbf{T}}]$ and $F' \subseteq F \neq \emptyset$, then either (a) $N \equiv N_2$ or $N \rightarrow^* N_2$ or (b) $N \equiv N_3$ or $N \rightarrow^* N_3$.
3. If $N = \mathscr{C}[\mathscr{E}[\text{try}\{v\}\mathsf{h}\{H\}]_{\mathbf{T}}]$ and $f \in dom(H)$ and process $H(f)$ is acting on $s[p_1]$, then $N \not\equiv N_2$ and $N \not\rightarrow^* N_2$.

This corollary states that our system is *free from deadlock* and *starvation*: if there is a receiving action in N, then N is either structurally congruent to the network which contains the message for input, or N will reduce to such a network. We state that $[\mathsf{try}\{v\}\mathsf{h}\{H\}]_\mathbf{T}$ is safe to become idle by proving that no $f \in dom(H)$ is heading to it (Case 3).

Corollary 1 provides the means to prove that our system *never gets stuck and is free from orphan messages* (*property of progress*):

Theorem 2 (Progress). $\Gamma \vdash N \rhd \Delta$ with Δ coherent and $N \to N'$ imply that N' is communication safe or $N' = \mathbf{0} \parallel s : \varepsilon$.

This theorem states that every interaction in a well-typed network is a safe interaction and reducible until the whole network terminates without any message left.

7   Related Works

Failure handling has been addressed in several process calculi and communication-centered programming languages. For instance, the conversation calculus [20] models exception handling in abstract service-based systems with message-passing based communication. It studies expressiveness and behaviour theory of bisimilarity rather than theory of types. Colombo and Pace [7] investigate several different process calculi for failure-recovery within long-running transactions. They give insight regarding the application of these failure-recovery formalisms in practice via comparing the design choices and formal notions of correctness properties. Both works do not provide a type system to statically type check local implementations.

Previous works for failure handling with type systems [3–5,13] extend the theory of session types to specify error handling under asynchronous interactions. These works do not capture handling of partial failures and the scenarios which exhibit the properties **P1** to **P4**. They may be able to encode multiple possible failures at the interaction level (**P1**), for example, by (i) explicitly using a labeled branching inside the failure handler, or (ii) piggybacking a label with the failure notification ("multiplexing"). However, (i) implies double communication and synchronisation (once for the failure notification, then for the branch) and (ii) implies that either the well-formedness constraints on the shape of interactions in handlers are needed or any participants related to any failure handling activity should be informed as a failure occurs in order to know how to proceed. Our approach is different since we do not have such constrains and we do not inform the unaffected participants. Moreover, while the termination of try-handle terms in those works demands an agreement of all participants, ours allows local try-handle terms to terminate since we have locally added synchronisation points by *transformation* (see Sect. 2.2). Our approach can encode the global types for exception-handling proposed in the work by Capecchi *et al.* [3], which is the closest related work (and other related ones have similar try-handle syntax). The formal encoding can be found in the long version of this paper [9].

Collet and Van Roy [6] informally present a distributed programming model of Oz for asynchronous failure handling and focus on programming applications in a distributed manner. Jakšić and Padovani [14] study a type theory for error handling for copy-less messaging and memory sharing to prevent memory leaks/faults through typing of exchange heaps. Lanese *et al.* [11,15] formalise a feature which can dynamically install fault and compensation handlers at execution time in an orchestration programming style. They investigate the interplay between fault handling and the request-response pattern. In contrast, our framework statically defines the handlers for non-trivial failure handling, which can only be done with a global perspective.

8 Concluding Remarks

Protocol types enable the design of protocols in an intuitive manner, and statically type check multiple failure-handling processes in a transparent way. Our type discipline exhibits the desirable properties of **P1(alignment)**, **P2(precision)**, **P3(causality)**, and **P4(decentralisation)** for robust failure handling, and ensures fundamental properties of safety and progress. We are currently implementing the proposed framework and are extending it to support system-induced failures as opposed to application-specific ones focused on in this paper, in addition to parameterisation and dynamic multiroles.

References

1. Bettini, L., Coppo, M., D'Antoni, L., De Luca, M., Dezani-Ciancaglini, M., Yoshida, N.: Global progress in dynamically interleaved multiparty sessions. In: van Breugel, F., Chechik, M. (eds.) CONCUR 2008. LNCS, vol. 5201, pp. 418–433. Springer, Heidelberg (2008)
2. Caires, L., Vieira, H.T.: Conversation types. In: Castagna, G. (ed.) ESOP 2009. LNCS, vol. 5502, pp. 285–300. Springer, Heidelberg (2009)
3. Capecchi, S., Giachino, E., Yoshida, N.: Global escape in multiparty sessions. MSCS **29**, 1–50 (2015)
4. Carbone, M., Honda, K., Yoshida, N.: Structured interactional exceptions in session types. In: van Breugel, F., Chechik, M. (eds.) CONCUR 2008. LNCS, vol. 5201, pp. 402–417. Springer, Heidelberg (2008)
5. Carbone, M., Yoshida, N., Honda, K.: Asynchronous session types: exceptions and multiparty interactions. In: Bernardo, M., Padovani, L., Zavattaro, G. (eds.) SFM 2009. LNCS, vol. 5569, pp. 187–212. Springer, Heidelberg (2009)
6. Collet, R., Van Roy, P.: Failure handling in a network-transparent distributed programming language. In: Cheraghchi, H.S., Lindskov Knudsen, J., Romanovsky, A., Babu, C.S. (eds.) Exception Handling. LNCS, vol. 4119, pp. 121–140. Springer, Heidelberg (2006)
7. Colombo, C., Pace, G.J.: Recovery within long-running transactions. ACM Comput. Surv. **45**(3), 28: 1–28: 35 (2013)
8. Deniélou, P.-M., Yoshida, N.: Dynamic multirole session types. In: POPL 2011, pp. 435–446 (2011)

9. Technical report. Long version of this paper. https://github.com/Distributed-Systems-Programming-Group/paper/blob/master/2016/forte16_long_dsp.pdf
10. Gärtner, F.C.: Fundamentals of fault-tolerant distributed computing in asynchronous environments. ACM Comput. Surv. **31**(1), 1–26 (1999)
11. Guidi, C., Lanese, I., Montesi, F., Zavattaro, G.: On the interplay between fault handling and request-response service invocations. In: 8th International Conference on Application of Concurrency to System Design, 2008, ACSD 2008, pp. 190–198, June 2008
12. Honda, K., Yoshida, N., Carbone, M.: Multiparty asynchronous session types. In: POPL 2008, pp. 273–284. ACM (2008)
13. Hu, R., Neykova, R., Yoshida, N., Demangeon, R., Honda, K.: Practical interruptible conversations. In: Legay, A., Bensalem, S. (eds.) RV 2013. LNCS, vol. 8174, pp. 130–148. Springer, Heidelberg (2013)
14. Jakšić, S., Padovani, L.: Exception handling for copyless messaging. Sci. Comput. Program. **84**, 22–51 (2014)
15. Lanese, I., Montesi, F.: Error handling: from theory to practice. In: Margaria, T., Steffen, B. (eds.) ISoLA 2010, Part II. LNCS, vol. 6416, pp. 66–81. Springer, Heidelberg (2010)
16. Lanese, I., Montesi, F., Zavattaro, G.: Amending choreographies. In: WWV 2013, vol. 123 of EPTCS, pp. 34–48 (2013)
17. Mostrous, D.: Session Types, in Concurrent Calculi: Higher-Order Processes and Objects. Ph.D. thesis, Imperial College London (2009)
18. Pierce, B.C.: Types and Programming Languages. MIT Press, Cambridge (2002)
19. Takeuchi, K., Honda, H., Kubo, M.: An interaction-based language and its typing system. In: Halatsis, Constantinos, Philokyprou, G., Maritsas, D., Theodoridis, Sergios (eds.) PARLE 1994. LNCS, vol. 817. Springer, Heidelberg (1994)
20. Vieira, H.T., Caires, L., Seco, J.C.: The conversation calculus: a model of service-oriented computation. In: Drossopoulou, S. (ed.) ESOP 2008. LNCS, vol. 4960, pp. 269–283. Springer, Heidelberg (2008)
21. Yoshida, N., Vasconcelos, V.T.: Language primitives and type discipline for structured communication-based programming revisited: two systems for higher-order session communication. Electr. Notes Theor. Comput. Sci. **171**(4), 73–93 (2007)

Choreographies in Practice

Luís Cruz-Filipe[(✉)] and Fabrizio Montesi

Department of Mathematics and Computer Science,
University of Southern Denmark, Odense, Denmark
{lcf,fmontesi}@imada.sdu.dk

Abstract. Choreographic Programming is a development methodology
for concurrent software that guarantees correctness by construction. The
key to this paradigm is to disallow mismatched I/O operations in programs, and mechanically synthesise process implementations.

There is still a lack of practical illustrations of the applicability of
choreographies to computational problems with standard concurrent
solutions. In this work, we explore the potential of choreographic programming by writing concurrent algorithms for sorting, solving linear
equations, and computing Fast Fourier Transforms. The lessons learned
from this experiment give directions for future improvements of the paradigm.

1 Introduction

Choreographic Programming is an emerging paradigm for developing concurrent software based on message passing [16]. Its key aspect is that programs
are choreographies – global descriptions of communications based on an "Alice
and Bob" security protocol notation. Since this notation disallows mismatched
I/O actions, choreographies always describe deadlock-free systems by construction. Given a choreography, a distributed implementation can be projected automatically (synthesis) onto terms of a process model – a transformation called
EndPoint Projection (EPP) [2,3]. A correct definition of EPP yields a
correctness-by-construction result: since a choreography cannot describe deadlocks, the generated process implementations are also deadlock-free. Previous
works presented formal models capturing different aspects of choreographic programming, e.g., web services [2,12], asynchronous multiparty sessions [3], runtime adaptation [9], modular development [18], protocol compliance [3,4], and
computational expressivity [7]. Choreography models have also been investigated
in the realms of type theory [14], automata theory [11], formal logics [5], and
service contracts [1].

Despite the rising interest in choreographic programming, there is still a
lack of evidence about what nontrivial programs can actually be written with
this paradigm. This is due to its young age [17]. Indeed, most works on languages for choreographic programming still focus on showcasing representative

Supported by *CRC (Choreographies for Reliable and efficient Communication software)*, grant DFF–4005-00304 from the Danish Council for Independent Research.

© IFIP International Federation for Information Processing 2016
E. Albert and I. Lanese (Eds.): FORTE 2016, LNCS 9688, pp. 114–123, 2016.
DOI: 10.1007/978-3-319-39570-8_8

toy examples (e.g., [2,3,6,12,16,18]), rather than giving a comprehensive practical evaluation based on standard computational problems.

In this work, we contribute to filling this gap. Our investigation uses the language of Procedural Choreographies (PC) [8], summarised in Sect. 2, which extends previous choreography models with primitives for parameterised procedures. Like other choreography languages (e.g., [3,18]), PC supports implicit parallelism: non-interfering communications can take place in any order. We provide an empirical evaluation of the expressivity of PC, by using it to program some representative and standard concurrent algorithms: Quicksort (Sect. 3), Gaussian elimination (Sect. 4), and Fast Fourier Transform (Sect. 5). As a consequence of using choreographies, all these implementations are guaranteed to be deadlock-free. We also illustrate how implicit parallelism has the surprising effect of automatically giving concurrent behaviour to traditional sequential implementations of these algorithms. Our exploration brings us to the limits of the expressivity of PC, which arise when trying to tackle distributed graph algorithms (Sect. 6), due to the lack of primitives for accessing the structure of process networks, e.g., broadcasting a message to neighbouring processes.

2   Background

In this section, we recap the language and properties of Procedural Choreographies (PC). We refer the reader to [8] for a more comprehensive presentation.

Procedural Choreographies. The syntax of PC is given below:

$$C ::= \eta; C \mid I; C \mid 0 \qquad \eta ::= \mathsf{p}.e \to \mathsf{q}.f \mid \mathsf{p} \to \mathsf{q}[l] \mid \mathsf{p}\,\mathsf{start}\,\mathsf{q} \mid \mathsf{p}: \mathsf{q} <\text{-}> \mathsf{r}$$
$$\mathcal{D} ::= X(\tilde{\mathsf{q}}) = C, \mathcal{D} \mid \emptyset \qquad I ::= \mathsf{if}\ \mathsf{p}.e\ \mathsf{then}\ C_1\ \mathsf{else}\ C_2 \mid X\langle\tilde{\mathsf{p}}\rangle \mid 0$$

A procedural choreography is a pair $\langle \mathcal{D}, C \rangle$, where C is a choreography and $\mathcal{D}$ is a set of procedure definitions. Process names, ranged over by $\mathsf{p}, \mathsf{q}, \mathsf{r}, \ldots$, identify processes that execute concurrently. Each process p is equipped with a memory cell storing a single value of a fixed type. In the remainder, we omit type information since they can always be inferred using the technique given in [8]. Statements in a choreography can either be communication actions (η) or compound instructions (I), and both can have continuations. Term 0 is the terminated choreography, often omitted, and $0; A$ is used only at runtime.

Processes communicate (synchronously) via direct references (names) to each other. In a value communication $\mathsf{p}.e \to \mathsf{q}.f$, process p evaluates expression e and sends the result to q; e can contain the placeholder c, replaced at runtime with the data stored at p. When q receives the value from p, it applies to it the (total) function f and stores the result. The body of f can also contain c, which is replaced by the contents of q's memory. Expressions and functions are written in a pure functional language, left unspecified.

In a selection $\mathsf{p} \to \mathsf{q}[l]$, p communicates to q its choice of label l.

In term $\mathsf{p}\,\mathsf{start}\,\mathsf{q}$, process p spawns the new process q, whose name is bound in the continuation C of $\mathsf{p}\,\mathsf{start}\,\mathsf{q}; C$. After executing $\mathsf{p}\,\mathsf{start}\,\mathsf{q}$, p is the only process who knows the name of q. This knowledge is propagated to other processes by the action p: q <-> r, read "p introduces q and r", where p, q and r are distinct.

In a conditional term if p.e then C_1 else C_2, process p evaluates expression e to choose between the possible continuations C_1 and C_2.

The set $\mathcal{D}$ defines global procedures that can be invoked in choreographies. Term $X(\tilde{q}) = C$ defines a procedure X with body C, which can be used anywhere in $\langle \mathcal{D}, C \rangle$ – in particular, inside the definitions of X and other procedures. The names $\tilde{q}$ are bound to C, and are assumed to be exactly the free process names in C. The set $\mathcal{D}$ contains at most one definition for each procedure name. Term $X\langle \tilde{p} \rangle$ invokes procedure X, instantiating its parameters with the processes $\tilde{p}$.

The semantics of PC, which we do not detail, is a reduction semantics that relies on two extra elements: a total state function that assigns to each process the value it stores, and a connection graph that keeps track of which processes know (are connected to) each other [8]. In particular, processes can only communicate if there is an edge between them in the connection graph. Therefore, choreographies can deadlock because of errors in the programming of communications: if two processes try to communicate but they are not connected, the choreography gets stuck. This issue is addressed by a simple typing discipline, which guarantees that well-typed PC choreographies are deadlock-free [8].

Procedural Processes. Choreographies in PC are compiled into terms of the calculus of Procedural Processes (PP), which has the following syntax:

$$B ::= \mathsf{q}!e; B \mid \mathsf{p}?f; B \mid \mathsf{q}!!\mathsf{r}; B \mid \mathsf{p}?\mathsf{r}; B \mid \mathsf{q} \oplus l; B \mid \mathsf{p}\&\{l_i : B_i\}_{i \in I}; B \mid \mathbf{0}$$
$$\mid \mathsf{start}\, \mathsf{q} \triangleright B_2; B_1 \mid \text{if } e \text{ then } B_1 \text{ else } B_2; B \mid X\langle \tilde{p} \rangle; B \mid \mathbf{0}; B$$
$$N, M ::= \mathsf{p} \triangleright_v B \quad \mid \quad N \mid M \quad \mid \quad \mathbf{0} \qquad \mathcal{B} ::= X(\tilde{q}) = B, \mathcal{B} \mid \emptyset$$

A term $\mathsf{p} \triangleright_v B$ is a process, where p is its name, v is the value it stores, and B is its behaviour. Networks, ranged over by N, M, are parallel compositions of processes, where $\mathbf{0}$ is the inactive network. Finally, $\langle \mathcal{B}, N \rangle$ is a procedural network, where $\mathcal{B}$ defines the procedures that the processes in N may invoke.

We comment on behaviours. A send term $\mathsf{q}!e; B$ sends the evaluation of expression e to process q, and then proceeds as B. Dually, term $\mathsf{p}?f; B$ receives a value from process p, combines it with the value in memory cell of the process executing the behaviour as specified by f, and then proceeds as B. Term $\mathsf{q}!!\mathsf{r}$ sends process name r to q and process name q to r, making q and r "aware" of each other. The dual action is $\mathsf{p}?\mathsf{r}$, which receives a process name from p that replaces the bound variable r in the continuation. Term $\mathsf{q} \oplus l; B$ sends the selection of a label l to process q. Selections are received by the branching term $\mathsf{p}\&\{l_i : B_i\}_{i \in I}$ (I nonempty), which receives a selection for a label l_i and proceeds as B_i. Term $\mathsf{start}\, \mathsf{q} \triangleright B_2; B_1$ starts a new process (with a fresh name) executing B_2, proceeding in parallel as B_1. Other terms (conditionals, procedure calls, and termination) are standard; procedural definitions are stored globally as in PC.

Term $\mathsf{start}\, \mathsf{q} \triangleright B_2; B_1$ binds q in B_1, and $\mathsf{p}?\mathsf{r}; B$ binds r in B. We omit the formal semantics of PP, which follows the intuitions given above.

EndPoint Projection (EPP). In [8] we show how every well-typed choreography can be projected into a PP network by means of an EndPoint Projection (EPP). EPP guarantees a strict operational correspondence: the projection of a choreography implements exactly the behaviour of the originating choreography. As a consequence, projections of typable PC terms never deadlock.

3   Quicksort

In this section, we illustrate PC's capability of supporting divide-and-conquer algorithms, by providing a detailed implementation of (concurrent) Quicksort.

We begin by defining procedure `split`, which splits the (non-empty) list stored at p among three processes: $q_<$, $q_=$ and $q_>$. We assume that all processes store objects of type `List(T)`, where T is some type, endowed with the following constant-time operations: get the first element (`fst`); get the second element (`snd`); check that the length of a list is at most 1 (`short`); append an element (`add`); and append another list (`append`). Also, `fst<snd` and `fst>snd` test whether the first element of the list is, respectively, smaller or greater than the second. Procedure `pop2` (omitted) removes the second element from the list.

We write `p -> q1,...,qn[l]` as an abbreviation for the sequence of selections `p -> q1[l]; ...; p -> qn[l]`. We can now define `split`.

```
split(p,q<,q=,q>) =
  if p.short then p -> q<,q=,q>[stop]; p.fst -> q=.add
  else if p.fst<snd then p -> q<[get]; p.snd -> q<.add; p -> q=,q>[skip]
       else if p.fst>snd then p -> q>[get]; p.snd -> q>.add; p -> q<,q=[skip]
            else p -> q=[get]; p.snd -> q=.add; p -> q<,q>[skip]
  ; pop2<p>; split<p,q<,q=,q>>
```

When `split` terminates, we know that all elements in $q_<$ and $q_>$ are respectively smaller or greater than those in $q_=$.[1] Using `split` we can implement a robust version of Quicksort (lists may contain duplicates), the procedure QS below. We write `p start q1,..., qn` for `p start q1;...; p start qn`. Note that `split` is only called when p stores a non-empty list.

```
QS(p) = if p.short then 0
        else p.start q<,q=,q>;
             split<p,q<,q=,q>>; QS<q<>; QS<q>>;
             q<.c -> p.id; q=.c -> p.append; q>.c -> p.append
```

Procedure QS implements Quicksort using its standard recursive structure. Since the created processes $q_<$, $q_=$ and $q_>$ do not have references to each other, they cannot exchange messages, and thus the recursive calls run completely in parallel. Applying EPP, we get the following process procedures (among others).

```
split_p(p,q<,q=,q>) =
  if short then q<⊕stop; q=⊕stop; q>⊕stop; q=!fst
  else if fst<snd then q<⊕get; q<!snd; q=⊕skip; q>⊕skip
       else if fst>snd then q>⊕get; q>!snd; q<⊕skip; q=⊕skip
            else q=⊕get; q=!snd; q<⊕skip; q>⊕skip
  ; pop2<p>; split_p<p,q<,q=,q>>

split_q<(p,q) = p&{stop: 0, get: p?add;split_q<(p,q), skip: split_q<(p,q)}
```

---

[1] The selections of label `skip` are required for projectability, see [8].

```
QS_p(p) = if small then 0
          else (start q< ▷ split_q< <p,q<>; QS_p<q<>; p!c);
               (start q= ▷ split_q= <p,q=>; p!c);
               (start q> ▷ split_q> <p,q>>; QS_p<q>>; p!c);
               q<?id; q=?append; q>?append
```

4 Gauss Elimination

Let $Ax = b$ be a system of linear equations in matrix form. We define a procedure gauss that applies Gaussian elimination to transform it into an equivalent system $Ux = y$, with U upper triangular (so this system can be solved by direct substitution). We use parameter processes a_{ij}, with $1 \leq i \leq n$ and $1 \leq j \leq n+1$. For $1 \leq i, j \leq n$, a_{ij} stores one value from the coefficient matrix; $a_{i,n+1}$ stores the independent term in one equation. (Including b in the coefficient matrix simplifies the notation.) After execution, each a_{ij} stores the corresponding term in the new system. We assume A to be non-singular and numerically stable.

This algorithm cannot be implemented in PC directly, as gauss takes a variable number of parameters (the a_{ij}). However, it is easy to extend PC so that procedures can also take process *lists* as parameters, as we describe.

Syntax of PC and PP. The arguments of parametric procedures are now lists of process names, all with the same type. These lists can only be used in procedure calls, where they can be manipulated by means of pure functions that take a list as their only argument. Our examples use uppercase letters to identify process lists and lowercase letters for normal process identifiers.

Semantics of PC. We assume that a procedure that is called with an empty list as one of its arguments is equivalent to the terminated process 0.

Connections. Connections between processes are uniform wrt argument lists, i.e., if p and A are arguments to some procedure X, then X requires/guarantees that p be connected to none or all of the processes in A.

The definition of gauss uses: hd and tl (computing the head and tail of a list of processes); fst and rest (taking a list of processes representing a matrix and returning the first row of the matrix, or the matrix without its first row); and minor (removing the first row and the first column from a matrix). Processes use standard arithmetic operations to combine their value with values received.

```
gauss(A) = solve(fst(A)); eliminate(fst(A),rest(A)); gauss(minor(A))

solve(A) = divide_all(hd(A),tl(A)); set_to_1(hd(A))

divide_all(a,A) = divide(a,hd(A)); divide_all(a,tl(A))
divide(a,b) = a.c -> b.div

eliminate(A,B) = elim_row(A,fst(B)); eliminate(A,rest(B))
elim_row(A,B) = elim_all(tl(A),hd(B),tl(B)); set_to_0(hd(B))
elim_all(A,m,B) = elim1(hd(A),m,hd(B)); elim_all(tl(A),m,tl(B))
elim1(a,m,b) = b start x; b: x <-> a; b: x <-> m;
                        a.c -> x.id; m.c -> x.mult; x.c -> b.minus

set_to_0(a) = a start p; p.0 -> a.id
set_to_1(a) = a start p; p.1 -> a.id
```

Procedure `solve` divides the first equation by the pivot. Then, `eliminate` uses this row to perform an elimination step, setting the first column of the coefficient matrix to zeroes. The auxiliary procedure `eli_row` performs this step at the row level, using `elim_all` to iterate through a single row and `elim1` to perform the actual computations. The first row and the first column of the matrix are then removed in the recursive call, as they will not change further.

This implementation follows the standard sequential algorithm for Gaussian elimination (Algorithm 8.4 in [13]). However, it runs concurrently due to the implicit parallelism in the semantics of choreographies. We explain this behaviour by focusing on a concrete example. Assume that A is a 3×3 matrix, so there are 12 processes in total. For legibility, we will write `b1` for the independent term `a14` etc.; `A=⟨a11,a12,a13,b1,a21,a22,a23,b2,a31,a32,a33,b3⟩` for the matrix; `A1=⟨a11,a12,a13,b1⟩` for the first row (likewise for A2 and A3); and, `A'2=⟨a22,a23,b2⟩` and likewise for `A'3`. Calling `gauss(A)` unfolds to

```
solve(A1); elim_row(A1,A2); elim_row(A1,A3);
solve(A'2); elim_row(A'2,A'3);
solve(⟨a33,b3⟩)
```

Fully expanding the sequence `elim_row(A1,A3); solve(A'2)` yields

```
elim1(a12,a31,a32); elim1(a13,a31,a33); elim1(b1,a31,b3); set_to_0(a31);
a21.c->a22.div; a21.c->a23.div; a21.c->b2.div; a21 start x2; x2.1->a21.id
```

and the semantics of PC allows the communications in the second line to be interleaved with those in the first line in any possible way; in the terminology of [7], the calls to `elim_row(A1,A3)` and `solve(A'2)` run in parallel.

This corresponds to implementing Gaussian elimination with pipelined communication and computation as in Sect. 8.3 of [13]. Indeed, as soon as any row has been reduced by all rows above it, it can apply `solve` to itself and try to begin reducing the rows below. It is a bit surprising that we get such parallel behaviour by straightforwardly implementing an imperative algorithm; the explanation is that EPP encapsulates the part of determining which communications can take place in parallel, removing this burden from the programmer.

5   Fast Fourier Transform

We now present a more complex example: computing the discrete Fourier transform of a vector via the *Fast Fourier Transform* (FFT), as in Algorithm 13.1 of [13]. We assume that n is a power of 2. In the first call, $\omega = e^{2\pi i/n}$.

```
procedure R_FFT(X,Y,n,ω)
  if n = 1 then y₀ = x₀
      else R_FFT(⟨x₀,x₂,...,xₙ₋₂⟩,⟨q₀,q₁,...,q_{n/2}⟩,n/2,ω²)
           R_FFT(⟨x₁,x₃,...,xₙ₋₁⟩,⟨t₀,t₁,...,t_{n/2}⟩,n/2,ω²)
           for j = 0 to n − 1 do    yⱼ = q_{(j%\frac{n}{2})} + ωʲt_{(j%\frac{n}{2})}
```

Implementing this procedure in PC requires two procedures `gsel_then(p,Q)` and `gsel_else(p,Q)`, where `p` broadcasts a selection of label **then** or else, respectively, to every process in Q.[2] We also use auxiliary procedures intro(n,m,P), where n introduces m to all processes in P, and power(n,m,nm), where at the end nm stores the result of exponentiating the value in m to the power of the value stored in n (see [7] for a possible implementation in a sublanguage of PC).

The one major difference between our implementation of FFT and the algorithm R_FFT reported above is that we cannot create a variable number of fresh processes and pass them as arguments to other procedures (the auxiliary vectors q and t). Instead, we use y to store the result of the recursive calls, and create two auxiliary processes inside each iteration of the final for loop.

```
fft(X,Y,n,w) = if n.is_one
                then gsel_then(n,join(X,Y)); n -> w[then]; base(hd(X),hd(Y))
                else gsel_else(n,join(X,Y)); n -> w[else];
                     n start n'; n.half -> n'; intro(n,n',Y);
                     w start w'; w.square -> w'; intro(w,w',Y);
                     n: n' <-> w; w: n' <-> w';
                     fft(even(X),half1(Y),n',w');
                     fft(odd(X),half2(Y),n',w');
                     n' start wn; n': w <-> wn; power(n',w,wn);
                     w start wj; w.1 -> wj; intro(w,wj,Y);
                     combine(half1(Y),half2(Y),wn,w,wi)

base(x,y) = x.c -> y

combine(Y1,Y2,wn,w,wj) = combine1(hd(Y1),hd(Y2),wn,wj); w.c -> wj.mult;
                         combine(tl(Y1),tl(Y2),wn,w,wj)

combine1(y1,y2,wn,wj) = y1 start q; y1.c -> q; y1: q <-> y2;
                        y2 start t; y2.c -> t; y2: t <-> y1; y2: t <-> wj;
                        q.c -> y1; wj.c -> t.mult; t.c -> y1.add;
                        q.c -> y2; wn.c -> t.mult; t.c -> y2.add
```

The level of parallelism in this implementation is suboptimal, as both recursive calls to fft use n' and w'. By duplicating these processes, these calls can run in parallel as in the previous example. (We chose the current formulation for simplicity.) Process n' is actually the main orchestrator of the whole execution.

6 Graphs

Another prototypical application of distributed algorithms is graph problems. In this section, we focus on a simple example (broadcasting a token to all nodes of a graph) and discuss the limitations of implementing these algorithms in PC.

The idea of broadcasting a token in a graph is very simple: each node receiving the token for the first time should communicate it to all its neighbours. The catch is that, in PC, there are no primitives for accessing the connection graph structure from within the language. Nevertheless, we can implement our simple example of token broadcasting if we assume that the graph structure is statically encoded in the set of available functions over parameters of procedures. To be precise, assume that we have a function neighb(p,V), returning the neighbours of p in the set of vertices V. (The actual graph is encapsulated in this function.) We also use ++ and \ for appending two lists and computing the set difference of

---

[2] For EPP to work, the merge operator in [8] has to be extended with these procedures.

two lists. We can then write a procedure broadcast(P,V), propagating a token from every element of P to every element of V, as follows.

```
broadcast(P,V) = bcast(hd(P),neighb(hd(P),V));
                 broadcast(tl(P)++neighb(hd(P),V),V\neighb(hd(P),V))

bcast(p,V) = bcast_one(p,hd(V)); bcast(p,tl(V))

bcast_one(p,v) = p.c -> v.id
```

Calling broadcast($\langle$p$\rangle$,G), where G is the full set of vertices of the graph and p is one vertex, will broadcast p's contents to all the vertices in the connected component of G containing p. Implicit parallelism ensures that each node starts broadcasting after it receives the token, independently of the remaining ones.

This approach is not very satisfactory as a graph algorithm, as it requires encoding the whole graph in the definition of broadcast, and does not generalise easily to more sophisticated graph algorithms. Adding primitives for accessing the network structure at runtime would however heavily influence EPP and the type system of PC [8]. We leave this as an interesting direction for future work, which we plan to pursue in order to be able to implement more sophisticated graph algorithms, e.g., for computing a minimum spanning tree.

7   Related Work and Conclusions

To the best of our knowledge, this is the first experience report on using choreographic programming for writing real-world, complex computational algorithms.

Related Work. The work nearest to ours is the evaluation of the Chor language [16], which implements the choreographic programming model in [3]. Chor supports multiparty sessions (as π-calculus channels [15]) and their mobility, similar to introductions in PC. Chor is evaluated by encoding representative examples from Service-Oriented Computing (e.g. distributed authentication and streaming), but these do not cover interesting algorithms as in here.

Previous works based on Multiparty Session Types (MPST) [14] have explored the use of choreographies as protocol specifications for the coordination of message exchanges in some real-world scenarios [10,19,20]. Differently from our approach, these works fall back to a standard process calculus model for defining implementations. Instead, our programs are choreographies. As a consequence, programming the composition of separate algorithms in PC is done on the level of choreographies, whereas in MPST composition requires using the low-level process calculus. Also, our choreography model is arguably much simpler and more approachable by newcomers, since much of the expressive power of PC comes from allowing parameterised procedures, a standard feature of most programming languages. The key twist in PC is that parameters are process names.

Conclusions. Our main conclusion is that choreographies make it easy to produce simple concurrent implementations of sequential algorithms, by carefully choosing process identifiers and relying on EPP for maximising implicit parallelism. This is distinct from how concurrent algorithms usually differ from their sequential counterparts. Although we do not necessarily get the most efficient possible distributed algorithm, this automatic concurrency is pleasant to observe.

The second interesting realisation is that it is relatively easy to implement nontrivial algorithms in choreographies. This is an important deviation from the typical use of toy examples, of limited practical significance, that characterises previous works in this programming paradigm.

References

1. Bravetti, M., Zavattaro, G.: Towards a unifying theory for choreography conformance and contract compliance. In: Lumpe, M., Vanderperren, W. (eds.) SC 2007. LNCS, vol. 4829, pp. 34–50. Springer, Heidelberg (2007)
2. Carbone, M., Honda, K., Yoshida, N.: Structured communication-centered programming for web services. ACM Trans. Program. Lang. Syst. **34**(2), 8 (2012)
3. Carbone, M., Montesi, F.: Deadlock-freedom-by-design: multiparty asynchronous global programming. In: Giacobazzi, R., Cousot, R. (eds.) POPL, pp. 263–274. ACM, Italy (2013)
4. Carbone, M., Montesi, F., Schürmann, C.: Choreographies, logically. In: Baldan, P., Gorla, D. (eds.) CONCUR 2014. LNCS, vol. 8704, pp. 47–62. Springer, Heidelberg (2014)
5. Carbone, M., Montesi, F., Schürmann, C., Yoshida, N.: Multiparty session types as coherence proofs. In: Aceto, L., de Frutos-Escrig, D. (eds.) CONCUR, vol. 42 of LIPIcs, pp. 412–426. Schloss Dagstuhl, Germany (2015)
6. Chor. Programming Language. http://www.chor-lang.org/
7. Cruz-Filipe, L., Montesi, F.: Choreographies, computationally, CoRR, abs/1510.03271. (2015, submitted)
8. Cruz-Filipe, L., Montesi, F.: Choreographies, divided and conquered, CoRR, abs/1602.03729. (2016, submitted)
9. Dalla Preda, M., Gabbrielli, M., Giallorenzo, S., Lanese, I., Mauro, J.: Dynamic choreographies. In: Holvoet, T., Viroli, M. (eds.) Coordination Models and Languages. LNCS, vol. 9037, pp. 67–82. Springer, Heidelberg (2015)
10. Deniélou, P.-M., Yoshida, N.: Dynamic multirole session types. In: Ball, T., Sagiv, M. (eds.) POPL, pp. 435–446. ACM, USA (2011)
11. Deniélou, P.-M., Yoshida, N.: Multiparty session types meet communicating automata. In: Seidl, H. (ed.) Programming Languages and Systems. LNCS, vol. 7211, pp. 194–213. Springer, Heidelberg (2012)
12. Gabbrielli, M., Giallorenzo, S., Montesi, F.: Applied choreographies. CoRR, abs/1510.03637 (2015)
13. Grama, A., Gupta, A., Karypis, G., Kumar, V.: Introduction to Parallel Computing, 2nd edn. Pearson, Noida (2003)
14. Honda, K., Yoshida, N., Carbone, M.: Multiparty asynchronous session types. In: Necula, G.C., Wadler, P. (eds.) POPL, pp. 273–284. ACM, New York (2008)
15. Milner, R., Parrow, J., Walker, D.: A calculus of mobile processes, I, II. Inf. Comput. **100**(1), 41–77 (1992)
16. Montesi, F.: Choreographic Programming, Ph.D. thesis, IT University of Copenhagen (2013). http://fabriziomontesi.com/files/choreographic_programming.pdf
17. Montesi, F.: Kickstarting choreographic programming, CoRR, abs/1502.02519 (2015)

18. Montesi, F., Yoshida, N.: Compositional choreographies. In: D'Argenio, P.R., Melgratti, H. (eds.) CONCUR 2013 – Concurrency Theory. LNCS, vol. 8052, pp. 425–439. Springer, Heidelberg (2013)
19. Ng, N., Yoshida, N.: Pabble: parameterised scribble. SOCA **9**(3–4), 269–284 (2015)
20. Yoshida, N., Deniélou, P.-M., Bejleri, A., Hu, R.: Parameterised multiparty session types. In: Ong, L. (ed.) FOSSACS 2010. LNCS, vol. 6014, pp. 128–145. Springer, Heidelberg (2010)

Specification-Based Synthesis of Distributed Self-Stabilizing Protocols

Fathiyeh Faghih[1], Borzoo Bonakdarpour[1(✉)], Sébastien Tixeuil[2],
and Sandeep Kulkarni[3]

[1] McMaster University, Hamilton, Canada
{faghihef,borzoo}@mcmaster.ca
[2] UPMC Sorbonne Universités, Paris, France
Sebastien.Tixeuil@lip6.fr
[3] Michigan State University, East Lansing, USA
sandeep@cse.msu.edu

Abstract. In this paper, we introduce an SMT-based method that automatically synthesizes a distributed *self-stabilizing* protocol from a given high-level specification and the network topology. Unlike existing approaches, where synthesis algorithms require the *explicit* description of the set of legitimate states, our technique only needs the temporal behavior of the protocol. We also extend our approach to synthesize *ideal-stabilizing* protocols, where every state is legitimate. Our proposed methods are implemented and we report successful synthesis of Dijkstra's token ring and a self-stabilizing version of Raymond's mutual exclusion algorithm, as well as ideal-stabilizing leader election and local mutual exclusion.

1 Introduction

Self-stabilization [4] has emerged as one of the prime techniques for forward fault recovery. A self-stabilizing protocol satisfies two requirements: (1) *Convergence* ensures that starting from any arbitrary state, the system reaches a set of *legitimate states* (denoted in the sequel by LS) with no external intervention within a finite number of execution steps, provided no new faults occur, and (2) *closure* indicates that the system remains in LS thereafter.

As Dijkstra mentions in his belated proof of self-stabilization [5], designing self-stabilizing systems is a complex task, but proving their correctness is even more tedious. Thus, having access to automated methods (as opposed to manual techniques such as [3]) for *synthesizing* correct self-stabilizing systems is highly desirable. However, synthesizing self-stabilizing protocols incurs high time and space complexity [12]. The techniques proposed in [1,2,6,13] attempt to cope with this complexity using heuristic algorithms, but none of these algorithms are complete; i.e., they may fail to find a solution although there exists one.

Recently, Faghih and Bonakdarpour [7] proposed a sound and complete method to synthesize finite-state self-stabilizing systems based on SMT-solving. However, the shortcoming of this work as well as the techniques in [2,6,13] is that

© IFIP International Federation for Information Processing 2016
E. Albert and I. Lanese (Eds.): FORTE 2016, LNCS 9688, pp. 124–141, 2016.
DOI: 10.1007/978-3-319-39570-8_9

an *explicit* description of *LS* is needed as an input to the synthesis algorithm. The problem is that developing a formal predicate for legitimate states is not at all a straightforward task. For instance, the predicate for the set of legitimate states for Dijkstra's token ring algorithm with three-state machines [4] for three processes is the following:

$$LS = ((x_0 + 1 \equiv_3 x_1) \wedge (x_1 + 1 \not\equiv_3 x_2))$$
$$\vee ((x_1 = x_0) \wedge (x_1 + 1 \not\equiv_3 x_2))$$
$$\vee ((x_1 + 1 \equiv_3 x_0) \wedge (x_1 + 1 \not\equiv_3 x_2))$$
$$\vee ((x_0 + 1 \not\equiv_3 x_1) \wedge (x_1 + 1 \not\equiv_3 x_0) \wedge (x_1 + 1 \equiv_3 x_2))$$

where $\equiv_3$ denotes modulo 3 equality and variable x_i belongs to process i. Obviously, developing such a predicate requires huge expertise and insight and is, in fact, the key to the solution. Ideally, the designer should only express the basic requirements of the protocols (i.e., the existence of a unique token and its fair circulation), instead of an obscure predicate such as the one above.

In this paper, we propose an automated approach to synthesize self-stabilizing systems given (1) the network topology, and (2) the high-level specification of legitimate states in the linear temporal logic (LTL). We also investigate automated synthesis of *ideal-stabilizing* protocols [14]. These protocols address two drawbacks of self-stabilizing protocols, namely exhibiting unpredictable behavior during recovery and poor compositional properties. In order to keep the specification as implicit as possible, the input LTL formula may include a set of uninterpreted predicates. In designing ideal-stabilizing systems, the transition relation of the system and interpretation function of uninterpreted predicates must be found such that the specification is satisfied in every state. Our synthesis approach is SMT-based; i.e., we transform the input specification into a set of SMT constraints. If the SMT instance is satisfiable, then a witness solution to its satisfiability encodes a distributed protocol that meets the input specification and topology. If the instance is not satisfiable, then we are guaranteed that no protocol that satisfies the input specification exists.

We also conduct several case studies using the model finder Alloy [10]. In the case of self-stabilizing systems, we successfully synthesize Dijkstra's [4] token ring and Raymond's [16] mutual exclusion algorithms without explicit legitimate states as input. We also synthesize ideal-stabilizing leader election and local mutual exclusion (in a line topology) protocols.

Organization. In Sects. 2 and 3, we present the preliminary concepts on the shared-memory model and self-stabilization. Section 4 formally states the synthesis problems. In Sect. 5, we describe our SMT-based technique, while Sect. 6 is dedicated to our case studies. We discuss the related work in Sect. 7, and finally, we make concluding remarks and discuss future work in Sect. 8.

2   Model of Computation

2.1   Distributed Programs

Throughout the paper, let V be a finite set of discrete *variables*. Each variable $v \in V$ has a finite domain D_v. A *state* is a mapping from each variable $v \in V$ to a value in its domain D_v. We call the set of all possible states the *state space*. A *transition* in the program state space is an ordered pair (s_0, s_1), where s_0 and s_1 are two states. We denote the value of a variable v in state s by $v(s)$.

Definition 1. *A process π over a set V of variables is a tuple $\langle R_\pi, W_\pi, T_\pi \rangle$, where*

- $R_\pi \subseteq V$ *is the* read-set *of π; i.e., variables that π can read,*
- $W_\pi \subseteq R_\pi$ *is the* write-set *of π; i.e., variables that π can write, and*
- T_π *is the set of transitions of π, such that $(s_0, s_1) \in T_\pi$ implies that for each variable $v \in V$, if $v(s_0) \neq v(s_1)$, then $v \in W_\pi$.* □

Notice that Definition 1 requires that a process can only change the value of a variable in its write-set (third condition), but not blindly (second condition). We say that a process $\pi = \langle R_\pi, W_\pi, T_\pi \rangle$ is *enabled* in state s_0 if there exists a state s_1, such that $(s_0, s_1) \in T_\pi$.

Definition 2. *A distributed program is a tuple $\mathcal{D} = \langle \Pi_\mathcal{D}, T_\mathcal{D} \rangle$, where*

- $\Pi_\mathcal{D}$ *is a set of processes over a common set V of variables, such that:*
  - *for any two distinct processes $\pi_1, \pi_2 \in \Pi_\mathcal{D}$, we have $W_{\pi_1} \cap W_{\pi_2} = \emptyset$*
  - *for each process $\pi \in \Pi_\mathcal{D}$ and each transition $(s_0, s_1) \in T_\pi$, the following read restriction holds:*

$$\forall s_0', s_1' : \ ((\forall v \in R_\pi : (v(s_0) = v(s_0') \ \wedge \ v(s_1) = v(s_1')))$$
$$\wedge (\forall v \notin R_\pi : v(s_0') = v(s_1'))) \implies (s_0', s_1') \in T_\pi \qquad (1)$$

- $T_\mathcal{D}$ *is the set of transitions and is the union of transitions of all processes: $T_\mathcal{D} = \bigcup_{\pi \in \Pi_\mathcal{D}} T_\pi$.* □

Intuitively, the read restriction in Definition 2 imposes the constraint that for each process π, each transition in T_π depends only on reading the variables that π can read. Thus, each transition is an equivalence class in $T_\mathcal{D}$, which we call a *group* of transitions. The key consequence of read restrictions is that during synthesis, if a transition is included (respectively, excluded) in $T_\mathcal{D}$, then its corresponding group must also be included (respectively, excluded) in $T_\mathcal{D}$ as well. Also, notice that $T_\mathcal{D}$ is defined in such a way that $\mathcal{D}$ resembles an asynchronous distributed program, where process transitions execute in an *interleaving* fashion.

Example. We use the problem of distributed self-stabilizing *mutual exclusion* as a running example to describe the concepts throughout the paper. Let $V = \{c_0, c_1, c_2\}$ be the set of variables, where $D_{c_0} = D_{c_1} = D_{c_2} = \{0, 1, 2\}$. Let $\mathcal{D} = \langle \Pi_\mathcal{D}, T_\mathcal{D} \rangle$ be a distributed program, where $\Pi_\mathcal{D} = \{\pi_0, \pi_1, \pi_2\}$. Each process π_i $(0 \leq i \leq 2)$ can write variable c_i. Also, $R_{\pi_0} = \{c_0, c_1\}$, $R_{\pi_1} = \{c_0, c_1, c_2\}$, and $R_{\pi_2} = \{c_1, c_2\}$. Notice that following Definition 2 and read/write restrictions of π_0, (arbitrary) transitions

$$t_1 = ([c_0 = 1, c_1 = 1, c_2 = 0], [c_0 = 2, c_1 = 1, c_2 = 0])$$
$$t_2 = ([c_0 = 1, c_1 = 1, c_2 = 2], [c_0 = 2, c_1 = 1, c_2 = 2])$$

are in the same group, since π_0 cannot read c_2. This implies that if t_1 is included in the set of transitions of a distributed program, then so should be t_2. Otherwise, execution of t_1 by π_0 depends on the value of c_2, which, of course, π_0 cannot read.

Definition 3. *A computation of $\mathcal{D} = \langle \Pi_\mathcal{D}, T_\mathcal{D} \rangle$ is an infinite sequence of states $\overline{s} = s_0 s_1 \cdots$, such that: (1) for all $i \geq 0$, we have $(s_i, s_{i+1}) \in T_\mathcal{D}$, and (2) if a computation reaches a state s_i, from where there is no state $\mathfrak{s} \neq s_i$, such that $(s_i, \mathfrak{s}) \in T_\mathcal{D}$, then the computation stutters at s_i indefinitely. Such a computation is called a* terminating computation. □

2.2 Predicates

Let $\mathcal{D} = \langle \Pi_\mathcal{D}, T_\mathcal{D} \rangle$ be a distributed program over a set V of variables. The *global state space* of $\mathcal{D}$ is the set of all possible global states of $\mathcal{D}$: $\Sigma_\mathcal{D} = \prod_{v \in V} D_v$. The *local state space* of $\pi \in \Pi_\mathcal{D}$ is the set of all possible local states of π: $\Sigma_\pi = \prod_{v \in R_\pi} D_v$.

Definition 4. *An* interpreted global predicate *of a distributed program $\mathcal{D}$ is a subset of $\Sigma_\mathcal{D}$ and an* interpreted local predicate *is a subset of Σ_π, for some $\pi \in \Pi_\mathcal{D}$.* □

Definition 5. *Let $\mathcal{D} = \langle \Pi_\mathcal{D}, T_\mathcal{D} \rangle$ be a distributed program. An* uninterpreted global predicate *up is an uninterpreted Boolean function from $\Sigma_\mathcal{D}$. An* uninterpreted local predicate *lp is an uninterpreted Boolean function from Σ_π, for some $\pi \in \Pi_\mathcal{D}$.* □

The interpretation of an uninterpreted global predicate is a Boolean function from the set of all states:

$$up_I : \Sigma_D \mapsto \{true, false\}$$

Similarly, the interpretation of an uninterpreted local predicate for the process π is a Boolean function:

$$lp_I : \Sigma_\pi \mapsto \{true, false\}$$

Throughout the paper, we use 'uninterpreted predicate' to refer to either uninterpreted global or local predicate, and use global (local) predicate to refer to interpreted global (local) predicate.

2.3 Topology

A topology specifies the communication model of a distributed program.

Definition 6. *A* topology *is a tuple* $\mathcal{T} = \langle V, |\Pi_{\mathcal{T}}|, R_{\mathcal{T}}, W_{\mathcal{T}} \rangle$, *where*

- *V is a finite set of finite-domain discrete variables,*
- *$|\Pi_{\mathcal{T}}| \in \mathbb{N}_{\geq 1}$ is the number of processes,*
- *$R_{\mathcal{T}}$ is a mapping $\{0 \ldots |\Pi_{\mathcal{T}}| - 1\} \mapsto 2^V$ from a process index to its read-set,*
- *$W_{\mathcal{T}}$ is a mapping $\{0 \ldots |\Pi_{\mathcal{T}}| - 1\} \mapsto 2^V$ from a process index to its write-set,*
  such that $W_{\mathcal{T}}(i) \subseteq R_{\mathcal{T}}(i)$, for all i $(0 \leq i \leq |\Pi_{\mathcal{T}}| - 1)$.   □

Definition 7. *A* distributed program *$\mathcal{D} = \langle \Pi_{\mathcal{D}}, T_{\mathcal{D}} \rangle$ has* topology *$\mathcal{T} = \langle V, |\Pi_{\mathcal{T}}|, R_{\mathcal{T}}, W_{\mathcal{T}} \rangle$ iff*

- *each process $\pi \in \Pi_{\mathcal{D}}$ is defined over V*
- *$|\Pi_{\mathcal{D}}| = |\Pi_{\mathcal{T}}|$*
- *there is a mapping $g : \{0 \ldots |\Pi_{\mathcal{T}}| - 1\} \mapsto \Pi_{\mathcal{D}}$ such that*

$$\forall i \in \{0 \ldots |\Pi_{\mathcal{T}}| - 1\} : (R_{\mathcal{T}}(i) = R_{g(i)}) \wedge (W_{\mathcal{T}}(i) = W_{g(i)}).$$ □

3 Formal Characterization of Self- and Ideal-Stabilization

We specify the behavior of a distributed self-stabilizing program based on (1) the *functional* specification, and (2) the *recovery* specification. The functional specification is intended to describe what the program is required to do in a fault-free scenario (e.g., mutual exclusion or leader election). The recovery behavior stipulates Dijkstra's idea of self-stabilization in spite of distributed control [4].

3.1 The Functional Behavior

We use LTL [15] to specify the functional behavior of a stabilizing program. Since LTL is a commonly-known language, we refrain from presenting its syntax and semantics and continue with our running example (where **F**, **G**, **X**, and **U** denote the 'finally', 'globally', 'next', and 'until' operators, respectively). In our framework, an LTL formula may include uninterpreted predicates. Thus, we say that a program $\mathcal{D}$ satisfies an LTL formula φ from an initial state in the set I, and write $\mathcal{D}, I \models \varphi$ iff there exists an interpretation function for each uninterpreted predicate in φ, such that all computations of $\mathcal{D}$, starting from a state in I satisfy φ. Also, the semantics of the satisfaction relation is the standard semantics of LTL over Kripke structures (i.e., computations of $\mathcal{D}$ that start from a state in I).

Example 3.1. Consider the problem of *token passing* in a ring topology (*i.e.*, token ring), where each process π_i has a variable c_i with the domain $D_{c_i} = \{0, 1, 2\}$. This problem has two functional requirements:

Safety. The *safety* requirement for this problem is that in each state, only one process can execute. To formulate this requirement, we assume each process π_i is associated with a local uninterpreted predicate tk_i, which shows whether π_i is enabled. Let $LP = \{tk_i \mid 0 \le i < n\}$. A process π_i can execute a transition, if and only if tk_i is true. The LTL formula, $\varphi_{\mathbf{TR}}$, expresses the above requirement for a ring of size n:

$$\varphi_{\mathbf{TR}} = \forall i \in \{0 \cdots n-1\} : tk_i \iff (\forall val \in \{0,1,2\} : (c_i = val) \Rightarrow \mathbf{X}\,(c_i \ne val))$$

Using the set of uninterpreted predicates, the safety requirement can be expressed by the following LTL formula:

$$\psi_{\mathbf{safety}} = \exists i \in \{0 \cdots n-1\} : (tk_i \wedge \forall j \ne i : \neg tk_j)$$

Note that although safety requirements generally need the **G** operator, we do not need it, as every state in a stabilizing system can be an initial state.

Fairness. This requirement implies that for every process π_i and starting from each state, the computation should reach a state, where π_i is enabled:

$$\psi_{\mathbf{fairness}} = \forall i \in \{0 \cdots n-1\} : (\mathbf{F}\,tk_i)$$

Another way to guarantee this requirement is that processes get enabled in a clockwise order in the ring, which can be formulated as follows:

$$\psi_{\mathbf{fairness}} = \forall i \in \{0 \cdots n-1\} : (tk_i \Rightarrow \mathbf{X}\,tk_{(i+1 \bmod n)})$$

Note that the latter approach is a stronger constraint, and would prevent us to synthesize bidirectional protocols, such as Dijkstra's three-state solution.

Thus, the functional requirements of the token ring protocol is

$$\psi_{\mathbf{TR}} = \psi_{\mathbf{safety}} \wedge \psi_{\mathbf{fairness}}$$

Observe that following Definition 3, $\psi_{\mathbf{TR}}$ ensures deadlock-freedom as well.

Example 3.2. Consider the problem of *local mutual exclusion* on a line topology, where each process π_i has a Boolean variable c_i. The requirements of this problem are as follows:

Safety. In each state, *(i)* at least one process is enabled (*i.e.*, deadlock-freedom), and *(ii)* no two neighbors are enabled (*i.e.*, mutual exclusion). To formulate this requirement, we associate with each process π_i a local uninterpreted predicate tk_i, which is true when π_i is enabled:

$$\varphi_{\mathbf{LME}} = \forall i \in \{0 \cdots n-1\} : tk_i \iff ((c_i \Rightarrow \mathbf{X}\neg c_i) \wedge (\neg c_i \Rightarrow \mathbf{X} c_i))$$

Thus, $LP = \{tk_i \mid 0 \le i < n\}$ and the safety requirement can be formulated by the following LTL formula:

$$\psi_{\mathbf{safety}} = (\exists i \in \{0 \cdots n-1\} : tk_i) \wedge (\forall i \in \{0 \cdots n-2\} : \neg(tk_i \wedge tk_{(i+1)})).$$

Fairness. Each process is eventually enabled:

$$\psi_{\mathbf{fairness}} = \forall i \in \{0 \cdots n-1\} : (\mathbf{F}\,tk_i)$$

Thus, the functional requirement of the local mutual exclusion protocol is

$$\psi_{\mathbf{LME}} = \psi_{\mathbf{safety}} \wedge \psi_{\mathbf{fairness}}.$$

3.2 Self-Stabilization

A *self-stabilizing system* [4] is one that always recovers a good behavior (typically, expressed in terms of a set of *legitimate states*), starting from any arbitrary initial state.

Definition 8. *A distributed program $\mathcal{D} = \langle \Pi_{\mathcal{D}}, T_{\mathcal{D}} \rangle$ with the state space $\Sigma_{\mathcal{D}}$ is self-stabilizing for an LTL specification ψ iff there exists a global predicate LS (called the set of legitimate states), such that:*

- Functional behavior: $\mathcal{D}, LS \models \psi$
- Strong convergence: $\mathcal{D}, \Sigma_{\mathcal{D}} \models \mathbf{F} LS$
- Closure: $\mathcal{D}, \Sigma_{\mathcal{D}} \models (LS \Rightarrow \mathbf{X} LS)$.   □

Notice that the strong convergence property ensures that starting from any state, any computation converges to a legitimate state of $\mathcal{D}$ within a finite number of steps. The closure property ensures that execution of the program is closed in the set of legitimate states.

3.3 Ideal-Stabilization

Self-stabilization does not predict program behavior during recovery, which may be undesirable for some applications. A trivial way to integrate program behavior during recovery is to include it in the specification itself, then the protocol must ensure that every configuration in the specification is legitimate (so, the only recovery behaviors are those included in the specification). Such a protocol is *ideal stabilizing* [14].

Definition 9. *Let ψ be an LTL specification and $\mathcal{D} = \langle \Pi_{\mathcal{D}}, T_{\mathcal{D}} \rangle$ be a distributed program. We say that $\mathcal{D}$ is ideal stabilizing for ψ iff $\mathcal{D}, \Sigma_{\mathcal{D}} \models \psi$.*   □

The existence of ideal stabilizing protocols for "classical" specifications (that only mandate legitimate states) is an intriguing question, as one has to find a "clever" transition predicate and an interpretation function for every uninterpreted predicate (if included in the specification), such that the system satisfies the specification. Note that there is a specification for every system to which it ideally stabilizes [14], and that is the specification that includes all of the system computations. In this paper, we do the reverse; meaning that getting a specification ψ, we synthesize a distributed system that ideally stabilizes to ψ.

4   Problem Statement

Our goal is to develop synthesis algorithms that take as input the (1) system topology, and (2) two LTL formulas φ and ψ that involve a set LP of uninterpreted predicates, and generate as output a self- or ideal-stabilizing protocol. For instance, in token passing on a ring, $\psi_{\mathbf{TR}}$ includes safety and fairness, which should hold in the set of legitimate states, while $\varphi_{\mathbf{TR}}$ is a general requirement that we specify on every uninterpreted predicate tk_i. Since in the case of self-stabilizing systems, we do not get LS as a set of states (global predicate), we refer to our problem as "synthesis of self-stabilizing systems with implicit LS".

Problem statement 1 (self-stabilization). Given is

1. a topology $\mathcal{T} = \langle V, |\Pi_\mathcal{T}|, R_\mathcal{T}, W_\mathcal{T} \rangle$;
2. two LTL formulas φ and ψ that involve a set LP of uninterpreted predicates.

The synthesis algorithm is required to identify as output (1) a distributed program $\mathcal{D} = \langle \Pi_\mathcal{D}, T_\mathcal{D} \rangle$, (2) an interpretation function for every local predicate $lp \in LP$, and (3) the global state predicate LS, such that $\mathcal{D}$ has topology $\mathcal{T}$, $\mathcal{D}, \Sigma_\mathcal{D} \models \varphi$, and $\mathcal{D}$ is self-stabilizing for ψ.

Problem statement 2 (ideal-stabilization). Given is

1. a topology $\mathcal{T} = \langle V, |\Pi_\mathcal{T}|, R_\mathcal{T}, W_\mathcal{T} \rangle$
2. two LTL formulas φ and ψ that involve a set LP of uninterpreted predicates.

The synthesis algorithm is required to generate as output (1) a distributed program $\mathcal{D} = \langle \Pi_\mathcal{D}, T_\mathcal{D} \rangle$, and (2) an interpretation function for every local predicate $lp \in LP$, such that $\mathcal{D}$ has topology $\mathcal{T}$ and $\mathcal{D}, \Sigma_\mathcal{D} \models (\varphi \wedge \psi)$.

---

5 SMT-based Synthesis Solution

Our technique is inspired by our SMT-based work in [7]. In particular, we transform the problem input into an *SMT instance*. An SMT instance consists of two parts: (1) a set of *entity* declarations (in terms of sets, relations, and functions), and (2) first-order modulo-theory *constraints* on the entities. An SMT-solver takes as input an SMT instance and determines whether or not the instance is satisfiable. If so, then the witness generated by the SMT solver is the answer to our synthesis problem. We describe the SMT entities obtained in our transformation in Subsect. 5.1. SMT constraints appear in Subsects. 5.2 and 5.3. Note that using our approach in [7], we can synthesize different systems considering types of timing models (i.e., synchronous and asynchronous), symmetric and asymmetric, as well as strong- and weak-stabilizing protocols. In a weak-stabilizing protocol there is only the *possibility* of recovery [9].

5.1 SMT Entities

Recall that the inputs to our problems include a topology $\mathcal{T} = \langle V, |\Pi_\mathcal{T}|, R_\mathcal{T}, W_\mathcal{T} \rangle$, and two LTL formulas on a set LP of uninterpreted predicates. Let $D = \langle \Pi_\mathcal{D}, T_\mathcal{D} \rangle$ denote a distributed program that is a solution to our problem. In our SMT instance, we include:

- A set D_v for each $v \in V$, which contains the elements in the domain of v.
- A set $Bool$ that contains the elements $true$ and $false$.
- A set called S, whose cardinality is $\left| \prod_{v \in V} D_v \right|$. This set represents the state space of the synthesized distributed program.
- An uninterpreted function v_val for each variable v; i.e., $v\_val : S \mapsto D_v$.
- An uninterpreted function lp_val for each uninterpreted predicate $lp \in LP$; i.e., $lp\_val : S \mapsto Bool$.
- A relation T_i that represents the transition relation for process π_i in the synthesized program.
- An uninterpreted function γ, from each state to a natural number ($\gamma : S \mapsto \mathbb{N}$). This function is used to capture convergence to the set of legitimate states.
- An uninterpreted function $LS : S \mapsto Bool$.

The last two entities are only included in the case of Problem Statement 1.

Example. For Example 3.1, we include the following SMT entities:

- $D_{c_0} = D_{c_1} = D_{c_2} = \{0, 1, 2\}$, $Bool = \{true, false\}$, set S, where $|S| = 27$
- $c_0\_val : S \mapsto D_{c_0}, c_1\_val : S \mapsto D_{c_1}, c_2\_val : S \mapsto D_{c_2}$
- $T_0 \subseteq S \times S, T_1 \subseteq S \times S, T_2 \subseteq S \times S, \gamma : S \mapsto \mathbb{N}, LS : S \mapsto Bool$.

5.2 General SMT Constraints

5.2.1 State Distinction
Any two states differ in the value of some variable:

$$\forall s_0, s_1 \in S : (s_0 \neq s_1) \Rightarrow (\exists v \in V : v\_val(s_0) \neq v\_val(s_1)). \tag{2}$$

5.2.2 Local Predicates Constraints
Let LP be the set of uninterpreted predicates used in formulas φ and ψ. For each uninterpreted local predicate lp_π, we need to ensure that its interpretation function is a function of the variables in the read-set of π. To guarantee this requirement, for each $lp_\pi \in LP$, we add the following constraint to the SMT instance:

$$\forall s, s' \in S : (\forall v \in R_\pi : (v(s) = v(s'))) \Rightarrow (lp_\pi(s) = lp_\pi(s')).$$

Example. For Example 3.1, we add the following constraint for process π_1:

$$\forall s, s' \in S : (x_0(s) = x_0(s')) \wedge (x_1(s) = x_1(s')) \wedge (x_2(s) = x_2(s')) \Rightarrow$$
$$(tk_1(s) = tk_1(s')). \tag{3}$$

5.2.3   Constraints for an Asynchronous System

To synthesize an asynchronous distributed program, we add the following constraint for each transition relation T_i:

$$\forall (s_0, s_1) \in T_i \ : \forall v \notin W_\mathcal{T}(i) \ : \ v\_val(s_0) = v\_val(s_1) \tag{4}$$

Constraint 4 ensures that in each relation T_i, only process π_i can execute. By introducing $|\Pi_\mathcal{T}|$ transition relations, we consider all possible interleaving of processes executions.

5.2.4   Read Restrictions

To ensure that $\mathcal{D}$ meets the read restrictions given by $\mathcal{T}$ and Definition 2, we add the following constraint for each process index:

$$\forall (s_0, s_1) \in T_i : \forall s_0', s_1' : \ ((\forall v \in R_\pi : (v(s_0) = v(s_0') \ \wedge \ v(s_1) = v(s_1'))) \ \wedge$$
$$(\forall v \notin R_\pi : v(s_0') = v(s_1'))) \Rightarrow (s_0', s_1') \in T_i. \tag{5}$$

5.3   Specific SMT Constraints for Self- and Ideal-Stabilizing Problems

Before presenting the constraints specific to each of our problem statements, we present the formulation of an LTL formula as an SMT constraint. We use this formulation to encode the ψ and φ formulas (given as input) as ψ_{SMT} and φ_{SMT}, and add them to the SMT instance.

5.3.1   SMT Formulation of an LTL Formula

SMT formulation of an LTL formula is presented in [8]. Below, we briefly discuss the formulation of LTL formulas without nested temporal operators. For formulas with nested operators, the formulation based on universal co-Büchi automata [8] needs to be applied.

SMT Formulation of **X***:* A formula of the form **X**P is translated to an SMT constraint as below[1]:

$$\forall s, s' \in S \ : \ \forall i \in \{0, \ldots, |\Pi_\mathcal{T}| - 1\} \ : \ (s, s') \in T_i \ \Rightarrow \ P(s'). \tag{6}$$

SMT Formulation of **U***:* Inspired by *bounded synthesis* [8], for each formula of the form P **U** Q, we define an uninterpreted function $\gamma_i : S \mapsto \mathbb{N}$ and add the following constraints to the SMT instance:

$$\forall s, s' \in S \ : \forall i \in \{0, \ldots, |\Pi_\mathcal{T}| - 1\} \ : \ \neg Q(s) \ \wedge \ (s, s') \in T_i \ \Rightarrow$$
$$(P(s) \ \wedge \ \gamma_i(s') > \gamma_i(s)) \tag{7}$$

$$\forall s \in S \ : \ \neg Q(s) \ \Rightarrow \ \exists i \in \{0, \ldots, |\Pi_\mathcal{T}| - 1\} \ : \ \exists s' \in S \ : \ (s, s') \in T_i \tag{8}$$

---

[1] Note that for a formula P, $P(s)$ is acquired the by replacing each variable v with $v(s)$.

The intuition behind Constraints 7 and 8 can be understood easily. If we can assign a natural number to each state, such that along each outgoing transition from a state in $\neg Q$, the number is strictly increasing, then the path from each state in $\neg Q$ should finally reach Q or get stuck in a state, since the size of state space is finite. Also, there cannot be any loops whose states are all in $\neg Q$, as imposed by the annotation function. Finally, Constraint 8 ensures that there is no deadlock state in $\neg Q$ states.

5.3.2 Synthesis of Self-Stabilizing Systems

In this section, we present the constraints specific to Problem Statement 1.

Closure (CL): The formulation of the closure constraint in our SMT instance is as follows:

$$\forall s, s' \in S \ : \ \forall i \in \{0 \cdots |\Pi_T| - 1\} \ : \ (LS(s) \wedge (s, s') \in T_i) \ \Rightarrow \ LS(s'). \quad (9)$$

Strong Convergence (SC): Similar to the constraints presented in Sect. 5.3.1, our SMT formulation for *SC* is an adaptation of the concept of *bounded synthesis* [8]. The two following constraints ensure strong self-stabilization in the resulting model:

$$\forall s, s' \in S : \forall i \in \{0 \cdots |\Pi_T| - 1\} : \neg LS(s) \wedge (s, s') \in T_i \Rightarrow \gamma(s') > \gamma(s) \quad (10)$$

$$\forall s \in S \ : \ \neg LS(s) \ \Rightarrow \ \exists i \in \{0 \cdots |\Pi_T| - 1\} \ : \ \exists s' \in S \ : \ (s, s') \in T_i. \quad (11)$$

General Constraints on Uninterpreted Predicates: As mentioned in Sect. 4, one of the inputs to our problem is an LTL formulas, φ describing the role of uninterpreted predicates. Considering φ_{SMT} to be the SMT formulation of φ, we add the following SMT constraint to the SMT instance:

$$\forall s \in S \ : \ \varphi_{SMT}. \quad (12)$$

Constraints on LS: Another input to our problem is the LTL formula, ψ that includes requirements, which should hold in the set of legitimate states. We formulate this formula as SMT constraints using the method discussed in Sect. 5.3.1. Considering ψ_{SMT} to be the SMT formulation of the ψ formula, we add the following SMT constraint to the SMT instance:

$$\forall s \in S \ : \ LS(s) \ \Rightarrow \ \psi_{SMT}. \quad (13)$$

Example. Continuing with Example 3.1, we add the following constraints to encode $\varphi_{\mathbf{TR}}$:

$$\forall s \in S \ : \ \forall i \in \{0 \cdots n - 1\} \ : \ tk_i(s) \iff (\forall j \in \{0 \cdots n - 1\} \ : \ j \neq i \Rightarrow \\ \nexists s' \in S \ : \ (s, s') \in T_j)$$

Note that the asynchronous constraint does not allow change of x_i for T_j, where $j \neq i$. The other requirements of the token ring problem are $\psi_{\mathbf{safety}}$ and $\psi_{\mathbf{fairness}}$, which should hold in the set of legitimate states. To guarantee them, the following SMT constraints are added to the SMT instance:

$$\forall s \in S : LS(s) \Rightarrow (\exists i \in \{0 \cdots n-1\} : (tk_i(s) \wedge \forall j \neq i : \neg tk_j(s)))$$
$$\forall s \in S : LS(s) \Rightarrow \forall i \in \{0 \cdots n-1\} : (tk_i(s) \wedge (s,s') \in T_i) \Rightarrow tk_{(i+1 \bmod n)}(s').$$

5.3.3   Synthesis of Ideal-Stabilizing Systems

We now present the constraints specific to Problem Statement 2. The only such constraints is related to the two LTL formulas φ and ψ. To this end, we add the following to our SMT instance:

$$\forall s \in S : \varphi_{SMT} \wedge \psi_{SMT}. \tag{14}$$

Example. We just present $\psi_{\mathbf{LME}}$ for Example 3.2, as $\varphi_{\mathbf{LME}}$ is similar to Example 3.1:

$$\forall s \in S : (\exists i \in \{0 \cdots n-1\} : (tk_i(s) \wedge \forall j \neq i : \neg tk_j(s)))$$

$$\forall s, s' \in S : \forall i, j \in \{0, \ldots, |\Pi_T| - 1\} : \neg tk_i(s) \wedge (s,s') \in T_j \implies \gamma_i(s') > \gamma_i(s)$$

$$\forall s \in S : \forall i \in \{0, \ldots, |\Pi_T| - 1\} : \neg tk_i(s) \implies \exists j \in \{0, \ldots, |\Pi_T| - 1\} :$$
$$\exists s' \in S : (s,s') \in T_j$$

Note that adding a set of constraints to an SMT instance is equivalent to adding their conjunction.

6   Case Studies and Experimental Results

We used the Alloy [10] model finder tool for our experiments. Alloy performs the relational reasoning over quantifiers, which means that we did not have to unroll quantifiers over their domains. The results presented in this section are based on experiments on a machine with Intel Core i5 2.6 GHz processor with 8GB of RAM. We report our results in both cases of success and failure for finding a solution. Failure is normally due to the impossibility of self- or ideal-stabilization for certain problems.

6.1   Case Studies for Synthesis of Self-Stabilizing Systems

6.1.1   Self-stabilizing Token Ring

Synthesizing a self-stabilizing system for Example 3.1 leads to automatically obtaining Dijkstra [4] *three-state* algorithm in a bi-directional ring. Each process π_i maintains a variable x_i with domain $\{0, 1, 2\}$. The read-set of a process is its own and its neighbors' variables, and its write-set contains its own variable. For example, in case of three processes for π_1, $R_T(1) = \{x_0, x_1, x_2\}$ and

$W_T(1) = \{x_1\}$. Token possession and mutual exclusion constraints follow Example 3.1. Table 1 presents our results for different input settings. In the symmetric cases, we synthesized protocols with symmetric middle (not top nor bottom) processes. We present one of the solutions we found for the token ring problem in ring of three processes[2]. First, we present the interpretation functions for the uninterpreted local predicates.

$$tk_0 \Leftrightarrow x_0 = x_2, \quad tk_1 \Leftrightarrow x_1 \neq x_0, \quad tk_2 \Leftrightarrow x_2 \neq x_1$$

Next, we present the synthesized transition relations for each process:

$$
\begin{aligned}
\pi_0 : & \qquad (x_0 = x_2) & \rightarrow & \quad x_0 := (x_0 + 1) \bmod 3 \\
\pi_1 : & \qquad (x_1 \neq x_0) & \rightarrow & \quad x_1 := x_0 \\
\pi_1 : & \qquad (x_2 \neq x_1) & \rightarrow & \quad x_2 := x_1
\end{aligned}
$$

Note that our synthesized solution is similar to Dijkstra's k-state solution.

Table 1. Results for synthesizing Dijkstra's three-state token ring.

# of processes	Self-stabilization	Timing model	Symmetry	Time (s)
3	Strong	Asynchronous	Asymmetric	4.21
3	Weak	Asynchronous	Asymmetric	1.91
4	Strong	Asynchronous	Asymmetric	71.19
4	Weak	Asynchronous	Asymmetric	73.55
4	Strong	Asynchronous	Symmetric	178.6

6.1.2   Mutual Exclusion in a Tree

In the second case study, the processes form a directed rooted tree, and the goal is to design a self-stabilizing protocol, where at each state of LS, one and only one process is enabled. In this topology, each process π_j has a variable h_j with domain $\{i \mid \pi_i \text{ is a neighbor of } \pi_j\} \cup \{j\}$. If $h_j = j$, then π_j has the token. Otherwise, h_j contains the process id of one of the process's neighbors. The holder variable forms a directed path from any process in the tree to the process currently holding the token. The problem specification is the following:

Safety. We assume each process π_i is associated with an uninterpreted local predicate tk_i, which shows whether π_i is enabled. Thus, mutual exclusion is the following formula:

$$\psi_{\text{safety}} = \exists i \in \{0 \cdots n - 1\} : (tk_i \wedge \forall j \neq i : \neg tk_j).$$

Fairness. Each process π_i is eventually enabled:

$$\psi_{\text{fairness}} = \forall i \in \{0 \cdots n - 1\} : (\mathbf{F} \, tk_i).$$

Table 2. Results for synthesizing mutual exclusion on a tree (Raymond's algorithm).

# of processes	Self-stabilization	Timing model	Time (s)
3	Strong	Synchronous	0.84
4	Strong	Synchronous	16.07
4	Weak	Synchronous	26.8

The formula, $\psi_\mathbf{R}$ given as input is $\psi_\mathbf{R} = \psi_\mathsf{safety} \wedge \psi_\mathsf{fairness}$

Using the above specification, we synthesized a synchronous self-stabilizing systems, which resembles Raymond's mutual exclusion algorithm on a tree [16]. Table 2 shows the experimental results. We present one of our solutions for token circulation on a tree, where there is a root with two leaves. The interpretation functions for the uninterpreted local predicates are as follows:

$$\forall i \;:\; tk_i \Leftrightarrow h_i = i$$

Another part of the solution is the transition relation. Assume π_0 to be the root process, and π_1 and π_2 to be the two leaves of the tree. Hence, the variable domains are $D_{h_0} = \{0, 1, 2\}$, $D_{h_1} = \{0, 1\}$, and $D_{h_2} = \{0, 2\}$. Figure 1 shows the transition relation over states of the form (h_0, h_1, h_2) as well as pictorial representation of the tree and token, where the states in LS are shaded.

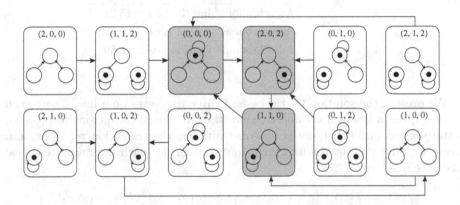

Fig. 1. Self-stabilizing mutual exclusion in a tree of size 3 (Raymond's algorithm).

6.2 Case Studies for Synthesis of Ideal-Stabilizing Systems

6.2.1 Leader Election

In leader election, a set of processes choose a leader among themselves. Normally, each process has a subset of states in which it is distinguished as the leader. In

---

[2] We manually simplified the output of Alloy for presentation, although this task can be also automated.

a legitimate state, exactly one process is in its leader state subset, whereas the states of all other processes are outside the corresponding subset.

We consider line and tree topologies. Each process has a variable c_i and we consider domains of size two and three to study the existence of an ideal-stabilizing leader election protocol. To synthesize such a protocol, we associate an uninterpreted local predicate l_i for each process π_i, whose value shows whether or not the process is in its leader state. Based on the required specification, in each state of the system, there is one and only one process π_i, for which $l_i = true$:

$$\psi_{\mathbf{safety}} = \exists i \in \{0 \cdots n - 1\} : (l_i \wedge \forall j \neq i : \neg l_j)$$

The results for this case study are presented in Table 3. In the topology column, the structure of the processes along with the domain of variables is reported. In the case of 4 processes on a line topology and tree/2-state, no solution is found. The time we report in the table for these cases are the time needed to report unsatisfiability by Alloy.

Table 3. Results for ideal stabilizing leader election.

# of processes	Timing model	Topology	Time (s)
3	Asynchronous	line/2-state	0.034
4	Asynchronous	line/2-state	0.73
4	Asynchronous	line/3-state	115.21
4	Asynchronous	tree/2-state	0.63
4	Asynchronous	tree/3-state	12.39

We present the solution for the case of three processes on a line, where each process π_i has a Boolean variable c_i. Since the only specification for this problem is state-based (safety), there is no constraint on the transition relations, and hence, we only present the interpretation function for each uninterpreted local predicate l_i.

$$l_0 = (c_0 \wedge \neg c_1) \quad l_1 = (\neg c_0 \wedge \neg c_1) \vee (c_1 \wedge \neg c_2) \quad l_2 = (c_1 \wedge c_2).$$

6.2.2 Local Mutual Exclusion

Our next case study is local mutual exclusion, as discussed in Example 3.2. We consider a line topology in which each process π_i has a Boolean variable c_i. The results for this case study are presented in Table 4.

The solution we present for the local mutual exclusion problem corresponds to the case of four processes on a ring. Note that for each process π_i, when tk_i is true, the transition T_i changes the value of c_i. Hence, having the interpretation functions of tk_i, the definition of transitions T_i are determined as well. Below,

Table 4. Results for synthesizing ideal stabilizing local mutual exclusion.

# of Processes	Timing model	Symmetry	Time (s)
3	Asynchronous	Asymmetric	0.75
4	Asynchronous	Asymmetric	24.44

we present the interpretation functions of the uninterpreted local predicates tk_i.

$$tk_0 = (c_0 \wedge c_1) \vee (\neg c_0 \wedge \neg c_1)$$
$$tk_1 = (\neg c_0 \wedge c_1 \wedge c_2) \vee (c_0 \wedge \neg c_1 \wedge \neg c_2)$$
$$tk_2 = (\neg c_1 \wedge c_2 \wedge \neg c_3) \vee (c_1 \wedge \neg c_2 \wedge c_3)$$
$$tk_3 = (c_2 \wedge c_3) \vee (\neg c_2 \wedge \neg c_3).$$

7   Related Work

Bounded Synthesis. In bounded synthesis [8], given is a set of LTL properties, a system architecture, and a set of bounds on the size of process implementations and their composition. The goal is to synthesize an implementation for each process, such that their composition satisfies the given specification. The properties are translated to a universal co-Büchi automaton, and then a set of SMT constraints are derived from the automaton. Our work is inspired by this idea for finding the SMT constraints for strong convergence and also the specification of legitimate states. For other constraints, such as the ones for synthesis of weak convergence, asynchronous and symmetric systems, we used a different approach from bounded synthesis. The other difference is that the main idea in bounded synthesis is to put a bound on the number of states in the resulting state-transition systems, and then increase the bound if a solution is not found. In our work, since the purpose is to synthesize a self-stabilizing system, the bound is the number of all possible states, derived from the given topology.

Synthesis of Self-Stabilizing Systems. In [12], the authors show that adding strong convergence is NP-complete in the size of the state space, which itself is exponential in the size of variables of the protocol. Ebnenasir and Farahat [6] also proposed an automated method to synthesize self-stabilizing algorithms. Our work is different in that the method in [6] is not complete for strong self-stabilization. This means that if it cannot find a solution, it does not necessarily imply that there does not exist one. However, in our method, if the SMT-solver declares "unsatisfiability", it means that no self-stabilizing algorithm that satisfies the given input constraints exists. A complete synthesis technique for self-stabilizing systems is introduced in [13]. The limitations of this work compared to ours is: (1) Unlike the approach in [13], we do not need the explicit description of the set of legitimate states, and (2) The method in [13] needs the set of actions on the underlying variables in the legitimate states. We also emphasize that although our experimental results deal with small numbers of processes, our approach can give key insights to designers of self-stabilizing protocols to generalize the protocol for any number of processes [11].

Automated Addition of Fault-Tolerance. The proposed algorithm in [2] synthesizes a fault-tolerant distributed algorithm from its fault-intolerant version. The distinction of our work with this study is (1) we emphasize on self-stabilizing systems, where any system state could be reachable due to the occurrence of any possible fault, (2) the input to our problem is just a system topology, and not a fault-intolerant system, and (3), the proposed algorithm in [2] is not complete.

8 Conclusion

In this paper, we proposed an automated SMT-based technique for synthesizing self- and ideal-stabilizing algorithms. In both cases, we assume that only a high-level specification of the algorithm is given in the linear temporal logic (LTL). In the particular case of self-stabilization, this means that the detailed description of the set of legitimate states is not required. This relaxation is significantly beneficial, as developing a detailed predicate for legitimate states can be a tedious task. Our approach is sound and complete for finite-state systems; i.e., it ensures correctness by construction and if it cannot find a solution, we are guaranteed that there does not exist one. We demonstrated the effectiveness of our approach by automatically synthesizing Dijkstra's token ring, Raymond's mutual exclusion, and ideal-stabilizing leader election and local mutual exclusion algorithms.

For future, we plan to work on synthesis of probabilistic self-stabilizing systems. Another challenging research direction is to devise synthesis methods where the number of distributed processes is parameterized as well as cases where the size of state space of processes is infinite. We note that parameterized synthesis of distributed systems, when there is a cut-off point is studied in [11]. Our goal is to study parameterized synthesis for self-stabilizing systems, and we plan to propose a general method that works not just for cases with cut-off points. We would also like to investigate the application of techniques such as counter-example guided inductive synthesis to improve the scalability of the synthesis process.

Acknowledgments. This research was supported in part by Canada NSERC Discovery Grant 418396-2012 and NSERC Strategic Grant 430575-2012.

References

1. Abujarad, F., Kulkarni, S.S.: Multicore constraint-based automated stabilization. In: Guerraoui, R., Petit, F. (eds.) SSS 2009. LNCS, vol. 5873, pp. 47–61. Springer, Heidelberg (2009)

2. Bonakdarpour, B., Kulkarni, S.S., Abujarad, F.: Symbolic synthesis of masking fault-tolerant programs. Springer J. Distrib. Comput. **25**(1), 83–108 (2012)
3. Demirbas, M., Arora, A.: Specification-based design of self-stabilization. IEEE Trans. Parallel Distrib. Syst. **27**(1), 263–270 (2016)
4. Dijkstra, E.W.: Self-stabilizing systems in spite of distributed control. Commun. ACM **17**(11), 643–644 (1974)
5. Dijkstra, E.W.: A belated proof of self-stabilization. Distrib. Comput. **1**(1), 5–6 (1986)
6. Ebnenasir, A., Farahat, A.: A lightweight method for automated design of convergence. In: International Parallel and Distributed Processing Symposium (IPDPS), pp. 219–230 (2011)
7. Faghih, F., Bonakdarpour, B.: SMT-based synthesis of distributed self-stabilizing systems. ACM Trans. Auton. Adapt. Syst. (TAAS) **10**(3), 21 (2015)
8. Finkbeiner, B., Schewe, S.: Bounded synthesis. Int. J. Softw. Tools Technol. Transfer (STTT) **15**(5–6), 519–539 (2013)
9. Gouda, M.G.: The theory of weak stabilization. In: Datta, A.K., Herman, T. (eds.) WSS 2001. LNCS, vol. 2194, pp. 114–123. Springer, Heidelberg (2001)
10. Jackson, D.: Software Abstractions: Logic, Language, and Analysis. MIT Press, Cambridge (2012)
11. Jacobs, S., Bloem, R.: Parameterized synthesis. Logical Meth. Comput. Sci. **10**(1), 1–29 (2014)
12. Klinkhamer, A., Ebnenasir, A.: On the complexity of adding convergence. In: Arbab, F., Sirjani, M. (eds.) FSEN 2013. LNCS, vol. 8161, pp. 17–33. Springer, Heidelberg (2013)
13. Klinkhamer, A., Ebnenasir, A.: Synthesizing self-stabilization through superposition and backtracking. In: Felber, P., Garg, V. (eds.) SSS 2014. LNCS, vol. 8756, pp. 252–267. Springer, Heidelberg (2014)
14. Nesterenko, M., Tixeuil, S.: Ideal stabilisation. IJGUC **4**(4), 219–230 (2013)
15. Pnueli, A.: The temporal logic of programs. In: Symposium on Foundations of Computer Science (FOCS), pp. 46–57 (1977)
16. Raymond, K.: A tree-based algorithm for distributed mutual exclusion. ACM Trans. Comput. Syst. **7**(1), 61–77 (1989)

Branching Bisimulation Games

David de Frutos Escrig[1], Jeroen J.A. Keiren[2,3], and Tim A.C. Willemse[4(✉)]

[1] Dpto. Sistemas Informáticos y Computación - Facultad CC. Matemáticas,
Universidad Complutense de Madrid, Madrid, Spain
defrutos@sip.ucm.es
[2] Open University in the Netherlands, Heerlen, The Netherlands
Jeroen.Keiren@ou.nl
[3] Radboud University, Nijmegen, The Netherlands
[4] Eindhoven University of Technology, Eindhoven, The Netherlands
t.a.c.willemse@tue.nl

Abstract. Branching bisimilarity and branching bisimilarity with explicit divergences are typically used in process algebras with silent steps when relating implementations to specifications. When an implementation fails to conform to its specification, *i.e.*, when both are not related by branching bisimilarity [with explicit divergence], pinpointing the root causes can be challenging. In this paper, we provide characterisations of branching bisimilarity [with explicit divergence] as games between SPOILER and DUPLICATOR, offering an operational understanding of both relations. Moreover, we show how such games can be used to assist in diagnosing non-conformance between implementation and specification.

1 Introduction

Abstraction is a powerful, fundamental concept in process theories. It facilitates reasoning about the conformance between implementations and specifications of a (software) system, described by a transition system. Essentially, it allows one to ignore (*i.e.*, abstract from) implementation details that are unimportant from the viewpoint of the specification. While there is a wealth of behavioural equivalences (and preorders), each treating abstraction in slightly different manners, there are a few prototypical equivalences that have been incorporated in contemporary tool sets that implement verification technology for (dis)proving the correctness of software systems. These equivalences include branching bisimulation [19] and branching bisimulation with explicit divergence [18], which are both used in tool sets such as CADP [5], μCRL [2], and mCRL2 [4].

From a practical perspective, branching bisimulation and branching bisimulation with explicit divergence have pleasant properties. For instance, both relations are essentially *compositional*, permitting one to stepwise replace subcomponents in a specification with their implementations. Moreover, both types of branching bisimulation can be computed efficiently in $\mathcal{O}(n \cdot m)$, where n is the number of states in a transition system and m is the number of transitions [8]. A recently published algorithm improves this to $\mathcal{O}(m \log n)$ [9].

© IFIP International Federation for Information Processing 2016
E. Albert and I. Lanese (Eds.): FORTE 2016, LNCS 9688, pp. 142–157, 2016.
DOI: 10.1007/978-3-319-39570-8_10

The key idea behind both kinds of branching bisimulation is that they abstract from 'internal' events (events that are *invisible* to the outside observer of a system) while, at the same time, they remain sensitive to the branching structure of the transition system. This means that these relations preserve both the essential, externally visible, computations and the potential future computations of all states. At the same time, this can make it difficult to explain why a particular pair of states is not branching bisimilar, as one must somehow capture the loss of potential future computations in the presence of internal actions. While (theoretical) tools such as distinguishing formulae can help to understand why two states are distinguishable, these are not very accessible and, to date, the idea of integrating such formulae in tool sets seems not to have caught on.

We address the above concern by providing game-based views on branching bisimulation and branching bisimulation with explicit divergence. More specifically, we show that both branching bisimulation and branching bisimulation with explicit divergence can be characterised by Ehrenfeucht-Fraïssé games [17]. This provides an alternative point of view on the traditional coinductive definitions of branching bisimulation and branching bisimulation with explicit divergence. Moreover, we argue, using some examples, how such games can be used to give an operational explanation of the inequivalence of states following the ideas in [15], thereby remaining closer to the realm of transition systems.

Related Work. Providing explanations of the inequivalence of states for a given equivalence relation has a long tradition, going back to at least Hennessy and Milner's seminal 1980 work [10] on the use of modal logics for characterising behavioural equivalences. Modal characterisations (and by extension, distinguishing formulae) for branching bisimulation appeared first in [11] and for branching bisimulation with explicit divergence in [18]. An alternative line of research has led to game-based characterisations of behavioural equivalences. For instance, in [16], Stirling provides a game-based definition of Milner and Park's strong bisimulation [13]. More recently, Yin *et al.* describe a branching bisimulation game in the context of normed process algebra [20], but their game uses moves that consist of sequences of silent steps, rather than single steps. As argued convincingly by Namjoshi [12], local reasoning using single steps often leads to simpler arguments. A game-based characterisation of divergence-blind stuttering bisimulation (a relation for Kripke structures that in essence is the same as branching bisimulation), provided by Bulychev *et al.* in [3] comes closer to our work for branching bisimulation. However, their game-based definition is sound only for transition systems that are essentially free of divergences, so that in order to deal with transition systems containing divergences they need an additional step that precomputes and eliminates these divergences. Such a preprocessing step is a bit artificial, and makes it hard to present the user with proper diagnostics. As far as we are aware, ours is the first work that tightly integrates dealing with divergences in a game-based characterisation of a behavioural equivalence.

Structure of the Paper. Section 2 introduces the necessary preliminaries. In Sect. 3, we present our game-based definitions of branching bisimulation and branching bisimulation with explicit divergence and prove these coincide with their traditional, coinductive definitions. We illustrate their application in Sect. 4, while Sect. 5 shows how our results can be easily extended to the case of branching simulation. We conclude in Sect. 6.

2   Preliminaries

In this paper we are concerned with relations on labelled transition systems that include both *observable* transitions, and *internal* transitions labelled by the special action τ.

Definition 1. *A* Labelled Transition System *(LTS) is a structure* $L = \langle S, A, \rightarrow \rangle$ *where:*

- *S is a set of states,*
- *A is a set of actions containing a special action τ,*
- *$\rightarrow \subseteq S \times A \times S$ is the transition relation.*

As usual, we write $s \xrightarrow{a} t$ to stand for $(s, a, t) \in \rightarrow$. The reflexive-transitive closure of the $\xrightarrow{\tau}$ relation is denoted by $\twoheadrightarrow$. Given a relation $R \subseteq S \times S$ on states, we simply write $s \, R \, t$ to represent $(s, t) \in R$. We say that s is a *divergent* state if there is an infinite sequence $s \xrightarrow{\tau} s_1 \xrightarrow{\tau} s_2 \cdots$.

Branching bisimulation was introduced by van Glabbeek and Weijland in [19].

Definition 2 ([19]). *A symmetric relation $R \subseteq S \times S$ is said to be a* branching bisimulation *whenever for all $s \, R \, t$, if $s \xrightarrow{a} s'$, then there exist states t', t'' such that $t \twoheadrightarrow t''$, with $s \, R \, t''$ and $s' \, R \, t'$; and either $t'' \xrightarrow{a} t'$, or both $a = \tau$ and $t' = t''$. We write $s \leftrightarrow_b t$ and say that s and t are* branching bisimilar, *iff there is a branching bisimulation R such that $s \, R \, t$. Typically we simply write $\leftrightarrow_b$ to denote branching bisimilarity.*

Van Glabbeek *et al.* investigated branching bisimulations with explicit divergence in [18]. We here use one of their (many) equivalent characterisations:

Definition 3 ([18, Condition D2]). *A symmetric relation $R \subseteq S \times S$ is called a* branching bisimulation with explicit divergence *if and only if R is a branching bisimulation and for all $s \, R \, t$, if there is an infinite sequence $s \xrightarrow{\tau} s_1 \xrightarrow{\tau} s_2 \cdots$, then there is a state t' such that $t \xrightarrow{\tau} t'$ and for some k, $s_k \, R \, t'$. We write $s \leftrightarrow_b^{ed} t$ iff there is a branching bisimulation with explicit divergence R such that $s \, R \, t$.*

Both kinds of branching bisimulations are equivalence relations.

Theorem 1 ([1,18]). *Both $\leftrightarrow_b$ and $\leftrightarrow_b^{ed}$ are equivalence relations. Moreover they are the largest branching bisimulation and branching bisimulation with explicit divergence, respectively.*

Both branching bisimulation relations and branching bisimulation with explicit divergence relations have the *stuttering property* [18, Corollary 4.4]. This will be useful in several of the proofs in this paper.

Definition 4 ([18]). *A relation R has the* stuttering property *if, whenever $t_0 \xrightarrow{\tau} t_1 \cdots \xrightarrow{\tau} t_k$ with $s \, R \, t_0$ and $s \, R \, t_k$, then $s \, R \, t_i$, for all $i \leq k$.*

3 Branching Bisimulation Games

The games we consider in this section are instances of two-player infinite-duration games with ω-regular winning conditions, played on game arenas that can be represented by graphs. In these games each vertex is assigned to one of two players, here called SPOILER and DUPLICATOR. The players move a token over the vertices as follows. The player that 'owns' the vertex where the token is pushes it to an adjacent vertex, and this continues as long as possible, possibly forever. The winner of the play is decided from the resulting sequence of vertices visited by the token, depending on the predetermined winning criterion. We say that a player *can win from a given vertex* if she has a strategy such that any play with the token initially at that vertex will be won by her. The games that we consider here are *memoryless* and *determined*: every vertex is won by (exactly) one player, and the winning player has a *positional* winning strategy, so that she can decide her winning moves based only on the vertex where the token currently resides, without inspecting the previous moves of the play. These winning strategies can be efficiently computed while solving the game. We refer to [7] for a more in-depth treatment of the underlying theory.

3.1 The Branching Bisimulation Games

We start by presenting our game-based characterisation of branching bisimilarity. This will be extended to capture branching bisimulation with explicit divergence in Sect. 3.2.

Definition 5. *A* branching bisimulation (bb) game *on an LTS L is played by players* SPOILER *and* DUPLICATOR *on an arena of* SPOILER-*owned configurations* $[(s,t),c,r]$ *and* DUPLICATOR-*owned configurations* $\langle(s,t),c,r\rangle$, *where* $((s,t),c,r) \in$ *Position* $\times$ *Challenge* $\times$ *Reward. Here Position* $= S \times S$ *is the set of* positions, *Challenge* $= (A \times S) \cup \{\dagger\}$ *is the set of* pending challenges, *and* Reward $= \{*, \checkmark\}$ *the set of* rewards. *By convention, we write* $((s,t),c,r)$ *if we do not care about the owner of the configuration.*

- SPOILER *moves from a configuration* $[(s_0,s_1),c,r]$ *by:*
  1. *selecting* $s_0 \xrightarrow{a} s_0'$ *and moving to* $\langle(s_0,s_1),(a,s_0'),*\rangle$ *if* $c = (a,s_0')$ *or* $c = \dagger$, *and to* $\langle(s_0,s_1),(a,s_0'),\checkmark\rangle$, *otherwise; or*
  2. *picking some* $s_1 \xrightarrow{a} s_1'$ *and moving to* $\langle(s_1,s_0),(a,s_1'),\checkmark\rangle$.
- DUPLICATOR *responds from a configuration* $\langle(s_0,s_1),c,r\rangle$ *by:*
  1. *not moving if* $c = (\tau,s_0')$ *and propose configuration* $[(s_0',s_1),\dagger,\checkmark]$, *or,*
  2. *if* $c = (a,s_0')$, *moving* $s_1 \xrightarrow{a} s_1'$ *if available and continue in configuration* $[(s_0',s_1'),\dagger,\checkmark]$, *or*
  3. *if* $c \neq \dagger$, *moving* $s_1 \xrightarrow{\tau} s_1'$ *if possible and continue in configuration* $[(s_0,s_1'),c,*]$.

DUPLICATOR *wins a finite play starting in a configuration* $((s,t),c,r)$ *if* SPOILER *gets stuck, and she wins an infinite play if the play yields infinitely many* ✓ *rewards. All other plays are won by* SPOILER. *We say that a configuration is won by a player when she has a strategy that wins all plays starting in it. Full plays of the game start in a configuration* $[(s,t),†,*]$; *we say that* DUPLICATOR *wins the bb game for a position* (s,t), *if the configuration* $[(s,t),†,*]$ *is won by it; in this case, we write* $s \equiv_b t$. *Otherwise, we say that* SPOILER *wins that game.*

Note that by definition both players strictly alternate their moves along plays.

Remark 1. Our branching bisimulation game definition resembles the divergence-blind stuttering bisimulation (dbsb) game definition [3] of Bulychev *et al.* Apart from the different computational models, there are two fundamental differences: we maintain SPOILER's pending challenges and DUPLICATOR's earned rewards, whereas the dbsb game does not, *and* our winning condition for DUPLICATOR requires an infinite number of ✓ rewards on infinite plays, whereas the dbsb game only requires DUPLICATOR not to get stuck. However, both games are equivalent when played on LTSs in which there are no divergences. Instead, there are transition systems with divergent states that show that, unlike our bb game, the rules of [3] fail to capture branching bisimulation, see Example 1.

Let us explain how our game works intuitively: by keeping track of pending challenges and earned rewards, we can distinguish between DUPLICATOR 'facilitating' *progress* (when choosing her first or second option) and DUPLICATOR *procrastinating* (when choosing her third option) when facing challenges presented by SPOILER. Procrastination is penalised by a * reward, but progress is rewarded by a ✓ reward. On her account, SPOILER can either maintain a previously presented challenge, or change it if the challenge is still not totally *solved* by DUPLICATOR. In the latter case, SPOILER is penalised by rewarding DUPLICATOR with a ✓. This notion of pending challenge will be essential when extending the game so that it coincides with branching bisimulation with explicit divergence, as we will do in the next section. Omitting the concepts of pending challenges and earned rewards is what prevented extending the dbsb game to properly deal with divergent transition systems, and to (divergence sensitive) stuttering equivalence, in [3].

Before we prove that our bb game coincides with the classical co-inductive definition of branching bisimulation, we illustrate our game definition and a few of the subtleties we discussed above.

Example 1. Consider the LTS depicted in Fig. 1. Observe that s_0 and t_0 are branching bisimilar. Suppose SPOILER tries (in vain) to disprove that s_0 and t_0 are branching bisimilar and challenges DUPLICATOR by playing $s_0 \xrightarrow{a} c_1$. DUPLICATOR may respond with an infinite sequence of τ-steps, moving between t_0 and t_1, so long as SPOILER sticks to her challenge. In this way she would win the play following the rules in [3], but such *procrastinating* behaviour of DUPLICATOR is not rewarded in our game. Instead, DUPLICATOR has to eventually move to c_1, matching the challenge, if she wants to win the play.

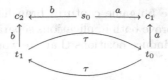

Fig. 1. LTS illustrating some consequences and subtleties of using challenges.

Now suppose SPOILER tries to disprove (again in vain) that s_0 and t_0 are branching bisimilar, and challenges DUPLICATOR by playing $t_0 \xrightarrow{\tau} t_1$. The only response for DUPLICATOR is not to move at all, which completes the pending challenge, turning it into †, thus generating the new configuration $[\,(s_0, t_1), \dagger, \checkmark\,]$. SPOILER may then challenge DUPLICATOR by playing $t_1 \xrightarrow{\tau} t_0$, and DUPLICATOR can again respond by not moving. The infinite play that is produced is winning for DUPLICATOR, even if an infinite sequence of τ-steps proving the divergence of t_0 has been matched by DUPLICATOR by staying totally idle, since DUPLICATOR got infinitely many $\checkmark$s. Of course, things will be different when divergences will be taken into account in Sect. 3.2, since t_0 is divergent, whereas s_0 is not.

Before proving our first main theorem stating that two states are branching bisimilar just whenever DUPLICATOR wins the associated game, we present two auxiliary results relating the winning configurations for this player.

Proposition 1. *Configurations $[\,(s,t), c, *\,]$ and $[\,(s,t), c, \checkmark\,]$ are both won by the same player. Likewise, configurations $\langle\,(s,t), c, *\,\rangle$ and $\langle\,(s,t), c, \checkmark\,\rangle$ are both won by the same player.*

Proof. This follows immediately from the Büchi winning condition: any player that wins some suffix of an infinite play also wins the infinite play itself. Furthermore, note that neither SPOILER nor DUPLICATOR can get stuck playing a game by changing a reward from $*$ to $\checkmark$ or *vice versa*. $\square$

Definition 6. *We say that a configuration $((s,t), c, r)$ is consistent when either $c = \dagger$, or $c = (a, s')$ for some a, s' such that $s \xrightarrow{a} s'$ in the given LTS.*

Proposition 2. *If DUPLICATOR wins a consistent configuration $[\,(s,t), c, r\,]$, then DUPLICATOR wins all consistent configurations $[\,(s,t), c', r'\,]$.*

Proof. Let $[\,(s,t), c, r\,]$ be a SPOILER-owned consistent configuration that is won by DUPLICATOR. Towards a contradiction, assume SPOILER wins some consistent configuration $[\,(s,t), c', r'\,]$. Suppose SPOILER's winning strategy involves playing to configuration $\langle\,(s,t), c'', r''\,\rangle$. Then from $[\,(s,t), c, r\,]$, SPOILER can force play to configuration $\langle\,(s,t), c'', *\,\rangle$ or $\langle\,(s,t), c'', \checkmark\,\rangle$: if $c = \dagger$, then she can simply choose challenge c'' while, if $c = (a, s')$, she can change her challenge to c''. But this leads to a contradiction: by Proposition 1, both configurations are won by SPOILER, once $\langle\,(s,t), c'', r''\,\rangle$ is won by SPOILER. So DUPLICATOR wins any SPOILER-owned consistent configuration $[\,(s,t), c', r'\,]$. $\square$

We next prove that the bb game captures branching bisimilarity. We split the proof obligations and prove both implications separately. First, we show that branching bisimilar states induce positions that are won by DUPLICATOR in the bb game.

Lemma 1. *If $s \leftrightarroweq_b t$ then $s \equiv_b t$.*

Proof. We have to design a winning strategy for DUPLICATOR for the game that starts in $[(s,t), \dagger, *]$. We will call the consistent configurations $((s',t'), c, r)$ corresponding to a position (s',t'), with $s' \leftrightarroweq_b t'$, *good* configurations (for player DUPLICATOR). Let us first see that whenever SPOILER makes a move from a good configuration $[(s',t'), c', r']$, then DUPLICATOR can reply with a move to another good configuration. We distinguish cases according to the move selected by SPOILER.

Assume SPOILER plays according to her first option and chooses a transition $s' \xrightarrow{a} s''$. We distinguish cases depending on the nature of the executed action:

1. if $a = \tau$ and $s'' \leftrightarroweq_b t'$, then DUPLICATOR can play choosing her first option getting the configuration $[(s'',t'), \dagger, \checkmark]$, which clearly is good for her.
2. if $a \neq \tau$ or $s'' \not\leftrightarroweq_b t'$, then there exist states t'_k, t'' such that $t' \twoheadrightarrow t'_k$, $s' \leftrightarroweq_b t'_k$, $s'' \leftrightarroweq_b t''$ and $t'_k \xrightarrow{a} t''$. Next we consider the length of the sequence of transitions that generates $t' \twoheadrightarrow t'_k$. If this length is zero, then DUPLICATOR can directly use her second option selecting the transition $t' \xrightarrow{a} t''$ that generates $[(s'',t''), \dagger, \checkmark]$, which is clearly good for her. If instead the sequence is not empty, then she can select the first transition $t' \xrightarrow{\tau} t'_1$ of this sequence, and applying the stuttering property we have $s' \leftrightarroweq_b t'_1$. Therefore, when DUPLICATOR moves according to her third option, this produces configuration $[(s',t'_1), (a, s''), *]$, which is also good.

If SPOILER plays her second option, then the strategy DUPLICATOR uses is the same that she would have used if SPOILER had played her first option from configuration $[(t', s'), c', r']$.

When playing in this way, DUPLICATOR will never get stuck, so that next it suffices to argue that she can select her moves as above in such a way that the generated play will contain an infinite number of $\checkmark$ rewards. It is clear that the contrary could only happen if (1) SPOILER sticks to some fixed challenge (a, s'') forever, as changing challenges is penalised with a $\checkmark$; and (2) DUPLICATOR replies generating a divergent sequence, *i.e.* choosing her third option, never earning a $\checkmark$. But DUPLICATOR can simply avoid generating such a sequence if the first time that the challenge is presented to her she selects any sequence $t' \twoheadrightarrow t'_k$ as stated above, and then she plays by executing one by one the transitions in it, finally concluding by executing $t'_k \xrightarrow{a} t''$, that will produce a new $\checkmark$, thus generating the desired play with infinitely many $\checkmark$ challenges.   □

Lemma 2. *The relation $\equiv_b$ is a branching bisimulation.*

Proof. First, observe that $\equiv_b$ is obviously symmetric, since starting from configuration $[(s,t), \dagger, *]$, SPOILER can propose exactly the same challenges as when starting from $[(t,s),\dagger,*]$, and the infinite suffixes of the resulting plays will therefore be identical, leading to the same winners.

Pick arbitrary s,t such that $s \equiv_b t$ and assume $s \xrightarrow{a} s'$. Let us see that $\equiv_b$ meets the transfer condition. Since DUPLICATOR has a winning strategy from $[(s,t),\dagger,*]$, she has a winning move when SPOILER proposes the move $s \xrightarrow{a} s'$ and configuration $\langle (s,t),(a,s'),*\rangle$. We distinguish cases based on DUPLICATOR's response in this winning strategy:

- DUPLICATOR replies according to her first option, by not making a move, producing the configuration $[(s',t),\dagger,\checkmark]$. Then we have $s' \equiv_b t$, and the transfer condition can be satisfied by choosing $t'' = t' = t$.
- DUPLICATOR replies following her second option, thus selecting $t \xrightarrow{a} t'$ to continue from the configuration $[(s',t'),\dagger,\checkmark]$. This means that $s' \equiv_b t'$, so that the transfer condition is satisfied by taking $t'' = t$, since obviously $s \equiv_b t''$ and $s' \equiv_b t'$.
- DUPLICATOR replies following her third option, thus selecting $t \xrightarrow{\tau} t'_1$ to continue from configuration $[(s,t'_1),(a,s'),*]$. This configuration is again won by DUPLICATOR, and then applying Proposition 2 we also have $s \equiv_b t'_1$. Now, SPOILER could maintain the challenge (a,s'), and then the procedure can be repeated with DUPLICATOR responding with her third move, until she can eventually play the second move, in order to get the reward that she eventually must be able to get, since she is playing a winning strategy. This final move by DUPLICATOR will correspond to a transition $t'_k \xrightarrow{a} t'$, and will produce the configuration $[(s',t'),\dagger,\checkmark]$. Moreover, we had $s \equiv_b t'_k$, so that taking $t'' = t'_k$ the transfer condition is again satisfied.

So R is a branching bisimulation relation.   □

From the above lemmata, the following theorem follows immediately.

Theorem 2. *We have* $\underline{\leftrightarrow}_b = \equiv_b$.

3.2   The Branching Bisimulation with Explicit Divergence Games

The results in the previous section demonstrate that maintaining pending challenges and earned rewards in the game play, and properly dealing with these in the winning condition, leads to an equivalence relation on states that coincides with branching bisimulation. It does not yet give rise to an equivalence that is sensitive to divergences. In fact, in Example 1 we already saw a pair of states s_0 and t_0 for which we have $s_0 \underline{\leftrightarrow}_b t_0$, and therefore $s_0 \equiv_b t_0$, while instead $s_0 \not\underline{\leftrightarrow}_b^{ed} t_0$.

As we argued in the previous section, by including challenges and rewards, our winning condition is able to reject plays in which DUPLICATOR procrastinates forever. This addresses a part of the divergence problem: DUPLICATOR cannot try to 'prove' two states equivalent modulo branching bisimulation simply by diverging when SPOILER does not ask for a divergence. However, DUPLICATOR is still capable of matching a challenge of SPOILER that consists of a divergence by *not* diverging. Capturing explicit divergences can therefore only be achieved by clearly indicating *when* DUPLICATOR replied to an internal move with another one, instead of just remaining idle. In the game definition we present below, we essentially do so by rewarding DUPLICATOR in a new way only whenever she just properly responded with a matching move. Note that the changes required are subtle: assigning rewards differently would probably lead to different relations.

Definition 7. *A branching bisimulation with explicit divergence (bbed) game on an LTS L is played by players* SPOILER *and* DUPLICATOR *on an arena of* SPOILER-*owned configurations* $[(s,t),c,r]$ *and* DUPLICATOR-*owned configurations* $\langle (s,t),c,r \rangle$, *where* $((s,t),c,r) \in$ *Position* $\times$ *Challenge* $\times$ *Reward. Here Position* $= S \times S$ *is the set of* positions, *Challenge* $= (A \times S) \cup \{\dagger\}$ *is the set of* pending challenges, *and Reward* $= \{*,\checkmark\}$ *the set of* rewards. *We again use the convention to write* $((s,t),c,r)$ *if we do not care about the owner of the configuration.*

- SPOILER *moves from a configuration* $[(s_0,s_1),c,r]$ *by:*
  1. *selecting* $s_0 \xrightarrow{a} s_0'$ *and moving to* $\langle (s_0,s_1),(a,s_0'),* \rangle$ *if* $c = (a,s_0')$ *or* $c = \dagger$, *and* $\langle (s_0,s_1),(a,s_0'),\checkmark \rangle$ *otherwise; or*
  2. *picking some* $s_1 \xrightarrow{a} s_1'$ *and moving to* $\langle (s_1,s_0),(a,s_1'),\checkmark \rangle$.
- DUPLICATOR *responds from a configuration* $\langle (s_0,s_1),c,r \rangle$ *by:*
  1. *not moving if* $c = (\tau,s_0')$ *and propose configuration* $[(s_0',s_1),\dagger,*]$, *or,*
  2. *if* $c = (a,s_0')$, *moving* $s_1 \xrightarrow{a} s_1'$ *if available and continue in configuration* $[(s_0',s_1'),\dagger,\checkmark]$, *or*
  3. *if* $c \neq \dagger$, *moving* $s_1 \xrightarrow{\tau} s_1'$ *if possible and continue in configuration* $[(s_0,s_1'),c,*]$.

DUPLICATOR *wins a finite play starting in a configuration* $((s,t),c,r)$ *if* SPOILER *gets stuck, and she wins an infinite play if the play yields infinitely many* $\checkmark$ *rewards. All other plays are won by* SPOILER. *We say that a configuration is won by a player when she has a strategy that wins all plays starting in it. Full plays of the game start in a configuration* $[(s,t),\dagger,*]$; *we say that* DUPLICATOR *wins the bbed game for a position* (s,t), *if the configuration* $[(s,t),\dagger,*]$ *is won by it; in this case, we write* $s \equiv_b^{ed} t$. *Otherwise, we say that* SPOILER *wins that game.*

In order to understand how the new game works, note first that it is a (quite subtle!) *refinement* of the bb game. To be exact, only the first option in the description of DUPLICATOR's moves is changed, simply turning the previously obtain reward $\checkmark$ into $*$, thus reducing the set of plays that are won by this player. As a consequence, any play DUPLICATOR wins in the bbed game is also won by her in the bb game. Moreover, the original bb game can be recovered from the bbed game by weakening the winning condition of the latter as follows: an infinite play is won by DUPLICATOR if the play yields infinitely many $\checkmark$ rewards or $\dagger$ challenges.

In contrast to the bb game, DUPLICATOR now only earns a $\checkmark$ reward when she fully satisfies a pending challenge (choosing her second option): she is now punished for choosing to not move (*i.e.* whenever she chooses her first option). As a result, whenever DUPLICATOR is confronted with an infinite sequence of τ-challenges produced by SPOILER, effectively creating a divergent computation, DUPLICATOR can no longer win such a play by choosing to stay put. Instead, DUPLICATOR will need to collect a ✓ mark from time to time, so that in the end she will be able to exhibit an infinite number of such marks.

Example 2. Reconsider the LTS in Fig. 1. In Example 1, we argued that SPOILER was not able to win the bb game starting in position (s_0, t_0). Now reconsider SPOILER's strategy to challenge DUPLICATOR, by playing $t_0 \xrightarrow{\tau} t_1$ in the bbed game. As before, DUPLICATOR's only option is not to move. However, by not moving, DUPLICATOR discharges SPOILER's (local) challenge, but she does not earn any ✓ reward. Clearly, SPOILER can then challenge DUPLICATOR by playing $t_1 \xrightarrow{\tau} t_0$ in the bbed game, thereby forcing DUPLICATOR to engage in an infinite play in which she earns no ✓ reward, thus losing the game.

The above example suggests that, indeed, the reconsideration of challenges and rewards leads to a game in which SPOILER can explicitly check divergences. We next prove that the relation induced by the bbed game exactly captures branching bisimilarity with explicit divergence. We split the proof obligations into three separate lemmata.

Lemma 3. *If $s \leftrightarrow_b^{ed} t$ then $s \equiv_b^{ed} t$.*

Proof. We again need to design the winning strategy for DUPLICATOR for the bbed game that starts in $[(s,t), \dagger, *]$. Since $s \leftrightarrow_b^{ed} t$ implies $s \leftrightarrow_b t$, she could use the strategy defined in the proof of Lemma 1 to win the corresponding bb game. However, if we do not change anything in this strategy, it could be the case that SPOILER now wins the bbed game, since the strategy does not take divergences into account. Let us see which changes are needed to guarantee that DUPLICATOR will also win the bbed game.

First, note that all the *positions* along any play consistent with that winning strategy for DUPLICATOR contain two $\leftrightarrow_b$ equivalent states, as we proved in Lemma 2. Second, observe that we start from a configuration $[(s,t), \dagger, *]$ containing two $\leftrightarrow_b^{ed}$ equivalent states, and in order to be able to repeat our arguments after any move of DUPLICATOR, we need to preserve that relation, and not just $\leftrightarrow_b$, as in the proof of Lemma 1.

Concerning this new requirement, note that DUPLICATOR's winning strategy designed to prove that lemma was based on $\leftrightarrow_b$, but it is easy to see that now we can base it on $\leftrightarrow_b^{ed}$, so that the new winning strategy will preserve $\leftrightarrow_b$ along the plays of that game that are consistent with that strategy.

If we apply this strategy to the bbed game, the only case in which player DUPLICATOR loses the game is that in which she is generating infinitely many $\dagger$ challenges, but only finitely many ✓ rewards. In particular, there would be some suffix of a play in which DUPLICATOR generates infinitely many $\dagger$ challenges, and earns no ✓ reward. Next we consider that suffix as a full play and make a few observations about the moves played by both players along it:

- SPOILER never plays her second move;
- DUPLICATOR never plays her second move;
- DUPLICATOR never plays her third move,

since in the first two cases, DUPLICATOR would *immediately* earn a $\checkmark$ reward, while in the third case, DUPLICATOR will, by definition of the strategy used in the proof of Lemma 1, *eventually* earn a $\checkmark$ reward after a finite sequence of τ-moves.

Since DUPLICATOR is always playing her first move, all challenges involved in the infinite suffix concern τ actions; moreover, all rewards on this suffix are $*$ rewards. Now observe that this infinite sequence of τ successors of s_0 consists of states that are all $\underleftrightarrow{}^{ed}_b$-related to the state t_0 DUPLICATOR chooses to stay put in. But then, by definition of $\underleftrightarrow{}^{ed}_b$, there must be some transition $t_0 \xrightarrow{\tau} t'$ such that for some k, $s_k \underleftrightarrow{}^{ed}_b t'$, and then DUPLICATOR can reply playing $t_0 \xrightarrow{\tau} t_1$, instead of choosing her first option, thus collecting the needed $\checkmark$ reward, and the play will continue from $[(s_k, t'), \dagger, \checkmark]$.

Then, we will change the choice selected by DUPLICATOR whenever the situation above appears, and in this way we get a revised strategy that will allow her to win the bbed game that starts in $[(s, t), \dagger, *]$, thus proving $s \equiv^{ed}_b t$.   □

Lemma 4. *The relation $\equiv^{ed}_b$ is a branching bisimulation.*

Proof. As stated above, the bbed game is a refinement of the bb game: any configuration that is won in the bbed game is also won in the bb game. Hence, we can repeat the reasoning in the proof of Lemma 2 substituting the $\checkmark$ reward by a $*$ reward whenever DUPLICATOR resorts to choosing her first option, to obtain the proof that $\equiv^{ed}_b$ is a branching bisimulation.   □

The lemma below confirms that the relation induced by a bbed game is indeed sensitive to divergences.

Lemma 5. *Let $s \equiv^{ed}_b t$, and assume that we have a divergent sequence $s = s_0 \xrightarrow{\tau} s_1 \xrightarrow{\tau} s_2 \xrightarrow{\tau} \cdots$. Then $t \xrightarrow{\tau} t'$ for some t' such that for some k, $s_k \equiv^{ed}_b t'$.*

Proof. Let us suppose that for all $t \xrightarrow{\tau} t'$, and for all k, we have $s_k \not\equiv^{ed}_b t'$. Consider SPOILER's strategy that starts the game from $[(s_0, t), \dagger, *]$ by making the move $s_0 \xrightarrow{\tau} s_1$. Then DUPLICATOR cannot reply moving to a τ-successor of t, so that she has to play choosing her first option, which produces the configuration $[(s_i, t), \dagger, *]$. Next SPOILER will play each of the moves $s_i \xrightarrow{\tau} s_{i+1}$ in a row, and in all the cases DUPLICATOR needs to stay idle, producing the configurations $[(s_i, t), \dagger, *]$, that generate an infinite play without $\checkmark$ rewards. Hence, SPOILER's strategy is winning for this bbed game, which contradicts the assumption that $s \equiv^{ed}_b t$.   □

Theorem 3. *We have $\underleftrightarrow{}^{ed}_b = \equiv^{ed}_b$.*

Proof. The inclusion $\underleftrightarrow{}^{ed}_b \subseteq \equiv^{ed}_b$ follows from Lemma 3. For the reverse, observe that $\equiv^{ed}_b$ is a branching bisimulation with explicit divergence relation, since by Lemma 4 it is a branching bisimulation, that also fulfils the added obligation concerning divergences, as proved by Lemma 5.   □

4 Some Small Applications

4.1 A Simple Application

The game-based definitions of branching bisimulation and branching bisimulation with explicit divergence provide an alternative, more dynamic view, on the standard coinductive definitions of these relations. A major benefit of any game-based characterisation of an equivalence relation is that it lends itself to explain, in a natural way, why two states in an LTS are not equivalent, when that is the case. Such an explanation is drawn directly from SPOILER's winning strategy in the branching bisimulation game. We illustrate this by showing how one can prove that an abstraction of a communication protocol over unreliable channels differs from a simple one-place buffer.

Example 3. Consider two LTSs below. The leftmost LTS models the abstraction of an implementation of a simple communication protocol for exchanging two types of messages (d_1 and d_2), using a system of acknowledgements to cater for the unreliability introduced by a lossy/corrupting channel between sending and receiving parties. The LTS depicted below on the right models a simple specification of a one-place buffer for exchanging these two types of messages.

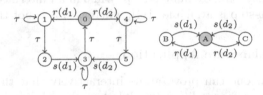

These LTSs are not branching bisimilar with explicit divergence. Since both *are* branching bisimilar, the difference between them must be in the lack of divergence in the specification. This is captured by SPOILER's winning strategy when playing the bbed game starting on $[(A,0), \dagger, *]$, SPOILER can play against the designer of the implementation in a way similar to that in [15], allowing the designer to better understand the mistake. Such a play could proceed as is shown below:

```
Spoiler moves A --r(d1)--> B
You respond with 0 --r(d1)--> 1
Spoiler switches positions and moves 1 --tau--> 1
You respond by not moving
...
Spoiler moves 1 --tau--> t
You respond by not moving
You explored all options. You lose.
```

Likewise, one can check that states B and 2 are not branching bisimilar with explicit divergence.

An alternative to illustrating the inequivalence between two states is through the use of a distinguishing formula. However, in many cases the nature of these formulae is rather 'descriptive' and requires a thorough understanding of modal logics, in order to understand its meaning. Instead, the game-based approach stays closer to the operational nature of LTSs. Moreover, the distinguishing formulae can become rather unwieldy, easily spanning several lines for states that are inequivalent for non-trivial reasons. The complexity of this approach is already illustrated by the following example, taken from [11].

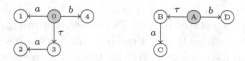

Our game-based approach to distinguishing states 0 and A (in this case also under plain branching bisimulation equivalence) would start by SPOILER challenging by moving $0 \xrightarrow{a} 1$, to which DUPLICATOR can only respond by moving $A \xrightarrow{\tau} B$. Now, continuing from $[(0, B), (a, 1), *]$ SPOILER plays her second option and challenges DUPLICATOR to mimic move $0 \xrightarrow{b} 4$, something that DUPLICATOR cannot match.

The distinguishing formula given in [11] is $\neg((tt\langle b\rangle tt)\langle a\rangle tt)$, which holds at state A, but not at state 0. It explains that states 0 and A are inequivalent because state 0 may "engage in an a-step, while in all intermediate states (state 0 in this case) a b-step is available" [11], whereas this is not true of state A.

4.2   A More Elaborate Application

We illustrate how one can prove/argue interactively that the Alternating Bit Protocol with two messages differs (modulo branching bisimulation with explicit divergence) from a simple one-place buffer.

Example 4. Reconsider the one-place buffer for exchanging two different types of messages (d_1 and d_2), as specified in Example 3. Suppose one tries to implement this one-place buffer using the Alternating Bit Protocol (see Fig. 2), only to find out that states A and 0 are not branching bisimilar with explicit divergences. In this case, SPOILER's winning strategy can be used to 'play' against the designer of the implementation in a way similar to that of [15], allowing the designer to better understand the reason why this implementation is not satisfactory. By solving the automatically generated game we obtain the following winning strategy for player SPOILER, that proceeds as follows:

```
Spoiler moves A --r(d1)--> B
You respond with 0 --r(d1)--> 1
Spoiler switches positions and moves 1 --tau--> 3
You respond by not moving
...
Spoiler moves 19 --tau--> 1
You respond by not moving
You explored all options. You lose.
```

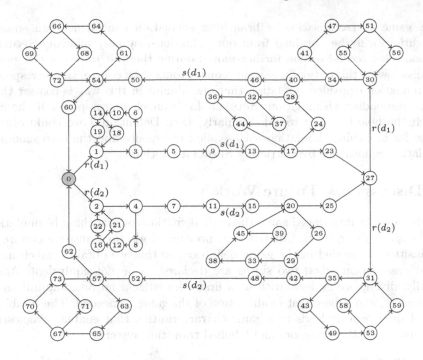

Fig. 2. The ABP with two messages; unlabelled transitions are τ transitions.

In a similar vein, one can check also that states B and 9 are not branching bisimilar with explicit divergence.

5 Branching Simulation Games

In this paper we have considered branching bisimulation [with explicit divergence]. Both relations are equivalence relations. When checking an implementation relation, sometimes it is desirable to drop this symmetry requirement, and use simulation relations, rather than bisimulation relations.

Whereas branching similarity has been studied before, see, *e.g.* [6], we are not aware of an exact simulation variant of branching bisimulation with explicit divergence, although the notion of divergence preserving branching simulation defined in [14] comes quite close.

A branching simulation game can be obtained from Definition 5 by disallowing SPOILER to choose her second option. The proof of the fact that the resulting preorder coincides with branching similarity proceeds along the same lines of that of Theorem 2. If we reconsider the example we took from [11] in Sect. 4.1, we note that state 0 is not branching simulated by state A, which can be proved following the same arguments as used in that section. Instead, state A is branching simulated by state 0, as the last can copy any move from the former, eventually arriving at states that are trivially equivalent.

A game characterisation of branching simulation equivalence can equally straightforwardly be obtained from our definitions, by only allowing SPOILER to choose her second option for her moves during the first round of the game, and disallowing this option in any subsequent rounds. Of course, the corresponding simulation equivalence relation that one obtains in this way is coarser than the corresponding bisimulation: SPOILER has a much bigger power if she can switch the board at any round. Similarly, from Definition 7 we could obtain games for branching simulation with explicit divergence and the corresponding simulation equivalence by restricting SPOILER's options.

6   Discussion & Future Work

In this paper we introduced game-theoretic definitions of branching bisimulation [with explicit divergence]. Compared to previous work, no transitive closure of τ-transitions is needed in the game definition, so that we obtain a much more "local" assessment when two states are declared to be not equivalent. Additionally, divergence is dealt with as a first-class citizen: no precomputation of divergences, and subsequent modification of the game, is needed. The combination of these aspects leads to a game characterisation that enables diagnostics that apply directly to the original labelled transition systems.

Future Work. We have experimented with a prototype of the game-theoretic definitions of branching bisimulation (also with explicit divergence); we intend to make a proper implementation available in the mCRL2 tool set [4]. We leave further evaluating the effectiveness of the counterexamples described in this paper to future work. Furthermore, it can be investigated whether our approach of dealing with internal transitions extends to other behavioural equivalences, such as weak (bi)simulation.

References

1. Basten, T.: Branching bisimilarity is an equivalence indeed!. Inform. Process. Lett. **58**(3), 141–147 (1996)
2. Blom, S., Fokkink, W.J., Groote, J.F., van Langevelde, I., Lisser, B., van de Pol, J.: mgrCRL: a toolset for analysing algebraic specifications. In: Berry, G., Comon, H., Finkel, A. (eds.) CAV 2001. LNCS, vol. 2102, pp. 250–254. Springer, Heidelberg (2001)
3. Bulychev, P.E., Konnov, I.V., Zakharov, V.A.: Computing (bi)simulation relations preserving CTL*-X for ordinary and fair Kripke structures. Inst. Syst. Program. Russ. Acad. Sci. Math. Meth. Algorithm **12**, 59–76 (2007)
4. Cranen, S., Groote, J.F., Keiren, J.J.A., Stappers, F.P.M., de Vink, E.P., Wesselink, W., Willemse, T.A.C.: An overview of the mCRL2 toolset and its recent advances. In: Piterman, N., Smolka, S.A. (eds.) TACAS 2013 (ETAPS 2013). LNCS, vol. 7795, pp. 199–213. Springer, Heidelberg (2013)
5. Garavel, H., Lang, F., Mateescu, R., Serwe, W.: CADP 2011: a toolbox for the construction and analysis of distributed processes. Int. J. Softw. Tools Technol. Transf. **15**(2), 89–107 (2013)

6. Gerth, R., Kuiper, R., Peled, D., Penczek, W.: A partial order approach to branching time logic model checking. Inform. Comput. **150**(2), 132–152 (1999)
7. Grädel, E., Thomas, W., Wilke, T. (eds.): Automata Logics, and Infinite Games. LNCS, vol. 2500. Springer, Heidelberg (2002)
8. Groote, J.F., Vaandrager, F.W.: An efficient algorithm for branching and stuttering equivalence. In: Paterson, M.S. (ed.) Automata, Languages and Programming. LNCS, vol. 443, pp. 626–638. Springer, Heidelberg (1990)
9. Groote, J.F., Wijs, A.: An O(m log n) algorithm for stuttering equivalence and branching bisimulation. In: Chechik, M., Raskin, J.-F. (eds.) TACAS 2016. LNCS, vol. 9636, pp. 607–624. Springer, Heidelberg (2016). doi:10.1007/978-3-662-49674-9_40
10. Hennessy, M., Milner, R.: On observing nondeterminism and concurrency. In: de Bakker, J., van Leeuwen, J. (eds.) Automata, Languages and Programming. LNCS, vol. 85, pp. 299–309. Springer, Heidelberg (1980)
11. Korver, H.: Computing distinguishing formulas for branching bisimulation. In: Larsen, K.G., Skou, A. (eds.) CAV 1991. LNCS, vol. 575, pp. 13–23. Springer, Heidelberg (1992)
12. Namjoshi, K.S.: A simple characterization of stuttering bisimulation. In: Ramesh, S., Sivakumar, G. (eds.) FST TCS 1997. LNCS, vol. 1346, pp. 284–296. Springer, Heidelberg (1997)
13. Park, D.: Concurrency and automata on infinite sequences. In: Deussen, P. (ed.) Theoretical Computer Science. LNCS, vol. 104, pp. 167–183. Springer, Heidelberg (1981)
14. Reniers, M.A., Schoren, R., Willemse, T.A.C.: Results on embeddings between state-based and event-based systems. Comput. J. **57**(1), 73–92 (2014)
15. Stevens, P., Stirling, C.: Practical model-checking using games. In: Steffen, B. (ed.) TACAS 1998. LNCS, vol. 1384, pp. 85–101. Springer, Heidelberg (1998)
16. Stirling, C.: Modal and temporal logics for processes. In: Moller, F., Birtwistle, G. (eds.) Structure versus Automata. LNCS, vol. 1043, pp. 149–237. Springer, Heidelberg (1996)
17. Thomas, W.: On the Ehrenfeucht-Fraïssé game in theoretical computer science. In: Gaudel, M.-C., Jouannaud, J.-P. (eds.) TAPSOFT'93: Theory and Practice of Software Development. LNCS, vol. 668, pp. 559–568. Springer, Heidelberg (1993)
18. van Glabbeek, R.J., Luttik, S.P., Trçka, N.: Branching bisimilarity with explicit divergence. Fundam. Inform. **93**(4), 371–392 (2009)
19. van Glabbeek, R.J., Weijland, W.P.: Branching time and abstraction in bisimulation semantics. J. ACM **43**(3), 555–600 (1996)
20. Yin, Q., Fu, Y., He, C., Huang, M., Tao, X.: Branching bisimilarity checking for PRS. In: Esparza, J., Fraigniaud, P., Husfeldt, T., Koutsoupias, E. (eds.) ICALP 2014, Part II. LNCS, vol. 8573, pp. 363–374. Springer, Heidelberg (2014)

A Configurable CEGAR Framework
with Interpolation-Based Refinements

Ákos Hajdu[1,2]([✉]), Tamás Tóth[2], András Vörös[1,2], and István Majzik[2]

[1] MTA-BME Lendület Cyber-Physical Systems Research Group, Budapest, Hungary
[2] Department of Measurement and Information Systems,
Budapest University of Technology and Economics, Budapest, Hungary
{hajdua,totht,vori,majzik}@mit.bme.hu

Abstract. Correctness of software components in a distributed system is a key issue to ensure overall reliability. Formal verification techniques such as model checking can show design flaws at early stages of development. Abstraction is a key technique for reducing complexity by hiding information, which is not relevant for verification. Counterexample-Guided Abstraction Refinement (CEGAR) is a verification algorithm that starts from a coarse abstraction and refines it iteratively until the proper precision is obtained. Many abstraction types and refinement strategies exist for systems with different characteristics. In this paper we show how these algorithms can be combined into a configurable CEGAR framework. In our framework we also present a new CEGAR configuration based on a combination of abstractions, being able to perform better for certain models. We demonstrate the use of the framework by comparing several configurations of the algorithms on various problems, identifying their advantages and shortcomings.

1 Introduction

As critical distributed systems, including safety-critical embedded systems and cloud applications are becoming more and more prevalent, assuring their correct operation is gaining increasing importance. Correctness of software components in a distributed system is a key issue to ensure overall reliability. Formal verification methods such as model checking can show design flaws at early stages of development. However, a typical drawback of using formal verification methods is their high computational complexity. Abstraction is a generic technique for reducing complexity by hiding information which is not relevant for verification. However, finding the proper precision of abstraction is a difficult task. Counterexample-Guided Abstraction Refinement (CEGAR) is an automatic verification algorithm that starts with a coarse abstraction and refines it iteratively until the proper precision is obtained [6]. CEGAR-based algorithms have been successfully applied for both hardware [6,8] and software [1,11] verification.

T. Tóth—Partially supported by Gedeon Richter's Talentum Foundation (Gyömrői út 19–21, 1103 Budapest, Hungary).

© IFIP International Federation for Information Processing 2016
E. Albert and I. Lanese (Eds.): FORTE 2016, LNCS 9688, pp. 158–174, 2016.
DOI: 10.1007/978-3-319-39570-8_11

CEGAR can be defined for various abstraction types including predicate [6,13] and explicit value abstraction [1,8]. There are several refinement strategies as well, many of them being based on Craig [17] or sequence [19] interpolation.

In our paper we describe a configurable CEGAR framework that is able to incorporate both predicate abstraction and explicit value abstraction, along with Craig and sequence interpolation-based refinements. We use this framework to extend predicate abstraction with explicit values at the initial abstraction, producing better results for certain models. We also implemented a prototype of the algorithms and techniques in order to evaluate their performance. In our framework we compare different CEGAR configurations on various (software and hardware) models and identify their advantages and shortcomings.

The rest of the paper is organized as follows. Section 2 introduces the preliminaries of our work. Section 3 presents related work in the field of CEGAR-based model checking. Section 4 describes our framework with our new extension. Section 5 evaluates the algorithms and finally, Sect. 6 concludes our work.

2   Background

This section introduces the preliminaries of our work. First, we present symbolic transition systems as the formalism used in our work (Sect. 2.1). Then we describe the model checking problem (Sect. 2.2) and we also introduce interpolation (Sect. 2.3), a mathematical tool widely used in verification.

2.1   Symbolic Transition Systems

In our work we describe models using *symbolic transition systems*, which offer a compact way of representing the set of *states*, *transitions* and *initial states* using first order logic (FOL) variables and formulas. Given a set of variables $V = \{v_1, v_2, \ldots, v_n\}$, let V' and V_i represent the primed and indexed version of the variables, i.e., $V' = \{v_1', v_2', \ldots, v_n'\}$ and $V_i = \{v_{1,i}, v_{2,i}, \ldots, v_{n,i}\}$. Given a formula φ over V, let φ' and φ_i denote the formulas obtained by replacing V with V' and V_i in φ respectively, e.g., if $\varphi = x < y$ then $\varphi' = x' < y'$ and $\varphi_2 = x_2 < y_2$. Given a formula φ over $V \cup V'$, let $\varphi_{i,j}$ denote the formula obtained by replacing V with V_i and V' with V_j in φ, e.g., if $\varphi = x' \doteq x + 1$ then $\varphi_{3,5} = x_5 \doteq x_3 + 1$. Given a formula φ let $\mathsf{var}(\varphi)$ denote the set of variables appearing in φ, e.g., $\mathsf{var}(x < y + 1) = \{x, y\}$.

Definition 1 (Symbolic Transition System). *A symbolic transition system is a tuple $T = (V, Inv, Tran, Init)$, where*

- *$V = \{v_1, v_2, \ldots, v_n\}$ is the set of variables with domains $D_{v_1}, D_{v_2}, \ldots, D_{v_n}$,*
- *Inv is the invariant formula over V, which must hold for every state,[1]*

---

[1] The invariant formula should not be confused with an invariant property, which is checked whether it holds for every reachable state. The invariant formula only restricts the possible set of states regardless of reachability. For example, an integer variable x with range $[2; 5]$ can be defined with domain $\mathbb{Z}$ and invariant $2 \leq x \land x \leq 5$.

– *Tran* is the transition formula over $V \cup V'$, which describes the transition relation between the actual state (V) and the successor state (V'),
– *Init* is the initial formula over V, which defines the set of initial states.

A *concrete state* s is a (many sorted) interpretation that assigns a value $s(v_i) = d_i \in D_{v_i}$ to each variable $v_i \in V$ of its domain D_{v_i}. A state can also be regarded as a tuple of values $(d_1, d_2, \ldots, d_n)$. A state with a prime (s') or an index (s_i) assigns values to V' or V_i respectively. The set of concrete states S, concrete transitions R and concrete initial states S_0 (i.e., the *state space*) of a symbolic transition system are defined in the following way.

– $S = \{s \mid s \models Inv\}$, i.e., S contains all possible interpretations that satisfy the invariant.
– $R = \{(s, s') \mid (s, s') \models Inv \wedge Tran \wedge Inv'\}$, i.e., s' is a successor of s if assigning s to the non-primed variables and s' to the primed variables of the transition formula evaluates to true.
– $S_0 = \{s \mid s \models Inv \wedge Init\}$, i.e., S_0 is the subset of S for which the initial formula holds.

A *concrete path* is a (finite, loop-free) sequence of concrete states $\pi = (s_1, s_2, \ldots, s_n)$ for which $(s_1, s_2, \ldots, s_n) \models Init_1 \wedge \bigwedge_{1 \leq i \leq n} Inv_i \wedge \bigwedge_{1 \leq i < n} Tran_{i,i+1}$ holds. In other words, the first state is initial, all states satisfy the invariant and successor states satisfy the transition formula. A concrete state s is *reachable* if a path $\pi = (s_1, s_2, \ldots, s_n)$ exists with $s = s_n$ for some n.

2.2   Model Checking

Model checking [7] is a formal verification technique to automatically determine whether a system meets a given requirement by explicitly or implicitly analyzing its behaviors (i.e., paths starting from initial states). Requirements are usually given using *temporal logics* [7]. In our work we focus on *safety properties*, where a FOL formula φ is given over V that must hold for every reachable state. When the system does not meet the safety property, a path $\pi = (s_1, s_2, \ldots, s_n)$ can be found where $s_n \not\models \varphi_n$. Such paths are called *counterexamples*.

2.3   Interpolation

Craig interpolation is a technique from logic that can produce for two inconsistent formulas an *interpolant*, which generalizes the first formula, while still contradicting the second one. The interpolant can be interpreted as an explanation of the contradiction.

Definition 2 (Craig Interpolant). *Let A and B be FOL formulas such that $A \wedge B$ is unsatisfiable. The formula I is a Craig interpolant (or simply an interpolant) for A, B if the following properties hold [17]:*

- *A implies I,*
- *I ∧ B is unsatisfiable,*
- *I only contains symbols common in A and B (excluding symbols of the logic).*

William Craig showed that an interpolant always exists for FOL formulas A and B with at least one symbol in common and $A \wedge B$ being unsatisfiable [9].

Interpolation can be generalized from two formulas to a sequence of formulas, for which an *interpolation sequence* is calculated instead of a single interpolant.

Definition 3 (Interpolation Sequence). *Let $A_1, A_2, \ldots, A_n$ be a sequence of FOL formulas such that $A_1 \wedge A_2 \wedge \ldots \wedge A_n$ is unsatisfiable. The sequence of formulas $I_0, I_1, \ldots, I_n$ is an interpolation sequence for $A_1, A_2, \ldots, A_n$ if the following properties hold [19]:*

- $I_0 = \top$, $I_n = \bot$,
- $I_j \wedge A_{j+1}$ *implies* I_{j+1} *for* $0 \leq j < n$,
- I_j *only contains symbols common in* $A_1, \ldots, A_j$ *and* $A_{j+1}, \ldots, A_n$ *for* $0 < j < n$ *(excluding symbols of the logic).*

3 Related Work and Contributions

Counterexample-Guided Abstraction Refinement (CEGAR) is a widely used abstraction-based approach to tackle the complexity of real-life software and hardware systems [6]. CEGAR-based algorithms usually have the following four main steps.

1. The first step is to create an abstract model that over-approximates the concrete model and is easier to handle computationally.
2. The abstract model is then checked by a model checking algorithm. Due to the behavior of over-approximation, if the abstract model satisfies the requirement, then it also holds in the concrete model.[2]
3. On the other hand, if the abstract model violates the requirement, an abstract counterexample is produced by the model checker. The third step is to check the feasibility of the abstract counterexample in the concrete model. If a concrete counterexample exists, it is a witness that the original model also violates the requirement.
4. If the abstract counterexample is not feasible, the abstraction has to be refined and the process has to be repeated from Step 2, until either the requirement holds for the abstract model or a concrete counterexample is found.

Types of Abstraction. CEGAR can work with different types of abstractions, including *predicate abstraction* [13] and *explicit value abstraction* [8]. There has also been work on a combination of the former two approaches for configurable program analysis [2]. We also propose a combination of predicate abstraction and explicit values at the initial abstraction, but instead of program analysis, we focus on symbolic transition systems (Sect. 4.1).

---

[2] This relation holds for ACTL* properties [6], including safety properties.

Refinement Strategies. Interpolation is often used to infer new predicates that refine the abstraction. Craig interpolation yields a single predicate [4,14], while its extension, sequence interpolation produces a sequence of predicates [1,11,16]. Our approach is similar to the one presented in [11], however in our framework the initial abstraction can be defined by arbitrary predicates and explicit variables (Sect. 4.4). As a special case, choosing the program counter as the only explicit variable yields a similar approach to the one presented in [11].

Contributions. In our work we make the following novel contributions. (1) We describe a *CEGAR framework for symbolic transition systems*, where refinement is based on splitting abstract states. We show that both predicate abstraction and explicit value abstraction can be incorporated into this framework along with Craig and sequence interpolation-based refinement strategies. This allows us to experiment with several algorithm configurations and their extensions. (2) As a first result, we used this framework to develop a *new configuration of CEGAR* that extends predicate abstraction with explicit values at the initial abstraction based on domain knowledge or heuristics. (3) We also use this framework to *evaluate different CEGAR configurations* (including our extended one) on various models, including industrial PLC codes and hardware.

In the following section, we present the CEGAR framework with our new configuration, this way also discussing the integration of the different algorithmic components.

4   A Configurable CEGAR Framework

This section presents the steps of our configurable CEGAR framework: initial abstraction (Sect. 4.1), model checking (Sect. 4.2) with an incremental optimization (Sect. 4.5), counterexample concretization (Sect. 4.3) and abstraction refinement (Sect. 4.4).

4.1   Initial Abstraction

The algorithms are based on the *existential abstraction* framework of Clarke et al. [6], *predicate abstraction* [13] and *explicit-value abstraction* [8].

Predicate Abstraction. Predicate abstraction maps concrete states to abstract states based on their evaluation on a set of FOL predicates. Given a symbolic transition system $T = (V, Inv, Tran, Init)$ and a set of FOL predicates $\mathcal{P}$ over V, there are $2^{|\mathcal{P}|}$ possible *abstract states*, denoted by $\hat{S}$. An abstract state $\hat{s} \in \hat{S}$ is a set of predicates, where for each $p_i \in \mathcal{P}$, $\hat{s}$ contains either p_i or $\neg p_i$. Given an abstract state $\hat{s} \in \hat{S}$, let its label be $Label(\hat{s}) = \bigwedge_{p \in \hat{s}} p$, i.e., the conjunction of predicates (or their negations) in $\hat{s}$. A concrete state s is mapped to $\hat{s}$ if $s \models Label(\hat{s})$.

In existential abstraction the *abstract transition relation* $\hat{R}$ and the set of *abstract initial states* $\hat{S}_0$ are defined in the following way [6].

- $\hat{R} = \{(\hat{s}, \hat{s}') \in \hat{S} \times \hat{S} \mid \exists s, s'. (s, s') \models Inv \wedge Inv' \wedge Label(\hat{s}) \wedge Label(\hat{s}')' \wedge Tran\}$,
  i.e., concrete successor states (s, s') exist, with s mapped to $\hat{s}$ and s' to $\hat{s}'$.
- $\hat{S}_0 = \{\hat{s} \in \hat{S} \mid \exists s. s \models Inv \wedge Init \wedge Label(\hat{s})\}$, i.e., a concrete initial state s
  exists, which is mapped to $\hat{s}$.

Example 1. Consider a symbolic transition system T with $V = \{x, y\}$, $D_x = D_y = \mathbb{Z}$, $Inv = (0 \leq x \wedge x \leq 3 \wedge 0 \leq y \wedge y \leq 1)$, $Init = (x \doteq 0 \wedge y \doteq 0)$ and $Tran = (x + y \doteq 0 \wedge x' - y' \doteq 2) \vee (x + y \doteq 1 \wedge x' \doteq 1 \wedge y' \doteq 1) \vee (x + y \doteq 3 \wedge x' \doteq 3 \wedge y' \doteq 0)$. The concrete state space of T can be seen in Fig. 1(a), where circles denote concrete states (x, y), the double circle denotes the initial state and edges denote transitions. Suppose, that $\mathcal{P} = \{x < 2, y \doteq 1\}$, which means that there are $2^{|\mathcal{P}|} = 4$ abstract states. Partitioning by $\mathcal{P}$ is indicated by dashed lines in Fig. 1(a), while the corresponding abstract transition system $(\hat{S}, \hat{R}, \hat{S}_0)$ can be seen in Fig. 1(b).

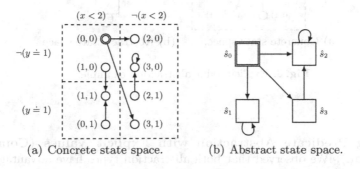

(a) Concrete state space.   (b) Abstract state space.

Fig. 1. Predicate abstraction example.

An *abstract path* is a (finite, loop-free) sequence of abstract states $\hat{\pi} = (\hat{s}_1, \hat{s}_2, \ldots, \hat{s}_n)$ with $\hat{s}_1 \in \hat{S}_0$ and $(\hat{s}_i, \hat{s}_{i+1}) \in \hat{R}$ $(1 \leq i < n)$. An abstract path $\hat{\pi} = (\hat{s}_1, \hat{s}_2, \ldots, \hat{s}_n)$ is *concretizable* if a sequence of states $\pi = (s_1, s_2, \ldots, s_n)$ exists for which $(s_1, s_2, \ldots, s_n) \models Init_1 \wedge \bigwedge_{1 \leq i \leq n} Label(\hat{s}_i)_i \wedge \bigwedge_{1 \leq i \leq n} Inv_i \wedge \bigwedge_{1 \leq i < n} Tran_{i,i+1}$. In other words, π is a concrete path where the ith concrete state is mapped to the ith abstract state.

Explicit Value Abstraction. In explicit value abstraction, the variables V of the system are divided into two disjoint sets: *visible* (V_V) and *invisible* (V_I) sets of variables. Concrete states are mapped to abstract states based on their evaluation on visible variables. Given a symbolic transition system $T = (V, Inv, Tran, Init)$ and the set of visible variables $V_V \subseteq V$, there are $\prod_{v_i \in V_V} |D_{v_i}|$ possible abstract states, denoted by $\hat{S}$. An abstract state $\hat{s} \in \hat{S}$ is a (many sorted) interpretation that assigns a value $\hat{s}(v_i) = d_i \in D_{v_i}$ to each visible variable $v_i \in V_V$ of its domain D_{v_i}. A concrete state s is mapped to $\hat{s}$ if $s(v_i) = \hat{s}(v_i)$ for each visible variable $v_i \in V_V$. The label of an abstract state $\hat{s}$ in explicit value abstraction can be defined by $Label(\hat{s}) = \wedge_{v_i \in V_V} (v_i \doteq \hat{s}(v_i))$, i.e., a conjunction of the assignments. Transitions and initial states are mapped as in predicate abstraction.

Example 2. Recall the symbolic transition system of Example 1 and suppose, that $V_V = \{y\}$, $V_I = \{x\}$. The concrete state space and the partitioning by V_V is indicated in Fig. 2(a), while the corresponding abstract transition system $(\hat{S}, \hat{R}, \hat{S}_0)$ can be seen in Fig. 2(b).

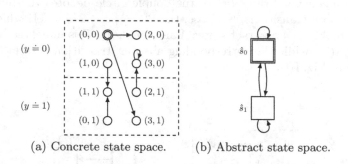

(a) Concrete state space.   (b) Abstract state space.

Fig. 2. Explicit value abstraction example.

Extending Predicate Abstraction with Explicit Values (Combined Abstraction). We observed that both abstraction types have advantages and shortcomings. For example, a variable with an infinite domain cannot be tracked explicitly. On the other hand, a variable appearing in different equalities (e.g., $x \doteq 1, x \doteq 2, \ldots$) may yield a handful of predicates and refinement iterations. In such cases it is more efficient to keep track of the variable explicitly. Therefore, we also developed a combined method that extends predicate abstraction with explicit values when creating the initial abstract model. Formally, let $T = (V, Inv, Tran, Init)$ be a symbolic transition system with variables $V = \{v_1, v_2, \ldots, v_n\}$, $\mathcal{P}$ be a set of FOL predicates over V and $V_E \subseteq V$ be the set of *explicit variables*. Without the loss of generality, in the following it is assumed that explicit variables are represented by the first k indices ($0 \leq k \leq n$), i.e., $V_E = \{v_1, v_2, \ldots, v_k\}$. We combine predicate abstraction with explicit values in the following way. An abstract state $\hat{s} \in \hat{S}$ is a set of predicates, where

– for each $p_i \in \mathcal{P}$, $\hat{s}$ contains either p_i or $\neg p_i$,
– for each $v_i \in V_E$, $\hat{s}$ contains a predicate of the form $v_i \doteq d_i$, where $d_i \in D_{v_i}$.

Consequently, there are $|\hat{S}| = 2^{|\mathcal{P}|} \cdot |D_{v_1}| \cdot |D_{v_2}| \cdot \ldots \cdot |D_{v_k}|$ possible abstract states. The abstract transition relation $\hat{R}$ and the initial states $\hat{S}_0$ can be calculated similarly to predicate abstraction. The initial set of predicates and explicit values can be determined by domain knowledge or by simple heuristics (see Sect. 5).

Example 3. Suppose, that $V = \{x, y\}$ with $D_x = D_y = \{0, 1\}$, the only predicate is $\mathcal{P} = \{x < y\}$ and the only explicit variable is $V_E = \{x\}$. There are thus four abstract states $\hat{s}_1 = \{x < y, x \doteq 0\}$, $\hat{s}_2 = \{x < y, x \doteq 1\}$, $\hat{s}_3 = \{\neg(x < y), x \doteq 0\}$ and $\hat{s}_4 = \{\neg(x < y), x \doteq 1\}$.

4.2   Model Checking

An abstract state $\hat{s} \in \hat{S}$ violates the safety property φ if $Label(\hat{s}) \wedge Inv \wedge \neg\varphi$ is satisfiable, i.e., a concrete state exists, which is mapped to $\hat{s}$ but violates φ. The model checking problem on the abstract transition system is to check if an abstract state $\hat{s}$ violating φ is reachable, i.e., whether an abstract path $\hat{\varphi} = (\hat{s}_1, \hat{s}_2, \ldots, \hat{s}_n)$ exists with $\hat{s}_n = \hat{s}$.

Example 4. Recall Example 1 and suppose that the safety property is $\varphi = (x \neq 3 \vee y \neq 0)$, i.e., only the concrete state $(3, 0)$ violates φ. Consequently, $\hat{s}_2$ also violates φ and the paths $\hat{\pi}_1 = (\hat{s}_0, \hat{s}_3, \hat{s}_2)$ and $\hat{\pi}_2 = (\hat{s}_0, \hat{s}_2)$ are abstract counterexamples.

CEGAR can work with different kinds of model checkers as long as they are capable of providing a counterexample. Our framework is currently equipped with an incremental explicit model checker. Incrementality relies on the refinement strategy (Sect. 4.4), therefore it is presented afterwards (Sect. 4.5).

4.3   Counterexample Concretization

An abstract counterexample $\hat{\pi} = (\hat{s}_1, \hat{s}_2, \ldots, \hat{s}_n)$ for the safety property φ is *concretizable* if a sequence of states $\pi = (s_1, s_2, \ldots, s_n)$ exists for which $(s_1, s_2, \ldots, s_n) \models Init_1 \wedge \bigwedge_{1 \leq i \leq n} Label(\hat{s}_i)_i \wedge \bigwedge_{1 \leq i \leq n} Inv_i \wedge \bigwedge_{1 \leq i < n} Tran_{i,i+1} \wedge \neg\varphi_n$ holds. In other words, $\hat{\pi}$ is concretizable as a path and in addition the last state violates the safety property. A concretizable counterexample is a witness that the concrete model also violates the requirement, while a non-concretizable counterexample is called *spurious*.

In order to avoid finding the spurious counterexample again, the abstraction has to be refined. The longest concretizable prefix of the counterexample provides useful information for the refinement. Therefore, an abstract counterexample $\hat{\pi} = (\hat{s}_1, \hat{s}_2, \ldots, \hat{s}_n)$ is concretized iteratively with the following $n + 1$ formulas.

$$F_i = \begin{cases} Init_1 \wedge Inv_1 \wedge Label(\hat{s}_1)_1 & \text{if } i = 1 \\ Inv_i \wedge Label(\hat{s}_i)_i \wedge Tran_{i-1,i} & \text{if } 1 < i \leq n \\ \neg\varphi_n & \text{if } i = n + 1 \end{cases}$$

The formula $F_1 \wedge F_2 \wedge \ldots \wedge F_n$ describes concrete paths mapped to $\hat{\pi}$ (similarly to bounded model checking [3]), while F_{n+1} ensures that the last state violates the property. If $F_1 \wedge F_2 \wedge \ldots \wedge F_{n+1}$ is satisfiable, the counterexample is concretizable. Otherwise, let $1 \leq f \leq n$ be the largest index for which $F_1 \wedge F_2 \wedge \ldots \wedge F_f$ is satisfiable. The state $\hat{s}_f$ is then called the *failure state* since a concrete path leads there but it cannot be extended.

Example 5. Recall Example 4 with the abstract counterexamples $\hat{\pi}_1 = (\hat{s}_0, \hat{s}_3, \hat{s}_2)$ and $\hat{\pi}_2 = (\hat{s}_0, \hat{s}_2)$. It can be seen that $\hat{\pi}_1$ is spurious since $\hat{s}_2$ cannot be reached by a concrete path. The longest concretizable prefix is $(\hat{s}_0, \hat{s}_3)$, hence the failure state is $\hat{s}_3$. The abstract counterexample $\hat{\pi}_2$ is concretizable as a path with $((0,0),(2,0))$, but $(2,0)$ fulfills the property, thus the failure state is $\hat{s}_2$.

4.4   Abstraction Refinement

The set of concrete states mapped to the failure state $\hat{s}_f$ are partitioned into the following three groups: states that can be reached from an initial state are *dead-end*, states having a transition to $\hat{s}_{f+1}$ or violating φ are *bad*, while other states are *irrelevant*. It is clear that a state cannot be dead-end and bad at the same time since then $\hat{s}_f$ would not be a failure state [6].

Example 6. Recall Example 5 and Fig. 1 with $\hat{\pi}_1 = (\hat{s}_0, \hat{s}_3, \hat{s}_2)$ and $\hat{\pi}_2 = (\hat{s}_0, \hat{s}_2)$. The failure state of $\hat{\pi}_1$ is $\hat{s}_3$, where $(3,1)$ is a dead-end state and $(2,1)$ is bad. The failure state of $\hat{\pi}_2$ is $\hat{s}_2$, where $(2,0)$ is dead-end and $(3,0)$ is bad.

The purpose of abstraction refinement is to map dead-end and bad states to different abstract states so that the spurious counterexample cannot occur in the next iteration. Predicate abstraction and our combined method uses predicate refinement to obtain new predicates, while explicit value abstraction employs explicit value refinement to make some previously invisible variables visible.

Predicate Refinement. Our framework supports both Craig and sequence interpolation to infer new predicates and it also utilizes lazy abstraction, i.e., only a subset of the abstract states is refined.

Craig Interpolation. Dead-end and bad states can be characterized with formulas D and B respectively in the following way.

$$D = Init_1 \wedge \bigwedge_{1 \le i \le f} Inv_i \wedge \bigwedge_{1 \le i \le f} Label(\hat{s}_i)_i \wedge \bigwedge_{1 \le i < f} Tran_{i,i+1}$$

$$B = \begin{cases} Inv_{f+1} \wedge Label(\hat{s}_{f+1})_{f+1} \wedge Tran_{f,f+1} & \text{if } f < n \\ \neg\varphi_n & \text{if } f = n \end{cases}$$

In other words, D describes paths mapped to the prefix $(\hat{s}_1, \hat{s}_2, \ldots, \hat{s}_f)$, while B describes either transitions from $\hat{s}_f$ to $\hat{s}_{f+1}$ or states violating φ. It is clear that $D \wedge B$ is unsatisfiable, otherwise a longer prefix could be found or $\hat{\pi}$ would be concretizable. Consequently, Craig interpolation can be applied, yielding an interpolant I with the following properties.

- $D \Rightarrow I$, i.e., I is a generalization of dead-end states,
- $I \wedge B$ is unsatisfiable, i.e., bad states cannot satisfy I,
- I refers to common symbols of D and B, which are variables with index f.

Therefore, removing the indices from the variables in I yields a new predicate that separates dead-end and bad states mapped to $\hat{s}_f$. We refine the abstraction by replacing $\hat{s}_f$ with $\hat{s}_{f1}$ and $\hat{s}_{f2}$ obtained by adding I and $\neg I$ to the predicates of $\hat{s}_f$, i.e., $\hat{s}_{f1} = \hat{s}_f \cup \{I\}$ and $\hat{s}_{f2} = \hat{s}_f \cup \{\neg I\}$. This approach, namely splitting only a subset of states is similar to *lazy abstraction* [15].

Example 7. Recall Example 6 and the spurious counterexample $\hat{\pi}_1 = (\hat{s}_0, \hat{s}_3, \hat{s}_2)$, where $\hat{s}_3$ is the failure state. Thus, D and B are defined in the following way for Craig interpolation.

- $D = Init_0 \wedge Inv_0 \wedge Inv_3 \wedge Label(\hat{s}_0)_0 \wedge Label(\hat{s}_3)_3 \wedge Tran_{0,3}$,
- $B = Inv_2 \wedge Label(\hat{s}_2)_2 \wedge Tran_{3,2}$.

The formula $I = (x_3 \doteq 3)$ is an interpolant for D and B, which can be used to split $\hat{s}_3$ (Fig. 3(a)). The refined abstract state space can be seen in Fig. 3(b), where the spurious behavior of $\hat{\pi}_1$ is eliminated. However, $\hat{\pi}_2 = (\hat{s}_0, \hat{s}_2)$ is still a spurious counterexample that needs another refinement iteration.

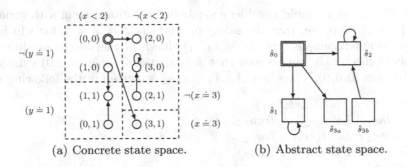

(a) Concrete state space.   (b) Abstract state space.

Fig. 3. Predicate refinement example with Craig interpolation.

Sequence Interpolation. Craig interpolation can be generalized to sequence interpolation [11] in order to split multiple states along the spurious counterexample $\hat{\pi} = (\hat{s}_1, \hat{s}_2, \ldots, \hat{s}_n)$. Formally, $A_1, A_2, \ldots, A_{n+1}$ is defied in the following way.

$$A_i = \begin{cases} Init_1 \wedge Inv_1 \wedge Label(\hat{s}_1)_1 & \text{if } i = 1 \\ Inv_i \wedge Label(\hat{s}_i)_i \wedge Tran_{i-1,i} & \text{if } 1 < i \leq n \\ \neg\varphi_n & \text{if } i = n+1 \end{cases}$$

In other words, the formula A_1 describes initial states mapped to $\hat{s}_1$, while $A_2, A_3, \ldots, A_n$ describe reachable states mapped to $\hat{s}_2, \hat{s}_3, \ldots, \hat{s}_n$ respectively. Finally, A_{n+1} describes states violating the safety property. It is clear that $A_1 \wedge A_2 \wedge \ldots \wedge A_{n+1}$ is unsatisfiable, since $\hat{\pi}$ is spurious. Hence, an interpolation sequence $I_0, I_1, \ldots I_{n+1}$ exists with the following properties:

- $I_0 = \top$, $I_{n+1} = \bot$, i.e., interpolants that do not correspond to any state in the counterexample carry no information,
- $I_j \wedge A_{j+1} \Rightarrow I_{j+1}$ for $0 \leq j \leq n$, i.e., the interpolants together generalize dead-end states and contradict bad states,
- I_j refers only to the common symbols of $A_1, \ldots, A_j$ and $A_{j+1}, \ldots, A_{n+1}$, i.e., variables with index j.

Abstraction is refined by replacing each $\hat{s}_i$ ($1 \leq i \leq n$) with $\hat{s}_{i1}$ and $\hat{s}_{i2}$ obtained by adding I_i and $\neg I_i$ to the predicates of $\hat{s}_i$ respectively. Formally, $\hat{s}_{i1} = \hat{s}_i \cup \{I_i\}$ and $\hat{s}_{i2} = \hat{s}_i \cup \{\neg I_i\}$. It may occur that $I_i = \top$ or $I_i = \bot$ for some $1 \leq i \leq n$. In this case the corresponding abstract state $\hat{s}_i$ is not split.

The motivation behind sequence interpolation is twofold. On the one hand, splitting multiple states in a single step can eliminate more spurious behavior, yielding fewer refinement iterations. On the other hand, we observed that separating dead-end and bad states with a single formula (Craig interpolant) may render the formula long and complex. Sequence interpolation in contrast, can produce more, but less complex formulas. Furthermore, it also makes concretization easier, since the failure state $\hat{s}_f$ does not have to be determined.

Example 8. As an example, consider a symbolic transition system with variables $V = \{x, y, z\}$. Suppose, that the safety property is $\varphi = x \neq 5$, for which the abstract counterexample $\hat{\pi} = (\hat{s}_1, \hat{s}_2, \hat{s}_3, \hat{s}_4)$ shown in Fig. 4(a) is produced by the model checker. It can be seen that $\hat{\pi}$ is spurious, since $(5, 0, 0)$ cannot be reached from $(0, 0, 0)$. Therefore, $A_1, A_2, \ldots, A_5$ is defined in the following way:

- $A_1 = Init_1 \wedge Inv_1 \wedge Label(\hat{s}_1)_1$,
- $A_2 = Inv_2 \wedge Label(\hat{s}_2)_2 \wedge Tran_{1,2}$,
- $A_3 = Inv_3 \wedge Label(\hat{s}_3)_3 \wedge Tran_{2,3}$,
- $A_4 = Inv_4 \wedge Label(\hat{s}_4)_4 \wedge Tran_{3,4}$,
- $A_5 = \neg\varphi_4$.

It can be checked that $I_0 = \top$, $I_1 = \top$, $I_2 = (x_2 < 2)$, $I_3 = (x_3 < 4)$, $I_4 = \bot$, $I_5 = \bot$ is an interpolation sequence for $A_1, A_2, \ldots, A_5$. Hence, $\hat{s}_1$ and $\hat{s}_4$ are not split, $\hat{s}_2$ is split with the predicate $(x < 2)$ and $\hat{s}_3$ with $(x < 4)$ as the dashed lines indicate. The abstract states after the refinement can be seen in Fig. 4(b). It is clear that the spurious counterexample is eliminated. It can also be seen that both splits are required.

Suppose now, that Craig interpolation is applied for the same problem. The failure state is $\hat{s}_2$, where $(1, 1, 1)$ is a dead-end state and all the others are bad. Therefore, $(1, 1, 1)$ has to be separated from the others with a single formula. This requires all three variables (e.g., $I = (x_2 \doteq 1 \wedge y_2 \doteq 1 \wedge z_2 \doteq 1)$), since $(1, 1, 1)$ is not distinguishable with two or less variables. In contrast, sequence interpolation could be solved with two predicates containing only x.

Explicit Value Refinement. As in predicate abstraction, the purpose of refinement is to map dead-end and bad states to different abstract states.

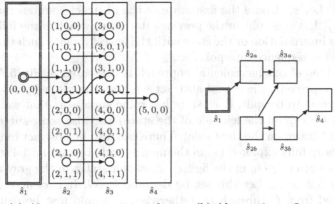

(a) Abstract counterexample.   (b) Abstraction refinement.

Fig. 4. Predicate refinement example with sequence interpolation.

In pure explicit value analysis this can be done by making a subset $V_I' \subseteq V_I$ of the previously invisible variables visible, i.e., $V_V \leftarrow V_V \cup V_I'$ and $V_I \leftarrow V_I \setminus V_I'$ [8]. In contrast to predicate abstraction, visible variables are common for each state, which means that each abstract state is split in the new iteration [8].[3] In our framework we generate V_I' with interpolation in the following way. Recall that we defined the label of an abstract state in explicit value abstraction as a conjunction of assignments ($Label(\hat{s}) = \wedge_{v_i \in V_V}(v_i \doteq \hat{s}(v_i))$). Thus, for a spurious counterexample $\hat{\pi} = (\hat{s}_1, \hat{s}_2, \ldots, \hat{s}_n)$ a Craig interpolant I or an interpolation sequence $I_0, I_1, \ldots, I_{n+1}$ can be calculated in the same way as in predicate refinement. Then $V_I' = \mathsf{var}(I) \cap V_I$ with Craig interpolation, or $V_I' = \cup_{1 \leq i \leq n} \mathsf{var}(I_i) \cap V_I$ with sequence interpolation. In other words, new visible variables are the invisible variables appearing in the interpolants. Again, sequence interpolation can generate simpler formulas, keeping V_I' (and thus, the abstract state space) smaller.

The reason for a spurious abstract counterexample is that dead-end and bad states are mapped to the same abstract state $\hat{s}_f$, where $\hat{s}_f$ assigns the same values to visible variables V_V. Interpolants distinguish dead-end states and bad states, which means that they must contain at least one invisible variable. This ensures that $V_I' \neq \emptyset$ and that the spurious counterexample is eliminated.

4.5 Incremental Model Checking

A non-incremental explicit model checker loops through each initial abstract state and traverses the set of reachable abstract states using for example depth-first search. If an abstract state violating the safety property is found, the actual abstract path is returned. Our incremental model checker exploits the fact that only a subset of the abstract states are split when using predicate refinement

---

[3] This splitting is of course, not performed explicitly. The model checker constructs the state space on-the-fly.

(see Sect. 4.4). Let $\hat{s}_s$ denote the first state of the abstract counterexample $\hat{\pi} = (\hat{s}_1, \hat{s}_2, \ldots, \hat{s}_n)$ that was split in the previous iteration, which is the failure state $\hat{s}_f$ using Craig interpolation or the state with the lowest index s such that $I_s \neq \top$ and $I_s \neq \bot$ using sequence interpolation.

The main idea of our incremental approach is presented in Fig. 5. The path $(\hat{s}_1, \hat{s}_2, \hat{s}_3, \hat{s}_4)$ represents the actual abstract counterexample, where $\hat{s}_3$ was the first abstract state to be split. Each state has some successors that were already fully explored (drawn on the left side of the state) and also some successors yet to be explored (drawn on the right side). There can also be abstract initial states that were already fully explored ($\hat{s}_5$ in the figure) and abstract initial states that will be explored after $\hat{s}_1$ ($\hat{s}_6$ in the figure). Abstract states in the gray area were fully explored before $\hat{s}_3$. Let this set be denoted by $\hat{G}$. It is clear that $\hat{s}_3$ can only be reached from $\hat{G}$ through $\hat{s}_2$. Otherwise, $\hat{s}_3$ would first be reached that way and not through $\hat{s}_2$. Therefore, splitting $\hat{s}_3$ does not affect states in $\hat{G}$. If exploration is continued with $(\hat{s}_1, \hat{s}_2)$ on the stack, $\hat{s}_2$ will "represent" states in $\hat{G}$, i.e., if some of the new abstract states could be reached from $\hat{G}$, they will be reached from $\hat{s}_2$. Therefore, if $\hat{s}_s$ is the first abstract state that was split ($\hat{s}_3$ in the example), abstract states explored before $\hat{s}_s$ do not need to be re-explored and the actual abstract path can be kept until $\hat{s}_{s-1}$.

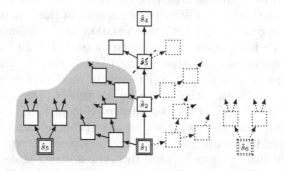

Fig. 5. Illustration of incremental model checking.

It may seem that incremental model checking requires extra memory to store the explored states. However, a non-incremental version also has to discover and keep track of the same states. The only difference is that the incremental version keeps the explored states in memory between the refinement iterations and continues the search, while the non-incremental version always re-explores.

5   Evaluation

We developed a prototype Java implementation for the framework presented in Sect. 4. We used Z3 [18] as the underlying logic solver. We compared various configurations on industrial PLC codes (Sect. 5.1), on a protocol with infinite state space (Sect. 5.2) and on hardware models (Sect. 5.3).

5.1 Industrial PLC Codes

Programmable Logic Controller (PLC) codes can be represented by an automaton-based model [12], which can then be translated into a symbolic transition system. Table 1 contains results for the following six configurations, corresponding to the main columns: (1) predicate abstraction with Craig interpolation, (2) predicate abstraction with sequence interpolation, (3) combined abstraction with Craig interpolation, (4) combined abstraction with sequence interpolation, (5) explicit value abstraction with Craig interpolation, (6) explicit value abstraction with sequence interpolation.

In predicate abstraction the initial set of predicates is empty, while in explicit value abstraction the initial visible variables are those appearing in the safety property. We observed that the program location variable appears in many equality formulas, e.g., $loc \doteq 0, loc \doteq 1, \ldots, loc \doteq n$. With this extra knowledge, we configured the combined approach to track the location variable explicitly and to start with an empty set of initial predicates. Note, that this idea can be generalized to any automaton-based model or such variables can also be detected by a heuristic that analyzes the formulas.

The sub-columns T, #R and #S represent the run time in seconds, the number of refinements and the sum of explored abstract states in each iteration respectively. The ✓ or × sign before the name of the model indicates whether it meets the property or not. The columns V and L denote the number of variables and locations in the automaton-based model respectively. The shortest run time is indicated by bold font for each model.

It can be seen that explicit value abstraction has the best performance for many models. However, predicate abstraction has shorter run time for models PLC01 and PLC02 (where no reductions were applied to the automata) and the combined approach performs best for models with the largest state space (PLC06 and PLC08). It can also be observed that the combined approach gives a better performance for most of the models compared to pure predicate abstraction. Furthermore, it can be seen that Craig interpolation yields many small steps (many iterations), in contrast to sequence interpolation, which performs fewer, but bigger steps.

5.2 Fischer's Protocol

Fischer's protocol [10] is a mutual exclusion algorithm for arbitrarily many components (column #C). The model contains clock variables (with domain $\mathbb{Q}$), rendering the state space infinite. Explicit value abstraction fails to verify these models because the clock variables become visible after a few iterations. Table 2 contains results for predicate and combined abstraction. The algorithms start with an empty set of initial states and the combined approach tracks the variables corresponding to the locks explicitly. It can be seen that Craig interpolation outperforms sequence interpolation for these models. It can also be observed that the combined method is more efficient when the model meets the property.

Table 1. Measurement results for PLC codes.

Model	V	L	Pred. (Cr.)			Pred. (seq.)			Comb. (Cr.)			Comb. (seq.)		
			T (s)	#R	#S	T (s)	#R	#S	T (s)	#R	#S	T (s)	#R	#S
× PLC01	66	36	**22.5**	33	100	50.2	34	191	42.0	20	452	48.5	1	81
× PLC02	66	36	**22.7**	33	100	49.4	34	191	41.0	20	452	47.3	1	81
✓ PLC03	29	17	479.2	195	6694	99.2	23	292	28.2	34	629	51.8	6	212
✓ PLC04	29	17	40.2	64	1076	14.4	16	82	17.6	21	353	6.1	2	47
× PLC04	29	17	44.0	65	1069	406.7	31	1198	34.3	35	650	36.1	5	192
✓ PLC05	29	17	42.2	63	1130	21.4	17	98	17.4	21	352	6.3	2	47
✓ PLC06	82	43	1512.8	159	4812	–	–	–	333.1	52	1369	**227.5**	2	120
✓ PLC07	82	43	190.8	58	552	462.2	66	1057	164.8	26	657	164.8	1	70
× PLC08	82	43	86.1	37	111	–	–	–	46.7	0	43	**46.2**	0	43
✓ PLC09	23	14	87.4	90	1716	94.6	32	633	61.3	94	1845	35.7	11	193

Model	V	L	Expl. (Cr.)			Expl. (Seq.)		
			T (s)	#R	#S	T (s)	#R	#S
× PLC01	66	36	36.4	7	1640	211.8	3	758
× PLC02	66	36	32.2	7	1697	428.5	5	1439
✓ PLC03	29	17	**5.2**	1	339	9.9	1	369
✓ PLC04	29	17	**3.3**	1	165	3.8	1	165
× PLC04	29	17	**7.6**	2	274	38.0	1	209
✓ PLC05	29	17	**3.5**	1	167	4.7	1	167
✓ PLC06	82	43	1254.5	3	20956	–	–	–
✓ PLC07	82	43	78.1	2	1163	**50.9**	1	518
× PLC08	82	43	65.1	2	628	123.0	3	541
✓ PLC09	23	14	**11.8**	5	1261	14.5	4	833

Table 2. Measurement results for Fischer's protocol.

Model	#C	Pred. (Cr.)			Pred. (seq.)			Comb. (Cr.)			Comb. (seq.)		
		T (s)	#R	#S	T (s)	#R	#S	T (s)	#R	#S	T (s)	#R	#S
✓ fischer	2	1.2	17	69	3.0	15	107	**0.8**	18	66	1.2	14	78
× fischer	2	**0.6**	11	41	1.1	9	45	0.8	18	62	1.2	12	58
✓ fischer	3	12.1	97	998	68.1	101	1584	**10.3**	93	1329	45.8	99	1334
× fischer	3	**1.4**	19	70	1.5	9	44	1.7	28	121	2.9	21	105

5.3 Hardware Models

We also evaluated the algorithms for some of the smaller models of the Hardware
Model Checking Competition [5]. Table 3 contains results for predicate abstraction and explicit value abstraction. We did not evaluate the combined approach,
since all variables are boolean type, hence it is identical to add a predicate for a
variable or to track it explicitly. Predicate abstraction starts with an empty set
of initial predicates and only the single output variable is visible using explicit
value abstraction. The columns I, L and A correspond to the number of inputs,
latches and and-gates respectively. It can be seen that predicate abstraction
performs better with Craig interpolation, but explicit value abstraction is more
efficient using sequence interpolation.

Table 3. Measurement results for hardware models.

Model	I	L	A	Pred. (Cr.)			Pred. (Seq.)			Expl. (Cr.)			Expl. (Seq.)		
				T (s)	#R	#S	T (s)	#R	#S	T (s)	#R	#S	T (s)	#R	#S
✓ mutexp0	11	20	159	**10.3**	63	494	24.5	43	420	14.3	8	742	22.7	7	806
✓ mutexp0neg	11	20	159	6.1	44	284	**3.7**	12	82	8.8	9	441	6.7	6	330
✗ nusmv.syncarb5p2.B	5	10	52	1.3	30	139	3.1	14	132	0.7	6	113	**0.2**	2	18
✗ nusmv.syncarb10p2.B	10	20	157	31.6	110	779	117.9	56	1491	239.8	11	5179	**1.6**	2	32
✗ pdtpmsarbiter	3	46	209	**0.5**	6	22	4.6	6	22	5.3	15	130	7.8	13	108
✓ ringp0	15	25	145	16.4	55	300	25.6	19	127	16.1	10	763	**14.5**	7	657
✓ ringp0neg	15	25	145	**7.8**	21	83	35.7	31	237	187.5	11	4870	108.2	7	2629
✓ srg5ptimonegnv	30	47	304	**0.3**	3	9	0.5	4	15	1.7	4	40	1.3	3	36

5.4 Summary

Measurements show that all configurations have advantages and shortcomings depending on the types of the models. Predicate abstraction with Craig interpolation performs well for software and hardware models, explicit value abstraction is efficient for PLC models, while the combined method with sequence interpolation was able to handle the largest state spaces. It can also be observed that extending predicate abstraction with explicit values (the combined method) boosts its performance. As our implementation is only a prototype without optimizations, the developed model checker can not compete with state-of-the-art tools now. Furthermore our current goal was to compare the configurations in the same framework, so also the formerly existing algorithms were reimplemented.

6 Conclusions

In our paper we examined various CEGAR-based algorithms for the verification of symbolic transition systems. From the theoretical point of view, we described a configurable framework, which can incorporate the different types of abstractions and refinement strategies. We also proposed a combination of predicate abstraction and explicit values at the initial abstraction, being able to provide better performance based on domain knowledge or heuristics. On the practical side, we examined the efficiency of different configurations of the algorithms on various models, including software and hardware and identified their advantages and shortcomings. Our future plan is to improve our prototype implementation, experiment with further algorithms and develop heuristics for automatically selecting the most efficient configuration based on the model.

Acknowledgement. This work was partially supported by the ARTEMIS JU and the Hungarian National Research, Development and Innovation Fund in the frame of the R5-COP (Reconfigurable ROS-based Resilient Reasoning Robotic Cooperating Systems) project.

References

1. Beyer, D., Löwe, S.: Explicit-state software model checking based on CEGAR and interpolation. In: Cortellessa, V., Varró, D. (eds.) FASE 2013 (ETAPS 2013). LNCS, vol. 7793, pp. 146–162. Springer, Heidelberg (2013)

2. Beyer, D., Löwe, S., Wendler, P.: Refinement selection. In: Fischer, B., Geldenhuys, J. (eds.) SPIN 2015. LNCS, vol. 9232, pp. 20–38. Springer, Heidelberg (2015)
3. Biere, A., Cimatti, A., Clarke, E., Zhu, Y.: Symbolic model checking without BDDs. In: Cleaveland, W.R. (ed.) TACAS 1999. LNCS, vol. 1579, pp. 193–207. Springer, Heidelberg (1999)
4. Brückner, I., Dräger, K., Finkbeiner, B., Wehrheim, H.: Slicing abstractions. In: Arbab, F., Sirjani, M. (eds.) FSEN 2007. LNCS, vol. 4767, pp. 17–32. Springer, Heidelberg (2007)
5. Cabodi, G., Loiacono, C., Palena, M., Pasini, P., Patti, D., Quer, S., Vendraminetto, D., Biere, A., Heljanko, K., Baumgartner, J.: Hardware model checking competition 2014: an analysis and comparison of solvers and benchmarks. J. Satisfiability Boolean Model. Comput. **9**, 135–172 (2016)
6. Clarke, E., Grumberg, O., Jha, S., Lu, Y., Veith, H.: Counterexample-guided abstraction refinement for symbolic model checking. J. ACM **50**(5), 752–794 (2003)
7. Clarke, E.M., Grumberg, O., Peled, D.: Model Checking. MIT Press, Cambridge (1999)
8. Clarke, E.M., Gupta, A., Strichman, O.: SAT-based counterexample-guided abstraction refinement. IEEE Trans. Comput. Aided Des. Integr. Circuits Syst. **23**(7), 1113–1123 (2004)
9. Craig, W.: Three uses of the Herbrand-Gentzen theorem in relating model theory and proof theory. J. Symbolic Logic **22**(03), 269–285 (1957)
10. Dutertre, B., Sorea, M., et al.: Timed systems in SAL. Technical report, SRI International, Computer Science Laboratory (2004)
11. Ermis, E., Hoenicke, J., Podelski, A.: Splitting via interpolants. In: Kuncak, V., Rybalchenko, A. (eds.) VMCAI 2012. LNCS, vol. 7148, pp. 186–201. Springer, Heidelberg (2012)
12. Fernández Adiego, B., Darvas, D., Blanco Viñuela, E., Tournier, J.C., Bliudze, S., Blech, J.O., González Suárez, V.M.: Applying model checking to industrial-sized PLC programs. IEEE Trans. Industr. Inf. **11**(6), 1400–1410 (2015)
13. Graf, S., Saidi, H.: Construction of abstract state graphs with PVS. In: Grumberg, O. (ed.) CAV 1997. LNCS, vol. 1254, pp. 72–83. Springer, Heidelberg (1997)
14. Henzinger, T.A., Jhala, R., Majumdar, R., McMillan, K.L.: Abstractions from proofs. In: Proceedings of the 31st ACM SIGPLAN-SIGACT Symposium on Principles of Programming Languages, pp. 232–244. ACM (2004)
15. Henzinger, T.A., Jhala, R., Majumdar, R., Sutre, G.: Lazy abstraction. In: Proceedings of the 29th ACM SIGPLAN-SIGACT Symposium on Principles of Programming Languages, pp. 58–70. ACM (2002)
16. McMillan, K.L.: Lazy abstraction with interpolants. In: Ball, T., Jones, R.B. (eds.) CAV 2006. LNCS, vol. 4144, pp. 123–136. Springer, Heidelberg (2006)
17. McMillan, K.L.: Applications of Craig interpolants in model checking. In: Halbwachs, N., Zuck, L.D. (eds.) TACAS 2005. LNCS, vol. 3440, pp. 1–12. Springer, Heidelberg (2005)
18. de Moura, L., Bjørner, N.S.: Z3: an efficient SMT solver. In: Ramakrishnan, C.R., Rehof, J. (eds.) TACAS 2008. LNCS, vol. 4963, pp. 337–340. Springer, Heidelberg (2008)
19. Vizel, Y., Grumberg, O.: Interpolation-sequence based model checking. In: Formal Methods in Computer-Aided Design, pp. 1–8. IEEE (2009)

A Theory for the Composition
of Concurrent Processes

Ludovic Henrio[1], Eric Madelaine[1,2(✉)], and Min Zhang[3]

[1] University of Nice Sophia Antipolis, CNRS, UMR 7271,
06900 Sophia Antipolis, France
ludovic.henrio@cnrs.fr
[2] INRIA Sophia Antipolis Méditérannée, BP 93, 06902 Sophia Antipolis, France
eric.madelaine@inria.fr
[3] Shanghai Key Laboratory of Trustworthy Computing, ECNU, Shanghai, China
mzhang@sei.ecnu.edu.cn

Abstract. In this paper, we provide a theory for the operators composing concurrent processes. Open pNets (parameterised networks of synchronised automata) are new semantic objects that we propose for defining the semantics of composition operators. This paper defines the operational semantics of open pNets, using "open transitions" that include symbolic hypotheses on the behaviour of the pNets "holes". We discuss when this semantics can be finite and how to compute it symbolically, and we illustrate this construction on a simple operator. This paper also defines a bisimulation equivalence between open pNets, and shows its decidability together with a congruence theorem.

1 Introduction

In the nineties, several works extended the basic behavioural models based on labelled transition systems to address value-passing or parameterised systems, using various symbolic encodings of the transitions [1–4]. In [4], Lin addressed value-passing calculi, for which he developed a symbolic behavioural semantics, and proved algebraic properties. Separately Rathke [5] defined another symbolic semantics for a parameterised broadcast calculus, together with strong and weak bisimulation equivalences, and developed a symbolic model-checker based on a tableau method for these processes. 30 years later, no practical verification approach and no verification platform are using this kind of approaches to provide proof methods for value-passing processes or open process expressions. This article proposes a new approach to study concurrent and distributed systems based on a semantic formalism featuring: (1) low-level description of behaviours (transition systems) with explicit data parameters, and hierarchical structure, (2) flexible composition and synchronisation mechanism, (3) finite representation of the behavioural semantics using symbolic representations of sets of behaviours.

This work was partially funded by the Associated Team FM4CPS between INRIA and ECNU, Shanghai.

© IFIP International Federation for Information Processing 2016
E. Albert and I. Lanese (Eds.): FORTE 2016, LNCS 9688, pp. 175–194, 2016.
DOI: 10.1007/978-3-319-39570-8_12

Parameterised Networks of synchronised automata (pNets) was proposed to give a behavioural specification formalism for distributed systems. It inherited from the work of Arnold on synchronisation vectors [6]. In previous work [7], we showed that pNets can be used to represent the behavioural semantics of a system including value-passing and many kinds of synchronisation methods. We used these results to give the semantics of various constructs and languages for distributed objects, and to build a platform for design and verification of distributed software components [8,9]. The parameterised and hierarchical nature of pNets allows for compact models easy to generate from applications in high-level languages. Their structure is static, but unbounded, and this allows for model-checking approaches even for reconfigurable applications. Closed pNets were used to encode fully defined programs or systems, while open pNets have "holes", playing the role of process parameters. Such open systems can be used to define composition operators. The challenge raised by the research on open pNets is due to its "open" nature and to the existence of holes and parameters.

Contribution. The aim of this paper is to provide a theory for the operators composing concurrent processes. This theory is based on the definition of operators as open pNets. By defining the operational semantics of open pNets, using open transitions that include symbolic hypotheses on the behaviour of the pNets holes, we can define a strong bisimulation equivalence between open pNets, and show its decidability. This work highlights the possibility to automatically infer proof obligations, in the form of predicate inclusion, that have to be verified to prove the equivalence of operators. These results allow us to envision the semi-automatic proof of equivalence between operators for composing processes.

Related Works. A number of fundamental works have been published on symbolic or open bisimulations, with varying vocabulary. In this section, we only list works that are directly related to our approach.

The closest research (and oldest) is from De Simone [1], who defines *Specification Rules* and a *FH-bisimulation* equivalence, that were one of our main inspiration for the open-transition concept. Some years later, Rensink [10] defines a generic notion of conditional transition systems and studies relations between FH-bisimulation and others. We believe that in the work of De Simone context and in ours, the relations coincide, and that Rensink work differs mainly in presence of recursive binding constructs that we do not consider.

In [3,4] Hennessy and Lin developed the theory of symbolic transition graphs (STG), and the associated symbolic (early and late) bisimulations, they also study STGs with assignments which can be a model for message-passing processes. These are clearly related to our parameterised LTSs, though they are more specifically addressing the action algebra of value-passing CCS expressions. [3] also gives an algorithm for computing symbolic bisimulation, but only for symbolic finite trees. An interesting variant was developed by Hennessy and Rathke [5], concerning a calculus of broadcasting systems (CBS) and a symbolic bisimulation. The main characteristic of this calculus is that communication is "one-to-many", and non blocking, so the definitions of semantics and equivalences differ significantly from previous works. Later, J. Rathke proposed a model-checker for CBS based on a sound tableau method over symbolic graphs. Another important similarity between the works on STGs, CBS, and ours is the use of an auxiliary proof system on value expressions. Remark that pNets can encode both value-passing CCS and CBS, but also other communication and synchronisation schemas.

More recently, Deng [11] gave an open bisimulation for π-calculus based on STG, which used a predicate equation system whose greatest solution characterizes the condition under which the two STGs are bisimilar. There is here a potential relation with our work: if the number of states and branching of the symbolic model is finite, then their algorithm can terminate; a similar approach may help us to compute our FH-bisimulation.

Finally, there are numerous works on subclasses of infinite-state programs or parameterised systems, seeking decidability properties, and sometimes model-checking or equivalence checking algorithms. For example [12] proposed a model checker to verify the safety and liveness properties on infinite-state programs. They symbolically encode transitions and states using predicates, including affine constraints on integer variables. Another very different approach is used by [13], relying on a dedicated model based on network grammars and regular languages.

Structure. Section 2 extends the previous definition of pNets [7] to fit the needs of the open pNets. Section 3 gives their operational semantics based on open transitions, and proves that this semantics is finite under reasonable conditions. In Sect. 4 we introduce an equivalence called FH-bisimulation, and prove its decidability. All sections are illustrated by a running example encoding a Lotos operator. Section 5 proves a crucial composition theorem. Finally Sect. 6 concludes and discusses future work.

2   Parameterised Networks (pNets): Definition

This section introduces pNets and the notations we will use in this paper. Then it gives the formal definition of pNet structures, together with an operational semantics for open pNets.

pNets are tree-like structures, where the leaves are either *parameterised labelled transition systems (pLTSs)*, expressing the behaviour of basic processes, or *holes*, used as placeholders for unknown processes, of which we only specify the set of possible actions, this set is named the *sort*. Nodes of the tree (pNet nodes) are synchronising artifacts, using a set of *synchronisation vectors* that express the possible synchronisation between the parameterised actions of a subset of the sub-trees.

Notations. We extensively use indexed structures over some countable indexed sets, which are equivalent to mappings over the countable set. $a_i^{i \in I}$ denotes a family of elements a_i indexed over the set I. $a_i^{i \in I}$ defines both I the set over which the family is indexed (called *range*), and a_i the elements of the family. E.g., $a^{i \in \{3\}}$ is the mapping with a single entry a at index 3 ; abbreviated $(3 \mapsto a)$ in the following. When this is not ambiguous, we shall use notations for sets, and typically write "indexed set over I" when formally we should speak of multisets, and write $x \in a_i^{i \in I}$ to mean $\exists i \in I. x = a_i$. An empty family is denoted $\emptyset$. We denote classically $\bar{a}$ a family when the indexing set is not meaningful. $\uplus$ is the disjoint union on indexed sets.

Term Algebra. Our models rely on a notion of parameterised actions, that are symbolic expressions using data types and variables. As our model aims at encoding the low-level behaviour of possibly very different programming languages, we do not want to impose one specific algebra for denoting actions, nor any specific communication mechanism. So we leave unspecified the constructors of the algebra that will allow building expressions and actions. Moreover, we use a generic *action interaction* mechanism, based on (some sort of) unification between two or more action expressions, to express various kinds of communication or synchronisation mechanisms.

Formally, we assume the existence of a term algebra $\mathcal{T}_{\Sigma,\mathcal{P}}$, where Σ is the signature of the data and action constructors, and $\mathcal{P}$ a set of variables. Within $\mathcal{T}_{\Sigma,\mathcal{P}}$, we distinguish a set of data expressions $\mathcal{E}_\mathcal{P}$, including a set of boolean expressions $\mathcal{B}_\mathcal{P}$ ($\mathcal{B}_\mathcal{P} \subseteq \mathcal{E}_\mathcal{P}$). On top of $\mathcal{E}_\mathcal{P}$ we build the action algebra $\mathcal{A}_\mathcal{P}$, with $\mathcal{A}_\mathcal{P} \subseteq \mathcal{T}_\mathcal{P}, \mathcal{E}_P \cap \mathcal{A}_P = \emptyset$; naturally action terms will use data expressions as subterms. To be able to reason about the data flow between pLTSs, we distinguish *input variables* of the form $?x$ within terms; the function $vars(t)$ identifies the set of variables in a term $t \in \mathcal{T}$, and $iv(t)$ returns its input variables.

pNets can encode naturally the notion of input actions in value-passing CCS [14] or of usual point-to-point message passing calculi, but it also allows for more general mechanisms, like gate negociation in Lotos, or broadcast communications. Using our notations, value-passing actions *à la* CCS would be encoded as $a(?x_1, ..., ?x_n)$ for inputs, $a(v_1, .., v_n)$ for outputs (in which v_i are action terms containing no input variables). We can also use more complex action structure such as Meije-SCCS action monoids, like in $a.b$, $a^{f(n)}$ (see [1]). The expressiveness of the synchronisation constructs will depend on the action algebra.

2.1   The (open) pNets Core Model

A pLTS is a labelled transition system with variables; variables can be manipulated, defined, or accessed inside states, actions, guards, and assignments. Without loss of generality and to simplify the formalisation, we suppose here that variables are local to each state: each state has its set of variables disjoint from the others. Transmitting variable values from one state to the other can be done by explicit assignment. Note that we make no assumption on finiteness of the set of states nor on finite branching of the transition relation.

We first define the set of actions a pLTS can use, let a range over action labels, op are operators, and x_i range over variable names. Action terms are:

$$\alpha \in \mathcal{A} ::= a(p_1, \ldots, p_n) \qquad\qquad \text{action terms}$$
$$p_i ::= ?x \mid Expr \qquad\qquad \text{parameters (input variable or expression)}$$
$$Expr ::= Value \mid x \mid op(Expr_1, .., Expr_n) \quad \text{Expressions}$$

The input variables in an action term are those marked with a ?. We additionally suppose that each input variable does not appear somewhere else in the same action term: $p_i = ?x \Rightarrow \forall j \neq i. x \notin vars(p_j)$

Definition 1 (pLTS). *A pLTS is a tuple $pLTS \triangleq \langle\!\langle S, s_0, \rightarrow \rangle\!\rangle$ where:*

- *S is a set of states.*
- *$s_0 \in S$ is the initial state.*
- *$\rightarrow \subseteq S \times L \times S$ is the transition relation and L is the set of labels of the form $\langle \alpha, e_b, (x_j := e_j)^{j \in J} \rangle$, where $\alpha \in \mathcal{A}$ is a parameterised action, $e_b \in \mathcal{B}$ is a guard, and the variables $x_j \in P$ are assigned the expressions $e_j \in \mathcal{E}$. If $s \xrightarrow{\langle \alpha, e_b, (x_j := e_j)^{j \in J} \rangle} s' \in \rightarrow$ then $iv(\alpha) \subseteq vars(s'),\ vars(\alpha) \backslash iv(\alpha) \subseteq vars(s),$ $vars(e_b) \subseteq vars(s'),$ and $\forall j \in J. vars(e_j) \subseteq vars(s) \land x_j \in vars(s').$*

Now we define pNet nodes, as constructors for hierarchical behavioural structures. A pNet has a set of sub-pNets that can be either pNets or pLTSs, and a set of Holes, playing the role of process parameters.

A composite pNet consists of a set of sub-pNets exposing a set of actions, each of them triggering internal actions in each of the sub-pNets. The synchronisation between global actions and internal actions is given by *synchronisation vectors*: a synchronisation vector synchronises one or several internal actions, and exposes a single resulting global action. Actions involved at the pNet level (in the synchronisation vectors) do not need to distinguish between input and output variables. Action terms for pNets are defined as follows:

$$\alpha \in \mathcal{A}_S ::= a(Expr_1, \ldots, Expr_n)$$

Definition 2 (pNets). *A pNet is a hierarchical structure where leaves are pLTSs and holes:*
$$pNet \triangleq pLTS \mid \langle\!\langle pNet_i^{i \in I}, S_j^{j \in J}, SV_k^{k \in K} \rangle\!\rangle \text{ where}$$

- *$I \in \mathcal{I}$ is the set over which sub-pNets are indexed.*
- *$pNet_i^{i \in I}$ is the family of sub-pNets.*
- *$J \in \mathcal{I}_P$ is the set over which holes are indexed. I and J are disjoint: $I \cap J = \emptyset$, $I \cup J \neq \emptyset$*
- *$S_j \subseteq \mathcal{A}_S$ is a set of action terms, denoting the Sort of hole j.*
- *$SV_k^{k \in K}$ is a set of synchronisation vectors ($K \in \mathcal{I}_P$). $\forall k \in K, SV_k = \alpha_l^{l \in I_k \uplus J_k} \rightarrow \alpha_k'$ where $\alpha_k' \in \mathcal{A}_P$, $I_k \subseteq I$, $J_k \subseteq J$, $\forall i \in I_k. \alpha_i \in \text{Sort}(pNet_i)$, $\forall j \in J_k. \alpha_j \in S_j$, and $vars(\alpha_k') \subseteq \bigcup_{l \in I_k \uplus J_k} vars(\alpha_l)$. The global action of a vector SV_k is $\text{Label}(SV_k) = \alpha_k'$.*

The preceding definition relies on the auxiliary functions below:

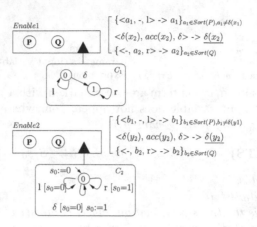

Fig. 1. Two pNet encodings for Enable

Definition 3 (Sorts, Holes, Leaves of pNets).

– *The sort of a pNet is its signature, i.e. the set of actions it can perform. In the definition of sorts, we do not need to distinguish input variables (that specify the dataflow within LTSs), so for computing LTS sorts, we use a substitution operator[1] to remove the* input marker *of variables. Formally:*

$$\text{Sort}(\langle\!\langle S, s_0, \rightarrow \rangle\!\rangle) = \{\alpha \{\!\{x \leftarrow ?x | x \in iv(\alpha)\}\!\} | s \xrightarrow{\langle \alpha,\ e_b,\ (x_j := e_j)^{j \in J}\rangle} s' \in \rightarrow\}$$
$$\text{Sort}(\langle\!\langle \overline{pNet}, \overline{S}, \overline{SV} \rangle\!\rangle) = \{\alpha'_k | \alpha_j^{j \in J_k} \rightarrow \alpha'_k \in \overline{SV}\}$$

– *The set of holes of a pNet is defined inductively; the sets of holes in a pNet node and its subnets are all disjoint:*

$$\text{Holes}(\langle\!\langle S, s_0, \rightarrow \rangle\!\rangle) = \emptyset$$
$$\text{Holes}(\langle\!\langle pNet_i^{i \in I}, S_j^{j \in J}, \overline{SV} \rangle\!\rangle) = J \cup \bigcup_{i \in I} \text{Holes}(pNet_i)$$
$$\forall i \in I.\ \text{Holes}(pNet_i) \cap J = \emptyset$$
$$\forall i_1, i_2 \in I.\ i_1 \neq i_2 \Rightarrow \text{Holes}(pNet_{i_1}) \cap \text{Holes}(pNet_{i_2}) = \emptyset$$

– *The set of leaves of a pNet is the set of all pLTSs occurring in the structure, defined inductively as:*

$$\text{Leaves}(\langle\!\langle S, s_0, \rightarrow \rangle\!\rangle) = \{\langle\!\langle S, s_0, \rightarrow \rangle\!\rangle\}$$
$$\text{Leaves}(\langle\!\langle pNet_i^{i \in I}, S_j^{j \in J}, \overline{SV} \rangle\!\rangle) = \bigcup_{i \in I} \text{Leaves}(pNet_i)$$

A pNet Q is *closed* if it has no hole: $\text{Holes}(Q) = \emptyset$; else it is said to be *open*.

---

[1] $\{\!\{y_k \leftarrow x_k\}\!\}^{k \in K}$ is the parallel substitution operation.

Alternative Syntax. When describing examples, we usually deal with pNets with finitely many sub-pNets and holes, and it is convenient to have a more concrete syntax for synchronisation vectors. When $I \cup J = [0..n]$ we denote synchronisation vectors as $< \alpha_1, .., \alpha_n > \rightarrow \alpha$, and elements not taking part in the synchronisation are denoted − as in: $< -, -, \alpha, -, - > \rightarrow \alpha$.

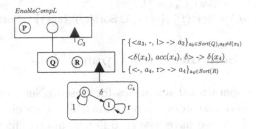

Fig. 2. Composed pNet for "P≫(Q≫R)"

Example 1. To give simple intuitions of the open pNet model and its semantics, we use here a small example coming from the Lotos specification language. It will be used as an illustrative example in the whole paper. We already have shown in [7] how to encode non trivial operators using synchronisation vectors and one or several pLTSs used as controllers, managing the state changes of the operators. In Fig. 1, we show 2 possible encodings of the Lotos "Enable" operator. In the Enable expression "P≫Q", an `exit(x)` statement within P terminates the current process, carrying a value x that is captured by the `accept(x)` statement of Q.

We use a simple action algebra, containing two constructors $\delta(x)$ and $acc(x)$, for any possible data type of the variable x, corresponding to the statements `exit(x)` and `accept(x)`. Both $\delta(x)$ and $acc(x)$ actions are implicitly included in the sorts of all processes. We need no specific predicate over the action expressions, apart from equality of actions. In the first encoding *Enable1*, in the upper part of Fig. 1, we use a controller C_1 with two states, and simple control actions l, r, δ. The second encoding *Enable2* uses a data-oriented style, with a single state controller, and a state-variable s_0, with values in $\{0, 1\}$.

In this example we use a specific notation for *local actions*, that cannot be further synchronised, like the τ silent action of CCS. We name them *synchronised actions*, and denote them as any action expression with the text underlined, as e.g. $\underline{\delta(x_2)}$. Such synchronised actions do not play any special role for defining strong bisimulation, but as one can expect, will be crucial for weak equivalences.

Note that synchronisation vectors are defined in a parameterised manner: the first and third lines represent one vector for each parameterised action in the Sort of hole P (resp. Q). This notation can also use predicates, as in the first case, in which we want the vector to apply to any action of P except $\delta(x)$.

In Fig. 2, we enrich our example by composing 2 occurences of the Enable1 pNet. To simplify, we only have represented one instance of the synchronisation vector set, and of the controller.

The reader can easily infer from these two figures the following sets:

Holes($EnableCompL$) = $\{P, Q, R\}$
Leaves($EnableCompL$)) = $\{C_3, C_4\}$
Sort(C_1) = Sort(C_2) = Sort(C_4) = $\{l, \delta, r\})$
Sort($EnableCompL$) = Sort(P)\$\{\delta(x)\}$ ∪ Sort(Q)\$\{\delta(x)\}$ ∪ Sort(R) ∪ $\underline{\{\delta(x)\}}$.

3   Operational Semantics for Open pNets

In [7] we defined an operational semantics for closed pNets, expressed in a *late style*, where states and transition were defined for a specific valuation of all the pNet variables. Here we have a very different approach: we build a direct symbolic operational semantics for open pNets, encoding formally hypotheses about the behaviour of the holes, and dealing symbolically with the variables. This will naturally lead us in the following sections to the definition of an open bisimulation equivalence, playing explicitly with predicates on the action of holes, and values of variables.

The idea is to consider an open pNet as an expression similar to an open process expression in a process algebra. pNet expressions can be combined to form bigger expressions, at the leaves pLTSs are constant expressions, and holes play the role of process parameters. In an open pNet, pLTSs naturally have states, and holes have no state; furthermore, the shape of the pNet expression is not modified during operational steps, only the state of its pLTSs can change.

The semantics of open pNets will be defined as an open automaton. An open automaton is an automaton where each transition composes transitions of several LTSs with action of some holes, the transition occurs if some predicates hold, and can involve a set of state modifications.

Definition 4 (Open Transitions). *An open transition over a set $(S_i, s_{0i}, \rightarrow_i)^{i \in I}$ of LTSs, a set J of holes with sorts $Sort_j^{j \in J}$, and a set of states $\mathcal{S}$ is a structure of the form:*

$$\frac{\{s_i \xrightarrow{a_i}_i s_i'\}^{i \in I}, \{\xrightarrow{b_j}_j\}^{j \in J}, Pred, Post}{s \xrightarrow{v} s'}$$

Where $s, s' \in \mathcal{S}$ and for all $i \in I$, $s_i \xrightarrow{a_i}_i s_i'$ is a transition of the LTS $(S_i, s_{0i}, \rightarrow_i)$, and $\xrightarrow{b_j}_j$ is a transition of the hole j, for any action b_j in the sort $Sort_j$. Pred is a predicate over the different variables of the terms, labels, and states s_i, b_j, s, v. Post is a set of equations that hold after the open transition, they are represented as a substitution of the form $\{x_k \leftarrow e_k\}^{k \in K}$ where x_k are variables of s', s_i', and e_k are expressions over the other variables of the open transition.

Example 2 An open-transition. The `EnableCompL` pNet of Fig. 2 has 2 controllers and 2 holes. One of its possible open-transition is:

$$OT_2 = \cfrac{0 \xrightarrow{\delta}_{C_3} 1 \quad 0 \xrightarrow{l}_{C_4} 0 \quad \xrightarrow{\delta(x4)}_{P} \quad \xrightarrow{accept(x4)}_{Q}}{A1_0 \xRightarrow{\delta(\tilde{x}4)} A1_1}$$

Definition 5 (Open Automaton). *An* open automaton *is a structure* $A = <LTS_i^{i \in I}, J, \mathcal{S}, s_0, \mathcal{T}>$ *where:*

- *I and J are sets of indices,*
- *$LTS_i^{i \in I}$ is a family of LTSs,*
- *$\mathcal{S}$ is a set of states and s_0 an initial state among $\mathcal{S}$,*
- *$\mathcal{T}$ is a set of open transitions and for each $t \in \mathcal{T}$ there exist I', J' with $I' \subseteq I$, $J' \subseteq J$, such that t is an open transition over $LTS_i^{i \in I'}$, J', and $\mathcal{S}$.*

Definition 6 (States of Open pNets). *A state of an open pNet is a tuple (not necessarily finite) of the states of its leaves (in which we denote tuples in structured states as $\triangleleft \ldots \triangleright$ for better readability).*

For any pNet p, let $\overline{Leaves} = \langle\!\langle S_i, s_{i0}, \rightarrow_i \rangle\!\rangle^{i \in L}$ be the set of pLTS at its leaves, then $States(p) = \{\triangleleft s_i^{i \in L} \triangleright | \forall i \in L.s_i \in S_i\}$. A pLTS being its own single leave: $States(\langle\!\langle S, s_0, \rightarrow \rangle\!\rangle) = \{\triangleleft s \triangleright | s \in S\}$.

The initial state is defined as: $InitState(p) = \triangleleft s_{i0}^{i \in L} \triangleright$.

Predicates: Let $\langle\!\langle \overline{pNet}, \overline{S}, SV_k^{k \in K} \rangle\!\rangle$ be a pNet. Consider a synchronisation vector SV_k, for $k \in K$. We define a predicate *Pred* relating the actions of the involved sub-pNets and the resulting actions. This predicate verifies:

$$Pred(SV_k, a_i^{i \in I}, b_j^{j \in J}, v) \Leftrightarrow \begin{aligned} &\exists (a_i')^{i \in I}, (b_j')^{j \in J}, v'. \, SV_k = (a_i')^{i \in I}, (b_j')^{j \in J} \rightarrow v' \\ &\wedge \forall i \in I. a_i = a_i' \wedge \forall j \in J. b_j = b_j' \wedge v = v' \end{aligned}$$

In any other case (if the action families do not match or if there is no valuation of variables such that the above formula can be ensured) the predicate is undefined.

This definition is not constructive but it is easy to build the predicate constructively by brute-force unification of the sub-pNets actions with the corresponding vector actions, possibly followed by a simplification step.

We build the semantics of open pNets as an open automaton where LTSs are the pLTSs at the leaves of the pNet structure, and the states are given by Definition 6. The open transitions first project the global state into states of the leaves, then apply pLTS transitions on these states, and compose them with the sort of the holes. The semantics regularly instantiates *fresh* variables, and uses a *clone* operator that clones a term replacing each variable with a fresh one.

Definition 7 (Operational Semantics of Open pNets). *The semantics of a pNet p is an open automaton $A = <Leaves(p), J, \mathcal{S}, s_0, \mathcal{T}>$ where:*

- *J is the indices of the holes: $Holes(p) = H_j^{j \in J}$.*

– $\overline{S} = States(p)$ and $s_0 = InitState(p)$
– $\mathcal{T}$ is the smallest set of open transitions satisfying the rules below:

The rule for a pLTS p checks that the guard is verified and transforms assignments into post-conditions:

Tr1:

$$\frac{s \xrightarrow{\langle \alpha,\, e_b,\, (x_j := e_j)^{j \in J} \rangle} s' \in \rightarrow}{p = \langle\!\langle S, s_0, \rightarrow \rangle\!\rangle \models \dfrac{\{s \xrightarrow{\alpha}_p s'\}, \emptyset, e_b, \{x_j \leftarrow e_j\}^{j \in J}}{\triangleleft s \triangleright \xrightarrow{\alpha} \triangleleft s' \triangleright}}$$

The second rule deals with pNet nodes: for each possible synchronisation vector applicable to the rule subject, the premisses include one open transition for each sub-pNet involved, one possible action for each Hole involved, and the predicate relating these with the resulting action of the vector. A key to understand this rule is that the open transitions are expressed in terms of the leaves and holes of the pNet structure, i.e. a flatten view of the pNet: e.g. L is the index set of the Leaves, L_k the index set of the leaves of one subnet, so all L_k are disjoint subsets of L. Thus the states in the open transitions, at each level, are tuples including states of all the leaves of the pNet, not only those involved in the chosen synchronisation vector.

Tr2:

$$k \in K \qquad SV = clone(SV_k) = \alpha_m^{m \in I_k \uplus J_k} \rightarrow \alpha'_k \qquad Leaves(p) = pLTS_l^{l \in L}$$

$$\forall m \in I_k.pNet_m \models \frac{\{s_i \xrightarrow{a_i}_i s'_i\}^{i \in I'_m}, \{\xrightarrow{b_j}_j\}^{j \in J'_m}, Pred_m, Post_m}{\triangleleft s_i^{i \in L_m} \triangleright \xrightarrow{v_m} \triangleleft s_i'^{\,i \in L_m} \triangleright}$$

$$I' = \biguplus_{m \in I_k} I'_m$$

$$J' = \biguplus_{m \in I_k} J'_m \uplus J_k \qquad Pred = \bigwedge_{m \in I_k} Pred_m \wedge Pred(SV, a_i^{i \in I_k}, b_j^{j \in J_k}, v)$$

$$\forall j \in J_k.\texttt{fresh}(b_j) \qquad \texttt{fresh}(v) \qquad \forall i \in L \backslash I'.s'_i = s_i$$

$$\overline{p = \langle\!\langle pNet_i^{i \in I}, S_j^{j \in J}, SV_k^{k \in K} \rangle\!\rangle \models \dfrac{\{s_i \xrightarrow{a_i}_i s'_i\}^{i \in I'}, \{\xrightarrow{b_j}_j\}^{j \in J'}, Pred, \uplus_{m \in I_k} Post_m}{\triangleleft s_i^{i \in L} \triangleright \xrightarrow{v} \triangleleft s_i'^{\,i \in L} \triangleright}}$$

Example 3. Using the operational rules to compute open-transitions In Fig. 3 we show the deduction tree used to construct and prove the open transition OT_2 of `EnableCompL` (see Example p. x). The rule uses TR1 for the δ transition of C_3, for the l transition of C_4, then combines the result using the a_4 vector of the bottom pNet node, and the $\underline{\delta(x)}$ vector of the top node.

Note that while the scenario above is expressed as a single instantiation of the possible behaviours, the constructions below are kept symbolic, and each open-transition deduced expresses a whole family of behaviours, for any possible values of the variables.

$$C_3 \models \cfrac{\cfrac{0 \xrightarrow{\delta}_{C_3} 1}{0 \xrightarrow{\delta}_{C_3} 1, \ \{\xrightarrow{\delta(x_1)} P\}, \ v_1 = \delta(x_1)}}{\triangleleft 0 \triangleright \xrightarrow{v_1} \triangleleft 1 \triangleright}$$

$$C_4 \models \cfrac{\cfrac{0 \xrightarrow{l}_{C_4} 0}{0 \xrightarrow{l}_{C_4} 0, \ \mathrm{Pred}_{C_4}}}{\triangleleft 0 \triangleright \xrightarrow{l} \triangleleft 0 \triangleright}$$

$$Q \gg R \models \cfrac{0 \xrightarrow{l}_{C_4} 0, \ \{\xrightarrow{acc(x_2)} Q\}, \ v_2 = acc(x_2)}{\triangleleft 0 \triangleright \xrightarrow{v_2} \triangleleft 0 \triangleright}$$

$$P \gg (Q \gg R) \models \cfrac{0 \xrightarrow{\delta}_{C_3} 1, \ 0 \xrightarrow{l}_{C_4} 0, \ \{\xrightarrow{\delta(x)} P, \xrightarrow{acc(x)} Q\}, \ a_3 = v_1 \wedge v = a_3 \wedge x_1 = x_2}{\triangleleft 00 \triangleright \xrightarrow{v} \triangleleft 10 \triangleright}$$

Fig. 3. Proof of transition OT_2 (with interaction of processes P and Q) for "P≫(Q≫R)"

Variable Management. The variables in each synchronisation vector are considered local: for a given pNet expression, we must have fresh local variables for each occurrence of a vector (= each time we instantiate rule Tr2). Similarly the state variables of each copy of a given pLTS in the system, must be distinct, and those created for each application of Tr2 have to be fresh and all distinct. This will be implemented within the open-automaton generation algorithm, e.g. using name generation using a global counter as a suffix.

3.1 Computing and Using Open Automata

In this section we present a simple algorithm to construct the open automaton representing the behaviour of an open pNet, and we prove that under reasonable conditions this automaton is finite.

Algorithm 1 (Behavioural Semantics of Open pNets: Sketch). *This is a standard residual algorithm over a set of open-automaton states, but where transitions are open transitions constructively "proven" by deduction trees.*

(1) Start with a set of unexplored states containing the initial state of the automaton, and an empty set of explored states.

(2) While there are unexplored states:

(2a) pick one state from the unexplored set and add it to the explored set. From this state build all possible deduction trees by application of the structural rules Tr1 and Tr2, using all applicable combinations of synchronisation vectors.

(2b) For each of the obtained deduction trees, extract the resulting open-transition, with its predicate and Post assignments by exploring the structure of the pNet.

(2c) Optionally, simplifying the predicate at this point may minimize the resulting transitions, or even prune the search-space.

(2d) For each open-transition from step 2b, add the resulting state in the unexplored set if it is not already in the explored set, and add the transition in the outgoing transitions of the current state.

To have some practical interest, it is important to know when this algorithm terminates. The following theorem shows that an open-pNet with finite synchronisation sets, finitely many leaves and holes, and each pLTS at leaves having a finite number of states and (symbolic) transitions, has a finite automaton:

Theorem 2 (Finiteness of Open-Automata). *Given an open pNet $\langle\!\langle \overline{pNet}, \overline{S}, SV_k^{k\in K} \rangle\!\rangle$ with leaves $pLTS_i^{i\in L}$ and holes $Hole_j^{j\in J}$, if the sets L and J are finite, if the synchronisation vectors of all pNets included in $\langle\!\langle \overline{pNet}, \overline{S}, SV_k^{k\in K} \rangle\!\rangle$ are finite, and if $\forall i \in L.\, finite(states(pLTS_i))$ and $pLTS_i$ has a finite number of state variables, then Algorithm 1 terminates and produces an open automaton $\mathcal{T}$ with finitely many states and transitions.*

Proof. The possible set of states of the open-automaton is the cartesian product of the states of its leaves $pLTS_i^{i\in L}$, that is finite by hypothesis. So the top-level residual loop of Algorithm 1 terminates provided each iteration terminates. The enumeration of open-transitions in step 2b is bounded by the number of applications of rules Tr2 on the structure of the pNet tree, with a finite number of synchronisation vectors applying at each node the number of global open transition is finite. Similarly rule Tr1 is applied finitely if the number of transitions of each pLTS is finite. So we get finitely many deduction trees, and open-transitions which ensures that each internal loop of Algorithm 1 terminates. □

4 Bisimulation

Now we use our symbolic operational semantics to define a notion of strong (symbolic) bisimulation. Moreover this equivalence is decidable whenever we have some decision procedure on the predicates of the action algebra.

The equivalence we need is a strong bisimulation between pNets having exactly the same Holes with the same sorts, but using a flexible matching between open transition, to accommodate comparisons between pNet expressions with different architectures. We name it FH-bisimulation, as a short cut for the "Formal Hypotheses" manipulated in the transitions, but also as a reference to the work of De Simone [1], that pioneered this idea. Formally:

Definition 8 (FH-bisimulation).
Suppose that $A_1 =< L_1, J, \mathcal{S}_1, s_0^1, \mathcal{T}_1 >$ and $A_2 =< L_2, J, \mathcal{S}_2, s_0^2, \mathcal{T}_2 >$ are open automata where the set of holes are equal and of the same sort. Let $(s^1, s^2 | Pred) \in \mathcal{R}$ be a relation over the sets $\mathcal{S}_1$ and $\mathcal{S}_2$ constrained by a predicate. More precisely, for

$$
\begin{array}{ccc}
s^1 & \mathcal{R} & s^2 \\
\Big\downarrow {\scriptstyle J \atop Pred} & {\scriptstyle J \atop Pred_1}\Big/ & \Big\backslash {\scriptstyle J \atop Pred_x} \\
s^{1\prime} \;\; \mathcal{R} & s_1^{2\prime} \;\; \cdots & s_x^{2\prime}
\end{array}
$$

any pair (s^1, s^2), *there is a single* $(s^1, s^2 | Pred) \in \mathcal{R}$
stating that s^1 *and* s^2 *are related if Pred is true.*
Then $\mathcal{R}$ *is an FH-bisimulation iff for any states* $s^1 \in \mathcal{S}_1$ *and* $s^2 \in \mathcal{S}_2$,
$(s^1, s^2 | Pred) \in \mathcal{R}$, *we have the following:*

– *For any open transition OT in* $\mathcal{T}_1$:

$$\frac{\{s_i^1 \xrightarrow{a_i}_i s_i^{1'}\}^{i \in I_1}, \{\xrightarrow{b_j}_j\}^{j \in J_1}, Pred_{OT}, Post_{OT}}{s^1 \xrightarrow{v} s^{1'}}$$

there exist open transitions $OT_x^{x \in X} \subseteq \mathcal{T}_2$:

$$\frac{\{s_i^2 \xrightarrow{a_{ix}}_i s_{ix}^2\}^{i \in I_{2x}}, \{\xrightarrow{b_{jx}}_j\}^{j \in J_{2x}}, Pred_{OT_x}, Post_{OT_x}}{s^2 \xrightarrow{v_x} s_x^2}$$

such that $\forall x, J_1 = J_{2x}, (s^{1'}, s_x^{2'} | Pred_{target_x}) \in \mathcal{R}$; *and*
$Pred \wedge Pred_{OT}$
$\implies \bigvee_{x \in X} (\forall j. b_j = b_{jx} \Rightarrow Pred_{OT_x} \wedge v = v_x \wedge Pred_{target_x} \{Post_{OT}\} \{Post_{OT_x}\})$
– *and symmetrically any open transition from* s^2 *in* $\mathcal{T}_2$ *can be covered by a set
of transitions from* t^1 *in* $\mathcal{T}_1$.

*Two pNets are FH-bisimilar if there exist a relation between their associated
automata that is an FH-bisimulation.*

Classically, $Pred_{target_x} \{Post_{OT}\} \{Post_{OT_x}\}$ applies in parallel the substitutions $Post_{OT}$ and $Post_{OT_x}$ (parallelism is crucial inside each $Post$ set but $Post_{OT}$ is independent from $Post_{OT_x}$), applying the assignments of the involved rules.

Weak symbolic bisimulation can be defined in a similar way, using as *invisible actions* a subset of the *synchronised actions* defined in Sect. 2. To illustrate our approach on a simple example, let us encode the Lotos **Enable** operator using 2 different encodings, and prove their equivalence.

Example 4. In Fig. 1, we proposed two different open pNets encoding the expression P≫Q. While it is easy to be convinced that they are equivalent, their structures are sufficiently different to show how the FH-bisimultion works and addresses the crucial points on the proof of equivalence between operators. The open automata of these two pNets are given, together with their open transitions in Fig. 4. To illustrate the proof of bisimulation, let us build a relation:

$$R = \{(A_0, B_0 | s_0 = 0), (A_1, B_0 | s_0 = 1)\}$$

and prove that R is a strong FH-bisimulation. For each transition in each automaton, we must find a covering set of transitions, with same holes involved, and equivalent target states. Finding the matching here is trivial, and all covering sets are reduced to singleton. All proofs are pretty similar, so we only show

$$A_0 \xrightarrow{\quad ot_2 \quad} A_1$$

$$\circlearrowleft ot_1 \qquad \circlearrowleft ot_3$$

$$ot'_1 \circlearrowleft B_0 \circlearrowright ot'_3$$

$$\circlearrowleft ot'_2$$

$$ot_1 = \frac{0 \xrightarrow{l}_{C_1} 0, \quad \xrightarrow{a1}_P, \quad a1 \neq \delta(x1)}{A_0 \xrightarrow{a1} A_0}$$

$$ot_2 = \frac{0 \xrightarrow{\delta}_{C_1} 1, \quad \{\xrightarrow{\delta(x2)}_P, \xrightarrow{acc(x2)}_Q\}}{A_0 \xrightarrow{\delta(x2)} A_1}$$

$$ot_3 = \frac{0 \xrightarrow{r}_{C_1} 1, \quad \xrightarrow{a2}_q}{A_1 \xrightarrow{a2} A_1}$$

$$ot'_1 = \frac{0 \xrightarrow{l}_{C_2} 0, \quad \xrightarrow{b1}_P, \quad b1 \neq \delta(y1) \wedge s_0 = 0}{B_0 \xrightarrow{b1} B_0}$$

$$ot'_2 = \frac{0 \xrightarrow{\delta}_{C_2} 1, \quad \{\xrightarrow{\delta(y2)}_P, \xrightarrow{acc(y2)}_Q\}, \quad s_0 = 0, \quad \{s_0 \leftarrow 1\}}{B_0 \xrightarrow{\delta(y2)} B_1}$$

$$ot'_3 = \frac{1 \xrightarrow{r}_{C_2} 1, \quad \xrightarrow{b2}_q, \quad s_0 = 1}{B_1 \xrightarrow{b2} B_1}$$

Fig. 4. The two open automata

here the details for matching (both ways) the open transitions ot_2 and ot'_2; these are the most interesting, because of the presence of the assignment.

Consider transition ot_2 of state A_0, and prove that it is covered by ot'_2. Let us detail the construction of the proof obligation:

$$\boxed{Pred} \wedge Pred_{OT} \implies \bigvee_{x \in X} (\boxed{\forall j.b_j = b_{jx}} \implies \boxed{Pred_{OT_x}} \wedge v = v_x) \wedge \boxed{Pred_{target_x} \{\{Post_{OT}\}\} \{\{Post_{OT_x}\}\}})$$

$$\boxed{s_0 = 0} \implies (\boxed{(\delta(x2) = \delta(y2) \wedge acc(x2) = acc(y2)} \implies \boxed{s_0 = 0} \wedge \boxed{\delta(y2) = \delta(x2)} \wedge \boxed{1 = 1})$$

The source $Pred$ for A_0 in ot_2 is $s_0 = 0$, and ot_2 itself has no predicate. Then we find the condition for holes to have the same behaviours, and from that we must prove the predicate in ot'_2 holds, and finally the predicate of the target state ($A_1, B_0 | s_0 = 1$), after substitution using the assignment $\{s_0 \leftarrow 1\}$, that is $1 = 1$. This formula (in which all variables are universally quantified) is easy to discharge.

Conversely, transition ot'_2 of state B_0 matches with ot_2 of A_0, but now the assignment is on the left hand side, and the proof goal mostly concern the triggered action as ot_2 has no predicate:

$$s_0 = 0 \wedge s_0 = 0 \implies (\delta(y2) = \delta(x2) \wedge acc(y2) = acc(x2) \implies \underline{\delta(x2) = \delta(y2)} \wedge 1 = 1)$$

$\square$

Despite the simplicity of the proven equivalence, the proof of bisimulation highlights precisely the use of the different predicates. It is also important to see that all the arguments necessary for proving the equivalence are well identified and properly used, and that we really made a proof about the operator without having to refer to the behaviour of the processes that will be put in the holes. This simple example shows the expressiveness of our approach by illustrating the use of variables, assignments, controllers and sort of holes. It is straightforward to prove e.g. that the enable operator is associative, after computing the open

automaton of the pNet *EnableComp* from Fig. 2, and a similar one representing
(P>>Q)>>R). Each of the automata has 3 states and 5 open-transitions. For
reasons of space we cannot show them here [15]. We can finally prove that it
is decidable whether a relation is a FH-bisimulation provided the logic of the
predicates is decidable.

Theorem 3 (Decidability of FH-bisimulation). *Let A_1 and A_2 be finite
open automata and $\mathcal{R}$ a relation over their states S_1 and S_2 constrained by a set
of predicates. Assume that the predicates inclusion is decidable over the action
algebra $\mathcal{A}_P$. Then it is decidable whether the relation $\mathcal{R}$ is a FH-bisimulation.*

Proof. The principle is to consider each pair of states (s_1, s_2), consider the ele-
ment $(s_1, s_2 | Pred)$ in $\mathcal{R}$; if *Pred* is not false we consider the (finite) set of open
transition having $s_1 \xrightarrow{v} s_1'$ as a conclusion. For each of them, to prove the simulation, we can consider all the transitions leaving s_2. Let OT_x be the set of all
transitions with a conclusion of the form $s_2 \xrightarrow{v} s_{2x}'$ such that the same holes
are involved in the open transition and such that there exist $Pred_{target_x}$ such
that $(s_1', s_{2x}' | Pred_{target_x}) \in R$. This gives us the predicates and *Post* assignments
corresponding to those open transitions. We then only have to prove:

$$Pred \wedge Pred_{OT} \Rightarrow \bigvee_{x \in X} (\forall j.b_j = b_{jx} \Rightarrow Pred_{OT_x} \wedge v = v_x \wedge Pred_{target_x} \{\!\{Post_{OT}\}\!\} \{\!\{Post_{OT_x}\}\!\})$$

Which is decidable since predicates inclusion is decidable. As the set of elements
in $\mathcal{R}$ is finite and the set of open transitions is finite, it is possible to check them
exhaustively. $\qquad\square$

5   Composability

The main interest of our symbolic approach is to define a method to prove
properties directly on open structures, that will be preserved by any correct
instantiation of the holes. In this section we define a composition operator for
open pNets, and we prove that it preserves FH-bisimulation. More precisely, one
can define two preservation properties, namely (1) when one hole of a pNet is
filled by two bisimilar other (open) pNets; and (2) when the same hole in two
bisimilar pNets are filled by the same pNet, in other words, composing a pNet
with two bisimilar contexts. The general case will be obtained by transitivity of
the bisimulation relation. We concentrate here on the second property, that is
the most interesting.

Definition 9 (pNet Composition). *An open pNet: $pNet = \langle\!\langle pNet_i^{i \in I},$
$S_j^{j \in J}, \overline{SV} \rangle\!\rangle$ can be (partially) filled by providing a pNets $pNet'$ of the right sort
to fill one of its holes. Suppose $j_0 \in J$:*

$$pNet \left[pNet' \right]_{j_0} = \langle\!\langle pNet_i^{i \in I} \uplus \{j_0 \mapsto pNet'\}, S_j^{j \in J \setminus \{j_0\}}, \overline{SV} \rangle\!\rangle$$

Theorem 4 (Context Equivalence). *Consider two FH-bisimilar open pNets:* $pNet = \langle\langle pNet_i^{i\in I}, S_j^{j\in J}, \overline{SV}\rangle\rangle$ *and* $pNet' = \langle\langle pNet'^{i\in I}_i, S_j^{j\in J}, \overline{SV'}\rangle\rangle$ *(recall they must have the same holes to be bisimilar). Let* $j_0 \in J$ *be a hole, and* Q *be a pNet such that* $\mathrm{Sort}(Q) = S_{j_0}$. *Then* $pNet[Q]_{j_0}$ *and* $pNet'[Q]_{j_0}$ *are FH-bisimilar.*

The proof of Theorem 4 relies on two main lemmas, dealing respectively with the decomposition of a composed behaviour between the context and the internal pNet, and with their recomposition. We start with decomposition: from one open transition of $P[Q]_{j_0}$, we exhibit corresponding behaviours of P and Q, and determine the relation between their predicates:

Lemma 1 (OT Decomposition). *Let* $\mathrm{Leaves}(Q) = p_l^{l\in L_Q}$; *suppose:*

$$P[Q]_{j_0} \models \frac{\{s_i \xrightarrow{a_i}_i s_i'\}^{i\in I}, \{\xrightarrow{b_j}_j\}^{j\in J}, Pred, Post}{\lhd s_i^{i\in L}\rhd \xrightarrow{v} \lhd s_i'^{i\in L}\rhd}$$

with Q *"moving" (i.e.* $J \cap \mathrm{Holes}(Q) \neq \emptyset$ *or* $I \cap L_Q \neq \emptyset$*). Then there exist* v_Q, *Pred', Pred'', Post', Post'' s.t.:*

$$P \models \frac{\{s_i \xrightarrow{a_i}_i s_i'\}^{i\in I\setminus L_Q}, \{\xrightarrow{b_j}_j\}^{j\in J\setminus\mathrm{Holes}(Q)\cup\{j_0\}}, Pred', Post'}{\lhd s_i^{i\in L\setminus L_Q}\rhd \xrightarrow{v} \lhd s_i'^{i\in L\setminus L_Q}\rhd}$$

and $Q \models \dfrac{\{s_i \xrightarrow{a_i}_i s_i'\}^{i\in I\cap L_Q}, \{\xrightarrow{b_j}_j\}^{j\in J\cap\mathrm{Holes}(Q)}, Pred'', Post''}{\lhd s_i^{i\in L_Q}\rhd \xrightarrow{v_Q} \lhd s_i'^{i\in L_Q}\rhd}$

and $Pred\{\!\!\{v_Q \leftarrow b_{j_0}\}\!\!\} = (Pred' \wedge Pred'')$, $Post = Post' \uplus Post''$ *where* $Post''$ *is the restriction of* $Post$ *over variables of* $\mathrm{Leaves}(Q)$.

Proof. Consider each premise of the open transition (as constructed by rule TR2 in Definition 7). We know each premise is true for $P[Q]$ and try to prove the equivalent premise for P. First, K and the synchronisation vector SV_k are unchanged[2] (however j_0 passes from the set of subnets to the set of holes). Then $SV = clone(\alpha_j^{j\in I_k\uplus\{j_0\}\uplus J_k})$. $\mathrm{Leaves}(P[Q]_{j_0}) = \mathrm{Leaves}(P)\uplus\mathrm{Leaves}(Q)$. Now focus on OTs of the subnets (see footnote 2):

$$\forall m \in I_k \cup \{j_0\}.pNet_m \models \frac{\{s_i \xrightarrow{a_i}_i s_i'\}^{i\in I_m}, \{\xrightarrow{b_j}_j\}^{j\in J_m}, Pred_m, Post_m}{\lhd s_i^{i\in L_m}\rhd \xrightarrow{v_m} \lhd s_i'^{i\in L_m}\rhd}$$

Only elements of I_k are useful to assert the premise for reduction of P; the last one ensures (note that Q is at place j_0, and $I_{j_0} = I \cap L_Q$, $L_{j_0} = L_Q$):

$$Q \models \frac{\{s_i \xrightarrow{a_i}_i s_i'\}^{i\in I\cap L_Q}, \{\xrightarrow{b_j}_j\}^{j\in J\cap\mathrm{Holes}(Q)}, Pred_{j_0}, Post''}{\lhd s_i^{i\in L_Q}\rhd \xrightarrow{v_{j_0}} \lhd s_i'^{i\in L_Q}\rhd}$$

---

[2] Cloning and freshness introduce alpha-conversion at many points of the proof; we only give major arguments concerning alpha-conversion to make the proof readable; in general, fresh variables appear in each transition inside terms b_j, v, and $Pred$.

This already ensures the second part of the conclusion if we choose (see footnote 2) $v_Q = v_{j_0}$ ($Pred'' = Pred_{j_0}$). Now let $I' = \biguplus I'_m = I \setminus L_Q$, $J' = \biguplus J'_m \uplus J_k \uplus \{j_0\} = J \setminus \text{Holes}(Q) \uplus \{j_0\}$; the predicate is $Pred' = \bigwedge_{m \in I_k} Pred_m \wedge Pred(SV, a_i^{i \in I_k}, b_j^{j \in J_k \cup \{j_0\}}, v)$ where (see footnote 2) $Pred(SV, a_i^{i \in I_k}, b_j^{j \in J_k}, v) \Leftrightarrow \forall i \in I_k.\alpha_i = a_i \wedge \forall j \in J_k \cup \{j_0\}.\alpha_j = b_j \wedge v = \alpha'_k$. Modulo renaming of fresh variables, this is identical to the predicate that occurs in the source open transition except $\alpha_{j_0} = v_{j_0}$ has been replaced by $\alpha_{j_0} = b_{j_0}$. Thus, $Pred\{v_Q \leftarrow b_{j_0}\} = (Pred' \wedge Pred'')$. Finally, Post into conditions of the context P and the pNet Q (they are builts similarly as they only deal with leaves): $Post = Post' \uplus Post''$. We checked all the premises of the open transition for both P and Q. $\qquad\square$

In general, the actions that can be emitted by Q is a subset of the possible actions of the holes, and the predicate involving v_Q and the synchronisation vector is more restrictive than the one involving only the variable b_{j_0}. Lemma 2 is combining an open transition of P with an open transition of Q, and building a corresponding transition of $P[Q]_{j_0}$, assembling their predicates.

Lemma 2. (Open Transition Composition). *Suppose* $j_0 \in J$ *and:*

$$P \models \frac{\{s_i \xrightarrow{a_i}_i s'_i\}^{i \in I}, \{\xrightarrow{b_j}_j\}^{j \in J},\ Pred, Post}{\lhd s_i^{i \in L} \rhd \xrightarrow{v} \lhd s_i'^{i \in L} \rhd} \quad and \quad Q \models \frac{\{s_i \xrightarrow{a_i}_i s'_i\}^{i \in I_Q}, \{\xrightarrow{b_j}_j\}^{j \in J_Q},\ Pred', Post'}{\lhd s_i^{i \in L_Q} \rhd \xrightarrow{v_Q} \lhd s_i'^{i \in L_Q} \rhd}$$

Then, we have: $P[Q]_{j_0} \models \dfrac{\{s_i \xrightarrow{a_i}_i s'_i\}^{i \in I \uplus I_Q}, \{\xrightarrow{b_j}_j\}^{j \in J \setminus \{j_0\} \uplus J_Q},\ Pred\{b_{j_0} \leftarrow v_Q\} \wedge Pred', Post \uplus Post'}{\lhd s_i^{i \in L \uplus L_Q} \rhd \xrightarrow{v} \lhd s_i'^{i \in L \uplus L_Q} \rhd}$

The proof is omitted, it is mostly similar to Lemma 1, see [15] for details. The proof of Theorem 4 exhibits a bisimulation relation for a composed system. It then uses Lemma 1 to decompose the open transition of $P[Q]$ and obtain an open transition of P on which the FH-bisimulation property can be applied to obtain an equivalent family of open transitions of P'; this family is then recomposed by Lemma 2 to build open transitions of $P'[Q]$ that simulate the original one.

Proof of (Theorem 4). Let $\text{Leaves}(Q) = p_l^{l \in L_Q}$, $\text{Leaves}(P) = p_l^{l \in L}$, $\text{Leaves}(P') = p_l'^{l \in L'}$. P is FH-bisimilar to P': there is an FH-bisimulation $\mathcal{R}$ between the open automata of P and of P'. Consider the relation $\mathcal{R}' = \{(s_1, s_2 | Pred) | s_1 = s_1' \uplus s \wedge s_2 = s_2' \uplus s \wedge s \in \mathcal{S}_Q \wedge (s_1', s_2' | Pred) \in \mathcal{R}\}$ where $\mathcal{S}_Q$ is the set of states of the open automaton of Q. We prove that $\mathcal{R}'$ is an open FH-bisimulation. Consider a pair of FH-bisimilar states: $(\lhd s_{1i}^{i \in L \uplus L_Q} \rhd, \lhd s_{2i}^{i \in L'} \uplus s_{1i}^{i \in L_Q} \rhd | Pred) \in \mathcal{R}'$. Consider an open transition OT of $P[Q]_{j_0}$:

$$\frac{\{s_i \xrightarrow{a_i}_i s'_i\}^{i \in I}, \{\xrightarrow{b_j}_j\}^{j \in J}, Pred_{OT}, Post_{OT}}{\lhd s_{1i}^{i \in L \uplus L_Q} \rhd \xrightarrow{v} \lhd s'_{1i}^{i \in L \uplus L_Q} \rhd}$$

Let $J' = J \setminus \text{Holes}(Q) \cup \{j_0\}$. By Lemma 1 we have :

$$P \models \frac{\{s_i \xrightarrow{a_i}_i s_i'\}^{i \in I \setminus L_Q}, \{\xrightarrow{b_j}_j\}^{j \in J'}, Pred', Post'}{\lhd s_{1i}^{i \in L} \rhd \xrightarrow{v} \lhd s_{1i}'^{i \in L} \rhd}$$

$$Q \models \frac{\{s_i \xrightarrow{a_i}_i s_i'\}^{i \in I \cap L_Q}, \{\xrightarrow{b_j}_j\}^{j \in J \cap \text{Holes}(Q)}, Pred'', Post''}{\lhd s_{1i}^{i \in L_Q} \rhd \xrightarrow{v_Q} \lhd s_{1i}'^{i \in L_Q} \rhd}$$

and $Pred_{OT}\{\!|v_Q \leftarrow b_{j_0}|\!\} = (Pred' \wedge Pred'')$, $Post_{OT} = Post' \uplus Post''$ ($Post''$ is the restriction of $Post$ over variables of $\text{Leaves}(Q)$). As P is FH-bisimilar to P' and $(\lhd s_{1i}^{i \in L} \rhd, \lhd s_{2i}^{i \in L'} \rhd | Pred) \in \mathcal{R}$ there is a family OT_x' of open transitions of the automaton of P'

$$\frac{\{s_{2i} \xrightarrow{a_{ix}}_i s_{2ix}\}^{i \in I_x}, \{\xrightarrow{b_{jx}}_j\}^{j \in J'}, Pred_{OT_x}, Post_{OT_x}}{\lhd s_{2i}^{i \in L'} \rhd \xrightarrow{v_x} \lhd s_{2ix}^{i \in L'} \rhd}$$

and $\forall x, (\lhd s_{1i}^{i \in L} \rhd, \lhd s_{2ix}^{i \in L'} \rhd | Pred_{tgt_x}) \in \mathcal{R}$; and
$Pred \wedge Pred' \Rightarrow \bigvee_{x \in X} (\forall j \in J'.b_j = b_{jx} \Rightarrow Pred_{OT_x} \wedge v = v_x \wedge Pred_{tgt_x} \{\!|Post'|\!\}\{\!|Post_{OT_x}|\!\})$

By Lemma 2 (for $i \in L_Q$, $s_{2i} = s_{1i}$ and $s_{2ix} = s_{1i}'$, and for $j \in \text{Holes}(Q)$, $b_{jx} = b_j$):

$$P'[Q]_{j_0} \models \frac{\{s_{2i} \xrightarrow{a_{ix}}_i s_{2ix}\}^{i \in I_x \uplus (I \cap L_Q)}, \{\xrightarrow{b_{jx}}_j\}^{j \in J}, \ Pred_{OT_x} \{\!|b_{j_0 x} \leftarrow v_Q|\!\} \wedge Pred'', Post_{OT_x} \uplus Post''}{\lhd s_{2ix}^{i \in L' \uplus L_Q} \rhd \xrightarrow{v_x} \lhd s_{2i}^{i \in L' \uplus L_Q} \rhd}$$

Observe $J = (J \setminus \text{Holes}(Q) \cup \{j_0\}) \setminus \{j_0\} \cup (J \cap \text{Holes}(Q))$. We verify the conditions for the FH-bisimulation between OT and OT_x. $\forall x, (\lhd s_{1i}'^{i \in L \uplus L_Q} \rhd, \lhd s_{2ix}^{i \in L' \uplus L_Q} \rhd | Pred_{tgt_x}) \in \mathcal{R}'$.
$Pred \wedge Pred_{OT} \Longrightarrow (Pred \wedge Pred')\{\!|b_{j_0} \leftarrow v_Q|\!\} \wedge Pred'' \Longrightarrow \ldots$
$\Longrightarrow \bigvee_{x \in X} (\forall j \in J'.b_j = b_{jx} \Rightarrow Pred_{OT_x}\{\!|b_{j_0} \leftarrow v_Q|\!\} \wedge Pred'' \wedge v = v_x \wedge Pred_{tgt_x}\{\!|Post'|\!\}\{\!|Post_{OT_x}|\!\})$

The obtained formula reaches the goal except for two points:

- We need $\forall j \in J$ instead of $\forall j \in J'$ with $J' = J \setminus \text{Holes}(Q) \cup \{j_0\}$ but the formula under the quantifier does not depend on b_{j_0} now (thanks to the substitution). Concerning $\text{Holes}(Q)$, adding quantification on new variables does not change the formula.
- We need $Pred_{tgt_x}\{\!|Post_{OT}|\!\}\{\!|Post_{OT_x} \uplus Post''|\!\}$ but by Lemma 2, this is equivalent to: $Pred_{tgt_x}\{\!|Post' \uplus Post''|\!\}\{\!|Post_{OT_x} \uplus Post''|\!\}$. We can conclude by observing that $Pred_{tgt_x}$ does not use any variable of Q and thus $\{\!|Post''|\!\}$ has no effect. □

This section proved the most interesting part of the congruence property for FH-bisimulation. The details of the additional lemmas are not only crucial for the proof but also shows that open transitions reveal to be a very powerful tool for proving properties on equivalences and systems. Indeed they show how open transitions can be composed and decomposed in the general case.

6   Conclusion and Discussion

In this paper, we built up theoretical foundation for the analysis of open parameterised automatas. pNets can be seen as a generalisation of labelled transition systems, and of generic composition systems. By studying open pNets, i.e. pNets with holes, we target not only a generalised point of view on process calculi, but also on concurrent process operators. The semantics and the bisimulation theory presented in this paper bring a strong formal background for the study of open systems and of system composition. In the past, we used pNets for building formal models of distributed component systems, and applied them in a wide range of case-studies on closed finitely instantiated distributed application. This work opens new directions that will allow us to study open parameterised systems in a systematic, and hopefully fully automatised way.

We are currently extending this work, looking at both further properties of FH-bisimulation, but also the relations with existing equivalences on closed systems. We also plan to apply open pNets to the study of complex composition operators in a symbolic way, for example in the area of parallel skeletons, or distributed algorithms. We have started developping some tool support for computing the symbolic semantics in term of open-automata. The following steps will be the development of algorithms and tools for checking FH-bisimulations, and interfacing with decision engines for predicates, typically SMT solvers. Those tools will include an algorithm that partitions the states and generates the right conditions (automatically or with user input) for checking whether two open pNets are bisimilar. Independently, it is clear that most interesting properties of such complex systems will not be provable by strong bisimulation. Next steps will include the investigation of weak versions of the FH-bisimulation, using the notion of *synchronised actions* mentionned in the paper.

References

1. De Simone, R.: Higher-level synchronising devices in MEIJE-SCCS. Theor. Comput. Sci. **37**, 245–267 (1985)
2. Larsen, K.G.: A context dependent equivalence between processes. Theor. Comput. Sci. **49**, 184–215 (1987)
3. Hennessy, M., Lin, H.: Symbolic bisimulations. Theor. Comput. Sci. **138**(2), 353–389 (1995)
4. Lin, H.: Symbolic transition graph with assignment. In: Sassone, V., Montanari, U. (eds.) CONCUR 1996. LNCS, vol. 1119, pp. 50–65. Springer, Heidelberg (1996)
5. Hennessy, M., Rathke, J.: Bisimulations for a calculus of broadcasting systems. Theor. Comput. Sci. **200**(1–2), 225–260 (1998)

6. Arnold, A.: Synchronised behaviours of processes and rational relations. Acta Informatica **17**, 21–29 (1982)
7. Henrio, L., Madelaine, E., Zhang, M.: pNets: an expressive model for parameterisednetworks of processes. In: 23rd Euromicro International Conference on Parallel, Distributed, and Network-Based Processing (PDP 2015) (2015)
8. Cansado, A., Madelaine, E.: Specification and verification for grid component-based applications: from models to tools. In: de Boer, F.S., Bonsangue, M.M., Madelaine, E. (eds.) FMCO 2008. LNCS, vol. 5751, pp. 180–203. Springer, Heidelberg (2009)
9. Henrio, L., Kulankhina, O., Li, S., Madelaine, E.: Integrated environment for verifying and running distributed components. In: Stevens, P. (ed.) FASE 2016. LNCS, vol. 9633, pp. 66–83. Springer, Heidelberg (2016). doi:10.1007/978-3-662-49665-7_5
10. Rensink, A.: Bisimilarity of open terms. In: Expressiveness in Languages for Concurrency (1997)
11. Deng, Y.: Algorithm for verifying strong open bisimulation in π calculus. J. Shanghai Jiaotong Univ. **2**, 147–152 (2001)
12. Bultan, T., Gerber, R., Pugh, W.: Symbolic model checking of infinite state systems using presburger arithmetic. In: Grumberg, O. (ed.) CAV 1997. LNCS, vol. 1254, pp. 400–411. Springer, Heidelberg (1997)
13. Clarke, E.M., Grumberg, O., Jha, S.: Verifying parameterized networks. ACM Trans. Program. Lang. Syst. **19**(5), 726–750 (1997)
14. Milner, R.: Communication and Concurrency. International Series in Computer Science. Prentice-Hall, Englewood Cliffs (1989). SU Fisher Research 511/24
15. Henrio, L., Madelaine, E., Zhang, M.: A theory for the composition of concurrent processes - extended version. Rapport de recherche RR-8898, INRIA, April 2016

Enforcing Availability in Failure-Aware Communicating Systems

Hugo A. López$^{(\boxtimes)}$, Flemming Nielson$^{(\boxtimes)}$, and Hanne Riis Nielson$^{(\boxtimes)}$

Technical University of Denmark, Kongens Lyngby, Denmark
{hulo,fnie,hrni}@dtu.dk

Abstract. Choreographic programming is a programming-language design approach that drives error-safe protocol development in distributed systems. Motivated by challenging scenarios in Cyber-Physical Systems (CPS), we study how choreographic programming can cater for dynamic infrastructures where the availability of components may change at runtime. We introduce the Global Quality Calculus (GC_q), a process calculus featuring novel operators for multiparty, partial and collective communications; we provide a type discipline that controls how partial communications refer only to available components; and we show that well-typed choreographies enjoy progress.

1 Introduction

Choreographies are a well-established formalism in concurrent programming, with the purpose of providing a *correct-by-construction* framework for distributed systems [9,12]. Using Alice-Bob's, protocol narrations, they provide the structure of interactions among components in a distributed system. Combined with a behavioral type system, choreographies are capable of deriving distributed (endpoint) implementations. Endpoints generated from a choreography ascribe all and only the behaviors defined by it. Additionally, interactions among endpoints exhibit correctness properties, such as liveness and deadlock-freedom. In practice, choreographies guide the implementation of a system, either by automating the generation of correct deadlock-free code for each component involved, or by monitoring that the execution of a distributed system behaves according to a protocol [3,9,32].

In this paper we study the role of *availability* when building communication protocols. In short, availability describes the ability of a component to engage in a communication. Insofar, the study of communications using choreographies assumed that components were always available. We challenge this assumption on the light of new scenarios. The case of Cyber-Physical Systems (CPS) is one of them. In CPS, components become unavailable due to faults or because of changes in the environment. Even simple choreographies may fail when including availability considerations. Thus, a rigorous analysis of availability conditions in communication protocols becomes necessary, before studying more advanced properties, such as deadlock-freedom or protocol fidelity.

© IFIP International Federation for Information Processing 2016
E. Albert and I. Lanese (Eds.): FORTE 2016, LNCS 9688, pp. 195–211, 2016.
DOI: 10.1007/978-3-319-39570-8_13

Practitioners in CPS take availability into consideration, programming applications in a *failure-aware* fashion. First, application-based QoS policies replace old node-based ones. Second, one-to-many and many-to-one communication patterns replace peer-to-peer communications. Still, programming a CPS from a component viewpoint such that it respects an application-based QoS is difficult, because there is no centralized way to ensure its enforcement.

This paper advocates a choreography-based approach for the development of failure-aware communication protocols, as exemplified by CPS. On the one hand, interactions described in choreographies take a *global* viewpoint, in the same way application-based QoS describe availability policies in a node-conscious fashion. On the other hand, complex communication including one-to-many and many-to-one communications can be explicitly defined in the model, which is a clear advantage over component-based development currently used in CPS. Finally, choreographies give a formal foundation to practical development of distributed systems, with Chor [11], ParTypes [27] and Scribble [36].

Contributions. First, we present the Global Quality Calculus (GC_q), a process calculus aimed at capturing the most important aspects of CPS, such as variable availability conditions and multicast communications. It is a generalization of the Global Calculus [9,12], a basic model for choreographies and the formal foundation of the Chor programming language [11]. With respect to the Global Calculus, GC_q introduces two novel aspects: First, it extends the communication model to include collective communication primitives (broadcast and reduce). Second, it includes explicit availability considerations. Central to the calculus is the inclusion of *quality predicates* [33] and optional datatypes, whose role is to allow for communications where only a subset of the original participants is available.

Our second contribution relates to the verification of failure-aware protocols. We focus on *progress*. As an application-based QoS, a progress property requires that at least a minimum set of components is available before firing a communication action. Changing availability conditions may leave collective communications without enough required components, forbidding the completion of a protocol. We introduce a type system, orthogonal to session types, that ensures that well-typed protocols with variable availability conditions do not get stuck, preserving progress.

Document Structure. In Sect. 2 we introduce the design considerations for a calculus with variable availability conditions and we present a minimal working example to illustrate the calculus in action. Section 3 introduces syntax and semantics of GC_q. The progress-enforcing type system is presented in Sect. 4. Section 5 discusses related work. Finally, Sect. 6 concludes. The Appendix includes additional definitions.

2   Towards a Language for CPS Communications

The design of a language for CPS requires a *technology-driven* approach, that answers to requirements regarding the nature of communications and devices involved in CPS. Similar approaches have been successfully used for Web-Services [10,31,36], and Multicore Programming [14,27]. The considerations on CPS used in this work come from well-established sources [2,35]. We will proceed by describing their main differences with respect to traditional networks.

2.1 Unique Features in CPS Communications

Before defining a language for communication protocols in CPS, it is important to understand the taxonomy of networks where they operate. CPS are composed by *sensor networks* (SN) that perceive important measures of a system, and *actuator networks* that change it. Some of the most important characteristics in these networks include asynchronous operation, sensor mobility, energy-awareness, application-based protocol fidelity, data-centric protocol development, and multicast communication patterns. We will discuss each of them.

Asynchrony. Depending on the application, deployed sensors in a network have less accessible mobile access points, for instance, sensors deployed in harsh environmental conditions, such as arctic or marine networks. Environment may also affect the lifespan of a sensor, or increase its probability of failure. To maximize the lifespan of some sensors, one might expect an *asynchronous operation*, letting sensors remain in a standby state, collecting data periodically.

Sensor Mobility. The implementation of sensors in autonomic devices brings about important considerations on *mobility*. A sensor can move away from the base station, making their interactions energy-intensive. In contrast, it might be energy-savvy to start a new session with a different base station closer to the new location.

Energy-Awareness. Limited by finite energetic resources, SN must optimize their energy consumption, both from node and application perspectives. From a node-specific perspective, a node in a sensor network can optimize its life by turning parts of the node off, such as the RF receiver. From a application-specific perspective, a protocol can optimize it energy usage by reducing its traffic. SN cover areas with dense node deployment, thus it is unnecessary that all nodes are operational to guarantee coverage. Additionally, SN must provide *self-configuration* capabilities, adapting its behavior to changing availability conditions. Finally, it is expected that some of the nodes deployed become permanently unavailable, as energetic resources ran out. It might be more expensive to recharge the nodes than to deploy new ones. The SN must be ready to cope with a decrease in some of the available nodes.

Data-Centric Protocols. One of the most striking differences to traditional networks is the *collaborative* behavior expected in SN. Nodes aim at accomplishing a similar, universal goal, typically related to maintaining an application-level quality of service (QoS). Protocols are thus data-centric rather than node-centric. Moreover, decisions in SN are made from the aggregate data from sensing nodes,

1 **start** $t_0[M]\{A_{c0}\}, t_1[S]\{A_{c1}\}, t_2[S]\{A_{c2}\}, t_3[S]\{A_{c3}\} : temperature(k);$
2 $t_0\{A_{c0}; M_{s0}\} \rightarrow \&_{q_1}(t_1\{A_{c1}; M_{s1}\}, t_2\{A_{c2}; M_{s2}\}, t_3\{A_{c3}; M_{s3}\}) : k[measure];$
3 $\&_{q_2}(t_1\{M_{s1}; E_1\}."1", t_2\{M_{s2}; E_2\}."-2", t_3\{M_{s3}; E_3\}."5") \rightarrow t_0\{M_{s0}; E_0\} : x_m : \langle k, avg\rangle; \mathbf{0}$

Fig. 1. Example: Sensor network choreography (Color figure online)

rather than the specific data of any of them [34]. Collective decision-making based in aggregates is common in SN, for instance, in protocols suites such as SPIN [20] and Directed Diffusion [24]. Shifting from node-level to application-level QoS implies that *node fairness* is considerably less important than in traditional networks. In consequence, the analysis of *protocol fidelity* [22] requires a shift from node-based guarantees towards application-based ones.

Multicast Communication. Rather than peer-to-peer message passing, one-to-many and many-to-one communications are better solutions for energy-efficient SN, as reported in [15,19]. However, as the number of sensor nodes in a SN scales to large numbers, communications between a base and sensing nodes can become a limiting factor. Many-to-one traffic patterns can be combined with data aggregation services (e.g.: TAG [29] or TinyDB [30]), minimizing the amount and the size of messages between nodes.

2.2   Model Preview

We will illustrate how the requirements for CPS communications have been assembled in our calculus through a minimal example in Sensor Networks (SN). The syntax of our language is inspired on the Global Calculus [9,12] extended with collective communication operations [27].

Example 1. Figure 1 portrays a simple SN choreography for temperature measurement. Line 1 models a *session establishment* phase between sensors t_1, t_2, t_3 (each of them implementing role S) and a monitor t_m with role M. In Line 2, t_m invoques the execution of method *measure* at each of the sensors. In Line 3, an asynchronous many-to-one communication (e.g. *reduce*) of values of the same base type (int in this case) is performed between sensors and the monitor. Quality predicates q_1, q_2 model application-based QoS, established in terms of availability requirements for each of the nodes. For instance, $q_1 = q_2 = \forall$ only allows communications with all sensors in place, and $q_1 = \forall, q_2 = 2/3$ tolerates the absence of one of the sensors in data harvesting. Once nodes satisfy applications' QoS requirements, an aggregation operation will be applied to the messages received, in this case computing the average value.

One important characteristic of fault-tolerant systems, of which CPS are part, is known as *graceful degradation*. Graceful degradation allows a system to maintain functionality when portions of a system break down, for instance, when some of the nodes are unavailable for a communication. The use of different quality predicates $q_1 = \forall, q_2 = 2/3$ allow us to describe choreographies that gracefully degrade, since the system preserves functionality despite one of the nodes is unavailable.

Considerations regarding the impact of available components in a communication must be tracked explicitly. Annotations $\{X; Y\}$ (in blue font) define *capabilities*, that is, control points achieved in the system. The X in $t\{X; Y\}$ denotes the *required* capability for t to act, and Y describes the capability *offered* after t has engaged in an interaction. No preconditions are necessary for establishing a new session, so no required capabilities are necessary in Line 1. After a session has been established, capabilities $(Ac_i)_{i \in \{0...3\}}$ are available in the system. Lines 2 and 3 modify which capabilities are present depending on the number of available threads. For example, a run of the choreography in Fig. 1 with $q_1 = 2/3$ will update capabilities from $\{Ac_0, Ac_1, Ac_2, Ac_3\}$ to any of the sets $\{Ms_0, Ac_1, Ms_2, Ms_3\}$, $\{Ms_0, Ms_1, Ac_2, Ms_3\}$, $\{Ms_0, Ms_1, Ms_2, Ac_3\}$, or $\{Ms_0, Ms_1, Ms_2, Ms_3\}$. The interplay between capabilities and quality predicates may lead to choreographies that cannot progress. For example, the choreography above with $q_2 = \forall$ will be stuck, since three of the possible evolutions fail to provide capabilities $\{Ms_0, Ms_1, Ms_2, Ms_3\}$. We will defer the discussion about the interplay of capabilities and quality predicates to Sect. 4.

3   The Global Quality Calculus (GC_q)

In the following, C denotes a choreography; p denotes an annotated thread $t[A]\{X; Y\}$, where t is a thread, X, Y are atomic formulae and A is a role annotation. We will use $\tilde{t}$ to denote $\{t_1, \ldots, t_j\}$ for a finite j. Variable a ranges over *service channels*, intuitively denoting the public identifier of a service, and $k \in \mathbf{N}$ ranges over a finite, countable set of session (names), created at runtime. Variable x ranges over variables local to a thread. We use terms t to denote data and expressions e to denote optional data, much like the use of option data types in programming languages like Standard ML [18]. Expressions include arithmetic and other first-order expressions excluding service and session channels. In particular, the expression $\mathsf{some}(t)$ signals the presence of some data t and none the absence of data. In our model, terms denote closed values v. Names m, n range over threads and session channels. For simplicity of presentation, all models in the paper are finite.

Definition 1. (GC_q *syntax*).

(Choreographies)	$C ::= \quad \eta; C \mid C + C \mid \text{if } e@p \text{ then } C \text{ else } C \mid \mathbf{0}$	
(Annotated threads)	$p, r ::= \quad t[A]\{X; Y\}$	
(Interactions)	$\eta ::= \quad \tilde{p_r} \, \mathbf{start} \, \tilde{p_s} : ak$	*(init)*
	$\mid \quad p_r.e \text{->} \&_{\mathsf{q}}(\widetilde{p_s : x_s}) : k$	*(broadcast)*
	$\mid \quad \&_{\mathsf{q}}(\widetilde{p_r.e_r}) \text{->} p_s : x : \langle k, op \rangle$	*(reduce)*
	$\mid \quad p_r \text{->} \&_{\mathsf{q}}(\tilde{p_s}) : k[l]$	*(select)*

A novelty in this variant of the Global calculus is the addition of *quality predicates* q, binding thread vectors in a multiparty communication. Essentially, q determines when sufficient inputs/outputs are available. As an example, q can

$$[\![\forall]\!](\widetilde{t_r}) = (|\{t_i \in \widetilde{t_r} \mid t_i = \mathtt{tt}\}| = n|) \qquad\qquad n = |\widetilde{t_r}|$$

$$[\![\exists]\!](\widetilde{t_r}) = (|\{t_i \in \widetilde{t_r} \mid t_i = \mathtt{tt}\}| \geq 1|) \qquad\qquad n = |\widetilde{t_r}|$$

$$[\![\mathrm{m/n}]\!](\widetilde{t_r}) = (|\{t_i \in \widetilde{t_r} \mid t_i = \mathtt{tt}\}| \geq m|) \qquad\qquad n = |\widetilde{t_r}|$$

Fig. 2. Quality predicates: syntax q and semantics $[\![q]\!]$. (Color figure online)

be $\exists$, meaning that one sender/receiver is required in the interaction, or it can be $\forall$ meaning that all of them are needed. The syntax of q and other examples can be summarised in Fig. 2. We require q to be monotonic (in the sense that $q(\widetilde{t_r})$ implies $q(\widetilde{t_s})$ for all $\widetilde{t_s} \subseteq \widetilde{t_r}$) and satisfiable.

We will focus our discussion on the novel interactions. First, **start** defines a (multiparty) *session initiation* between active annotated threads $\widetilde{p_r}$ and annotated service threads $\widetilde{p_s}$. Each active thread (resp. service thread) implements the behaviour of one of the roles in $\widetilde{A_r}$ (resp. $\widetilde{A_s}$), sharing a new session name k. We assume that a session is established with at least two participating processes, therefore $2 \leq |\widetilde{p_r}| + |\widetilde{p_s}|$, and that threads in $\widetilde{p_r} \cup \widetilde{p_s}$ are pairwise different.

The language features broadcast, reduce and selection as collective interactions. A *broadcast* describes one-to-many communication patterns, where a session channel k is used to transfer the evaluation of expression e (located at p_r) to threads in $\widetilde{p_s}$, with the resulting binding of variable x_i at p_i, for each $p_i \in \widetilde{p_s}$. At this level of abstraction, we do not differentiate between ways to implement one-to-many communications (so both broadcast and multicast implementations are allowed). A *reduce* combines many-to-one communications and aggregation [29]. In $\&_q(\widetilde{p_r.e_r}) \mathbin{\text{->}} p_s : x : \langle k, op \rangle$, each annotated thread p_i in $\widetilde{p_r}$ evaluates an expression e_i, and the aggregate of all receptions is evaluated using op (an operator defined on multisets such as max, min, etc.). Interaction $p_r \mathbin{\text{->}} \&_q(\widetilde{p_s}) : k[l]$ describes a collective *label selection*: p_r communicates the selection of label l to peers in $\widetilde{p_s}$ through session k.

Central to our language are *progress capabilities*. Pairs of atomic formulae $\{X; Y\}$ at each annotated thread state the necessary preconditions for a thread to engage (X), and the capabilities provided after its interaction (Y). As we will see in the semantics, there are no associated preconditions for session initiation (i.e. threads are created at runtime), so we normally omit them. Explicit $x@p/e@p$ indicate the variable/boolean expression x/e is located at p. We often omit $\mathbf{0}$, empty vectors, roles, and atomic formulae $\{X; Y\}$ from annotated threads when unnecessary.

The free term variables $\mathsf{fv}(C)$ are defined as usual. An interaction η in $\eta; C$ can bind session channels, choreographies and variables. In **start**, variables $\{\widetilde{p_r}, a\}$ are free while variables $\{\widetilde{p_s}, k\}$ are bound (since they are freshly created). In broadcast, variables $\widetilde{x_s}$ are bound. A reduce binds $\{x\}$. Finally, we assume that all bound variables in an expression have been renamed apart from each other, and apart from any other free variables in the expression.

$$\frac{\mathbf{T}(\eta) \,\#\, \mathbf{T}(\eta')}{\eta;\ (\eta';\ C) \simeq_C \eta';\ (\eta;\ C)} \qquad \frac{p \notin \mathbf{T}(\eta)}{\text{if } e@p \text{ then } \eta;\ C_1 \text{ else } \eta;\ C_2 \simeq_C \eta;\ \text{if } e@p \text{ then } C_1 \text{ else } C_2}$$

$$\frac{p \neq r}{\begin{array}{c}\text{if } e@p \text{ then } (\text{if } e'@r \text{ then } C_1 \text{ else } C_2) \text{ else} \\ (\text{if } e'@r \text{ then } C_1' \text{ else } C_2')\end{array} \simeq_C \begin{array}{c}\text{if } e'@r \text{ then } (\text{if } e@p \text{ then } C_1 \text{ else } C_1') \text{ else} \\ (\text{if } e@p \text{ then } C_2 \text{ else } C_2')\end{array}}$$

Fig. 3. Swap congruence relation, $\simeq_C$

Expressivity. The importance of roles is only crucial in a **start** interaction. Technically, one can infer the role of a given thread t used in an interaction η by looking at the **start** interactions preceding it in the abstract syntax tree. GC_q can still represent unicast message-passing patterns as in [9]. Unicast communication $p_1.e\text{->}p_2 : x : k$ can be encoded in multiple ways using broadcast/reduce operators. For instance, $p_1.e\text{->}\&_\forall(p_2 : x) : k$ and $\&_\forall(p_1.e)\text{->}p_2 : x : \langle id, k\rangle$ are just a couple of possible implementations. The implementation of unicast label selection $p\text{->}r : k[l]$ can be expressed analogously.

3.1 Semantics

Choreographies are considered modulo standard structural and swapping congruence relations (resp. $\equiv$, $\simeq_C$). Relation $\equiv$ is defined as the least congruence relation on C supporting α−renaming, such that $(C, \mathbf{0}, +)$ is an abelian monoid. The swap congruence [12] provides a way to reorder non-conflicting interactions, allowing for a restricted form of asynchronous behavior. Non-conflicting interactions are those involving sender-receiver actions that do not conform a control-flow dependency. For instance, $t_A.e_A\text{->}\&_{q_1}(t_B : x_B) : k_1;\ t_C.e_C\text{->}\&_{q_2}(t_D : x_D) : k_2 \simeq_C t_C.e_C\text{->}\&_{q_2}(t_D : x_D) : k_2;\ t_A.e_A\text{->}\&_{q_1}(t_B : x_B) : k_1$. Formally, let $\mathbf{T}(C)$ be the set of threads in C, defined inductively as $\mathbf{T}(\eta;\ C) \stackrel{\text{def}}{=} \mathbf{T}(\eta) \cup \mathbf{T}(C)$, and $\mathbf{T}(\eta) \stackrel{\text{def}}{=} \bigcup_{i=\{1..j\}} t_i$ if $\eta = t_1[A_1].e\text{->}\&_q(t_2[A_2] : x_2, \ldots, t_j[A_j] : x_j) : k$ (similarly for init, reduce and selection, and standardly for the other process constructs in C). The swapping congruence rules are presented in Fig. 3.

A state σ keeps track of the capabilities achieved by a thread in a session, and it is formally defined as set of maps $(t, k) \mapsto X$. The rules in Fig. 4 define state manipulation operations, including update ($\sigma[\sigma']$), and lookup ($\sigma(t, k)$).

Because of the introduction of quality predicates, a move from $\eta;\ C$ into C might leave some variables in η without proper values, as the participants involved might not have been available. We draw inspiration from [33], introducing *effect* rules describing how the evaluation of an expression in a reduce operation affects interactions. The relation $\twoheadrightarrow$ (Fig. 5) describes how evaluations are partially applied without affecting waiting threads. Label ξ records the substitutions of atomic formulae in each thread.

Finally, given $\phi \in \{\texttt{tt}, \texttt{ff}\}$, the relation $\beta ::_\phi \theta$ tracks whether all required binders in β have been performed, as well as substitutions used θ. Binder β is

$$\frac{Y = X \text{ if } (t,k,X) \in \sigma \quad Y = \emptyset \text{ o.w.}}{\sigma(t,k) = Y} \qquad \frac{\delta = \{(t,k,X) \mid (t,k,X) \in \sigma \wedge (t,k,Y) \in \sigma'\}}{\sigma[\sigma'] = (\sigma \setminus \delta), \sigma'}$$

Fig. 4. State lookup and update rules (Color figure online)

$$\frac{\eta = \&_q(t_1[A_1]\{X_1; Y_1\}.e_1, \ldots, t_j[A_j]\{X_j; Y_j\}.e_j) \to t_B[B]\{X_B; Y_B\} : x : \langle k, op \rangle \quad e_i @ t_i \downarrow v_i}{X_i \in \sigma(t_i, k) \quad \sigma' = \sigma[(t_i,k) \mapsto [\![X_i; Y_i]\!](\sigma(t_i,k))] \quad i \in \{1 \ldots j\}}$$

$$\langle \sigma, \eta; C \rangle \xrightarrow{(t_i,k): X_i :: Y_i} \left\langle \sigma', \begin{matrix} (\&_q(t_1[A_1]\{X_1; Y_1\}.e_1, \ldots, t_i[A_i]\{Y_i; Y_i\}.\mathsf{some}(v_i), \ldots, \\ t_j[A_j]\{X_j; Y_j\}.e_j) \to t_B[B]\{X_B; Y_B\} : x : \langle k, op \rangle); C \end{matrix} \right\rangle$$

Fig. 5. Effects (Color figure online)

defined in terms of partially evaluated outputs c:

$$sc :: = \quad p.e \quad \mid \quad p.\mathsf{some}(v) \qquad c :: = \quad \&_q(sc_1, \ldots, sc_n)$$

The rules specifying $\beta ::_\phi \theta$ appear in Fig. 6. A substitution $\theta = [(p_1, \mathsf{some}(v_1)), \ldots, (p_n, \mathsf{some}(v_n))/x_1 @ p_1, \ldots, x_n @ p_n]$ maps each variable x_i at p_i to optional data $\mathsf{some}(v_i)$ for $1 \leq i \leq n$. A composition $\theta_1 \circ \theta_2(x)$ is defined as $\theta_1 \circ \theta_2(x) :: = \theta_1(\theta_2(x))$, and $q(t_1, \ldots, t_n) = \bigwedge_{i \in 1 \leq i \leq n} t_i$ if $q = \forall$, $q(t_1, \ldots, t_n) = \bigvee_{i \in 1 \leq i \leq n} t_i$ if $q = \exists$, and possible combinations therein. As for process terms, $\theta(C)$ denotes the application of substitution θ to a term C (and similarly for η).

We now have all the ingredients to understand the semantics of GC_q. The set of transition rules in $\xrightarrow{\lambda}$ is defined as the minimum relation on names, states, and choreographies satisfying the rules in Fig. 7. The operational semantics is given in terms of labelled transition rules. Intuitively, a transition $(\nu \widetilde{m}) \langle \sigma, C \rangle \xrightarrow{\lambda} (\nu \widetilde{n}) \langle \sigma', C' \rangle$ expresses that a configuration $\langle \sigma, C \rangle$ with used names $\widetilde{m}$ fires an action λ and evolves into $\langle \sigma', C' \rangle$ with names $\widetilde{n}$. We use the shorthand notation $A \# B$ to denote set disjointness, $A \cap B = \emptyset$. The exchange function $[\![X; Y]\!]Z$ returns $(Z \setminus X) \cup Y$ if $X \subseteq Z$ and Z otherwise. Actions are defined as $\lambda :: = \{\tau, \eta\}$, where η denotes interactions, and τ represents an internal computation. Relation $e @ p \downarrow v$ describes the evaluation of a expression e (in p) to a value v.

We now give intuitions on the most representative operational rules. Rule ⌊INIT⌋ models initial interactions: state σ is updated to account for the new threads in the session, updating the set of used names in the reductum. Rule ⌊BCAST⌋ models broadcast: given an expression evaluated at the sender, one needs to check that there are enough receivers ready to get a message. Such a check is performed by evaluating $q(J)$. In case of a positive evaluation, the execution of the rule will: (1) update the current state with the new states of each participant engaged in the broadcast, and (2) apply the partial substitution θ to the continuation C. The behaviour of a reduce operation is described using rules ⌊REDD⌋ and ⌊REDE⌋: the evaluation of expressions of each of the available senders generates an application of the effect rule in Fig. 5. If all required substitutions have been performed, one can proceed by evaluating the operator to the set of received

$$\frac{}{p.e ::_{\mathit{ff}} [\,]} \qquad \frac{}{p.\mathsf{some}(v) ::_{\mathsf{tt}} [(p,\mathsf{some}(v))]} \qquad \frac{sc_1 ::_{t_1} \theta_1 \quad \cdots \quad sc_n ::_{t_n} \theta_n}{\&_q(sc_1, \ldots, sc_n) ::_{q(t_1,\ldots,t_n)} \theta_1 \circ \ldots \circ \theta_n}$$

Fig. 6. Rules for $\beta ::_\phi \theta$

values, binding variable x to its results, otherwise the choreography will wait until further inputs are received (i.e.: the continuation is delayed).

Remark 1 (Broadcast vs. Selection). The inclusion of separate language constructs for communication and selection takes origin in early works of structured communications [22]. Analogous to method invocation in object-oriented programming, selections play an important role in making choreographies projectable to distributed implementations. We illustrate their role with an example. Assume a session key k shared among threads p, r, s, and an evaluation of $e@p$ of boolean type. The choreography $p.e\text{->}r : x : k$; if $(x@r)$ then $(r.d\text{->}s : y : k)$ else $(s.f\text{->}r : z : k)$ branches into two different communication flows: one from r to s if the evaluation of $x@r$ is true, and one from s to r otherwise. Although the evaluation of the guard in the if refers only to r, the projection of such choreography to a distributed system requires s to behave differently based on the decisions made by r. The use of a selection operator permits s to be notified by r about which behavior to implement: $p.e\text{->}r : x : k$; if $(x@r)$ then $(p\text{->}r : k[l_1]; r.d\text{->}s : y : k)$ else $(p\text{->}r : k[l_2]; s.f\text{->}r : z : k)$

Remark 2 (Broadcast vs. Reduce). We opted in favor of an application-based QoS instead of a classical node-based QoS, as described in Sect. 2. This consideration motivates the asymmetry of broadcast and reduce commands: both operations are blocked unless enough receivers are available, however, we give precedence to senders over receivers. In a broadcast, only one sender needs to be available, and provided availability constraints for receivers are satisfied, its evolution will be immediate. In a reduce, we will allow a delay of the transition, capturing in this way the fact that senders can become active in different instants.

The reader familiar with the Global Calculus may have noticed the absence of a general asynchronous behaviour in our setting. In particular, rule:

$$\frac{(\nu\widetilde{m})\,\langle\sigma, C\rangle \xrightarrow{\lambda} (\nu\widetilde{n})\,\langle\sigma', C'\rangle \quad \eta \neq \mathbf{start} \quad snd(\eta) \subseteq \mathsf{fn}(\lambda)}{rcv(\eta) \;\#\; \mathsf{fn}(\lambda) \quad \widetilde{n} = \widetilde{m}, \widetilde{r} \quad \forall_{r \in \widetilde{r}} \; (r \in \mathsf{bn}(\lambda) \quad r \notin \mathsf{fn}(\eta))}{(\nu\widetilde{m})\,\langle\sigma, \eta; C\rangle \xrightarrow{\lambda} (\nu\widetilde{n})\,\langle\sigma', \eta; C'\rangle} \;[\text{Asynch}]$$

corresponding to the extension of rule $\lfloor^C\!\rfloor$ASYNCH⌉ in [12] with collective communications, is absent in our semantics. The reason behind it lies in the energy considerations of our application: consecutive communications may have different energetic costs, affecting the availability of sender nodes. Consider for example the configuration

$$(\nu\widetilde{m})\langle\sigma, (\mathsf{t}_A[A]\{X;Y\}.e\text{->}\&_\exists(\mathsf{t}_r\overline{[B_r]} : x_r) : k); \mathsf{t}_A[A]\{X;Y\}.e\text{->}\&_\vee(\mathsf{t}_s\overline{[B_s]} : x_s) : k\rangle$$

$$\frac{\eta = t_r[\widehat{A_r}]\{\widehat{X_r; Y_r}\}\ \mathbf{start}\ t_s[\widehat{B_s}]\{Y_s\} : a(k)}{\sigma' = [(t_i,k) \mapsto Y_i]_{i=1}^{|\widetilde{t_r}|+|\widetilde{t_s}|}\quad \widetilde{n} = \widetilde{t_s}, \{k\}\quad \widetilde{n}\ \#\ \widetilde{m}}{(\nu\widetilde{m})\ \langle \sigma, t_r[\widehat{A_r}]\{Y_r\}\ \mathbf{start}\ t_s[\widehat{B_s}]\{Y_s\} : a(k); C\rangle \xrightarrow{\eta} (\nu\widetilde{m},\widetilde{n})\ \langle \sigma[\sigma'], C\rangle}\ \lfloor\mathsf{Init}\rfloor$$

$$\frac{\eta = t_A[A]\{X_A; Y_A\}.e \rightarrow \&_q(t_r[B_r]\{\widehat{X_r; Y_r}\} : x_r) : k\quad J \subseteq \widetilde{t_r}\quad q(J)\quad e@t_A \downarrow v}{\forall_{i \in \{A\} \cup J} : X_i \subseteq \sigma(t_i,k) \wedge \sigma'(t_i,k) = [X_i; Y_i](\sigma(t_i,k))\quad \forall_{i \in \widetilde{t_r}} : \theta(x_i) = \begin{cases} \mathsf{some}(v) & i \in J \\ \mathsf{none} & \text{o.w.} \end{cases}}{(\nu\widetilde{m})\ \langle \sigma, \left(t_A[A]\{X_A; Y_A\}.e \rightarrow \&_q(t_r[B_r]\{\widehat{X_r; Y_r}\} : x_r) : k\right); C\rangle \xrightarrow{\theta(\eta)} (\nu\widetilde{m})\ \langle \sigma[\sigma'], \theta(C)\rangle}\ \lfloor\mathsf{Bcast}\rfloor$$

$$\frac{\eta = t_A[A]\{X_A; Y_A\} \rightarrow \&_q(t_r[B_r]\{\widehat{X_r; Y_r}\}) : k[l_h]\quad J \subseteq \widetilde{t_r}\quad q(J)}{\forall_{i \in \{A\} \cup J} : X_i \subseteq \sigma(t_i,k) \wedge \sigma'(t_i,k) = [X_i; Y_i](\sigma(t_i,k))}{(\nu\widetilde{m})\ \langle \sigma, \left(t_A[A]\{X_A; Y_A\} \rightarrow \&_q(t_r[B_r]\{\widehat{X_r; Y_r}\}) : k[l_h]\right); C\rangle \xrightarrow{\eta} (\nu\widetilde{m})\ \langle \sigma[\sigma'], C\rangle}\ \lfloor\mathsf{Sel}\rfloor$$

$$\frac{\eta = \&_q(t_r[A_r]\{\widehat{X_r; Y_r}\}.e_r) \rightarrow t_B[B]\{X_B; Y_B\} : x : \langle k, op\rangle}{\langle \sigma, \eta; C\rangle \xrightarrow{\xi}_{\twoheadrightarrow} \langle \sigma', \eta'; C\rangle\quad \eta' ::_{\mathsf{tt}} \theta}{(\nu\widetilde{m})\ \langle \sigma, \eta; C\rangle \xrightarrow{\tau} (\nu\widetilde{m})\ \langle \sigma', \eta'; C\rangle}\ \lfloor\mathsf{RedD}\rfloor$$

$$\frac{\eta = \&_q(t_r[A_r]\{\widehat{X_r; Y_r}\}.e_r) \rightarrow t_B[B]\{X_B; Y_B\} : x : \langle k, op\rangle}{\langle \sigma, \eta; C\rangle \xrightarrow{\xi}_{\twoheadrightarrow} \langle \sigma', \eta'; C\rangle\quad \eta' ::_{\phi} \theta\quad (t_B, k, X_B) \in \sigma'}{(\nu\widetilde{m})\ \langle \sigma, \eta; C\rangle \xrightarrow{\theta(\eta')} (\nu\widetilde{m})\ \langle [\![(t_B, k, X_B);(t_B, k, Y_B)]\!]\sigma', C[op(\theta)/x@t_B]\rangle}\ \lfloor\mathsf{RedE}\rfloor$$

$$\frac{C\,\mathcal{R}\,C'\quad (\nu\widetilde{m})\ \langle \sigma, C'\rangle \xrightarrow{\lambda} (\nu\widetilde{n})\ \langle \sigma', C''\rangle\quad C''\,\mathcal{R}\,C'''\quad \mathcal{R} \in \{\equiv, \simeq_C\}}{(\nu\widetilde{m})\ \langle \sigma, C\rangle \xrightarrow{\lambda} (\nu\widetilde{n})\ \langle \sigma', C'''\rangle}\ \lfloor\mathsf{Cong}\rfloor$$

$$\frac{i=1\ \text{if}\ e@t \downarrow \mathsf{tt},\quad i=2\ \text{o.w.}}{(\nu\widetilde{m})\ \langle \sigma, \mathbf{if}\ e@t\ \mathbf{then}\ C_1\ \mathbf{else}\ C_2\rangle \xrightarrow{\tau} (\nu\widetilde{m})\ \langle \sigma, C_i\rangle}\ \lfloor\mathsf{If}\rfloor \qquad \frac{(\nu\widetilde{m})\ \langle \sigma, C_i\rangle \xrightarrow{\lambda} (\nu\widetilde{n})\ \langle \sigma', C'\rangle\quad i \in \{1,2\}}{(\nu\widetilde{m})\ \langle \sigma, C_1 + C_2\rangle \xrightarrow{\lambda} (\nu\widetilde{n})\ \langle \sigma', C'\rangle}\ \lfloor\mathsf{Sum}\rfloor$$

Fig. 7. GC_q: Operational Semantics (Color figure online)

with $\widetilde{t_r}\#\widetilde{t_s}$ and $X \subseteq \sigma(t_A, k)$. If the order of the broadcasts is shuffled, the second broadcast may consume all energy resources for t_A, making it unavailable later. Formally, the execution of a broadcast update the capabilities offered in σ for t_A, k to Y, inhibiting two communication actions with same capabilities to be reordered. We will refrain the use Rule $\lfloor\mathsf{Asynch}\rfloor$ in our semantics.

Definition 2 (Progress). C *progresses if there exists* $C', \sigma', \widetilde{n}, \lambda$ *such that* $(\nu\widetilde{m})\ \langle \sigma, C\rangle \xrightarrow{\lambda} (\nu\widetilde{n})\ \langle \sigma', C'\rangle$, *for all* $\sigma, \widetilde{m}$.

4   Type-Checking Progress

One of the challenges regarding the use of partial collective operations concerns the possibility of getting into runs with locking states. Consider a variant of Example 1 with $q_1 = \exists$ and $q_2 = \forall$. This choice leads to a blocked configuration. The system blocks since the collective selection in Line (2) continues after a subset of the receivers in t_1, t_2, t_3, have executed the command. Line (3) requires all senders to be ready, which will not be the most general case. The system

2   ... Lines 1,2 in Figure 1.

3    $\&_\exists(t_1\{Ms_1; E_1\}.\text{"1"}, t_3\{Ms_3; E_3\}.\text{"5"}) \rightarrow t_m\{Ms_0; E_0\} : x_0 : \langle k, avg \rangle;\ 0$

Fig. 8. Variant of Example 1 with locking states (Color figure online)

will additionally block if participant dependencies among communications is not preserved. The choreography in Fig. 8 illustrates this. It blocks for $q_1 = \exists$, since the selection operator in Line 2 can proceed by updating the capability associated to t_2 to Ms_2, leaving the capabilities for t_1, t_3 assigned to Ac_1, Ac_3. With such state, Line 3 cannot proceed.

We introduce a type system to ensure progress on variable availability conditions. A judgment is written as $\Psi \vdash C$, where Ψ is a list of formulae in Intuitionistic Linear Logic (ILL) [17]. Intuitively, $\Psi \vdash C$ is read as *the formulae in Ψ describe the program point immediately before C*. Formulae $\psi \in \Psi$ take the form of the constant $\mathtt{tt}$, ownership types of the form $p : k\,[A] \rhd X$, and the linear logic version of conjunction, disjunction and implication ($\otimes, \oplus, \multimap$). Here $p : k\,[A] \rhd X$ is an *ownership type*, asserting that p behaves as the role A in session k with atomic formula X. Moreover, we require Ψ to contain formulae free of linear implications in $\Psi \vdash C$.

Figure 9 presents selected rules for the type system for GC_q. The full definition is included in Appendix A.1. Since the rules for inaction, conditionals and non-determinism are standard, we focus our explanation on the typing rules for communications. Rule $\lfloor\text{TINIT}\rfloor$ types new sessions: Ψ is extended with function $\mathbf{init}(t_p\overbrace{[A]\{X\}}, k)$, that returns a list of ownership types $t_p : k\,[A] \rhd X$. The condition $\{\tilde{t_s}, k\}\ \#\ (\mathbf{T}(\Psi) \cup \mathbf{K}(\Psi))$ ensures that new names do not exist neither in the threads nor in the used keys in Ψ.

The typing rules for broadcast, reduce and selection are analogous, so we focus our explanation in $\lfloor\text{TBCAST}\rfloor$. Here we abuse of the notation, writing $\Psi \vdash C$ to denote type checking, and $\Psi \vdash \psi$ to denote formula entailment. The semantics of $\forall^{\geq 1}J$ s.t. $\mathbf{C} : D$ is given by $\forall J$ s.t. $\mathbf{C} : D \wedge \exists J$ s.t. $\mathbf{C}$. The judgment

$$\Psi \vdash (t_A[A]\{X_A; Y_A\}.e\text{->}\&_q(t_r[B_r]\{\overbrace{X_r; Y_r}\} : x_r) : k);\ C$$

succeeds if environment Ψ can provide capabilities for sender $t_A[A]$ and for a valid subset J of the receivers in $\overbrace{t_r[B_r]}$. J is a valid subset if it contains enough threads to render the quality predicate true ($q(J)$), and the proof of $\psi_A, (\psi_j)_{j \in J} \vdash t_A : k\,[A] \rhd X_A \bigotimes_{j \in J}(t_j : k\,[B_j] \rhd X_j)$ is provable. This proof succeeds if ψ_A and $(\psi_j)_{j \in J}$ contain ownership types for the sender and available receivers with corresponding capabilities. Finally, the type of the continuation C will consume the resources used in the sender and all involved receivers, updating them with new capabilities for the threads engaged.

Example 2 In Example 1, $\mathtt{tt} \vdash C$ if $(q_1 = \forall) \wedge (q_2 = \{\forall, \exists\})$. In the case $q_1 = \exists, q_2 = \forall$, the same typing fails. Similarly, $\mathtt{tt} \nvdash C$ if $q_1 = \exists$, for the variant of Example 1 in Fig. 8.

Choregraphy Formation $(\Psi \vdash C)$,

$$\frac{\Psi, \mathbf{init}(\mathbf{t}_r\widetilde{[A_r]\{Y_r\}}, \mathbf{t}_s\widetilde{[B_s]\{Y_s\}}, k) \vdash C \quad \{\widetilde{t_s}, k\} \;\#\; (\mathbf{T}(\Psi) \cup \mathbf{K}(\Psi))}{\Psi \vdash \mathbf{t}_r\widetilde{[A_r]\{Y_r\}} \; \mathbf{start} \; \mathbf{t}_s\widetilde{[B_s]\{Y_s\}} : a(k); \; C} \lfloor \text{Tinit} \rceil$$

$$\frac{\forall^{\geq 1} J. \; s.t. \left(\begin{array}{c} J \subseteq \widetilde{t_r} \;\wedge\; q(J) \;\wedge\; \Psi = \psi_A, (\psi_j)_{j \in J}, \Psi' \\ \wedge\; \psi_A, (\psi_j)_{j \in J} \vdash \mathbf{t}_A : k\,[A] \rhd X_A \bigotimes_{j \in J} (\mathbf{t}_j : k\,[B_j] \rhd X_j) \end{array} \right): }{\mathbf{t}_A : k\,[A] \rhd Y_A, (\mathbf{t}_j : k\,[B_j] \rhd Y_j)_{j \in J}, \Psi' \vdash C \quad \vdash e@\mathbf{t}_A : \mathbf{opt.data} \; (\vdash x_i@\mathbf{t}_i : \mathbf{opt.data})_{i=1}^{|\widetilde{t_r}|}}{\Psi \vdash \left(\mathbf{t}_A[A]\{X_A; Y_A\}.e \to \&_q(\mathbf{t}_r\widetilde{[B_r]\{X_r; Y_r\}} : x_r) : k \right); \; C} \lfloor \text{Tbcast} \rceil$$

$$\frac{\forall^{\geq 1} J. \; s.t. \left(\begin{array}{c} J \subseteq \widetilde{t_r} \;\wedge\; q(J) \;\wedge\; \Psi = \psi_B, (\psi_j)_{j=1}^{|J|}, \Psi' \\ \wedge\; \psi_B, (\psi_j)_{j=1}^{|J|} \vdash \mathbf{t}_B : k\,[B] \rhd X_B \bigotimes_{j \in J} (\mathbf{t}_j : k\,[A_j] \rhd X_j) \end{array} \right): }{\mathbf{t}_B : k\,[B] \rhd Y_B, (\mathbf{t}_j : k\,[A_j] \rhd Y_j)_{j=1}^{|J|}, \Psi' \vdash C \quad (\vdash e_i@\mathbf{t}_i : \mathbf{opt.data})_{i=1}^{|\widetilde{t_r}|} \quad \vdash x@\mathbf{t}_B : \mathbf{opt.data}}{\Psi \vdash \left(\&_q(\mathbf{t}_r\widetilde{[A_r]\{X_r; Y_r\}}.e_r) \to \mathbf{t}_B[B]\{X_B; Y_B\} : x : \langle k, op \rangle \right); \; C} \lfloor \text{Tred} \rceil$$

$$\frac{((\text{as in } \lfloor \text{Tbcast} \rceil^*))}{\Psi \vdash \left(\mathbf{t}_A[A]\{X_A; Y_A\} \to \&_q(\mathbf{t}_r\widetilde{[B_r]\{X_r; Y_r\}}) : k[l_h] \right); \; C} \lfloor \text{Tsel} \rceil$$

$$\frac{}{\Psi \vdash \mathbf{0}} \lfloor \text{Tinact} \rceil \qquad \frac{\Psi \vdash C_1 \quad \Psi \vdash C_2}{\Psi \vdash \mathbf{if}\, e@\mathbf{t}\, \mathbf{then}\, C_1\, \mathbf{else}\, C_2} \lfloor \text{Tcond} \rceil \qquad \frac{\Psi = \psi \oplus \psi' \quad \psi \vdash C \quad \psi' \vdash C'}{\Psi \vdash C + C'} \lfloor \text{Tsum} \rceil$$

Fig. 9. GC_q: Type checking rules (excerpt): Premises for $\lfloor \text{TSEL} \rceil$ are the same as for $\lfloor \text{TBCAST} \rceil$, without **opt.data** premises (Color figure online)

A type preservation theorem must consider the interplay between the state and formulae in Ψ. We write $\sigma \models \Psi$ to say that the tuples in σ entail the formulae in Ψ. For instance, $\sigma \models \mathbf{t}: k\,[A] \rhd X$ iff $(\mathbf{t}, k, X) \in \sigma$. Its formal definition is included in Appendix A.1.

Theorem 1 (Type Preservation). *If* $(\nu \widetilde{m}) \langle \sigma, C \rangle \xrightarrow{\lambda} (\nu \widetilde{n}) \langle \sigma', C' \rangle$, $\sigma \models \Psi$, *and* $\Psi \vdash C$, *then* $\exists \Psi'. \; \Psi' \vdash C'$ *and* $\sigma' \models \Psi'$.

Theorem 2 (Progress). *If* $\Psi \vdash C$, $\sigma \models \Psi$ *and* $C \not\equiv \mathbf{0}$, *then* C *progresses.*

The decidability of type checking depends on the provability of formulae in our ILL fragment. Notice that the formulae used in type checking corresponds to the Multiplicative-Additive fragment of ILL, whose provability is decidable [26]. For typing collective operations, the number of checks grows according to the amount of participants involved. Decidability exploits the fact that for each interaction the number of participants is bounded.

Theorem 3 (Decidability of Typing). $\Psi \vdash C$ *is decidable*

5   Related Work

Availability considerations in distributed systems has recently spawned novel research strands in regular languages [1], continuous systems [2], and endpoint languages [33]. To the best of our knowledge, this is the first work considering availability from a choreographical perspective.

A closely related work is the Design-By-Contract approach for multiparty interactions [4]. In fact, in both works communication actions are enriched with pre-/post- conditions, similar to works in sequential programming [21]. The work on [4] enriches global types with assertions, that are then projected to a session π−calculus. Assertions may generate ill-specifications, and a check for consistency is necessary. Our capability-based type system guarantees temporal-satisfiability as in [4], not requiring history-sensitivity due to the simplicity of the preconditions used in our framework. The most obvious difference with [4] is the underlying semantics used for communication, that allows progress despite some participants are unavailable.

Other works have explored the behavior of communicating systems with collective/broadcast primitives. In [23], the expressivity of a calculus with bounded broadcast and collection is studied. In [27], the authors present a type theory to check whether models for multicore programming behave according to a protocol and do not deadlock. Our work differs from these approaches in that our model focuses considers explicit considerations on availability for the systems in consideration. Also for multicore programming, the work in [14] presents a calculus with fork/join communication primitives, with a flexible phaser mechanism that allows some threads to advance prior to synchronization. The type system guarantees a node-centric progress guarantee, ideal for multicore computing, but inadequate for CPS. Finally, the work [25], present endpoint (session) types for the verification of communications using broadcast in the Ψ-calculus. We do not observe similar considerations regarding availability of components in this work.

The work in [13] presented multiparty global types with join and fork operators, capturing in this way some notions of broadcast and reduce communications, which is similar to our capability type-system. The difference with our approach is described in Sect. 3. On the same branch, [16] introduces multiparty global types with recursion, fork, join and merge operations. The work does not provide a natural way of encoding broadcast communication, but one could expect to be able to encode it by composing fork and merge primitives.

6   Conclusions and Future Work

We have presented a process calculus aimed at studying protocols with variable availability conditions, as well as a type system to ensure their progress. It constitutes the first step towards a methodology for the safe development of communication protocols in CPS. The analysis presented is orthogonal to existing type systems for choreographies (c.f. session types [12].) Our next efforts include the modification of the type theory to cater for recursive behavior, the generation of distributed implementations (e.g. EndPoint Projection [9]), and considerations of compensating [7,8,28] and timed behavior [5,6]. Type checking is computationally expensive, because for each collective interaction one must perform the analysis on each subset of participants involved. The situation will be critical once recursion is considered. We believe that the efficiency of type checking can be improved by modifying the theory so it generates one formulae for all subsets.

Traditional design mechanisms (including sequence charts of UML and choreographies) usually focus on the desired behavior of systems. In order to deal with the challenges from security and safety in CPS it becomes paramount to cater for failures and how to recover from them. This was the motivation behind the development of the Quality Calculus that not only extended a π-calculus with quality predicates and optional data types, but also with mechanisms for programming the continuation such that both desired and undesired behavior was adequately handled. In this work we have incorporated the quality predicates into choreographies and thereby facilitate dealing with systems in a failure-aware fashion. However, it remains a challenge to incorporate the consideration of both desired and undesired behavior that is less programming oriented (or EndPoint Projection oriented) than the solution presented by the Quality Calculus. This may require further extensions of the calculus with *fault-tolerance* considerations.

Acknowledgments. We would like to thank Marco Carbone and Jorge A. Pérez for their insightful discussions, and to all anonymous reviewers for their helpful comments improving the paper. This research was funded by the Danish Foundation for Basic Research, project *IDEA4CPS* (DNRF86-10). López has benefitted from travel support by the EU COST Action IC1201: *Behavioural Types for Reliable Large-Scale Software Systems* (BETTY).

A   Additional Definitions

A.1   Type System

Figure 10 presents the complete type system for GC_q.

Definition 3 (State Satisfaction).   *The entailment relation between a state σ and a formula Ψ, and between σ and a formula ψ are written $\sigma \models \Psi$ and $\sigma \models \psi$, respectively. They are defined as follows:*

$$\sigma \models \cdot \qquad\qquad\qquad \Longleftrightarrow \sigma \text{ is defined}$$

$$\sigma \models \psi, \Psi \qquad\qquad \Longleftrightarrow \sigma \models \psi \text{ and } \sigma \models \Psi$$

$$\sigma \models \mathtt{tt} \qquad\qquad\qquad \Longleftrightarrow \sigma \text{ is defined}$$

$$\sigma \models \mathsf{t} : k\,[A] \rhd X \qquad \Longleftrightarrow (\mathsf{t}, k, X) \in \sigma$$

$$\sigma \models \psi_1 \otimes \psi_2 \qquad\quad \Longleftrightarrow \sigma = \sigma', \sigma'' \mid \sigma' \models \psi_1 \,\wedge\, \sigma'' \models \psi_2$$

$$\sigma \models \psi_1 \oplus \psi_2 \qquad\quad \Longleftrightarrow \sigma \models \psi_1 \text{ or } \sigma \models \psi_2$$

$$\sigma \models \psi \backslash \delta \qquad\qquad\quad \Longleftrightarrow \exists \sigma' \text{ s.t. } \sigma' \models \psi \,\wedge\, \sigma = \sigma' \backslash \delta$$

Choregraphy Formation ($\Psi \vdash C$),

$$\frac{\Psi, \mathbf{init}(t_r[\widetilde{A_r}]\{Y_r\}, t_s[\widetilde{B_s}]\{Y_s\}, k) \vdash C \quad \{\widetilde{t_s}, k\} \# (\mathbf{T}(\Psi) \cup \mathbf{K}(\Psi))}{\Psi \vdash t_r[\widetilde{A_r}]\{Y_r\} \ \mathbf{start} \ t_s[\widetilde{B_s}]\{Y_s\} : a(k); C} \lfloor \text{Tinit} \rfloor$$

$$\frac{\forall^{\geq 1} J.\ s.t. \left(\begin{array}{c} J \subseteq \widetilde{t_r} \ \wedge \ q(J) \ \wedge \ \Psi = \psi_A, (\psi_j)_{j \in J}, \Psi' \\ \wedge \ \psi_A, (\psi_j)_{j \in J} \vdash t_A : k[A] \rhd X_A \bigotimes_{j \in J} (t_j : k[B_j] \rhd X_j) \end{array} \right) :}{t_A : k[A] \rhd Y_A, (t_j : k[B_j] \rhd Y_j)_{j \in J}, \Psi' \vdash C \quad \vdash e@t_A : \mathbf{opt.data} \ (\vdash x_i@t_i : \mathbf{opt.data})_{i=1}^{|\widetilde{t_r}|}}{\Psi \vdash \left(t_A[A]\{X_A; Y_A\}.e \to \&_q(t_r[B_r]\{\widetilde{X_r}; Y_r\} : x_r) : k \right); C} \lfloor \text{Tbcast} \rfloor$$

$$\frac{\forall^{\geq 1} J.\ s.t. \left(\begin{array}{c} J \subseteq \widetilde{t_r} \ \wedge \ q(J) \ \wedge \ \Psi = \psi_B, (\psi_j)_{j=1}^{|J|}, \Psi' \\ \wedge \ \psi_B, (\psi_j)_{j=1}^{|J|} \vdash t_B : k[B] \rhd X_B \bigotimes_{j \in J} (t_j : k[A_j] \rhd X_j) \end{array} \right) :}{t_B : k[B] \rhd Y_B, (t_j : k[A_j] \rhd Y_j)_{j=1}^{|J|}, \Psi' \vdash C \ (\vdash e_i@t_i : \mathbf{opt.data})_{i=1}^{|\widetilde{t_r}|} \ \vdash x@t_B : \mathbf{opt.data}}{\Psi \vdash \left(\&_q(t_r[A_r]\{\widetilde{X_r}; Y_r\}.e_r) \to t_B[B]\{X_B; Y_B\} : x : \langle k, op \rangle \right); C} \lfloor \text{Tred} \rfloor$$

$$\frac{\forall^{\geq 1} J.\ s.t. \left(\begin{array}{c} J \subseteq \widetilde{t_r} \ \wedge \ q(J) \ \wedge \ \Psi = \psi_A, (\psi_j)_{j \in J}, \Psi' \\ \wedge \ \psi_A, (\psi_j)_{j \in J} \vdash t_A : k[A] \rhd X_A \bigotimes_{j \in J} (t_j : k[B_j] \rhd X_j) \end{array} \right) :}{t_A : k[A] \rhd Y_A, (t_j : k[B_j] \rhd Y_j)_{j \in J}, \Psi' \vdash C}{\Psi \vdash \left(t_A[A]\{X_A; Y_A\} \to \&_q(t_r[B_r]\{\widetilde{X_r}; Y_r\}) : k[l_h] \right); C} \lfloor \text{Tsel} \rfloor \qquad \frac{}{\Psi \vdash 0} \lfloor \text{Tinact} \rfloor$$

$$\frac{\Psi \vdash C_1 \quad \Psi \vdash C_2}{\Psi \vdash \mathbf{if} \ e@t \ \mathbf{then} \ C_1 \ \mathbf{else} \ C_2} \lfloor \text{Tcond} \rfloor \qquad \frac{\Psi = \psi \oplus \psi' \quad \psi \vdash C \quad \psi' \vdash C'}{\Psi \vdash C + C'} \lfloor \text{Tsum} \rfloor$$

Data Typing,

$$\frac{}{\vdash t@p : \mathbf{data}} \lfloor \text{TD1} \rfloor \qquad \frac{}{\vdash v@p : \mathbf{data}} \lfloor \text{TD2} \rfloor$$

$$\frac{}{\vdash e@p : \mathbf{opt.data}} \lfloor \text{TOD1} \rfloor \qquad \frac{\vdash v : \mathbf{data}}{\vdash \mathbf{some}(v)@p : \mathbf{opt.data}} \lfloor \text{TOD2} \rfloor \qquad \frac{}{\vdash \mathbf{none}@p : \mathbf{opt.data}} \lfloor \text{TOD3} \rfloor$$

State Formation ($\sigma : \mathbf{state}$),

$$\frac{}{\emptyset : \mathbf{state}} \lfloor \text{TS1} \rfloor \qquad \frac{\sigma : \mathbf{state} \quad \sigma(t[A], k) = \emptyset \quad X \in dom(\Sigma)}{\sigma, (t[A], k, X) : \mathbf{state}} \lfloor \text{TS2} \rfloor$$

$$\frac{\sigma : \mathbf{state} \quad (t[A], k, X) \in \sigma \quad Y \in dom(\Sigma)}{[\![X; Y]\!](\sigma(t, k)) : \mathbf{state}} \lfloor \text{TS3} \rfloor \qquad \frac{\sigma : \mathbf{state} \quad \delta : \mathbf{state}}{\sigma \backslash \delta : \mathbf{state}} \lfloor \text{TS4} \rfloor$$

Formulae Formation ($\Psi : \mathbf{form}$),

$$\frac{}{\cdot : \mathbf{form}} \lfloor \text{TF1} \rfloor \qquad \frac{\psi : \mathbf{form} \quad \Psi : \mathbf{form}}{\psi, \Psi : \mathbf{form}} \lfloor \text{TF2} \rfloor \qquad \frac{}{\mathbf{tt} : \mathbf{form}} \lfloor \text{TF3} \rfloor \qquad \frac{}{t : k[A] \rhd X : \mathbf{form}} \lfloor \text{TF4} \rfloor$$

$$\frac{\psi : \mathbf{form} \quad \psi' : \mathbf{form} \quad \circ \in \{\otimes, \oplus\}}{\psi \circ \psi' : \mathbf{form}} \lfloor \text{TF5} \rfloor \qquad \frac{\psi : \mathbf{form} \quad \delta : \mathbf{state}}{\psi \backslash \delta : \mathbf{form}} \lfloor \text{TF6} \rfloor$$

Fig. 10. GC_q: Type checking - Complete rules (Color figure online)

References

1. Abdulla, P.A., Atig, M.F., Meyer, R., Salehi, M.S.: What's decidable about availability languages? In: Harsha, P., Ramalingam, G. (eds.) FSTTCS. LIPIcs, vol. 45, pp. 192–205. Schloss Dagstuhl - Leibniz-Zentrum fuer Informatik (2015)
2. Alur, R.: Principles of Cyber-Physical Systems. MIT Press, Cambridge (2015)
3. Bocchi, L., Chen, T.-C., Demangeon, R., Honda, K., Yoshida, N.: Monitoring networks through multiparty session types. In: Beyer, D., Boreale, M. (eds.) FORTE 2013 and FMOODS 2013. LNCS, vol. 7892, pp. 50–65. Springer, Heidelberg (2013)
4. Bocchi, L., Honda, K., Tuosto, E., Yoshida, N.: A theory of design-by-contract for distributed multiparty interactions. In: Gastin, P., Laroussinie, F. (eds.) CONCUR 2010. LNCS, vol. 6269, pp. 162–176. Springer, Heidelberg (2010)

5. Bocchi, L., Lange, J., Yoshida, N.: Meeting deadlines together. In: Aceto, L., de Frutos-Escrig, D. (eds.) CONCUR, LIPIcs, vol. 42, pp. 283–296. Schloss Dagstuhl - Leibniz-Zentrum fuer Informatik (2015)
6. Bocchi, L., Yang, W., Yoshida, N.: Timed multiparty session types. In: Baldan, P., Gorla, D. (eds.) CONCUR 2014. LNCS, vol. 8704, pp. 419–434. Springer, Heidelberg (2014)
7. Carbone, M.: Session-based choreography with exceptions. Electron. Notes Theor. Comput. Sci. **241**, 35–55 (2009)
8. Carbone, M., Honda, K., Yoshida, N.: Structured interactional exceptions in session types. In: van Breugel, F., Chechik, M. (eds.) CONCUR 2008. LNCS, vol. 5201, pp. 402–417. Springer, Heidelberg (2008)
9. Carbone, M., Honda, K., Yoshida, N.: Structured communication-centered programming for web services. ACM Trans. Program. Lang. Syst. **34**(2), 8 (2012)
10. Carbone, M., Honda, K., Yoshida, N., Milner, R., Brown, G., Ross-Talbot, S.: A theoretical basis of communication-centred concurrent programming. In: Web Services Choreography Working Group mailing list, WS-CDL working report (2006, to appear)
11. Carbone, M., Montesi, F.: Chor: a choreography programming language for concurrent systems. http://sourceforge.net/projects/chor/
12. Carbone, M., Montesi, F.: Deadlock-freedom-by-design: multiparty asynchronous global programming. In: Giacobazzi, R., Cousot, R. (eds.) POPL, pp. 263–274. ACM (2013)
13. Castagna, G., Dezani-Ciancaglini, M., Padovani, L.: On global types and multiparty session. Logical Methods Comput. Sci. **8**(1), 1–45 (2012)
14. Cogumbreiro, T., Martins, F., Thudichum Vasconcelos, V.: Coordinating phased activities while maintaining progress. In: De Nicola, R., Julien, C. (eds.) COORDINATION 2013. LNCS, vol. 7890, pp. 31–44. Springer, Heidelberg (2013)
15. Deng, J., Han, Y.S., Heinzelman, W.B., Varshney, P.K.: Balanced-energy sleep scheduling scheme for high-density cluster-based sensor networks. Comput. Commun. **28**(14), 1631–1642 (2005)
16. Deniélou, P.-M., Yoshida, N.: Multiparty session types meet communicating automata. In: Seidl, H. (ed.) ESOP 2012. LNCS, vol. 7211, pp. 194–213. Springer, Heidelberg (2012)
17. Girard, J.-Y.: Linear logic. Theor. Comput. Sci. **50**, 1–102 (1987)
18. Harper, R.: Programming in Standard ML. Working Draft (2013)
19. Heinzelman, W.B., Chandrakasan, A.P., Balakrishnan, H.: An application-specific protocol architecture for wireless microsensor networks. IEEE Trans. Wireless Commun. **1**(4), 660–670 (2002)
20. Heinzelman, W.R., Kulik, J., Balakrishnan, H.: Adaptive protocols for information dissemination in wireless sensor networks. In MOBICOM, pp. 174–185. ACM (1999)
21. Hoare, C.A.R.: An axiomatic basis for computer programming (reprint). Commun. ACM **26**(1), 53–56 (1983)
22. Honda, K., Vasconcelos, V.T., Kubo, M.: Language primitives and type discipline for structured communication-based programming. In: Hankin, C. (ed.) ESOP 1998. LNCS, vol. 1381, pp. 122–138. Springer, Heidelberg (1998)
23. Hüttel, H., Pratas, N.: Broadcast and aggregation in BBC. In: Gay, S., Alglave, J. (eds.) PLACES, EPTCS, pp. 51–62 (2015)
24. Intanagonwiwat, C., Govindan, R., Estrin, D.: Directed diffusion: a scalable and robust communication paradigm for sensor networks. In: Pickholtz, R.L., Das, S.K., Cáceres, R., Garcia-Luna-Aceves, J.J. (eds.) MOBICOM, pp. 56–67. ACM (2000)

25. Kouzapas, D., Gutkovas, R., Gay, S.J.: Session types for broadcasting. In: Donaldson, A.F., Vasconcelos, V.T. (eds.) PLACES, EPTCS, vol. 155, pp. 25–31 (2014)
26. Lincoln, P.: Deciding provability of linear logic formulas. In: Advances in Linear Logic, pp. 109–122. Cambridge University Press (1994)
27. López, H.A., Marques, E.R.B., Martins, F., Ng, N., Santos, C., Vasconcelos, V.T., Yoshida, N.: Protocol-based verification of message-passing parallel programs. In: Aldrich, J., Eugster, P. (eds.) OOPSLA, pp. 280–298. ACM (2015)
28. López, H.A., Pérez, J.A.: Time and exceptional behavior in multiparty structured interactions. In: Carbone, M., Petit, J.-M. (eds.) WS-FM 2011. LNCS, vol. 7176, pp. 48–63. Springer, Heidelberg (2012)
29. Madden, S., Franklin, M.J., Hellerstein, J.M., Hong, W.: TAG: A tiny aggregation service for ad-hoc sensor networks. In: Culler, D.E., Druschel, P. (eds.) OSDI. USENIX Association (2002)
30. Madden, S., Franklin, M.J., Hellerstein, J.M., Hong, W.: The design of an acquisitional query processor for sensor networks. In: Halevy, A.Y., Ives, Z.G., Doan, A. (eds.) SIGMOD Conference, pp. 491–502. ACM (2003)
31. Montesi, F., Guidi, C., Zavattaro, G.: Service-oriented programming with jolie. In: Bouguettaya, A., Sheng, Q.Z., Daniel, F. (eds.) Web Services Foundations, pp. 81–107. Springer, New York (2014)
32. Neykova, R., Bocchi, L., Yoshida, N.: Timed runtime monitoring for multiparty conversations. In: Carbone, M. (ed.) BEAT, EPTCS, vol. 162, pp. 19–26 (2014)
33. Nielson, H.R., Nielson, F., Vigo, R.: A calculus for quality. In: Păsăreanu, C.S., Salaün, G. (eds.) FACS 2012. LNCS, vol. 7684, pp. 188–204. Springer, Heidelberg (2013)
34. Pattem, S., Krishnamachari, B., Govindan, R.: The impact of spatial correlation on routing with compression in wireless sensor networks. TOSN 4(4), 1–23 (2008)
35. Perillo, M.A., Heinzelman, W.B.: Wireless sensor network protocols. In: Boukerche, A. (ed.) Handbook of Algorithms for Wireless Networking and Mobile Computing, pp. 1–35. Chapman and Hall/CRC, London (2005)
36. Yoshida, N., Hu, R., Neykova, R., Ng, N.: The Scribble Protocol Language. In: Abadi, M., Lluch Lafuente, A. (eds.) TGC 2013. LNCS, vol. 8358, pp. 22–41. Springer, Heidelberg (2014)

Ransomware Steals Your Phone. Formal Methods Rescue It

Francesco Mercaldo[(⊠)], Vittoria Nardone, Antonella Santone,
and Corrado Aaron Visaggio

Department of Engineering, University of Sannio, Benevento, Italy
{fmercaldo,vnardone,santone,visaggio}@unisannio.it

Abstract. Ransomware is a recent type of malware which makes inaccessible the files or the device of the victim. The only way to unlock the infected device or to have the keys for decrypting the files is to pay a ransom to the attacker. Commercial solutions for removing ransomware and restoring the infected devices and files are ineffective, since this malware uses a very robust form of asymmetric cryptography and erases shadow copies and recovery points of the operating system. Literature does not count many solutions for effectively detecting and blocking ransomware and, at the best knowledge of the authors, formal methods were never applied to identify ransomware. In this paper we propose a methodology based on formal methods that is able to detect the ransomware and to identify in the malware's code the instructions that implement the characteristic instructions of the ransomware. The results of the experimentation are strongly encouraging and suggest that the proposed methodology could be the right way to follow for developing commercial solutions that could successful intercept the ransomware and blocking the infections it provokes.

Keywords: Malware · Android · Security · Formal methods · Temporal logic

1 Introduction and Motivation

Ransomware is a recent kind of malware that spread out mainly in last couple of years, and it is particularly aggressive for two reasons: on one hand it uses very effective mechanisms of infection based mainly on techniques of social engineering like sophisticated phishing (by mail or chat), and on the other hand it makes completely inaccessible the data on the infected machine, as it cyphers all the files with a strong asymmetric key cryptographic algorithm.

The ransomware is still increasing its capability to harm the victim's device, prevent the restore of the data or device, and evade detection. As a matter of fact, the more recent releases of this malware are able to recognize when they are executed in a virtual environment, which is often used for creating a sandbox where safely executing a program for studying its behavior and understanding if it launches a malicious payload or not. Additionally, recent ransomware is

© IFIP International Federation for Information Processing 2016
E. Albert and I. Lanese (Eds.): FORTE 2016, LNCS 9688, pp. 212–221, 2016.
DOI: 10.1007/978-3-319-39570-8_14

equipped with anti-debugging techniques, which is another way to evade detection as hindering the scanning of anti-malware.

Statistics from US governative agencies show that Cryptolocker infected in 2014: 336,856 machines in USA, 4,593 in UK, 25,841 in Canada, 15,427 in Australia, 1,832 in India, 100,448 in other countries. At its peak, CryptoLocker, a kind of ransomware, was infecting around 50,000 computers per month. According to SCMagazine[1] the CryptoWall, another ransomware, in a roughly five-month period infected 625,000 victims worldwide, encrypting 5.25 billion files, collecting more than $1.1 million in ransoms. The malware tries to delete shadow copies of the system through vssadmin.exe, so that the victim cannot return to previous system restore points too.

Moreover ransomware is invading the smartphone world: Kaspersky labs found 1,113 new ransomware samples targeting Android devices in the first quarter of 2015, which is a 65 % increase in the number of mobile ransomware samples with respect to those collected in 2014[2]. This is a dangerous trend since ransomware is designed to extort money, damage personal data, and block infected devices. Once the device is infected, the attacker asks the victim to pay a ransom in order to obtain the key for decrypting the files or restoring the control of the smartphone.

As the evidence of the high infections rate demonstrates, commercial anti-malware solutions are mainly ineffective to detect ransomware.

For this reason we propose a technique for specifically detecting ransomware on smartphone devices that is completely based on formal methods. The technique has been proved to be very effective as the evaluation produced an F-measure of detection equal to 0.99 on a dataset of $2,477$ samples. Additionally, the technique is able to localize in the code the peculiar instructions that implement the stages of infection, and the activation of the payload, which provides fundamental pieces of information to build both effective detectors and removal systems for ransomware. Moreover, at the best knowledge of the authors, literature counts only two works that propose a method to detect mobile ransomware [2,20] and that are compared with ours in the section of related work.

The paper proceeds as follows: Sect. 2 describes and motivates our detection method; Sect. 3 illustrates the results of experiments; Sect. 4 discusses the related work; finally, conclusions are drawn in Sect. 5.

2 The Methodology

In this section we present our methodology for the detection of Android ransomware malware using model checking. While model checking was originally developed to verify the correctness of systems against specifications, recently it

---

[1] http://www.scmagazine.com/cryptowall-surpasses-cryptolocker-in-infection-rates/article/368920/.

[2] https://securelist.com/analysis/quarterly-malware-reports/69872/it-threat-evolution-in-q1-2015/.

has been highlighted in connection with a variety of disciplines see [1,7]. Moreover, great advancements have been made to tackle the limitation of this technique due to its high time and memory requirements, see [4,9–11]. In this paper we present the use of model checking in the security field.

2.1 Formal Methods for Ransomware Detection

The approach is structured in three main sub-processes.

Formal Model Construction. This first sub-process aims at deriving formal models starting from the Java Bytecode. The Bytecode of the app under study is parsed and suitable formal models of the system are produced. More precisely, the bytecode of the analysed app that resides in a class folder or in JAR files is fed to a custom parser, based on the Apache Commons Bytecode Engineering Library (BCEL)[3]. The parsed Java Bytecode of the .class files are successively translated into formal models. In our approach Calculus of Communicating Systems (CCS) [15] has been exploited. CCS [15] is one of the most well known process algebras. A Java Bytecode-to-CCS transforming function has been defined for each instruction of the Java Bytecode. We associate a new CCS process to each Java Bytecode instruction. This translation has to be performed only one time for each app to be analysed and it has been completely automated. Each Java Bytecode instruction that is not a (conditional or unconditional) jump is represented by a process that, using the operator ("."), invokes the process corresponding to its successive instruction. Conditional jumps are instead specified as non-deterministic choices. An unconditional jump is represented by a CCS process that invokes the corresponding process of the jump target.

Temporal Logic Properties Construction. This second sub-process aims to define the characteristic behaviour of a ransomware by means of the construction of the temporal logic properties. This step tries to recognize specific and distinctive features of the ransomware behaviour with respect to all the other malware families and to goodware too. Thus, this specific behaviour is written as a set of properties. To specify the properties, we manually inspected a few samples in order to find the ransomware malicious behavior implementation at Bytecode level. In our approach, the mu-calculus logic [19] is used, which is a branching temporal logic to express behavioural properties.

Ransomware Family Detection. Finally, a formal verification environment, including a model checker, is invoked to recognise the ransomware family. This sub-process checks the sets of logic properties obtained from the ransomware malware family characterization against the CCS model of the app. In our approach, we invoke the Concurrency Workbench of New Century (CWB-NC) [8] as formal verification environment. When the result of the CWB-NC model checker is *true*, it means that the app under analysis belongs to the ransomware family, *false* otherwise. Thanks to very detailed CCS model and the logic formulae we are able to reach a good accuracy of the overall results, as explained in the following section.

---

[3] http://commons.apache.org/bcel/.

To the Authors' knowledge, model checking has never used before for the ransomware detection. The main distinctive features of the approach proposed in this paper are the use of formal methods, the identification of the ransomware through the Java Bytecode and the definition of a fully static approach. More precisely, our methodology exploits the Bytecode representation of the analysed apps. Detecting Android ransomware through the Bytecode and not directly on the source code has several benefits: (i) independence of the source programming language; (ii) recognition of malware families without decompilation even when source code is lacking; (iii) easiness of parsing a lower-level code; (iv) independence from obfuscation.

Another important feature of our approach is that we try to reuse existing model checkers avoiding the design of custom-made model checker. In fact our goal is to recognise ransomware with the criteria of reusing existing checking technologies. Model checkers, especially the most widely used ones, are extremely sophisticated programs that have been crafted over many years by experts in the specific techniques employed by the tool. A re-implementation of the algorithms in these tools could likely yield worst performance.

3 Results and Discussion

3.1 Empirical Evaluation Procedure

To estimate the detection performance of our methodology we compute the metrics of precision and recall, F-measure (Fm) and Accuracy (Acc), defined as follows:

$$PR = \frac{TP}{TP+FP}; \quad RC = \frac{TP}{TP+FN};$$

$$Fm = \frac{2PR\,RC}{PR+RC}; \quad Acc = \frac{TP+TN}{TP+FN+FP+TN}$$

where TP is the number of malware that was correctly identified in the right family (True Positives), TN is the number of malware correctly identified as not belonging to the family (True Negatives), FP is the number of malware that was incorrectly identified in the target family (False Positives), and FN is the number of malware that was not identified as belonging to the right family (False Negatives).

3.2 Experimental Dataset

The real world samples examined in the experiment were gathered from three different datasets. The first one is a collection of freely available 672 samples[4] and 11[5] Android ransomware samples. The samples are labelled as ransomware, koler, locker, fbilocker and scarepackage [2] and appeared from December 2014

---

[4] http://ransom.mobi/.
[5] http://contagiominidump.blogspot.it/.

Table 1. Dataset used in the experiment

Dataset	Original samples	Morphed samples	#Samples for category
Ransomware	683	594	1,277
Other malware	600	0	600
Trusted	600	0	600
Total	1,883	594	**2,477**

to June 2015. The second one is the Drebin project's dataset [3,18], a very well known collection of malware used in many scientific works, which includes the most diffused Android families.

Each malware sample in these datasets is labelled according to the *malware family* it belongs to: each family comprehends samples which have in common the same payload. This collection does not contain ransomware samples: we use this dataset to check the true positives.

The last one is a dataset of trusted applications crawled from Google Play[6], by using a script which queries a python API[7] to search and download apps. The downloaded applications belong to all the 26 different available categories (i.e., Books & Reference, Lifestyle, Business, Live Wallpaper, Comics, Media & Video, Communication, Medical, Education, Music & Audio, Finance & News, Magazines, Games, Personalization, Health & Fitness, Photography, Libraries & Demo, Productivity, Shopping, Social, Sport, Tools, Travel, Local & Transportation, Weather, Widgets). The applications retrieved were among the most downloaded in their category and were free.

The trusted applications were collected between April 2015 and January 2016 and were later analysed with the VirusTotal service[8], a service able to run 57 different antimalware software (i.e., Symantec, Avast, Kasperky, McAfee, Panda, and others) on the app: the analysis confirmed that the crawled applications did not contain malicious payload. We use this dataset to check the true positives.

Furthermore, we developed a framework[9] able to inject several obfuscation levels in Android applications: (i) changing package name; (ii) identifier renaming; (iii) data encoding; (iv) call indirections; (v) code reordering; (vi) junk code insertion.

These injections were aimed at generating morphed versions of the applications belonging to the ransomware dataset. Previous works [6] demonstrated that antimalware solutions fail to recognize the malware after these transformations. We applied our method to the morphed dataset in order to verify if it loses its effectiveness, too, or it keeps on recognizing the malware also after they have been altered. Table 1 provides the details of the full collection of 2,477 samples used to test the effectiveness of our method. Regarding the ransomware

---

[6] https://play.google.com.
[7] https://github.com/egirault/googleplay-api.
[8] https://www.virustotal.com/.
[9] https://github.com/faber03/AndroidMalwareEvaluatingTools.

Table 2. Families in Drebin dataset with details of the installation method (s̲tandalone, r̲epackaging, u̲pdate), the kind of attack (t̲rojan, b̲otnet), the events that trigger the malicious payload and a brief family description.

Family	Installation	Attack	Activation	Description
FakeInstaller	s	t,b		server-side polymorphic family
Plankton	s,u	t,b		it uses class loading to forward details
DroidKungFu	r	t	boot,batt,sys	it installs a backdoor
GinMaster	r	t	boot	malicious service to root devices
BaseBridge	r,u	t	boot,sms,net,batt	it sends information to a remote server
Adrd	r	t	net,call	it compromises personal data
Kmin	s	t	boot	it sends info to premium-rate numbers
Geinimi	r	t	boot,sms	first Android botnet
DroidDream	r	b	main	botnet, it gained root access
Opfake	r	t		first Android polymorphic malware

samples, Table 1 shows the number of original and morphed samples we tested; in some cases our framework was not able to disassemble some of the selected samples, this is the reason why we had to discard them and we consider a lower number of morphed samples if compared with original ones. In order to test the capacity of our rules to identify exclusively ransomware samples, we include in the dataset both trusted and malware samples from other families (respectively *Trusted* and *Other Malware*).

Table 2 provides a brief description of the payload brought by the malware families labelled as *Other Malware*, i.e., malware that is not ransomware.

We test 60 samples for each family. The malware was retrieved from the Drebin project [3,18] (we take into account the top 10 most populous families).

3.3 Evaluation

As a baseline for evaluating the performances of our solution, we compare the results obtained with our method with those produced by the top 10 ranked mobile antimalware solutions from AVTEST[10], an independent Security Institute which each year provides an analysis of the performances of the antimalware software. We built this baseline, by submitting our original and morphed samples to the VirusTotal API[11], which allows to run the above mentioned antimalware.

---

[10] https://www.av-test.org/en/antivirus/mobile-devices/.
[11] https://www.virustotal.com/.

Table 3. Top 10 signature-based antimalware evaluation against our method.

Antimalware	Original			Morphed		
	%ident.	#ident.	#unident.	%ident.	#ident.	#unident.
AhnLab	13.76 %	94	589	5.22 %	31	563
Alibaba	0.44 %	3	680	0 %	0	594
Antiy	13.18 %	90	593	4.04 %	24	570
Avast	27.52 %	188	495	6.4 %	38	556
AVG	3.22 %	22	661	1.51 %	9	585
Avira	19.76 %	135	548	12.46 %	74	520
Baidu	14.34 %	98	585	6.7 %	41	553
BitDefender	28.26 %	193	490	14.47 %	86	508
ESET-NOD32	20.35 %	139	544	8.58 %	51	543
GData	27.96 %	191	492	7.91 %	47	547
Our Method	**99.56 %**	**680**	**3**	**99.49 %**	**591**	**3**

Table 4. Performance evaluation

Formula	#Samples	TP	FP	FN	TN	PR	RC	Fm	Acc
Ransomware	2,477	1,271	0	6	1,200	1	0.99	**0.99**	**0.99**

Table 3 shows the evaluation between the top 10 antimalware solutions and our method with the original ransomware samples and with the morphed ones.

We consider only the samples and the percentage identified in the right family (column "ident" and the percentage in column "%ident") in Table 3. We also report the samples detected as malicious but not identified in the right family and the samples not recognized as malware (column "unident").

With regards to Table 3 we notice that BitDefender shows better performance in family identification for *Ransomware* original samples. Instead, with regards to morphed samples, antimalware performance decreases dramatically, indeed BitDefender is able to identify only 86 samples. The worst antimalware in *Ransomware* identification is Alibaba, able to correctly classify just 3 original samples and 0 morphed samples.

Due to the novelty of the problem, antimalware solutions are not still specialized in family identification; this is the reason why most of antimalware are unskilled to detect families. Another problem is that current antimalware are not able to detect malware when the signature mutates: their performance decreases dramatically with morphed samples. On the contrary, the detection done by our method is barely affected by the code transformations, so it is independent from the signature.

Table 4 shows the results obtained using our method. We consider the sum of original and morphed samples: the detail about the number of original and morphed samples is shown in Table 1.

Results in Table 4 seems to be very promising: we obtain an Accuracy and a F-measure equal to 0.99. Concerning the ransomware results, we are not able to identify the malicious payloads of just 6 samples (i.e., 3 originals and 3 morphed) on 1,277.

4 Related Work

In this section we review the current literature related to ransomware detection and formal methods applied to the detection of mobile malware.

As we stated previously, literature counts only two works about the detection of Android ransomare.

The first one proposes HelDroid [2]: the approach includes a text classifier based on NLP features, a lightweight Smali emulation technique to detect locking strategies, and the application of taint tracking for detecting file-encrypting flows. The main weakness of HelDroid is represented by the text classifier: the authors train it on generic threatening phrases, similar to those that typically appear in ransomware or scareware samples. In addiction, like whatever machine learning approach, HelDroid needs to train the classifier in order to label a samples as a ransomware: the detection capability of the model is related to the training dataset.

The other work in literature exploring the ransomare detection in mobile world is [20]. The authors illustrate a possible design of a static and dynamic analysis based solution, without implementing it. Their goal is to build a better performance tool in order to help to understand what should do to approach for a successful detection of Android ransomware.

Formal methods have been applied for studying malware in some recent papers, see [12,13,16,17]. Recently, the possibility to identify the malicious payload in Android malware using a model checking based approach has been explored in [5,14]. Starting from payload behavior definition they formulate logic rules and then test them by using a real world dataset composed by Droid-KungFu, Opfake families and update attack samples. However, as it emerges from the literature in the last years, formal methods have been applied to detect mobile malware, but at the best knowledge of the authors they have never been applied for identifying specifically the ransomware attack on Android malware.

5 Conclusions

Ransomware is a new type of malware that restricts access to the infected smartphone and it demands the user to pay a ransom to the attacker in order to remove the restriction. Ransomware samples are able to encrypt files on the infected device, which become difficult or impossible to decrypt without paying the ransom for the encryption key.

In this paper we propose a technique based on formal methods able to detect ransomware behaviour in Android platform. We obtain encouraging results on a dataset of 2,477 samples: 1 precision and 0.99 recall, overcoming in terms of effectiveness the top 10 popolous commercial antimalware.

As future work we are going to extend our solution using a ransomware dataset for different environment, like Windows Mobile and iOS in order to experiment the portability of our method.

References

1. Anastasi, G., Bartoli, A., Francesco, N.D., Santone, A.: Efficient verification of a multicast protocol for mobile computing. Comput. J. **44**(1), 21–30 (2001)
2. Andronio, N., Zanero, S., Maggi, F.: HelDroid: dissecting and detecting mobile ransomware. In: Bos, H., Monrose, F., Blanc, G. (eds.) RAID 2015. LNCS, vol. 9404, pp. 382–404. Springer, Heidelberg (2015). doi:10.1007/978-3-319-26362-5_18
3. Arp, D., Spreitzenbarth, M., Huebner, M., Gascon, H., Rieck, K.: Drebin: efficient and explainable detection of android malware in your pocket. In: Proceedings of 21st Annual Network and Distributed System Security Symposium (NDSS). IEEE (2014)
4. Barbuti, R., Francesco, N.D., Santone, A., Vaglini, G.: LORETO: a tool for reducing state explosion in verification of LOTOS programs. Softw. Pract. Exper. **29**(12), 1123–1147 (1999)
5. Battista, P., Mercaldo, F., Nardone, V., Santone, A., Visaggio, C.A.: Identification of android malware families with model checking. In: International Conference on Information Systems Security and Privacy. SCITEPRESS (2016)
6. Canfora, G., Di Sorbo, A., Mercaldo, F., Visaggio, C.: Obfuscation techniques against signature-based detection: a case study. In: Proceedings of Workshop on Mobile System Technologies. IEEE (2015)
7. Ceccarelli, M., Cerulo, L., Ruvo, G.D., Nardone, V., Santone, A.: Infer gene regulatory networks from time series data with probabilistic model checking. In: 3rd IEEE/ACM FME Workshop on Formal Methods in Software Engineering, FormaliSE 2015, Florence, Italy, 18 May 2015, pp. 26–32. IEEE (2015)
8. Cleaveland, R., Sims, S.: The NCSU concurrency workbench. In: Alur, R., Henzinger, T.A. (eds.) CAV 1996. LNCS, vol. 1102, pp. 394–397. Springer, Heidelberg (1996)
9. De Francesco, N., Lettieri, G., Santone, A., Vaglini, G.: Heuristic search for equivalence checking. Softw. Syst. Model. **15**(2), 513–530 (2016)
10. Francesca, G., Santone, A., Vaglini, G., Villani, M.L.: Ant colony optimization for deadlock detection in concurrent systems. In: Proceedings of the 35th Annual IEEE International Computer Software and Applications Conference, COMPSAC 2011, Munich, Germany, 18–22 July 2011, pp. 108–117. IEEE (2011)
11. Francesco, N.D., Santone, A., Vaglini, G.: State space reduction by non-standard semantics for deadlock analysis. Sci. Comput. Program. **30**(3), 309–338 (1998)
12. Jacob, G., Filiol, E., Debar, H.: Formalization of viruses and malware through process algebras. In: International Conference on Availability, Reliability and Security (ARES 2010). IEEE (2010)
13. Kinder, J., Katzenbeisser, S., Schallhart, C., Veith, H.: Detecting malicious code by model checking. In: Julisch, K., Kruegel, C. (eds.) DIMVA 2005. LNCS, vol. 3548, pp. 174–187. Springer, Heidelberg (2005)

14. Mercaldo, F., Nardone, V., Santone, A., Visaggio, C.A.: Download malware? No, thanks. How formal methods can block update attacks. In: 2016 IEEE/ACM 4th FME Workshop on Formal Methods in Software Engineering (FormaliSE). IEEE (2016)

15. Milner, R.: Communication and Concurrency. PHI Series in Computer Science. Prentice Hall, Upper Saddle River (1989)

16. Song, F., Touili, T.: Pommade: pushdown model-checking for malware detection. In: Proceedings of the 2013 9th Joint Meeting on Foundations of Software Engineering. ACM (2013)

17. Song, F., Touili, T.: Model-checking for android malware detection. In: Garrigue, J. (ed.) APLAS 2014. LNCS, vol. 8858, pp. 216–235. Springer, Heidelberg (2014)

18. Spreitzenbarth, M., Echtler, F., Schreck, T., Freling, F.C., Hoffmann, J.: Mobilesandbox: looking deeper into android applications. In: 28th International ACM Symposium on Applied Computing (SAC). ACM (2013)

19. Stirling, C.: An introduction to modal and temporal logics for CCS. In: Ito, T. (ed.) UK/Japan WS 1989. LNCS, vol. 491, pp. 1–20. Springer, Heidelberg (1991)

20. Yang, T., Yang, Y., Qian, K., Lo, D.C.T., Qian, Y., Tao, L.: Automated detection and analysis for android ransomware. In: HPCC/CSS/ICESS, pp. 1338–1343. IEEE (2015)

Multiple Mutation Testing from FSM

Alexandre Petrenko[1], Omer Nguena Timo[1(✉)], and S. Ramesh[2]

[1] Computer Research Institute of Montreal, CRIM, Montreal, Canada
{petrenko,omer.nguena}@crim.ca
[2] GM Global R&D, Warren, MI, USA
ramesh.s@gm.com

Abstract. Fault model based testing receives constantly growing interest of both, researchers and test practitioners. A fault model is typically a tuple of a specification, fault domain, and conformance relation. In the context of testing from finite state machines, the specification is an FSM of a certain type. Conformance relation is specific to the type of FSM and for complete deterministic machines it is equivalence relation. Fault domain is a set of implementation machines each of which models some faults, such as output, transfer or transition faults. In the traditional checking experiment theory the fault domain is the universe of all machines with a given number of states and input and output sets of the specification. Another way of defining fault domains similar to the one used in classical program mutation is to list a number of FSM mutants obtained by changing transitions of the specification. We follow in this paper the approach of defining fault domain as a set of all possible deterministic submachines of a given nondeterministic FSM, called a mutation machine, proposed in our previous work. The mutation machine contains a specification machine and extends it with a number of mutated transitions modelling potential faults. Thus, a single mutant represents multiple mutations and mutation machine represents numerous mutants. We propose a method for analyzing mutation coverage of tests which we cast as a constraint satisfaction problem. The approach is based on logical encoding and SMT-solving, it avoids enumeration of mutants while still offering a possibility to estimate the test adequacy (mutation score). The preliminary experiments performed on an industrial controller indicate that the approach scales sufficiently well.

Keywords: FSM · Conformance testing · Mutation testing · Fault modelling · Fault model-based test generation · Test coverage · Fault coverage analysis

1 Introduction

In the area of model based testing, one of the key questions concerns a termination rule for test generation procedures. It seems to us that there are two main schools of thought considering this rule. One of them follows a traditional approach of covering a specification model [19]. In terms of the Finite State Machine (FSM) model, one could consider for coverage various features of an FSM, such as transitions or sequences of them which model test purposes often used to guide and terminate test generation. Another school focuses on fault coverage and thus follows fault model based testing, see, e.g., [15, 16, 20–22, 26].

© IFIP International Federation for Information Processing 2016
E. Albert and I. Lanese (Eds.): FORTE 2016, LNCS 9688, pp. 222–238, 2016.
DOI: 10.1007/978-3-319-39570-8_15

Fault model based testing receives constantly growing interests of both, researchers and test practitioners. Fault models are defined in the literature in a variety of ways [26]. In [11], we propose to define a fault model as a tuple of a specification, a fault domain, and a conformance relation. In the context of testing from finite state machines, the specification is a certain type of an FSM. A conformance relation is specific to the FSM type and for complete deterministic machines it is equivalence relation. A fault domain is a set of implementation machines, aka mutants, each of which models some faults, such as output, transfer and transition faults.

In the traditional checking experiment theory the fault domain is the universe of all machines with a given number of states and input and output alphabets of the specification, see, e.g., [6, 8, 9, 12–14, 23]. While this theory offers clear understanding what does it mean to have sound and exhaustive, i.e., complete tests, it leads to tests whose number grows in the worst case exponentially with the FSM parameters. To us, this is a price to pay for considering the universe of all FSMs. Intuitively, choosing a reasonable subset of this fault domain might be the way to mitigate the test explosion effect. As an example, if one considers the fault domain of mutants that model output faults, a test complete for this fault model is simply a transition tour. The space between these two extreme fault models has received in our opinion insufficient attention. In what follows, we present a brief account of what has been done in this respect.

In the area of program mutation testing, mutants are generated by modifying programs. The number of tests is limited by the number of mutants, which usually need to be compared one by one with the original program to determine tests that kill them [3, 4]. Test minimization could then be achieved via explicit enumeration of all the mutants in the fault domain followed then by solving a set cover problem.

Mutation testing in hardware area seems to predate program mutation. An early work of Poage and McCluskey in 1964 [2] focuses on hardware faults in FSM implementations and builds a fault domain by extracting FSM mutants from modified circuits. The idea of this approach is to consolidate the comparisons of individual mutants aiming at reduction of the number of tests, however, mutants still need to be analyzed one by one. The approach in [1] focuses on detection of single FSM mutations with the same test, but provides no guarantees that mutants with multiple mutations (higher order mutants) can always be killed.

Explicit mutant enumeration can be avoided by defining a fault domain as a set of all possible submachines of a given nondeterministic FSM, called a mutation machine, proposed in our previous work [5, 7, 10]. The mutation machine contains a specification machine and extends it with a number of mutated transitions modelling potential faults. Mutated transitions might be viewed as faults injected in the specification machine, see, e.g., [25]. Thus, a single mutant represents multiple mutations and mutation machine represents numerous mutants. In our previous work, methods were developed for test generation using this fault model [5, 7, 10]. The main idea was to adjust classical checking experiments for a fault domain smaller than the universe of all FSMs. A checking experiment once obtained is in fact a complete test suite, however, this approach does not offer a means of analyzing mutation coverage of an arbitrary test suite or individual tests.

Traditional program mutation testing uses explicit mutant enumeration to determine test adequacy or mutation score. It is a ratio of the number of dead mutants to the number of non-equivalent mutants. We are not aware of any attempt to characterize a fault detection power of tests considering multiple mutants that avoids their enumeration.

The paper aims at solving this problem. We propose a method for analyzing mutation coverage of tests which we cast as a constraint satisfaction problem. The approach is based on logical encoding and SMT-solving, it avoids enumeration of mutants while still offering a possibility to estimate the test adequacy (mutation score). The analysis procedure can be used for test prioritization and test minimization, and could eventually lead to an incremental test generation.

The remaining of this paper is organized as follows. Section 2 defines a specification model as well as a fault model. In Sect. 3, we develop a method for mutation coverage analysis. Section 4 reports on our preliminary experiments performed on an industrial controller. Section 5 summarizes our contributions and indicates future work.

2 Background

2.1 Finite State Machines

A *Finite State Machine* (FSM) M is a 5-tuple (S, s_0, I, O, T), where S is a finite set of states with initial state s_0; I and O are finite non-empty disjoint sets of inputs and outputs, respectively; T is a transition relation $T \subseteq S \times I \times O \times S$, (s, i, o, s') is a transition.

M is *completely specified* (complete FSM) if for each tuple $(s, x) \in S \times I$ there exists transition $(s, x, o, s') \in T$. It is *deterministic* (DFSM) if for each $(s, x) \in S \times I$ there exists at most one transition $(s, x, o, s') \in T$; if there are several transitions for some $(s, x) \in S \times I$ then it is *nondeterministic* (NFSM); M is *observable* if for each tuple $(s, x, o) \in S \times I \times O$ there exists at most one transition; if there are several transitions for some $(s, x, o) \in S \times I \times O$ then it is *non-observable*.

An *execution* of M from state s is a sequence of transitions forming a path from s in the state transition diagram of M. The machine M is *initially connected*, if for any state $s \in S$ there exists an execution from s_0 to s. An execution is *deterministic* if each transition (s, x, o, s') in it is the only transition for $(s, x) \in S \times I$; otherwise, i.e., if for some transition (s, x, o, s') in the execution there exists in it a transition (s, x, o', s'') such that $o \neq o'$ or $s' \neq s''$, the execution is *nondeterministic*. Clearly, a DFSM has only deterministic executions, while an NFSM can have both.

A *trace* of M in state s is a string of input-output pairs which label an execution from s. Let $Tr_M(s)$ denote the set of all traces of M in state s and Tr_M denote the set of traces of M in the initial state. Given sequence $\beta \in (IO)^*$, the *input (output) projection* of β, denoted $\beta_{\downarrow I}$ ($\beta_{\downarrow O}$), is a sequence obtained from β by erasing symbols in O (I).

We say that an input sequence *triggers* an execution of M (in state s) if it is the input projection of a trace of an execution of M (in state s).

Given input sequence α, let $out_M(s, \alpha)$ denote the set of all output sequences which can be produced by M in response to α at state s, that is $out_M(s, \alpha) = \{\beta_{\downarrow O} \mid \beta \in Tr_M(s)$ and $\beta_{\downarrow I} = \alpha\}$.

We define several relations between states in terms of traces of a complete FSM.

Given states s_1, s_2 of a complete FSM $M = (S, s_0, I, O, T)$, s_1 and s_2 are (trace-) equivalent, $s_1 \simeq s_2$, if $Tr_M(s_1) = Tr_M(s_2)$; s_1 and s_2 are distinguishable, $s_1 \not\simeq s_2$, if $Tr_M(s_1) \neq Tr_M(s_2)$; s_2 is trace-included into (is a reduction of) s_1, $s_2 \leq s_1$, if $Tr_M(s_2) \subseteq Tr_M(s_1)$. M is reduced if any pair of its states is distinguishable, i.e., for every s_1, $s_2 \in S$ there exists $\alpha \in I^*$ such that $out_M(s_1, \alpha) \neq out_M(s_2, \alpha)$, α is called a distinguishing sequence for states s_1 and s_2, this is denoted $s_1 \not\simeq_\alpha s_2$.

We also use relations between machines. Given FSMs $M = (S, s_0, I, O, T)$ and $N = (P, p_0, I, O, N)$, $N \leq M$ if $s_0 \leq p_0$; $N \simeq M$ if $s_0 \simeq p_0$; $N \not\simeq M$ if $s_0 \not\simeq p_0$. In this paper, we use equivalence relation between machines as a conformance relation between implementation and specification machines.

Given a complete initially connected NFSM $M = (S, s_0, I, O, T)$, a complete initially connected machine $N = (S', s_0, I, O, N)$ is a submachine of M if $S' \subseteq S$ and $N \subseteq T$. The set of all complete deterministic submachines of M is denoted $Sub(M)$. Obviously, each machine in $Sub(M)$ is a reduction of M; moreover, if M is deterministic then $Sub(M)$ contains just M.

2.2 Fault Model

Let $A = (S, s_0, I, O, N)$ be a complete initially connected DFSM, called the specification machine.

Definition 1. A complete initially connected NFSM $M = (S, s_0, I, O, T)$ is a mutation machine of $A = (S, s_0, I, O, N)$, if $N \subseteq T$, i.e., if A is a submachine of M.

We assume that all possible implementation machines for the specification machine A constitute the fault domain $Sub(M)$, the set of all deterministic submachines of the mutation machine M of A. A submachine $B \in Sub(M)$, $B \neq A$ is called a mutant. Transitions of M that are also transitions of A are called unaltered, while others, in the set TN, are mutated transitions. Given $(s, x) \in S \times I$, we let $T(s, x)$ denote a set of transitions from state s and input x in M. If $T(s, x)$ is a singleton then its transition is called a trusted transition. The set $T(s, x)$ is called a suspicious set of transitions if it is not a singleton, transitions in a suspicious set are called suspicious. Trusted transitions are present in all mutants, but suspicious transitions in each set $T(s, x)$ are alternative and only one can be present in a deterministic mutant.

A mutant B is nonconforming if it is not equivalent to A, otherwise, it is called a conforming mutant. We say that input sequence $\alpha \in I^*$ such that $B \not\simeq_\alpha A$ detects or kills the mutant B.

The tuple $< A, \simeq, Sub(M) >$ is a fault model following [11]. For a given specification machine A the equivalence partitions the set $Sub(M)$ into conforming implementations and faulty ones. In this paper, we do not require the FSM A to be reduced, this implies that a conforming mutant may have fewer states than the specification A; on the other hand, we assume that no fault creates new states in implementations, hence mutants with more states than the specification FSM are not in the fault domain $Sub(M)$.

Consider the following example.

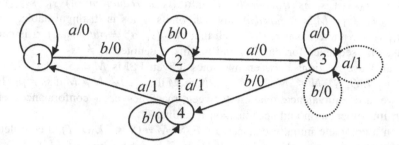

Fig. 1. A mutation machine with the specification machine as its submachine, where mutated transitions are depicted with dash lines, state 1 is the initial state.

The mutation machine M contains six suspicious transitions, one mutated transition represents output fault and the other two transfer faults. M contains eight deterministic submachines, the specification machine and seven mutants which share the same five trusted transitions.

As discussed in previous work [5, 7, 10], the mutation machine formally models test hypotheses about potential implementation faults. The mutation machine M allows compact representation of numerous mutants in the fault domain $Sub(M)$. More precisely, their number is given by the following formula:

$$|Sub(M)| = \prod_{(s,x) \in S \times I} |T(s, x)|$$

In the extreme case, considered in classical checking experiments a fault domain is the universe of all machines with a given number of states and fixed alphabets. The corresponding mutation machine becomes in this case a chaos machine with all possible transitions between each pair of states. The number of FSMs it represents is the product of the numbers of states and outputs to the power of the product of the numbers of states and inputs.

3   Mutation Testing

A finite set $E \subset I^*$ of finite input sequences is a *test suite* for A. A test suite is said to be *complete* w.r.t. the fault model $<A, \simeq, Sub(M)>$ if for each nonconforming mutant $B \in Sub(M)$ it contains a test detecting B.

In the domain of program mutation testing, such a test suite is often called adequate for a program (in our case, a specification machine) relative to a finite collection of programs (in our case the set of mutants), see, e.g., [4].

Differently from the classical program mutation testing, where the mutant killing tests are constructed mostly manually, in case of deterministic FSMs, tests that kill a given mutant FSM can be obtained from the product of the two machines, see, e.g., [1, 2, 27]. The problem can also be cast as model checking for a reachability property, considered in several work, see, e.g., [18]. This approach can also be used to check whether a given test kills mutants, but it requires mutant enumeration.

In this work, we develop an analysis approach that avoids mutant enumeration while still offering a possibility to estimate the test adequacy (mutation score).

3.1 Distinguishing Automaton

Tests detecting mutants of the specification are presented in a product of the specification and mutation machines obtained by composing their transitions as follows.

Definition 2. Given a complete deterministic specification machine $A = (S, s_0, I, O, N)$ and a mutation machine $M = (S, s_0, I, O, T)$, a finite automaton $D = (C \cup \{\nabla\}, c_0, I, D, \nabla)$, where $C \subseteq S \times S$, and ∇ is an accepting (sink) state is the *distinguishing* automaton for A and M, if it holds that

- $c_0 = (s_0, s_0)$
- For any $(s, t) \in C$ and $x \in I$, $((s, t), x, (s', t')) \in D$, if there exist $(s, x, o, s') \in N$, $(t, x, o', t') \in T$, such that $o = o'$ and $((s, t), x, \nabla) \in D$, if there exist $(s, x, o, s') \in N$, $(t, x, o', t') \in T$, such that $o \neq o'$
- $(\nabla, x, \nabla) \in D$ for all $x \in I$.

We illustrate the definition using the specification and mutation machines in Fig. 1. Figure 2 presents the distinguishing automaton for A and M.

The accepting state defines the language L_D of the distinguishing automaton D for A and M and possesses the following properties. First, all input sequences detecting each and every mutant belong to this language.

Theorem 1. Given the distinguishing automaton D for A and M, if $B \not\approx_\alpha A$, $B \in Sub$ (M), then $\alpha \in L_D$.

Notice that for any nonconforming mutant there exists an input sequence of length at most n^2, where n is the number of states of the specification machine, since distinguishing automaton has no more than n^2 states.

At the same time, not each and every word of the language detects a mutant. An input sequence $\alpha \in L_D$ triggers several executions in the distinguishing automaton D which are defined by a single execution in the specification machine A and some execution in the mutation machine M both triggered by α. The latter to represent a mutant must be deterministic. Such a deterministic execution of the mutation machine M defining (together with the execution of A) an execution of the distinguishing automaton D to the sink state is called α-*revealing*. Input sequences triggering revealing executions enjoy a nice property of being able to detect mutants.

Theorem 2. Given an input sequence $\alpha \in I^*$ such that $\alpha \in L_D$, an α-revealing execution includes at least one mutated transition, moreover, each mutant which has this execution is detected by the input sequence α.

Given an input sequence $\alpha \in L_D$, the question arises how all the mutants (un) detected by this input sequence can be characterized. We address this question in the next section.

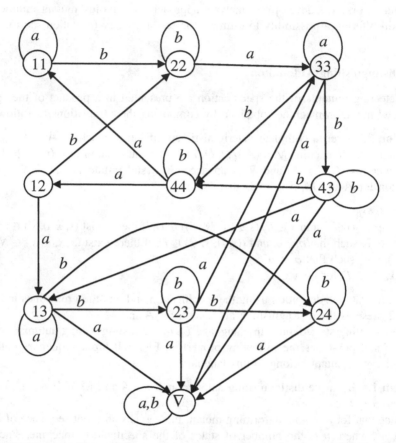

Fig. 2. The distinguishing automaton D for the specification A and mutation M machines in Fig. 1, state 11 is the initial state.

3.2   Mutation Coverage Analysis

Consider an input sequence $\alpha \in I*$ which detects a nonconforming mutant by triggering α-revealing executions. Analyzing these executions we can determine all mutated transitions involved in each of them. This analysis can performed by using a distinguishing automaton constrained to a given input sequence.

Let $\alpha \in I*$ and $Pref(\alpha)$ be the set of all prefixes of α. We define a linear automaton $(Pref(\alpha), \varepsilon, I, D_\alpha)$, such that each prefix of α is a state, and $(\beta, x, \beta x) \in D_\alpha$ if $\beta x \in Pref(\alpha)$.

Definition 3. Given input sequence $\alpha \in I^*$, a specification machine $A = (S, s_0, I, O, N)$ and a mutation machine $M = (S, s_0, I, O, T)$, a finite automaton $D_\alpha = (C_\alpha \cup \{\nabla\}, c_0, I, D_\alpha, \nabla)$, where $C_\alpha \subseteq Pref(\alpha) \times S \times S$, and ∇ is a designated sink state is the α-*distinguishing* automaton for A and M, if it holds that

- $c_0 = (\varepsilon, s_0, p_0)$
- For any $(\beta, s, t) \in C_\alpha$ and $x \in I$, such that $\beta x \in Pref(\alpha)$, $((\beta, s, t), x, (\beta x, s', t')) \in D_\alpha$, if there exist $(s, x, o, s') \in N$, $(t, x, o', t') \in T$, such that $o = o'$ and $((\beta, s, t), x, \nabla) \in D$, if there exist $(s, x, o, s') \in N$, $(t, x, o', t') \in T$, such that $o \neq o'$.

We illustrate the definition using the input sequence $\alpha = baaba$ for the specification and mutation machines in Fig. 1. Notice that the sequence hits all the mutated transitions in the mutation machine. The resulting α-distinguishing automaton for A and M is shown in Fig. 3.

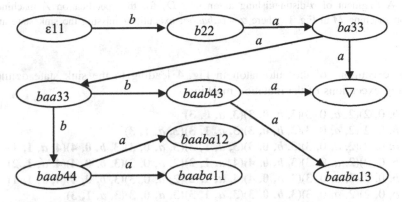

Fig. 3. The α-distinguishing automaton D_α for the specification A machine and mutation machine M in Fig. 1, where $\alpha = baaba$.

Notice that the input sequence $baaba$ and its prefix baa trigger two executions which end up in the sink state ∇. These are

1. $(1, b, 0, 2)(2, a, 0, 3)\mathbf{(3, a, 1, 3)}$
2. $(1, b, 0, 2)(2, a, 0, 3)\mathbf{(3, a, 0, 3)(3, b, 0, 3)}(3, a, 0, 3)$.

The suspicious transitions are in bold. The executions are deterministic and include two mutated transitions $(3, a, 1, 3)$ and $(3, b, 0, 3)$. The third mutated transition $(4, a, 1, 2)$ is in the execution that does not lead to the sink state ∇. Hence, the input sequence $baaba$ detects any mutant with two out of three mutated transitions.

The example indicates that α-distinguishing automata for the specification and mutation machines provide a suitable means for mutation analysis of a given test suite. Before we formulate a method for such an analysis, we consider yet another example of α-distinguishing automata with $\alpha = babaaba$.

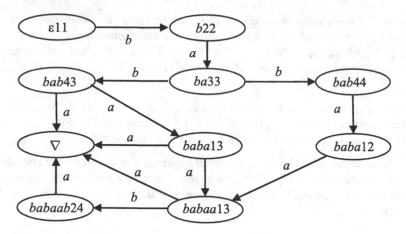

Fig. 4. A fragment of α-distinguishing automaton D_α for the specification A machine and mutation machine M in Fig. 1, where $\alpha = babaaba$; executions missing the sink state are not shown.

The executions of the automaton in Fig. 4 leading to the sink state define the following executions of the mutation machine:

1. $(1, b, 0, 2)(2, a, 0, 3)\mathbf{(3, b, 0, 3)(3, a, 0, 3)}$
2. $(1, b, 0, 2)(2, a, 0, 3)\mathbf{(3, b, 0, 3)(3, a, 1, 3)(3, a, 1, 3)}$
3. $(1, b, 0, 2)(2, a, 0, 3)\mathbf{(3, b, 0, 3)(3, a, 1, 3)}(3, a, 0, 3)\mathbf{(3, b, 0, 4)(4, a, 1, 1)}$
4. $(1, b, 0, 2)(2, a, 0, 3)\mathbf{(3, b, 0, 4)(4, a, 1, 2)}(2, a, 0, 3)\mathbf{(3, b, 0, 4)(4, a, 1, 2)}$
5. $(1, b, 0, 2)(2, a, 0, 3)\mathbf{(3, b, 0, 4)(4, a, 1, 2)}(2, a, 0, 3)\mathbf{(3, b, 0, 4)(4, a, 1, 1)}$
6. $(1, b, 0, 2)(2, a, 0, 3)\mathbf{(3, b, 0, 3)(3, a, 1, 3)}(3, a, 0, 3)\mathbf{(3, a, 1, 3)}$
7. $(1, b, 0, 2)(2, a, 0, 3)\mathbf{(3, b, 0, 4)(4, a, 1, 2)}(2, a, 0, 3)\mathbf{(3, a, 1, 3)}$
8. $(1, b, 0, 2)(2, a, 0, 3)\mathbf{(3, b, 0, 3)(3, a, 1, 3)}(3, a, 0, 3)\mathbf{(3, b, 0, 4)(4, a, 1, 2)}$

The executions 3, 5, 6 and 8 are nondeterministic in the mutation machine, since each of them has both unaltered and mutated transitions for the same pair of state and input.

Consider the first execution, it involves two suspicious transitions, mutated transition $(3, b, 0, 3)$ and unaltered transition $(3, a, 0, 3)$. The prefix $baba$ of the input sequence $babaaba$ detects any mutant in which unaltered transition $(3, b, 0, 4)$ is replaced by the mutated one $(3, b, 0, 3)$ and the suspicious transition $(3, a, 0, 3)$ is left unaltered. Let B be a set of transitions of a mutant $B \in Sub(M)$.

A mutant B is then detected by the input sequence $babaaba$ or its prefix if its set of transitions B satisfies at least one of the following constraints on suspicious transitions:

1. $(3, b, 0, 3), (3, a, 0, 3) \in B$
2. $(3, b, 0, 3), (3, a, 1, 3) \in B$
3. $(3, b, 0, 3), (3, a, 1, 3), (3, a, 0, 3), (3, b, 0, 4), (4, a, 1, 1) \in B$
4. $(3, b, 0, 4), (4, a, 1, 2) \in B$
5. $(3, b, 0, 4), (4, a, 1, 2), (4, a, 1, 1) \in B$

6. $(3, b, 0, 3), (3, a, 1, 3), (3, a, 0, 3) \in B$
7. $(3, b, 0, 4), (4, a, 1, 2), (3, a, 1, 3) \in B$
8. $(3, b, 0, 3), (3, a, 1, 3), (3, a, 0, 3), (3, b, 0, 4), (4, a, 1, 2) \in B$

Clearly nondeterministic executions 3, 5, 6 and 8 have unsatisfiable constraints since they require, e.g., that suspicious transition $(3, b, 0, 4)$ is unaltered and replaced by the mutated transition $(3, b, 0, 3)$ in the same mutant.

As stated above any mutant with the transition relation satisfying one of these constraints is detected by the input sequence *babaaba* or its prefix, since a wrong output sequence should be produced by such a mutant. On the other hand, a mutant that does not satisfy any of them escapes detection by this input sequence. To characterize these mutants, we formulate constraints which exclude all the executions of detected mutants by considering the negation of the disjunction of the constraints for all the triggered revealing executions. The resulting constraint becomes a conjunction of negated constraints of the executions.

For instance, the negated first constraint is $(3, b, 0, 3) \notin B$ or $(3, a, 0, 3) \notin B$. This reads that the unaltered transition $(3, b, 0, 4)$ or mutated transition $(3, a, 1, 3)$ must be present. The constraint $(3, b, 0, 3) \notin B$ is equivalent to $(3, b, 0, 4) \in B$; similarly, $(3, a, 0, 3) \notin B$ is equivalent to $(3, a, 1, 3) \in B$. We have that the negated constraint is $(3, b, 0, 4) \in B$ or $(3, a, 1, 3) \in B$.

To formalize the above discussions we cast the execution analysis as a constraint satisfaction problem by using auxiliary variables to specify the choices between suspicious transitions. Let $T_1, T_2, ..., T_m$ be the sets of suspicious transitions, where unaltered transitions are the first elements and the remaining elements of each set are lexicographically ordered. We introduce auxiliary variables $z_1, z_2, ..., z_m$, such that variable z_i represents the suspicious set T_i. For the variable z_i the domain is $D_i = \{1, 2, ..., |T_i|\}$, such that $z_i = 1$ represents the unaltered transition in the set T_i and the other values correspond to mutated transitions. We use conditional operators $\{=, \neq\}$ and logical operators AND ($\land$) and OR ($\lor$) for constraint formulas.

Each execution of a mutation machine that involves suspicious transitions yields assignments on variables representing these transitions, which expresses a constraint formula as the conjunction of individual assignments $(z_i = c)$, where $c \in D_i$. Then the negated constraint formula becomes the disjunction of individual constraints $(z_i \neq c)$.

A set of revealing executions triggered by one or more input sequences is then the conjunction of disjunctions of individual constraints.

In our example, the sets of suspicious transitions are

$T_1(3, a) = \{(3, a, 0, 3), (3, a, 1, 3)\}$,
$T_2(3, b) = \{(3, b, 0, 4), (3, b, 0, 3)\}$ and
$T_3(4, a) = \{(4, a, 1, 1), (4, a, 1, 2)\}$.

Each of these sets define two values of variables z_1, z_2 and z_3, where the value 1 of each variable represents a corresponding unaltered transition.

The constraint formula becomes:

$((z_2 \neq 2) \lor (z_1 \neq 1)) \land ((z_2 \neq 2) \lor (z_1 \neq 2)) \land ((z_2 \neq 2) \lor (z_1 \neq 2) \lor (z_1 \neq 1) \lor (z_2 \neq 1) \lor (z_3 \neq 1)) \land ((z_2 \neq 1) \lor (z_3 \neq 2)) \land ((z_2 \neq 1) \lor (z_3 \neq 2) \lor (z_3 \neq 1)) \land ((z_2 \neq 2) \lor (z_1 \neq 2) \lor (z_1 \neq 1)) \land ((z_2 \neq 1) \lor (z_3 \neq 2) \lor (z_1 \neq 2)) \land ((z_2 \neq 2) \lor (z_1 \neq 2) \lor (z_1 \neq 1) \lor (z_2 \neq 1) \lor (z_3 \neq 2)).$

Clearly, the formula always has a solution where values of variables determine unaltered transitions representing a specification machine, but we need a solution if it exists which has at least one mutated transition. To this end, we add the constraint $(z_1 \neq 1) \lor (z_2 \neq 1) \lor (z_3 \neq 1)$ excluding the solution defining the specification machine. The final constraint formula is

$((z_2 \neq 2) \lor (z_1 \neq 1)) \land ((z_2 \neq 2) \lor (z_1 \neq 2)) \land ((z_2 \neq 2) \lor (z_1 \neq 2) \lor (z_1 \neq 1) \lor (z_2 \neq 1) \lor (z_3 \neq 1)) \land ((z_2 \neq 1) \lor (z_3 \neq 2)) \land ((z_2 \neq 1) \lor (z_3 \neq 2) \lor (z_3 \neq 1)) \land ((z_2 \neq 2) \lor (z_1 \neq 2) \lor (z_1 \neq 1)) \land ((z_2 \neq 1) \lor (z_3 \neq 2) \lor (z_1 \neq 2)) \land ((z_2 \neq 2) \lor (z_1 \neq 2) \lor (z_1 \neq 1) \lor (z_2 \neq 1) \lor (z_3 \neq 2)) \land ((z_1 \neq 1) \lor (z_2 \neq 1) \lor (z_3 \neq 1)).$

To solve it, we use the SMT solver Yices [23] which finds the solution $(z_1 = 2)$, $(z_2 = 1)$, $(z_3 = 1)$. The solution defines a mutant with the single mutated transition $(3, a, 1, 3)$. The mutant is nonconforming, which can be verified with the help of a distinguishing automaton obtained for the specification machine and the mutant. This means that the input sequence $babaaba$ does not detect the mutant defined by the solution. To ensure its detection we have two options, to add a new input sequence or to try to extend the input sequence $babaaba$ until it detects the remaining mutant. The latter option avoids using the reset operation in testing, required in the former option.

Following the first option we notice that the input sequence which detects the escaped mutant is baa already obtained in the example of the α-distinguishing automaton in Fig. 3, where $\alpha = baaba$. Considering the revealing execution $(1, b, 0, 2)$ $(2, a, 0, 3)(3, a, 1, 3)$ triggered by its prefix baa, we generate an additional constraint $(z_1 \neq 2)$ which prevents the suspicious transition $(3, a, 1, 3)$ to be chosen and add it to the final constraint formula which has no solution. The set $\{babaaba, baa\}$ is therefore a complete test suite for the specification machine A and mutation machine M in Fig. 1.

Following the second option, we find that it is possible to extend the input sequence $babaaba$ which leaves the specification machine in state 3 with the input a to detect the mutated transition $(3, a, 1, 3)$. As before, we add constraint $(z_1 \neq 2)$ and the final constraint has no solution. The set $\{babaabaa\}$ is also a complete test suite.

This example indicates that various test generation strategies could be investigated, complementing checking experiments and checking sequences approaches. The latter allows one to avoid using multiple resets in testing. Notice that a classical checking experiment for this example derived by using, e.g., the W-method [12, 13], contains many more input sequences, moreover, the specification machine in Fig. 1 has no distinguishing sequence, which is usually required to generate a checking sequence. By this reason the existing methods cannot construct a single test, however, the example indicates that the mutation analysis allows us to do so. We leave the detailed elaboration of a test generation method for future work and formulate in this paper a procedure for mutant coverage analysis.

The procedure uses as inputs a test suite *TS* for a specification machine *A* and mutation machine *M* and consists of the following steps:

1. For each input sequence $\alpha \in TS$
   (a) Determine the α-distinguishing automaton
   (b) Find all executions leading to the sink state
   (c) Determine α-revealing executions of the mutation machine
   (d) Build the disjunction of constraints excluding the α-revealing executions
2. Build the conjunction of the obtained disjunctions and add the constraint that excludes the solution defining the specification machine
3. Solve the constraint formula by calling a solver
4. If it finds no solution terminate with the message "*TS* is complete", otherwise check whether the mutant defined by a solution is conforming
5. If it is nonconforming terminate with the message "*TS* is incomplete", otherwise add the constraint that excludes the solution defining the conforming mutant and go to Step 3.

The main steps of the procedure have already been discussed and illustrated on the examples, except of the last two steps which deserve more explanation. Constraint solvers normally provide a single solution if it exists. An extra constraint prevents the solution to point to just the specification machine, but the found solution may correspond to a conforming mutant. In the domain of general mutation testing the problem of dealing with mutants equivalent, i.e., conforming, to the specification is well understood. In testing from an FSM, most approaches assume that the specification machine is reduced, so conforming mutants are isomorphic machines. Checking FSM equivalence is based on an FSM product. Notice that the proposed approach does not require the specification machine be reduced.

The complexity of the proposed method is defined by the number of constraints. We expect that the method scales well, since the recent advances in solving techniques drastically improve their scalability [23, 24]. The number of constraints for a single execution is limited by the number of states of a mutation machine, but the number of executions increases with the number of mutated transitions. On the other hand, the number of executions of the distinguishing automaton which do not end up in the sink state grows with the number of mutated transitions, as faults may compensate each other. These executions are not revealing and do not contribute to the number of constraints. In Sect. 4 we present the results of our preliminary experiments performed on an industrial controller to assess the scalability of the approach.

3.3 Applications

The proposed mutation coverage analysis approach allows one to check if a given test suite is a complete test suite. A logical formula constructed by the proposed method represents the coverage of the test suite for a given fault model. If the test suite is found to be incomplete the question arises on how its quality in terms of fault coverage can be characterized. In the traditional software mutation testing, the fault detection power of tests is characterized by mutation score. It is a ratio of the number of killed mutants to the number of non-equivalent mutants. Note that the number of all possible mutants remains unknown and the mutation score is determined based on a limited set of generated mutants. As opposed to this approach, in our approach the total number of mutants can always be determined using the formula given in Sect. 2.2. Moreover, while the mutation analysis method avoids complete mutant enumeration, it does generate conforming mutants while searching for nonconforming ones. The enumeration of conforming mutants is achieved by adding constraints to a logical formula excluding repeated generation of already found mutants.

In the same vain, our method can be enhanced to generate and enumerate (at least partially) undetected nonconforming mutants. Once a nonconforming mutant is given by a solution found by a SMT solver and the method terminates declaring the test suite to be incomplete, we may continue this process by adding a constraint excluding its repeated generation. As a result a list of nonconforming mutants can be obtained. Two extreme cases of incomplete tests are worth to be discussed here.

First, a given test suite may have no detection capability at all. This property is in fact detected very early by the method; in this case all the α-distinguishing automata have no sink state reachable from the initial states, tests generate no constraints, the method can terminate at this step since there is no need to call a solver. No mutant in $Sub(M)$ is killed, the score is zero.

Second, a given test suite is "almost" complete and kills most of the mutants in Sub (M). In this case, the process of nonconforming mutant generation does not take much time and once terminated yields the number of conforming mutants c as well as the number of survived nonconforming ones n. Then the mutation score is computed as follows:

$$(|Sub(M)| - c - n) / (|Sub(M)| - c).$$

It is worth to note that the way the mutation score is determined is completely different from that in software mutation testing, as our method generates mutants based on a given test suite and not the other way around.

When a given test suite is "far" from being complete the number of survived nonconforming mutants can explode especially when a mutation machine is close to a complete chaos machine which represents the complete universe of FSMs. In this situation one possible solution to cope with the mutant explosion problem is to terminate generating nonconforming mutants once their number reaches a predefined maximum, e.g., a percentage of $|Sub(M)|$ or the time period allocated for mutation analysis ends. The obtained score is an (optimistic) estimation of an upper bound of the actual mutation score.

The proposed procedure could also be used for test minimization by defining a subsume relation between tests based on comparison of the logical formulas generated from them. Tests subsumed by other tests can always be removed from the original test suite. Similarly the generated formulas can be used to prioritize tests when needed, see, e.g., [28].

4   Experimental Results

In this section we report on a prototype tool implementing the proposed approach and its use on a case study of an FSM model of an automotive controller of industrial size.

4.1 Prototype Tool

The prototype tool takes as inputs a mutation machine and a test suite, both described in text format. The inputs are parsed with an ANTLR-based module [30] to build an internal representation of the two objects. The mutation analysis algorithm manipulates these representations to build α-distinguishing automata, determine revealing executions of the mutation machine and generate constraints for the Yices SMT solver [23]. The solver is used as a backend to decide the satisfiability of the constraints. The tool parses the outputs from Yices to extract a solution if it is found to build a mutant. The prototype can also be used with other SMT solvers compatible with the SMT-LIB 2.0.

4.2 Case Study

In our experiments, we use as a case study an automotive controller of the air quality system, which we also used in our previous work [29]. The functionality of the controller is to set an air source position depending on its current state and a current input from the environment.

The controller is initially specified as a hierarchical Simulink Stateflow model. Figure 5 gives an overview of the model which is composed of three super-states $s1$, $s2$ and $s23$ and 13 simple states. Each super-state is composed of states and transitions. The initial state is the simple state $s3$. To obtain an FSM we introduced an input alphabet replacing transitions guards and flattened the hierarchical machine. We have identified 24 abstract inputs and two outputs. The resulting FSM has 14 states, since we added (for modeling of a branching behavior implemented with C code in the original state) one extra state to the given 13 simple states. It has $24 \times 14 = 336$ transitions.

The mutation machine was constructed from the following assumption about potential implementation faults. These faults may occur in outgoing transitions from any of the simple states in two super-states, namely $s2$ and $s23$ and four inputs, as Table 1 shows. The obtained mutation machine has 46 mutated transitions. The formula in Sect. 2 gives the number of mutants being equal to $3^{12} \times 2^{17} = 69,657,034,752$ including the specification machine.

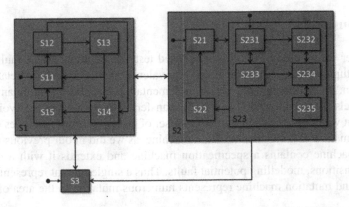

Fig. 5. An overview of the Simulink/Stateflow model in the controller

Tab. 1. The numbers of transitions for some pairs of states and inputs in the mutation machine (for the remaining pairs no mutated transitions were added).

	s21	s22	s231	s232	s233	s234	s235
a2	3	3	3	3	3	3	3
a4	2	2	2	2	2	2	2
a14	1	1	3	3	3	3	3
a16	1	1	4	4	4	4	4

4.3   Mutation Analysis

To perform the mutation analysis, we needed a test suite, which could be generated randomly, however, we find it difficult to obtain tests that hit suspicious transitions in this case study, since 26 out of 336 transitions of the specification machine become suspicious in the mutation machine. We decided to use an early prototype of a test generation tool (which is work in progress) as an input for the mutation analysis tool. The tool generates test cases one by one, so that the mutation analysis tool processes a test suite of an increasing size. The process terminates once a current test suite is found to be complete. In this experiment, the test suite completeness was determined when it had 31 test cases. The length of the test cases varies from 4 to 25 and the number of revealing executions triggered by each of them varies from 1 to 13. In the last, 31st execution of Yices, it was given the formula of 69 clauses, for which it found no solution, meaning that the test suite is complete for the given mutation machine. The mutation analysis process took less than one minute on a desktop computer with the following settings: 3.4 Ghz Intel Core i7-3770 CPU, 16.0 GB of RAM, Yices 2.4.1, and ANTLR 4.5.1.

The fact that the tool was able to determine that the given test suite kills each nonconforming mutant out of 69,657,034,752 possible mutants indicates that the approach scales sufficiently well on a typical automotive controller even when the number of mutants is big. In this experiment, we varied only the number of tests (from 1 to 31), hence more experiments by varying the specification as well as mutation machines are needed to assess the tool scalability.

5   Conclusions

In this paper we focused on fault model based testing, assuming that a fault model is given as a tuple of a specification FSM, equivalence as a conformance relation and a fault domain. A fault domain is a set of implementation machines, aka mutants, each of which models some faults, such as output, transfer or transition faults. Avoiding their enumeration we define the fault domain as a set of all possible submachines of a given nondeterministic FSM, called a mutation machine, as we did in our previous work. The mutation machine contains a specification machine and extends it with a number of mutated transitions, modelling potential faults. Thus a single mutant represents multiple mutations and mutation machine represents numerous mutants. In the area of mutation testing we could not find any attempt to analyze fault detection power of tests considering multiple mutants that avoids their enumeration.

We proposed a method for analyzing mutation coverage of tests which we cast as a constraint satisfaction problem. The method relies on the notion of a distinguishing automaton that is a product of the specification and mutation machines. To analyze mutation coverage of a single input sequence we define a distinguishing automaton constrained by this sequence. This allows us to determine all mutants revealing executions that are triggered by the input sequence. The executions are then used to build constraint formulas to be solved by an existing solver, Yices, in our experiments. The approach avoids enumeration of mutants while still offering a possibility to estimate the test adequacy (mutation score).

The preliminary experiments performed on an industrial controller indicate that the approach scales sufficiently well. We are planning to further enhance the approach to Extended FSMs [17] using mutation operators already defined for this type of FSMs.

Acknowledgements. This work is supported in part by GM R&D and the MEIE of Gouvernement du Québec. The authors would like to thank the reviewers for their useful comments.

References

1. Pomeranz, I., Sudhakar, M.R.: Test generation for multiple state-table faults in finite-state machines. IEEE Trans. Comput. **46**(7), 783–794 (1997)
2. Poage, J.F., McCluskey, Jr., E.J.: Derivation of optimal test sequences for sequential machines. In: Proceedings of the IEEE 5th Symposium on Switching Circuits Theory and Logical Design, pp. 121–132 (1964)
3. DeMillo, R.A., Lipton, R.J., Sayward, F.G.: Hints on test data selection: help for the practicing programmer. IEEE Comput. **11**(4), 34–41 (1978)
4. DeMilli, R.A., Offutt, J.A.: Constraint-based automatic test data generation. IEEE Trans. Softw. Eng. **17**(9), 900–910 (1991)
5. Grunsky, I.S., Petrenko, A.: Design of checking experiments with automata describing protocols. Automatic Control and Computer Sciences. Allerton Press Inc. USA. No. 4 (1988)
6. Hennie, F.C.: Fault detecting experiments for sequential circuits. In: Proceedings of the IEEE 5th Annual Symposium on Switching Circuits Theory and Logical Design, pp. 95–110. Princeton (1964)
7. Koufareva, I., Petrenko, A., Yevtushenko, N.: Test generation driven by user-defined fault models. In: Csopaki, G., Dibuz, S., Tarnay, K. (eds.) Testing of Communicating Systems. IFIP — The International Federation for Information Processing, vol. 21, pp. 215–233. Springer, New York (1999)
8. Lee, D., Yannakakis, M.: Principles and methods of testing finite-state machines - a survey. Proc. IEEE **84**(8), 1090–1123 (1996)
9. Moore, E.F.: Gedanken - Experiments on sequential machines. In: Automata Studies. Princeton University Press, pp. 129–153 (1956)
10. Petrenko, A., Yevtushenko, N.: Test suite generation for a FSM with a given type of implementation errors. In: Proceedings of IFIP 12th International Symposium on Protocol Specification, Testing, and Verification, pp. 229–243 (1992)

11. Petrenko, A., Yevtushenko, N., Bochmann, G.V.: Fault models for testing in context. In: Gotzhein, R., Bredereke, J. (eds.) Formal Description Techniques IX, pp. 163–178. Springer, USA (1996)
12. Vasilevskii, M.P.: Failure diagnosis of automata. Cybernetics 4, 653–665 (1973). Plenum Publishing Corporation. New York
13. Chow, T.S.: Testing software design modeled by finite-state machines. IEEE Trans. Softw. Eng. 4(3), 178–187 (1978)
14. Vuong, S.T., Ko, K.C.: A novel approach to protocol test sequence generation. In: Global Telecommunications Conference, vol. 3, pp. 2–5. IEEE (1990)
15. Godskesen, J.C.: Fault models for embedded systems. In: Pierre, L., Kropf, T. (eds.) CHARME 1999. LNCS, vol. 1703, pp. 354–359. Springer, Heidelberg (1999)
16. Cheng, K.T., Jou, J.Y.: A functional fault model for sequential machines. IEEE Trans. Comput. Aided Des. Integr. Circ. Syst. 11(9), 1065–1073 (1992)
17. Petrenko, A., Boroday, S., Groz, R.: Confirming configurations in EFSM testing. IEEE Trans. Softw. Eng. 30(1), 29–42 (2004)
18. Gordon, F., Wotawa, F., Ammann, P.: Testing with model checkers: a survey. Softw. Test. Verification Reliab. 19(3), 215–261 (2009)
19. Anand, S., et al.: An orchestrated survey of methodologies for automated software test case generation. J. Syst. Softw. 86(8), 1978–2001 (2013)
20. Petrenko, A.: Fault model-driven test derivation from finite state models: Annotated bibliography. Modeling and verification of parallel processes, pp. 196–205. Springer, Heidelberg (2001)
21. Petrenko, A., Bochmann, G.V., Yao, M.: On fault coverage of tests for finite state specifications. Comput. Netw. ISDN Syst. 29(1), 81–106 (1996)
22. Simao, A., Petrenko, A., Maldonado, J.C.: Comparing finite state machine test coverage criteria. IET Softw. 3(2), 91–105 (2009)
23. De Moura, L., Dutertre B.: Yices 1.0: An efficient SMT solver. In: The Satisfiability Modulo Theories Competition (SMT-COMP) (2006)
24. de Moura, L., Bjørner, N.S.: Z3: an efficient SMT solver. In: Ramakrishnan, C.R., Rehof, J. (eds.) TACAS 2008. LNCS, vol. 4963, pp. 337–340. Springer, Heidelberg (2008)
25. Rösch, S., Ulewicz, S., Provost, J., Vogel-Heuser, B.: Review of model-based testing approaches in production automation and adjacent domains - current challenges and research gaps. J. Softw. Eng. Appl. 8, 499–519 (2015)
26. Bochmann, G.V., et al.: Fault models in testing. In: Proceedings of the IFIP TC6/WG6. 1 Fourth International Workshop on Protocol Test Systems, pp. 17–30. North-Holland Publishing Co. (1991)
27. Petrenko, A., Yevtushenko, N.: Testing from partial deterministic FSM specifications. IEEE Trans. Comput. 54(9), 1154–1165 (2005)
28. Korel, B., Tahat, L.H., Harman M.: Test prioritization using system models. In: Proceedings of the 21st IEEE International Conference on Software Maintenance, pp. 559–568 (2005)
29. Petrenko, A., Dury, A., Ramesh, S., Mohalik, S.: A method and tool for test optimization for automotive controllers. In: ICST Workshops, pp. 198–207 (2013)
30. Parr, T.: The Definitive ANTLR 4 Reference, vol. 2. Pragmatic Bookshelf, Raleigh (2013)

The Challenge of Typed Expressiveness in Concurrency

Jorge A. Pérez(✉)

University of Groningen, Groningen, The Netherlands
j.a.perez@rug.nl

Abstract. By classifying behaviors (rather than data values), *behavioral types* abstract structured protocols and enforce disciplined message-passing programs. Many different behavioral type theories have been proposed: they offer a rich landscape of models in which types delineate concurrency and communication. Unfortunately, studies on formal relations between these theories are incipient. This paper argues that clarifying the *relative expressiveness* of these type systems is a pressing challenge for formal techniques in distributed systems. We overview works that address this issue and discuss promising research avenues.

1 Introduction

Communication and *types* are increasingly relevant in (concurrent) programming. To bear witness of this trend, several languages promoted by industry offer advanced type systems (or type-based analysis tools) and/or support (message-passing) communication. For instance, Facebook's Flow [1] is a type checker for JavaScript based on gradual typing; Mozilla's Rust [4] exploits affine, ownership types to balance safety and control; Google's Go [3] supports process concurrency and channel-based communication. Other languages (e.g., Erlang [2]) also offer forms of (message-passing) communication.

If communication and types are here to stay, on what foundations languages integrating both features should rest? Much research within formal techniques in distributed systems has been devoted to models for concurrency and communication. In particular, *process calculi* have been widely promoted as a basis for type systems for concurrent programs. Indeed, building upon the π-calculus, a variety of *behavioral type systems* have been put forward [24,35]: by classifying behaviors (rather than values), these type structures abstract structured protocols and enforce disciplined message-passing programs. Existing work suggests that rather than a shortage of foundations for types and communication, we have the opposite problem: there are many formal foundations and it is unclear how to build upon them to transfer analysis techniques into practice.

The current situation calls for rigorous comparisons between well-established (but distinct) behavioral typed frameworks. Besides revealing bridges between different models of typed processes, such comparisons should clarify the complementarities and shortcomings of analysis techniques based on types.

© IFIP International Federation for Information Processing 2016
E. Albert and I. Lanese (Eds.): FORTE 2016, LNCS 9688, pp. 239–247, 2016.
DOI: 10.1007/978-3-319-39570-8_16

Developing a theory of *typed expressiveness* is thus a challenge for the specification and analysis of distributed systems. The consolidation of *communication-centered* software systems (collections of interacting, heterogeneous services) and the renewed interest of software practitioners in communication and types endow this research challenge with practical significance.

We argue that the much needed formal comparisons may draw inspiration from results and frameworks for *relative expressiveness*, as studied in concurrency theory. This area has elucidated important formal relations between *untyped* process languages (see [49] for a survey); it thus appears as an adequate basis for analogous formal results in a typed setting.

This short paper is organized as follows. Next we overview main achievements in untyped expressiveness (Sect. 2). Then, we briefly review expressiveness results that consider behavioral types and/or behaviorally typed processes (Sect. 3). We conclude by discussing promising research directions (Sect. 4).

2   Expressiveness in Concurrency: The Untyped Case

Important studies of expressiveness in concurrency concern *process calculi*, a well-established approach to the analysis of concurrent systems. These formalisms, in particular the π-calculus, also provide a basis for typed systems for communicating programs. Process calculi promote the view of *concurrency as communication*: they abstract the interactions of a system by means of atomic communication actions. This view is simple and powerful, and has deep ramifications to *computing* at large.

The process calculi approach to concurrency has proved prolific. Starting from a few "basic" process calculi (including CSP, CCS, the π-calculus, amongst others), many extensions have been put forward, following modeling requirements (e.g., quantitative information) but also the need of representing forms of interaction typical of application domains such as, e.g., systems biology, security, and service-oriented computing. Given this *jungle* of process models [45], the need for establishing formal relationships between them was soon evident. To rise to this challenge, since the early 1990s a sustained body of work has assessed the *expressiveness* of process languages. These studies may pertain, for instance, to the nature of a process construct (e.g., whether it can be implemented using more basic ones) or to the transfer of reasoning techniques (e.g., process equivalences) across languages.

The main device used in expressiveness studies is the notion of *encoding*: a translation of a *source language* $\mathcal{L}_S$ into a *target language* $\mathcal{L}_T$ that satisfies certain properties. Such properties are usually defined as *syntactic and semantic criteria*; they are abstract indicators of an encoding's quality. Two common criteria are *homomorphism with respect to parallel composition*, which promotes compositional encodings, and *operational correspondence*, which relates the (visible) behavior of source and target processes. Abstract formulations of encodings and their criteria have been put forward (cf. [30]). An encoding of $\mathcal{L}_S$ into $\mathcal{L}_T$ (a *positive* encodability result) indicates that $\mathcal{L}_T$ is at least as expressive as $\mathcal{L}_S$:

all behaviors expressible in $\mathcal{L}_S$ can also be expressed in $\mathcal{L}_T$. The non existence of an encoding (a *negative* encodability result) may indicate that $\mathcal{L}_S$ is more expressive than $\mathcal{L}_T$: there are behaviors expressible in $\mathcal{L}_S$ but not in $\mathcal{L}_T$.

Encodability results have clarified our understanding of notions of interaction and communication as abstracted by process calculi. They have been crucial to:

(a) *Formally relate different computational models.* Two notable examples are (i) the encodability of the λ-calculus in the π-calculus [44], and (ii) decidability results for termination/convergence for CCS, which distinguish the expressive power of processes with replication and recursion [6].

(b) *Assess the expressive power of process languages.* As an example, several influential works have clarified the interplay of choice operators and (a)synchronous communication, and its influence on the expressive power of the π-calculus (see, for instance, [48]).

(c) *Transfer proof techniques between different calculi.* For instance, the fully abstract encodability of process mobility (process passing) into name mobility has important consequences on the behavioral theory of higher-order process calculi [50].

Expressiveness results can be useful in the design of concurrent languages. For instance, the formalization of compilers usually requires encodings and behavior-preserving translations. Similarly, the development of type systems for process calculi, in particular *behavioral types*, has further reconciled process models and actual concurrent languages.

3   Towards Relative Expressiveness for Behavioral Types

The development of process languages with verification techniques based on *type systems* has received much attention. From Milner's *sortings* [43] until recently discovered logic foundations of concurrency [9, 52]—passing through, e.g., *graph types* [53], *linear types* [39], *session types* [31], and *generic types* [36]—type systems have revealed a rich landscape of concurrent models with disciplined communication.

Within these different type systems, behavioral types stand out by their ability to abstract notions such as causality, alternatives (choices), and repetition [35]. A behavioral type defines the resource-usage policy of a communication channel, but also describes a series of actions realized through that channel along time. Behavioral types are often defined on top of process calculi; this enables the definition of general verification techniques that may be then adapted to different languages. Given this jungle of *typed* process models, the need for establishing formal relations between them rises again. Mirroring the achievements of untyped expressiveness (cf. (a)–(c) above), we believe that research on formal methods for distributed systems would benefit from efforts aimed at:

(i) Formally relating different typed models.
(ii) Assessing the expressiveness of languages governed by behavioral types.
(iii) Transferring analysis techniques between different typed languages and formalisms.

These are challenging issues: as different type systems rely on unrelated concepts, discrepancies on typability arise easily. Hence, objective comparisons are hard to establish. Next we briefly review some works that address (i)–(iii) from various angles. Most of them concern session types, one of the most representative classes of behavioral types. Session types abstract structured communications (protocols) by allowing sequential actions (input and output), labeled choices (internal and external), and recursion. *Binary* session types [31] abstract protocols between two partners; *multiparty* session types [32] overcome this limitation: a *global type* (*choreography*) offers a high-level perspective for the *local types* realized by each partner. Different formulations for binary/multiparty session types have been developed, with varying motivations [35].

Linear Types and Session Types. Kobayashi appears to be the first to have related distinct type disciplines for the π-calculus by encoding the (finite) session π-calculus into a π-calculus with linear types with usages and variant types [38, Sect. 10]. His encoding represents a session name by multiple linear channels, using a continuation-passing style. Since Kobayashi does not explore the correctness properties of his encoding, Dardha et al. [17] revisit it by establishing type and operational correspondences and by giving extensions with subtyping, polymorphism, and higher-order communication. An extension of [17] with recursion in processes and types is reported in [16].

In a similar vein as [17], Demangeon and Honda [19] encode a session π-calculus into a linear/affine π-calculus with subtyping based on choice and selection types, which generalize input and output types, resp. Their encoding preserves subtyping. In contrast to [17], the encoding in [19] is fully abstract up to may/must barbed congruences. Their linear/affine π-calculus can also encode a call-by-value λ-calculus.

Gay et al. [28] encode a monadic π-calculus with (finite) binary session types (as in [27]) into a polyadic π-calculus with generic process types (as in [36], instantiated with linear, race-free communications). They aim at retaining original constructs in both models and to ensure operational and type correspondences. Their encoding enjoys these correspondences, but does not preserve subtyping. The authors notice that encoding labeled choice into guarded, unlabeled summation is challenging; also, that the target languages considered in [17,19] admit simple encodings of labeled choice.

Concerning transfer of techniques, Carbone et al. [11] use the encoding in [17] to relate *progress* in the session π-calculus to *lock-freedom* [37] in the linear π-calculus. This path to progress in binary sessions is an improvement with respect to previous works [12,25], as more session processes with progress are accepted as well-typed.

Session Types and Automata-like Models. Just as (untyped) process calculi have been related to sequential models of computation to characterize (un)decidability properties (therefore identifying expressiveness gaps—see, e.g., [6]), session types have been related to automata-like models. Initial results are due to Villard [51] who, in the context of dual channel contracts, shows that a subclass of communicating finite state machines (CFSMs) characterizes binary session types. Deniélou and Yoshida [22] extend this characterization to the multiparty setting by giving a class of generalized multiparty session types and their interpretation into CFSMs. This class inherits key safety and liveness properties from CFSMs. The work [23] complements [22] by offering a sound and complete characterization of multiparty session types as CFSMs, identifying the key notion of multiparty compatibility. Lange et al. [41] extend this work by developing techniques to synthesize global graphs from CFSMs, covering more global protocols than [22,23]. Fossati et al. [26] overcome modeling limitations of textual multiparty session types through an integration with Petri nets. Using Petri nets token semantics they define a conformance relation between syntactic local types and *session nets*.

Types in the ψ-calculi. The ψ-calculi [5] are a family of name-passing process calculi that extends the π-calculus with terms, conditions, and assertions. Generality arises by treating terms as subjects in communication prefixes and by allowing input patterns. Hüttel [33] proposes a type system for ψ-calculi that generalizes simple types for the π-calculus; it enjoys generic formulations of type soundness and type safety. Instantiations are shown for other process languages, including the fusion calculus, the distributed π (Dπ), and the spi-calculus. The work [34] extends [33] to the case of resource-aware type systems: it proposes a type system for ψ-calculi that subsumes the system for linear channel usage of [39], the action types of [54], and a type system similar to that in [21].

Other Approaches. López et al. [42] encode binary session processes into a declarative process calculus, enabling the transfer of LTL reasoning to scenarios of session communications. Cano et al. [10] encode a session π-calculus into declarative process calculus with explicit linearity and establish strong operational correspondences. Padovani [47] relates labeled choice operators in session types with intersection and union types. Orchard and Yoshida [46] encode PCF with an effect type system into a session π-calculus; a reverse encoding that embeds the session π-calculus into PCF with concurrency primitives is used to offer a new implementation of sessions into Haskell.

4   Concluding Remarks and Future Directions

The works discussed above define insightful relations between different frameworks of behavioral types. Although some works define the transfer of techniques between typed models and/or enable practical applications (cf. [11,42,46]), most existing works define isolated studies: since each work uses different techniques to relate typed models, further research is needed to integrate their results. There are promising research directions towards this ambitious goal. For space reasons, below we discuss only three of them.

4.1   Expressiveness Without Processes

Using process calculi to study behavioral types allows to establish their properties by exploiting well-established process techniques. In practical multiparty communications [13,23,41], however, one is mostly interested in types (rather than in processes), as they offer contracts/interfaces to derive safe implementations. These works use process calculi techniques to define, e.g., operational semantics and equivalences for global types. If one focuses on types then expressiveness results should relate different behavioral types and their semantics. Demangeon and Yoshida [20] develop this approach: they contrasted the expressivity of different models of multiparty session types by comparing their trace-based denotations. As global types become richer in structure, comparisons will need to use techniques from relative expressiveness. The recent work of Cruz-Filipe and Montesi [15] goes in this direction.

4.2   A Logic Yardstick for Typed Expressiveness

The variety of behavioral types rises a natural question: what should be a "fair yardstick" to compare them? Recently developed Curry-Howard correspondences for concurrency [9,14,52] define a fundamental model of behavioral types: by relating session types and linear logic, they identify type preserving and deadlock-free process models.

Some works connect [9,52] and other models. Wadler [52] gives a deadlock-free fragment of the session-typed functional language in [29] by encodings into concurrent processes. The work [18] contrasts two classes of deadlock-free, session processes: the first class results from [9,52]; the other results by combining the encoding in [17] and usage types [37]. The former class is shown to be strictly included in the latter. The work [7,8] defines an analysis of multiparty session types (lock-free choreographies, as in [23]) using techniques for binary session types (as in [9]). Further work should relate [9,14,52] and other behavioral types.

4.3   Typed Encodability Criteria

Related to Sect. 4.1, another direction is clarifying how existing frameworks for relative expressiveness (such as [30]) can account for behavioral types. This is needed to understand how types induce encodability results, but also to relate different behavioral types in source/target languages.

In their recent study of the relative expressivity of higher-order session communication, Kouzapas et al. [40] define a notion of typed encoding that extends [30] with session types. This work considers translations of processes and types and two new encodability criteria: type soundness and type preservation. The former says that translations preserve typability (well-typed source processes are encoded into well-typed target processes), the latter says that encodings of types preserve the structure of the session protocol, as represented by session type operators. While demanding and focused to the case of binary session types, these criteria are shown to be appropriate in classifying session-based π-calculi. Further work is needed to generalize/relax these typed encodability criteria, so to consider source and target languages with different type systems.

Acknowledgments. I would like to thank Ilaria Castellani, Ornela Dardha, Mariangiola Dezani-Ciancaglini, Dimitrios Kouzapas, Hugo A. López, and Camilo Rueda for their useful feedback on previous drafts of this paper.

References

1. Flow: A Static Type Checker for JavaScript. http://flowtype.org
2. The Erlang Programming Language. http://www.erlang.org
3. The Go Programming Language. https://golang.org
4. The Rust Programming Language. https://www.rust-lang.org
5. Bengtson, J., Johansson, M., Parrow, J., Victor, B.: Psi-calculi: mobile processes, nominal data, and logic. In: Proceedings of LICS 2009, pp. 39–48. IEEE Computer Society (2009). http://doi.ieeecomputersociety.org/10.1109/LICS.2009.20
6. Busi, N., Gabbrielli, M., Zavattaro, G.: On the expressive power of recursion, replication and iteration in process calculi. Math. Struc. Comp. Sci. **19**(6), 1191–1222 (2009). http://dx.doi.org/10.1017/S096012950999017X
7. Caires, L., Pérez, J.A.: A typeful characterization of multiparty structured conversations based on binary sessions. CoRR abs/1407.4242 (2014). http://arxiv.org/abs/1407.4242
8. Caires, L., Pérez, J.A.: Multiparty session types within a canonical binary theory, and beyond. In: Albert, E., Lanese, I. (eds.) FORTE 2016. LNCS, vol. 9688, pp. 75–85. Springer, Heidelberg (2016)
9. Caires, L., Pfenning, F.: Session types as intuitionistic linear propositions. In: Gastin, P., Laroussinie, F. (eds.) CONCUR 2010. LNCS, vol. 6269, pp. 222–236. Springer, Heidelberg (2010)
10. Cano, M., Rueda, C., López, H.A., Pérez, J.A.: Declarative interpretations of session-based concurrency. In: Proceedings of PPDP 2015, pp. 67–78. ACM (2015). http://doi.acm.org/10.1145/2790449.2790513
11. Carbone, M., Dardha, O., Montesi, F.: Progress as compositional lock-freedom. In: Kühn, E., Pugliese, R. (eds.) COORDINATION 2014. LNCS, vol. 8459, pp. 49–64. Springer, Heidelberg (2014). http://dx.doi.org/10.1007/978-3-662-43376-8_4
12. Carbone, M., Debois, S.: A graphical approach to progress for structured communication in web services. In: Proceedings of ICE 2010. EPTCS, vol. 38, pp. 13–27 (2010). http://dx.doi.org/10.4204/EPTCS.38.4
13. Carbone, M., Montesi, F.: Deadlock-freedom-by-design: multiparty asynchronous global programming. In: Proceedings of POPL 2013, pp. 263–274. ACM (2013). http://doi.acm.org/10.1145/2429069.2429101
14. Carbone, M., Montesi, F., Schürmann, C., Yoshida, N.: Multiparty session types as coherence proofs. In: Proceedings of CONCUR 2015. LIPIcs, vol. 42, pp. 412–426 (2015). http://dx.doi.org/10.4230/LIPIcs.CONCUR.2015.412
15. Cruz-Filipe, L., Montesi, F.: Choreographies, computationally. CoRR abs/1510.03271 (2015). http://arxiv.org/abs/1510.03271
16. Dardha, O.: Recursive session types revisited. In: Proceedings of BEAT 2014. EPTCS, vol. 162, pp. 27–34 (2014). http://dx.doi.org/10.4204/EPTCS.162.4
17. Dardha, O., Giachino, E., Sangiorgi, D.: Session types revisited. In: Proceedings of PPDP 2012, pp. 139–150. ACM (2012). http://doi.acm.org/10.1145/2370776.2370794
18. Dardha, O., Pérez, J.A.: Comparing deadlock-free session typed processes. In: Proceedings of EXPRESS/SOS. EPTCS, vol. 190, pp. 1–15 (2015). http://dx.doi.org/10.4204/EPTCS.190.1

19. Demangeon, R., Honda, K.: Full abstraction in a subtyped pi-calculus with linear types. In: Katoen, J.-P., König, B. (eds.) CONCUR 2011. LNCS, vol. 6901, pp. 280–296. Springer, Heidelberg (2011). http://dx.org/10.1007/978-3-642-23217-6_19

20. Demangeon, R., Yoshida, N.: On the expressiveness of multiparty sessions. In: Proceedings of FSTTCS 2015. LIPIcs, vol. 45, pp. 560–574. Schloss Dagstuhl (2015). http://dx.org/10.4230/LIPIcs.FSTTCS.2015.560

21. Deng, Y., Sangiorgi, D.: Ensuring termination by typability. Inf. Comput. **204**(7), 1045–1082 (2006)

22. Deniélou, P.-M., Yoshida, N.: Multiparty session types meet communicating automata. In: Seidl, H. (ed.) ESOP 2012. LNCS, vol. 7211, pp. 194–213. Springer, Heidelberg (2012). http://dx.org/10.1007/978-3-642-28869-2_10

23. Deniélou, P.-M., Yoshida, N.: Multiparty compatibility in communicating automata: characterisation and synthesis of global session types. In: Fomin, F.V., Freivalds, R., Kwiatkowska, M., Peleg, D. (eds.) ICALP 2013, Part II. LNCS, vol. 7966, pp. 174–186. Springer, Heidelberg (2013). http://dx.org/10.1007/978-3-642-39212-2_18

24. Dezani-Ciancaglini, M., de'Liguoro, U.: Sessions and session types: an overview. In: Laneve, C., Su, J. (eds.) WS-FM 2009. LNCS, vol. 6194, pp. 1–28. Springer, Heidelberg (2010)

25. Dezani-Ciancaglini, M., de'Liguoro, U., Yoshida, N.: On progress for structured communications. In: Barthe, G., Fournet, C. (eds.) TGC 2007. LNCS, vol. 4912, pp. 257–275. Springer, Heidelberg (2008). http://dx.org/10.1007/978-3-540-78663-4_18

26. Fossati, L., Hu, R., Yoshida, N.: Multiparty session nets. In: Maffei, M., Tuosto, E. (eds.) TGC 2014. LNCS, vol. 8902, pp. 112–127. Springer, Heidelberg (2014). http://dx.org/10.1007/978-3-662-45917-1_8

27. Gay, S., Hole, M.: Subtyping for session types in the pi calculus. Acta Inf. **42**, 191–225 (2005). http://portal.acm.org/citation.cfm?id=1104643.1104646

28. Gay, S.J., Gesbert, N., Ravara, A.: Session types as generic process types. In: Proceedings of EXPRESS 2014 and SOS 2014. EPTCS, vol. 160, pp. 94–110 (2014). http://dx.org/10.4204/EPTCS.160.9

29. Gay, S.J., Vasconcelos, V.T.: Linear type theory for asynchronous session types. J. Funct. Program. **20**(1), 19–50 (2010). http://dx.org/10.1017/S0956796809990268

30. Gorla, D.: Towards a unified approach to encodability and separation results for process calculi. Inf. Comput. **208**(9), 1031–1053 (2010). http://dx.org/10.1016/j.ic.2010.05.002

31. Honda, K., Vasconcelos, V.T., Kubo, M.: Language primitives and type discipline for structured communication-based programming. In: Hankin, C. (ed.) ESOP 1998. LNCS, vol. 1381, pp. 122–138. Springer, Heidelberg (1998)

32. Honda, K., Yoshida, N., Carbone, M.: Multiparty asynchronous session types. In: POPL 2008, pp. 273–284. ACM (2008)

33. Hüttel, H.: Typed ψ-calculi. In: Katoen, J.-P., König, B. (eds.) CONCUR 2011. LNCS, vol. 6901, pp. 265–279. Springer, Heidelberg (2011). http://dx.doi.org/10.1007/978-3-642-23217-6_18

34. Hüttel, H.: Types for resources in ψ-calculi. In: Abadi, M., Lluch Lafuente, A. (eds.) TGC 2013. LNCS, vol. 8358, pp. 83–102. Springer, Heidelberg (2014). http://dx.org/10.1007/978-3-319-05119-2_6

35. Huttel, H., Lanese, I., Vasconcelos, V., Caires, L., Carbone, M., Deniélou, P.M., Mostrous, D., Padovani, L., Ravara, A., Tuosto, E., Vieira, H.T., Zavattaro, G.: Foundations of session types and behavioural contracts. ACM Comput. Surv. (2016, to appear)

36. Igarashi, A., Kobayashi, N.: A generic type system for the pi-calculus. Theor. Comput. Sci. **311**(1–3), 121–163 (2004). http://dx.org/10.1016/S0304-3975(03)00325–6
37. Kobayashi, N.: A type system for lock-free processes. Inf. Comput. **177**(2), 122–159 (2002). http://dx.org/10.1006/inco.2002.3171
38. Kobayashi, N.: Type systems for concurrent programs. In: Aichernig, B.K. (ed.) Formal Methods at the Crossroads. From Panacea to Foundational Support. LNCS, vol. 2757, pp. 439–453. Springer, Heidelberg (2003). http://dx.org/10.1007/978-3-540-40007-3_26
39. Kobayashi, N., Pierce, B.C., Turner, D.N.: Linearity and the pi-calculus. In: POPL, pp. 358–371 (1996)
40. Kouzapas, D., Pérez, J.A., Yoshida, N.: On the relative expressiveness of higher-order session processes. In: Thiemann, P. (ed.) ESOP 2016. LNCS, vol. 9632, pp. 446–475. Springer, Heidelberg (2016). doi:10.1007/978-3-662-49498-1_18
41. Lange, J., Tuosto, E., Yoshida, N.: From communicating machines to graphical choreographies. In: Proceedings of POPL 2015, pp. 221–232. ACM (2015). http://doi.acm.org/10.1145/2676726.2676964
42. López, H.A., Olarte, C., Pérez, J.A.: Towards a unified framework for declarative structured communications. In: Proceedings of PLACES 2009. EPTCS, vol. 17, pp. 1–15 (2009). http://dx.org/10.4204/EPTCS.17.1
43. Milner, R.: The Polyadic pi-Calculus: A Tutorial. Technical report, ECS-LFCS-91-180 (1991)
44. Milner, R.: Functions as processes. Math. Struc. Comp. Sci. **2**(2), 119–141 (1992)
45. Nestmann, U.: Welcome to the jungle: a subjective guide to mobile process calculi. In: Baier, C., Hermanns, H. (eds.) CONCUR 2006. LNCS, vol. 4137, pp. 52–63. Springer, Heidelberg (2006). http://dx.org/10.1007/11817949_4
46. Orchard, D.A., Yoshida, N.: Effects as sessions, sessions as effects. In: Proceedings of POPL 2016, pp. 568–581. ACM (2016). http://doi.acm.org/10.1145/2837614.2837634
47. Padovani, L.: Session types = intersection types + union types. In: Proceedings of ITRS 2010. EPTCS, vol. 45, pp. 71–89 (2010). http://dx.org/10.4204/EPTCS.45.6
48. Palamidessi, C.: Comparing the expressive power of the synchronous and asynchronous pi-calculi. Math. Struct. Comput. Sci. **13**(5), 685–719 (2003). http://dx.org/10.1017/S0960129503004043
49. Parrow, J.: Expressiveness of process algebras. In: ENTCS, vol. 209, pp. 173–186 (2008). http://dx.org/10.1016/j.entcs.2008.04.011
50. Sangiorgi, D.: Expressing Mobility in Process Algebras: First-Order and Higher-Order Paradigms. Ph.D. thesis CST-99-93, University of Edinburgh (1992)
51. Villard, J.: Heaps and Hops. Ph.D. thesis, École Normale Supérieure de Cachan, February 2011
52. Wadler, P.: Propositions as sessions. J. Funct. Program. **24**(2–3), 384–418 (2014). http://dx.org/10.1017/S095679681400001X
53. Yoshida, N.: Graph types for monadic mobile processes. In: Chandru, V., Vinay, V. (eds.) FSTTCS 1996. LNCS, vol. 1180, pp. 371–386. Springer, Heidelberg (1996). http://dx.org/10.1007/3-540-62034-6_64
54. Yoshida, N., Berger, M., Honda, K.: Strong normalisation in the pi -calculus. Inf. Comput. **191**(2), 145–202 (2004)

Type-Based Analysis for Session Inference
(Extended Abstract)

Carlo Spaccasassi[✉] and Vasileios Koutavas

Trinity College Dublin, Dublin, Ireland
spaccasc@tcd.ie, vasileios.koutavas@scss.tcd.ie

Abstract. We propose a type-based analysis to infer the session protocols of channels in an ML-like concurrent functional language. Combining and extending well-known techniques, we develop a type-checking system that separates the underlying ML type system from the typing of sessions. Without using linearity, our system guarantees communication safety and partial lock freedom. It also supports provably complete session inference for finite sessions with no programmer annotations. We exhibit the usefulness of our system with interesting examples, including one which is not typable in substructural type systems.

1 Introduction

Concurrent programming often requires processes to communicate according to intricate protocols. In mainstream programming languages these protocols are encoded implicitly in the program's control flow, and no support is available for verifying their correctness.

Honda [6] first suggested the use of *binary session types* to explicitly describe and check protocols over communication channels with two endpoints. Fundamentally, session type systems guarantee that a program respects the order of communication events (session fidelity) and message types (communication safety) described in a channel's session type. A number of session type systems (e.g., [2,3,16]) also ensure that processes fully execute the protocols of their open endpoints, as long as they do not diverge or block on opening new sessions (partial lock freedom).

To date, binary session type disciplines have been developed for various process calculi and high-level programming languages (see [8] for an overview) by following one of two main programming language design approaches: using a single substructural type system for both session and traditional typing [5,7,18,19], or using monads to separate the two [13,16].

In this paper we propose a third design approach which uses *effects*. Similar to previous work, our approach enables the embedding of session types in programming languages with sophisticated type systems. Here we develop a high-level

---

This research was supported, in part, by Science Foundatin Ireland grant 13/RC/2094. The first author was supported by MSR (MRL 2011-039).

E. Albert and I. Lanese (Eds.): FORTE 2016, LNCS 9688, pp. 248–266, 2016.
DOI: 10.1007/978-3-319-39570-8_17

language where intricate protocols of communication can be programmed and checked statically (Sect. 2). Contrary to both monads and substructural type systems, our approach allows pure code to call library code with communication effects, without having to refactor the pure code (e.g., to embed it in a monad or pass continuation channels through it—see Example 2.3). We apply our approach to ML$_S$, a core of ML with session communication (Sect. 3).

Our approach separates traditional typing from session typing in a two-level system, which follows the principles of *typed based analysis* [12]. The first level employs a type-and-effect system, which adapts and extends the one of Amtoft et al. [1] to session communication (Sect. 4). At this level the program is typed against an ML type and a *behaviour* which abstractly describes program structure and communication. Session protocols are not considered here—they are entirely checked at the second level. Thus, each endpoint is given type Ses$^\rho$, where ρ statically approximates its source. The benefit of extending [1] is that we obtain a complete behaviour inference algorithm, which extracts a behaviour for every program respecting ML types.

At the second level, our system checks that a behaviour, given an operational semantics, complies with the session types of channels and endpoints (Sect. 5). The session discipline realised here is inspired by the work of Castagna et al. [3]. This discipline guarantees that programs comply with session fidelity and communication safety, but also, due to stacked interleaving of sessions, partial lock freedom. However, one of the main appeals of our session typing discipline is that it enables a provably *complete session types inference* from behaviours which, with behaviour inference, gives us a complete method for session inference from ML$_S$, without programmer annotations (Sect. 6). The two levels of our system only interact through behaviours, which we envisage will allow us to develop front-ends for different languages and back-ends for different session disciplines.

To simplify the technical development we consider only sessions of finite interactions. However, we allow recursion in the source language, as long as it is *confined*: recursive code may only open new sessions and completely consume them (see Sect. 2). In Sect. 7 we discuss an extension to recursive types. Related work and conclusions can be found in Sect. 8. Details missing from this extended abstract can be found in the appendix for the benefit of the reviewers.

2 Motivating Examples

Example 2.1 (A Swap Service). A coordinator process uses the primitive acc-swp to accept two connections on a channel swp (we assume functions acc-c and req-c for every channel c), opening two concurrent sessions with processes that want to exchange values. It then coordinates the exchange and recurs.

```
let fun coord(_) =                          let fun swap(x) =
    let val p1 = acc-swp ()                     let val p = req-swp ()
        val x1 = recv p1                        in send p x; recv p
        val p2 = acc-swp ()                 in spawn (fn _ => swap 1);
        val x2 = recv p2                        spawn (fn _ => swap 2);
    in send p2 x1; send p1 x2; coord ()
in spawn coord;
```

Each endpoint the coordinator receives from calling acc-swp are used according to the session type $?T.!T$.end. This says that, on each endpoint, the coordinator will first read a value type T ($?T$), then output a value of the same type ($!T$) and close the endpoint (end). The interleaving of sends and receives on the two endpoints achieves the desired swap effect.

Function swap : $\mathsf{Int} \to T'$ calls req-swp and receives and endpoint which is used according to the session type $!\mathsf{Int}.?T'$.end. By comparing the two session types above we can see that the coordinator and the swap service can communicate without type errors, and indeed are typable, when $T = \mathsf{Int} = T'$. Our type inference algorithm automatically deduces the two session types from this code.

Because swp is a global channel, ill-behaved client code can connect to it too:

```
let val p1 = req-swp () in send p1 1;
let val p2 = req-swp () in send p2 2;
let val (x1, x2) = (recv p1, recv p2) in e_cl
```

This client causes a deadlock, because the coordinator first sends on p2 and then on p1, but this code orders the corresponding receives in reverse. The interleaving of sessions in this client is rejected by our type system because it is not *well-stacked*: recv p1 is performed before the most recent endpoint (p2) is closed. The interleaving in the coordinator, on the other hand, is well-stacked.

Example 2.2 (Delegation for Efficiency). In the previous example the coordinator is a bottleneck when exchanged values are large. A more efficient implementation delegates exchange to the clients:

```
let fun coord(_) =                    let fun swap(x) =
    let val p1 = acc-swp ()               let val p = req-swp ()
 in sel-SWAP p1;                       in case p {
    let val p2 = acc-swp                   SWAP: send p x; recv p
 in sel-LEAD p2;                          LEAD: let val q = resume p
       deleg p2 p1;                              val y = recv q
       coord()                           in send q x; y }
```

Function swap again connects to the coordinator over channel swp, but now offers two choices with the labels SWAP and LEAD. If the coordinator selects the former, the swap method proceeds as before; if it selects the latter, swap resumes (i.e., inputs) another endpoint, binds it to q, and performs a rcv and then a send on q. The new coordinator accepts two sessions on swp, receiving two endpoints: p1 and p2. It selects SWAP on p1, LEAD on p2, sends p1 over p2 and recurs.

When our system analyses the coordinator in isolation, it infers the protocol $\eta_{\mathsf{coord}} = (!\mathsf{SWAP}.\eta' \oplus !\mathsf{LEAD}.!\eta'.\mathsf{end})$ for both endpoints p1 and p2. When it analyses swap : $T_1 \to T_2$, it infers $\eta_{\mathsf{p}} = \Sigma\{?\mathsf{SWAP}.!T_1.?T_2.\mathsf{end}, ?\mathsf{LEAD}.?\eta_{\mathsf{q}}.\mathsf{end}\}$ and $\eta_{\mathsf{q}} = ?T_2.!T_1.\mathsf{end}$ as the protocols of p and q, respectively. The former *selects* either options SWAP or LEAD and the latter *offers* both options.

If the coordinator is type-checked in isolation, then typing succeeds with any η': the coordinator can delegate any session. However, because of duality, the typing of req-swp in the swap function implies that $\eta' = \eta_{\mathsf{q}}$ and $T_1 = T_2$. Our inference algorithm can type this program and derive the above session types.

Example 2.3 (A Database Library). In this example we consider the implementation of a library which allows clients to connect to a database.

```
let fun coord(_) =
    let val p = acc-db ()
        fun loop(_) = case p {
            QRY: let val sql = recv p
                     val res = process sql
                 in  send p res; loop ()
            END: () }
    in spawn coord; loop ()
in spawn coord;
```

```
let fun  clientinit (_) =
    let val con = req-db ()
        fun query(sql) = sel-QRY con;
                         sendcon sql;
                         recv con
        fun close(_) = sel-END con
    in (query, close)
in e_client
```

The coordinator accepts connections from clients on channel db. If a connection is established, after spawning a copy of the coordinator to serve other clients, the coordinator enters a loop that serves the connected client. In this loop it offers the client two options: QRY and END. If the client selects QRY, the coordinator receives an SQL query, processes it (calling process : sql → dbresult, with these types are defined in the library), sends back the result, and loops. If the client selects END the connection with the coordinator closes and the current coordinator process terminates.

Function clientinit is exposed to the client, which can use it to request a connection with the database coordinator. When called, it establishes a connection con and returns two functions to the client: query and close. Then, the client code e_{client} can apply the query function to an sql object and receive a dbresult as many times as necessary, and then invoke close to close the connection. Using our two-level inference system with recursion Sect. 7, we can infer the session type of the coordinator's endpoint p: $\mu X.\Sigma\{?\text{QRY}.?\text{sql}.!\text{dbresult}.X, ?\text{END.end}\}$, and check whether the client code e_{client} respects it.

This example is not typable with a substructural type system because query and close share the same (linear) endpoint con. Moreover, in a monadic system e_{client} will need to be converted to monadic form.

3   Syntax and Operational Semantics of MLS

Figure 1 shows the syntax and operational semantics of MLS, a core of ML with session communication. An expression can be one of the usual lambda expressions or spawn *e* which evaluates *e* to a function and asynchronously applies it to the unit value; it can also be case $e\{L_i : e_i\}_{i\in I}$ which, as we will see, implements finite *external choice*. We use standard syntactic sugar for writing programs. A *system S* is a parallel composition of closed expressions *(processes)*.

The operational semantics of MLS are standard; here we only discuss session-related rules. Following the tradition of binary session types [7], communication between processes happens over dynamically generated entities called *sessions* which have exactly two *endpoints*. Thus, MLS values contain a countably infinite set of endpoints, ranged over by *p*. We assume a total involution ($\cdot$) over this set, with the property $\overline{p} \neq p$, which identifies *dual endpoints*.

Exp: $e ::= v \mid (e,e) \mid e\,e \mid \mathsf{let}\,x = e\,\mathsf{in}\,e \mid \mathsf{if}\,e\,\mathsf{then}\,e\,\mathsf{else}\,e \mid \mathsf{spawn}\,e \mid \mathsf{case}\,e\,\{L_i : e_i\}_{i \in I}$

Sys: $S ::= e \mid S \parallel S$

Val: $v ::= x \mid k \in \mathsf{Const} \mid (v,v) \mid \mathsf{fn}\,x \Rightarrow e \mid \mathsf{fun}\,f(x) = e \mid p$
$\qquad\quad \mid \mathsf{req}\text{-}c \mid \mathsf{acc}\text{-}c \mid \mathsf{send} \mid \mathsf{recv} \mid \mathsf{sel}\text{-}L \mid \mathsf{deleg} \mid \mathsf{resume}$

ECxt: $E ::= [\cdot] \mid (E,e) \mid (v,E) \mid E\,e \mid v\,E \mid \mathsf{let}\,x = E\,\mathsf{in}\,e \mid \mathsf{if}\,E\,\mathsf{then}\,e\,\mathsf{else}\,e$
$\qquad\quad \mid \mathsf{spawn}\,E \mid \mathsf{case}\,E\,\{L_i : e_i\}_{i \in I}$

$\text{RIFT} \quad \mathsf{if}\,\mathsf{tt}\,\mathsf{then}\,e_1\,\mathsf{else}\,e_2 \hookrightarrow e_1 \qquad\qquad \text{RLET} \quad \mathsf{let}\,x = v\,\mathsf{in}\,e \hookrightarrow e[v/x]$

$\text{RIFF} \quad \mathsf{if}\,\mathsf{ff}\,\mathsf{then}\,e_1\,\mathsf{else}\,e_2 \hookrightarrow e_2 \qquad\qquad \text{RFIX} \quad (\mathsf{fun}\,f(x) = e)\,v \hookrightarrow e[\mathsf{fun}\,f(x) = e/f][v/x]$

$\text{RBETA} \qquad\qquad\qquad\qquad\qquad E[e] \parallel S \longrightarrow E[e'] \parallel S \qquad\qquad \text{if } e \hookrightarrow e'$

$\text{RSPN} \qquad\qquad\qquad\qquad\qquad E[\mathsf{spawn}\,v] \parallel S \longrightarrow E[()] \parallel v\,() \parallel S$

$\text{RINIT} \qquad\quad E_1[\mathsf{req}\text{-}c\,()] \parallel E_2[\mathsf{acc}\text{-}c\,()] \parallel S \longrightarrow E_1[p] \parallel E_2[\overline{p}] \parallel S \quad \text{if } p, \overline{p} \text{ fresh}$

$\text{RCOM} \qquad\quad E_1[\mathsf{send}\,(p,v)] \parallel E_2[\mathsf{recv}\,p] \parallel S \longrightarrow E_1[()] \parallel E_2[v] \parallel S$

$\text{RDEL} \qquad E_1[\mathsf{deleg}\,(p,p')] \parallel E_2[\mathsf{resume}\,\overline{p}] \parallel S \longrightarrow E_1[()] \parallel E_2[p'] \parallel S$

$\text{RSEL} \quad E_1[\mathsf{sel}\text{-}L_j\,p] \parallel E_2[\mathsf{case}\,\overline{p}\,\{L_i : e_i\}_{i \in I}] \parallel S \longrightarrow E_1[()] \parallel E_2[e_j] \parallel S \qquad \text{if } j \in I$

Fig. 1. ML$_S$ syntax and operational semantics.

A process can request (or accept) a new session by calling req-c (resp., acc-c) with the unit value, which returns the endpoint (resp., dual endpoint) of a new session. Here c ranges over an infinite set of global initialisation *channels*. To simplify presentation, the language contains req-c and acc-c for each channel c.

Once two processes synchronise on a global channel and each receives a fresh, dual endpoint (RINIT reduction), they can exchange messages (RCOM), *delegate* endpoints (RDEL) and offer a number of choices $L_{i \in I}$, from which the partner can select one (RSEL). Here L ranges over a countably infinite set of choice labels, and I is a finite set of natural numbers; L_i denotes a unique label for each natural number i and we assume sel-L_i for each L_i.

The next two sections present the two-level type system of ML$_S$.

4 First Level Typing: ML Typing and Behaviours

Here we adapt and extend the type-and-effect system of Amtoft et al. [1] to session communication in ML$_S$. A judgement $C;\ \Gamma \vdash e : T \triangleright b$ states that e has type T and behaviour b, under type environment Γ and *constraint environment* C. The constraint environment relates type-level variables to terms and enables type inference. These components are defined in Fig. 2.

An ML$_S$ expression can have a standard type or an endpoint type Ses^ρ. Function types are annotated with a behaviour variable β. *Type variables* α are used for ML polymorphism. As in [1], Hindley-Milner polymorphism is extended with type schemas TS of the form $\forall(\vec{\gamma}:C_0).T$, where γ ranges over variables $\alpha, \beta, \rho, \psi$, and C_0 imposes constraints on the quantified variables with $\mathrm{fv}(C_0) \subseteq \{\vec{\gamma}\}$. Type environments Γ bind program variables to type schemas; we let $\forall(\emptyset).T = T$.

The rules of our type-and-effect system are shown in Fig. 3 which, as in [1, Sect. 2.8], is a conservative extension of ML. This system performs both ML

Variables: $\alpha(\text{Type})$ $\beta(\text{Behaviour})$ $\psi(\text{Session})$ $\rho(\text{Region})$

T. Schemas: $TS ::= \forall(\vec{\alpha}\vec{\beta}\vec{\rho}\vec{\psi} : C).\, T$ **Regions:** $r ::= l \mid \rho$

Types: $T ::= \text{Unit} \mid \text{Bool} \mid \text{Int} \mid T \times T \mid T \xrightarrow{\beta} T \mid \text{Ses}^\rho \mid \alpha$

Constraints: $C ::= T \subseteq T \mid cfd(T) \mid b \subseteq \beta \mid \rho \sim r \mid c \sim \eta \mid \overline{c} \sim \eta \mid \eta \bowtie \eta \mid C, C \mid \epsilon$

Behaviours: $b ::= \beta \mid \tau \mid b\,;b \mid b \oplus b \mid \text{rec}_\beta\, b \mid \text{spawn}\, b \mid \text{push}(l : \eta)$

$\quad\qquad\qquad\; \mid\ \rho!T \mid \rho?T \mid \rho!\rho \mid \rho?l \mid \rho!L_i \mid \underset{i \in I}{\&}\{\rho?L_i\,;b_i\}$

Type Envs: $\Gamma ::= x : TS \mid \Gamma, \Gamma \mid \epsilon$

Fig. 2. Syntax of types, behaviours, constraints, and session types.

type checking (including type-schema inference), and behaviour checking (which enables behaviour inference). Rules TLET, TVAR, TIF, TCONST, TAPP, TFUN, TSPAWN and the omitted rule for pairs perform standard type checking and straightforward sequential ($b_1\,;b_2$) and non-deterministic ($b_1 \oplus b_2$) behaviour composition; τ is the behaviour with no effect.

Just as a type constraint $T \subseteq \alpha$ associates type T with type variable α, a behaviour constraint $b \subseteq \beta$ associated behaviour b to behaviour variable β. Intuitively, β is the non-deterministic composition of all its associated behaviours. Rule TSUB allows the replacement of behaviour b with variable β; such replacement in type annotations yields a subtyping relation ($C \vdash T <: T'$). Rules TINS and TGEN are taken from [1] and extend ML's type schema instantiation and generalisation rules, respectively. Because we extend Hindley-Milner's let polymorphism, generalisation (TGEN) is only applied to the right-hand side expression of the let construct. The following definition allows the instantiation of a type schema under a global constraint environment C. We write $C \vdash C'$ when C' is included in the reflexive, transitive, compatible closure of C.

Definition 4.1 (Solvability). $\forall(\vec{\gamma} : C_0).\, T$ *is* solvable *by* C *and substitution* σ *when* $dom(\sigma) \subseteq \{\vec{\gamma}\}$ *and* $C \vdash C_0\sigma$.

In TREC, the communication effect of the body of a recursive function should be *confined*, which means it may only use endpoints it opens internally. For this reason, the function does not input nor return open endpoints or other non-confined functions ($C \vdash confd(T, T')$). Although typed under Γ which may contain endpoints and non-confined functions, the effect of the function body is recorded in its behaviour. The second level of our system checks that if the function is called, no endpoints from its environment are affected. It also checks that the function fully consumes internal endpoints before it returns or recurs.

A type T is confined when it does not contain any occurrences of the endpoint type Ses^ρ for any ρ, and when any b in T is confined. A behaviour b is confined when all of its possible behaviours are either τ or recursive.

To understand rule TENDP, we have to explain region variables (ρ), which are related to region constants through C. Region constants are simple program annotations l (produced during pre-processing) which uniquely identify the textual sources of endpoints. We thus type an extended MLs syntax

$$\text{TLET} \quad \frac{C;\ \Gamma \vdash e_1 : TS \triangleright b_1 \quad C;\ \Gamma, x : TS \vdash e_2 : T \triangleright b_2}{C;\ \Gamma \vdash \mathsf{let}\, x = e_1 \text{ in } e_2 : T \triangleright b_1\,;b_2}$$

$$\text{TVAR} \quad \frac{}{C;\ \Gamma \vdash x : \Gamma(x) \triangleright \tau}$$

$$\text{TIF} \quad \frac{C;\ \Gamma \vdash e_1 : \mathsf{Bool} \triangleright b_1 \quad C;\ \Gamma \vdash e_i : T \triangleright b_i \ \ _{(i \in \{1,2\})}}{C;\ \Gamma \vdash \mathsf{if}\, e_1 \text{ then } e_2 \text{ else } e_3 : T \triangleright b_1\,;(b_2 \oplus b_3)}$$

$$\text{TCONST} \quad \frac{}{C;\ \Gamma \vdash k : typeof(k) \triangleright \tau}$$

$$\text{TAPP} \quad \frac{C;\ \Gamma \vdash e_1 : T' \xrightarrow{\beta} T \triangleright b_1 \quad C;\ \Gamma \vdash e_2 : T' \triangleright b_2}{C;\ \Gamma \vdash e_1\, e_2 : T \triangleright b_1\,;b_2\,;\beta}$$

$$\text{TFUN} \quad \frac{C;\ \Gamma, x : T \vdash e : T' \triangleright \beta}{C;\ \Gamma \vdash \mathsf{fn}\, x \Rightarrow e : T \xrightarrow{\beta} T' \triangleright \tau}$$

$$\text{TMATCH} \quad \frac{C;\ \Gamma \vdash e : \mathsf{Ses}^\rho \triangleright b \quad C;\ \Gamma \vdash e_i : T \triangleright b_i \ \ _{(i \in I)}}{C;\ \Gamma \vdash \mathsf{case}\, e\, \{L_i : e_i\}_{i \in I} : T \triangleright b\,;\, \underset{i \in I}{\&}\, \{\rho?L_i\,;b_i\}}$$

$$\text{TENDP} \quad \frac{}{C;\ \Gamma \vdash p^l : \mathsf{Ses}^\rho \triangleright \tau \quad \boxed{C \vdash \rho \sim l}}$$

$$\text{TSPAWN} \quad \frac{C;\ \Gamma \vdash e : \mathsf{Unit} \xrightarrow{\beta} \mathsf{Unit} \triangleright b}{C;\ \Gamma \vdash \mathsf{spawn}\, e : \mathsf{Unit} \triangleright b\,;\mathsf{spawn}\,\beta}$$

$$\text{TSUB} \quad \frac{C;\ \Gamma \vdash e : T \triangleright b \quad \boxed{C \vdash T <: T'}}{C;\ \Gamma \vdash e : T' \triangleright \beta \quad \boxed{C \vdash b \subseteq \beta}}$$

$$\text{TREC} \quad \frac{C;\ \Gamma, f : T \xrightarrow{\beta} T', x : T \vdash e : T' \triangleright b \quad \boxed{C \vdash confd(T, T')}}{C;\ \Gamma \vdash \mathsf{fun}\, f(x) = e : T \xrightarrow{\beta} T' \triangleright \tau \quad \boxed{C \vdash \mathsf{rec}_\beta\, b \subseteq \beta}}$$

$$\text{TINS} \quad \frac{C;\ \Gamma \vdash e : \forall(\vec{\gamma} : C_0).T \triangleright b \quad \boxed{dom(\sigma) \subseteq \{\vec{\gamma}\}}}{C;\ \Gamma \vdash e : T\sigma \triangleright b \quad \boxed{\forall(\vec{\gamma} : C_0).T \text{ is solvable by } C \text{ and } \sigma}}$$

$$\text{TGEN} \quad \frac{C \cup C_0;\ \Gamma \vdash e : T \triangleright b \quad \boxed{\{\vec{\gamma}\} \cap fv(\Gamma, C, b) = \emptyset}}{C;\ \Gamma \vdash e : \forall(\vec{\gamma} : C_0).T \triangleright b \quad \boxed{\forall(\vec{\gamma} : C_0).T \text{ is solvable by } C \text{ and some } \sigma}}$$

Fig. 3. Type-and-Effect system for $\mathrm{ML_S}$ expressions (omitting rule for pairs).

Values: $\quad v :: = \ldots \mid p^l \mid \mathsf{req}\text{-}c^l \mid \mathsf{acc}\text{-}c^l \mid \mathsf{resume}^l$

If a sub-expression has type Ses^ρ and it evaluates to a value p^l, then it must be that $C \vdash \rho \sim l$, denoting that p was generated from the code location identified by l. This location will contain one of $\mathsf{req}\text{-}c^l$, $\mathsf{acc}\text{-}c^l$, or resume^l. These primitive functions (typed by TCONST) are given the following type schemas.

$$\mathsf{req}\text{-}c^l \quad : \forall(\beta\rho\psi : \mathsf{push}(l : \psi) \subseteq \beta, \rho \sim l, c \sim \psi).\mathsf{Unit} \xrightarrow{\beta} \mathsf{Ses}^\rho$$

$$\mathsf{acc}\text{-}c^l \quad : \forall(\beta\rho\psi : \mathsf{push}(l : \psi) \subseteq \beta, \rho \sim l, \bar{c} \sim \psi).\mathsf{Unit} \xrightarrow{\beta} \mathsf{Ses}^\rho$$

$$\mathsf{resume}^l : \forall(\beta\rho\rho' : \rho?l \subseteq \beta,\ \rho' \sim l).\mathsf{Ses}^\rho \xrightarrow{\beta} \mathsf{Ses}^{\rho'}$$

An application of $\mathsf{req}\text{-}c^l$ starts a new session on the static endpoint l. To type it, C must contain its effect $\mathsf{push}(l : \psi) \subseteq \beta$, where ψ is a session variable, representing the session type of l. At this level session types are ignored (hence the use of a simple ψ); they become important in the second level of our typing system. Moreover, C must record that session variable ρ is related to l ($\rho \sim l$) and that the "request" endpoint of channel c has session type ψ ($c \sim \psi$). The only difference in the type schema of $\mathsf{acc}\text{-}c^l$ is that the "accept" endpoint of c is related to ψ ($\bar{c} \sim \psi$). Resume receives an endpoint (ρ') over another one (ρ), recorded in its type schema ($\rho?\rho' \subseteq \beta$); ρ is an existing endpoint but ρ' is treated as an endpoint generated by resume^l, hence the constraint $\rho' \sim l$.

The following are the type schemas of the rest of the constant functions.

$$\text{recv} \;\; : \forall(\alpha\beta\rho : \rho?\alpha \subseteq \beta, \mathit{cfd}(\alpha)). \, \mathsf{Ses}^\rho \xrightarrow{\beta} \alpha$$

$$\text{send} \;\; : \forall(\alpha\beta\rho : \rho!\alpha \subseteq \beta, \mathit{cfd}(\alpha)). \, \mathsf{Ses}^\rho \times \alpha \xrightarrow{\beta} \mathsf{Unit}$$

$$\text{deleg} : \forall(\beta\rho\rho' : \rho!\rho' \subseteq \beta). \, \mathsf{Ses}^\rho \times \mathsf{Ses}^{\rho'} \xrightarrow{\beta} \mathsf{Unit}$$

$$\text{sel-}L \;\; : \forall(\beta\rho : \rho?L \subseteq \beta). \, \mathsf{Ses}^\rho \xrightarrow{\beta} \mathsf{Unit}$$

These record input ($\rho?\alpha$), output ($\rho!\alpha$), delegation ($\rho!\rho'$), or selection ($\rho!L_i$) behaviour. For input and output the constraint $\mathit{cfd}(\alpha)$ must be in C, recording that the α can be instantiated only with confined types.

5 Second Level Typing: Session Types

Session types describe the communication protocols of endpoints; their syntax is:

$$\eta ::= \mathsf{end} \mid !T.\eta \mid ?T.\eta \mid !\eta.\eta \mid ?\eta.\eta \mid \bigoplus_{i \in I}\{L_i : \eta_i\} \mid \&_{i \in (I_1, I_2)}\{L_i : \eta_i\} \mid \psi$$

A session type is finished (end) or it can describe further interactions: the input ($?T.\eta$) or output ($!T.\eta$) of a *confined* value T, or the delegation ($!\eta'.\eta$) or resumption ($?\eta'.\eta$) of an endpoint of session type η', or the offering of non-deterministic selection ($\oplus\{L_i : \eta_i\}_{i \in I}$) of a label L_i, signifying that session type η_i is to be followed next.

Moreover, a session type can offer an external choice $\&\{L_i : \eta_i\}_{i \in (I_1, I_2)}$ to its communication partner. Here I_1 contains the labels that the process *must* be able to accept and I_2 the labels that it *may* accept. We require that I_1 and I_2 are disjoint and I_1 is not empty. Although a single set would suffice, the two sets make type inference deterministic and independent of source code order.

We express our session typing discipline as an *abstract interpretation semantics* for behaviours shown in Fig. 4. It describes transitions of the form $\Delta \vDash b \to_C \Delta' \vDash b'$, where b, b' are behaviours. The Δ and Δ' are stacks on which static endpoint labels together with their corresponding session types ($l : \eta$) can be pushed and popped. Inspired by Castagna et al. [3], in the transition $\Delta \vDash b \to_C \Delta' \vDash b'$, behaviour b can only use the top label in the stack to communicate, push another label on the stack, or pop the top label provided its session type is end. This stack principle gives us a partial lock freedom property (Theorem 5.2).

Rule END from Fig. 4 simply removes a finished stack frame, and rule BETA looks up behaviour variables in C; PLUS chooses one of the branches of non-deterministic behaviour. The PUSH rule extends the stack by adding one more frame to it, as long as the label has not been added before on the stack (see Example 5.2). Rules OUT and IN reduce the top-level session type of the stack by an output and input, respectively. The requirement here is that the labels in the stack and the behaviour match, the usual subtyping [4] holds for the communicated types, and that the communicated types are *confined*. Note that sending confined (recursive) functions does not require delegation of endpoints.

Transfer of endpoints is done by delegate and resume (rules DEL and RES). Delegate sends the second endpoint in the stack over the first; resume mimics

$$\text{END}: \qquad (l:\mathsf{end})\cdot \varDelta \vDash b \to_C \varDelta \vDash b$$

$$\text{BETA}: \qquad\qquad \varDelta \vDash \beta \to_C \varDelta \vDash b \qquad\qquad \text{if } C \vdash b \subseteq \beta$$

$$\text{PLUS}: \qquad\qquad \varDelta \vDash b_1 \oplus b_2 \to_C \varDelta \vDash b_i \qquad\qquad \text{if } i \in \{1,2\}$$

$$\text{PUSH}: \qquad\qquad \varDelta \vDash \mathsf{push}(l:\eta) \to_C (l:\eta)\cdot\varDelta \vDash \tau \qquad\qquad \text{if } l \notin \varDelta.\mathsf{labels}$$

$$\text{OUT}: \qquad (l:!T.\eta)\cdot \varDelta \vDash \rho!T' \to_C (l:\eta)\cdot\varDelta \vDash \tau \qquad\qquad \text{if } C \vdash \rho \sim l,\ T' <: T$$

$$\text{IN}: \qquad (l:?T.\eta)\cdot \varDelta \vDash \rho?T' \to_C (l:\eta)\cdot\varDelta \vDash \tau \qquad\qquad \text{if } C \vdash \rho \sim l,\ T <: T'$$

$$\text{DEL}: (l:!\eta_d.\eta)\cdot(l_d:\eta_d')\cdot \varDelta \vDash \rho!\rho_d$$
$$\to_C (l:\eta)\cdot\varDelta \vDash \tau \qquad\qquad \text{if } C \vdash \rho \sim l,\ \rho_d \sim l_d,\ \eta_d' <: \eta_d$$

$$\text{RES}: \qquad (l:?\eta_r.\eta) \vDash \rho?l_r \to_C (l:\eta)\cdot(l_r:\eta_r) \vDash \tau \quad \text{if } (l \neq l_r),\ C \vdash \rho \sim l$$

$$\text{ICH}: (l:\bigoplus_{i\in I}\{L_i:\eta_i\})\cdot \varDelta \vDash \rho!L_j \to_C (l:\eta_j)\cdot\varDelta \vDash \tau \qquad \text{if } (j \in I),\ C \vdash \rho \sim l$$

$$\text{ECH}: (l:\underset{i\in(I_1,I_2)}{\&}\{L_i:\eta_i\})\cdot \varDelta \vDash \underset{j\in J}{\&}\{\rho?L_j\,;b_j\}$$
$$\to_C (l:\eta_k)\cdot\varDelta \vDash b_k \qquad \begin{array}{l}\text{if } k \in J,\ C \vdash \rho \sim l,\\ I_1 \subseteq J \subseteq I_1 \cup I_2\end{array}$$

$$\text{REC}: \qquad\qquad \varDelta \vDash \mathsf{rec}_\beta b \to_C \varDelta \vDash \tau \qquad\qquad \begin{array}{l}\text{if } \epsilon \vDash b \Downarrow_{C'},\\ C' = (C\backslash(\mathsf{rec}_\beta b \subseteq \beta))\cup(\tau \subseteq \beta)\end{array}$$

$$\text{SPN}: \qquad\qquad \varDelta \vDash \mathsf{spawn}\, b \to_C \varDelta \vDash \tau \qquad\qquad \text{if } \epsilon \vDash b \Downarrow_C$$

$$\text{SEQ}: \qquad\qquad \varDelta \vDash b_1;b_2 \to_C \varDelta' \vDash b_1';b_2 \qquad\qquad \text{if } \varDelta \vDash b_1 \to_C \varDelta' \vDash b_1'$$

$$\text{TAU}: \qquad\qquad \varDelta \vDash \tau;b \to_C \varDelta \vDash b$$

Fig. 4. Abstract interpretation semantics.

this by adding a new endpoint label in the second position in the stack. Resume requires a one-frame stack to guarantee that the two endpoints of the same session do not end up in the same stack, thus avoiding deadlock [3]. If we abandon the partial lock freedom property guaranteed by our type system, then the conditions in RES can be relaxed and allow more than one frame.

A behaviour reduces an internal choice session type by selecting one of its labels (ICH). A behaviour offering an external choice is reduced nondeterministically to any of its branches (ECH). The behaviour must offer all *active* choices ($I_1 \subseteq J$) and all behaviour branches must be typable by the session type ($J \subseteq I_1 \cup I_2$).

As we previously explained, recursive functions in ML_S must be confined. This means that the communication effect of the function body is only on endpoints that the function opens internally, and the session type of these endpoints is followed to completion (or delegated) before the function returns or recurs. This is enforced in Rule REC, where $\mathsf{rec}_\beta b$ must have no net effect on the stack, guaranteed by $\epsilon \vDash b \Downarrow_{C'}$. Here $C' = (C\backslash(\mathsf{rec}_\beta b \subseteq \beta))\cup(\tau \subseteq \beta)$ is the original C with constraint $(\mathsf{rec}_\beta b \subseteq \beta)$ replaced by $(\tau \subseteq \beta)$ (cf., Definition 5.1). This update of C prevents the infinite unfolding of $\mathsf{rec}_b \beta$. Spawned processes must also be confined (SPN). We work with *well-formed* constraints:

(a)   let val $(\mathsf{p1}, \mathsf{p2}) = (\mathsf{req}\text{-}c^{l_1}, \mathsf{req}\text{-}d^{l_2})$
         val $\mathsf{p3} = $ if e then $\mathsf{p1}$ else $\mathsf{p2}$
      in send $\mathsf{p3}$ tt

(b)   let fun $\mathsf{f} = \mathsf{req}\text{-}c^l$
         val $\mathsf{p1} = \mathsf{f}$ ()
      in send $\mathsf{p1}$ 1;
      let val $\mathsf{p2} = \mathsf{f}$ () in send $\mathsf{p1}$ 2;

Fig. 5. Examples of aliasing

Definition 5.1 (Well-Formed Constraints). C *is* well-formed *if:*

1. Type-Consistent: *for all type constructors* tc_1, tc_2, *if* $(tc_1(\vec{t_1}) \subseteq tc_2(\vec{t_2})) \in C$, *then* $tc_1 = tc_2$, *and for all* $t_{1i} \in \vec{t_1}$ *and* $t_{2i} \in \vec{t_2}$, $(t_{1i} \subseteq t_{2i}) \in C$.
2. Region-Consistent: *if* $C \vdash l \sim l'$ *then* $l = l'$.
3. Behaviour-Compact: *behaviour constraints cycles contain a* $(rec_\beta\, b \subseteq \beta) \in C$; *also if* $(rec_\beta\, b \subseteq \beta') \in C$ *then* $\beta = \beta'$ *and* $\forall (b' \subseteq \beta) \in C$, $b' = rec_\beta\, b$.
4. Well-Confined: *if* $C \vdash confd(T)$ *then* $T \neq Ses^\rho$; *also if* $C \vdash confd(b)$ *then* $b \notin \{\rho!T, \rho?T, \rho!\rho, \rho?l, \rho!L_i, \underset{i \in I}{\&}\{\rho?L_i ; b_i\}\}$.

The first and fourth conditions are straightforward. The third condition disallows recursive behaviours through the environment without the use of a $rec_\beta\, b$ effect. All well-typed ML$_\mathsf{S}$ programs contain only such recursive behaviours because recursion is only possible through the use of a recursive function. The second part of the condition requires that there is at most one recursive constraint in the environment using variable β. This is necessary for type preservation and decidability of session typing. The second condition of Definition 5.1 requires that only endpoints from a single source can flow in each ρ, preventing aliasing of endpoints generated at different source locations.

Example 5.1 (Aliasing of Different Sources). Consider the program in Fig. 5(a). Which endpoint flows to $\mathsf{p3}$ cannot be statically determined and therefore the program cannot yield a consistent session type for channels c and d. The program will be rejected in our framework because $\mathsf{p3}$ has type Ses^ρ and from the constrain environment $C \vdash \rho \sim l_1$, $\rho \sim l_2$, which fails Definition 5.1.

Because endpoints generated from the same source code location are identified in our system, stacks are treated *linearly*: an endpoint label l may only once be pushed onto a stack. Every stack Δ contains an implicit set of the labels $\Delta.\mathsf{labels}$ to record previously pushed labels.

Example 5.2 (Aliasing from Same Source). Consider the program in Fig. 5(b) where endpoint $\mathsf{p1}$ has type Ses^ρ, with $C \vdash \rho \sim l$. The program has behaviour $push(l : \eta); \rho!\mathsf{Int}; push(l : \eta); \rho!\mathsf{Int}; \tau$. Label l is pushed on the stack twice and the behaviour complies with the session type $\eta = !\mathsf{Int}.\mathsf{end}$. However the program does not respect this session type because it sends two integers on $\mathsf{p1}$ and none on $\mathsf{p2}$. Our system rejects this program due to the violation of stack linearity.

Our system also rejects the correct version of the program in Fig. 5(b), where the last send is replaced by send $\mathsf{p2}$ 2. This is because the label l associated with the variable ρ of a type Ses^ρ is *control flow insensitive*. Existing techniques can make labels control flow sensitive (e.g., [14,15]).

Using the semantics of Fig. 4 we define the following predicate which requires behaviours to follow to completion or delegate all $(l : \eta)$ frames in a stack.

Definition 5.2 (Strong Normalization). $\Delta \vDash b \Downarrow_C \vec{\Delta}'$ *when for all* b', Δ' *such that* $\Delta \vDash b \to^*_C \Delta' \vDash b' \not\to_C$ *we have* $b' = \tau$ *and* $\Delta' \in \{\vec{\Delta}'\}$. *We write* $\Delta \vDash b \Downarrow_C$ *when* $\Delta \vDash b \Downarrow_C \epsilon$, *where* ϵ *is the empty stack.*

Lastly, session types on dual session endpoints $(c \sim \eta, \bar{c} \sim \eta')$ must be dual $(C \vdash \eta \bowtie \eta')$ The definition of duality is standard, with the exception that internal choice is dual to external choice only if the labels in the former are included in the *active* labels in the latter.

Definition 5.3 (Valid Constraint Environment). C *is* valid *if there exists a substitution* σ *of variables* ψ *with closed session types, such that* $C\sigma$ *is well-formed and for all* $(c \sim \eta), (\bar{c} \sim \eta') \in C\sigma$ *we have* $C \vdash \eta \bowtie \eta'$.

Combining the Two Levels. The key property here is *well-stackedness*, the fact that in a running system where each process has a corresponding stack of endpoints, there is a way to repeatedly remove pairs of endpoints with dual session types from the top of two stacks, until all stacks are empty.

Definition 5.4 (Well-Stackedness). $C \Vdash_{\mathsf{ws}} S$ *is the least relation satisfying:*

$$\frac{}{C \Vdash_{\mathsf{ws}} \epsilon} \qquad \frac{C \Vdash_{\mathsf{ws}} S, \ (\Delta \vDash b, \ e), \ (\Delta' \vDash b', \ e') \qquad C \vdash \eta \bowtie \eta' \qquad p, \bar{p} \,\sharp\, \Delta, \Delta', S}{C \Vdash_{\mathsf{ws}} S, \left((p^l : \eta) \cdot \Delta \vDash b, \ e\right), \left((\bar{p}^{l'} : \eta') \cdot \Delta' \vDash b', \ e'\right)}$$

Note that this does not mean that programs are deterministic. Multiple pairs of endpoints may be at the top of a set of stacks. Duality of endpoints guarantees that communications are safe; the ordering of endpoints in removable pairs implies the absence of deadlocks.

We let P, Q range over tuples of the form $(\Delta \vDash b, \ e)$ and S over sequences of such tuples. In this section stack frames $(p^l : \eta)$ store both endpoints and their labels. We write $C \Vdash \overrightarrow{(\Delta \vDash b, \ e)}$ if C is well-formed and valid, $(C; \ \emptyset \vdash \overrightarrow{e : T \triangleright b})$, and $(\overrightarrow{\Delta \vDash b} \Downarrow_C)$, for some $\vec{T}$. We write $C \Vdash_{\mathsf{ws}} S$ if $\vec{\Delta}$ is well-stacked. Well-typed systems enjoy session fidelity and preserve typing and well-stackedness.

Theorem 5.1. *Let* $S = \overrightarrow{\Delta \vDash b, e}$ *and* $C \Vdash S$ *and* $C \Vdash_{\mathsf{ws}} S$ *and* $\vec{e} \longrightarrow \vec{e}'$; *then there exist* $\vec{\Delta}', \vec{b}'$ *such that* $S' = \overrightarrow{(\Delta' \vDash b', \ e')}$ *and:*

1. $C \Vdash S'$ *(Type Preservation)*
2. $\overrightarrow{\Delta \vDash b} \to^*_C \overrightarrow{\Delta' \vDash b'}$ *(Session Fidelity)*
3. $C \Vdash_{\mathsf{ws}} S'$ *(Well-Stackedness Preservation)*

Session fidelity and well-stackedness preservation imply *communication safety*, since the former guarantees that processes are faithful to session types in the stacks, while the latter that session types are dual for each pair of open endpoints p and $\bar{p}$. Moreover, well-stackedness implies *deadlock freedom*. P depends on Q if the endpoint at the top of P's stack has dual endpoint in Q.

Lemma 5.1 (Deadlock Freedom). $C \Vdash_{ws} S$; dependencies in S are acyclic.

Type soundness is more technical. We divide system transitions to communication transitions between processes ($\longrightarrow_c$) and internal transitions ($\longrightarrow_i$). Let $S \longrightarrow_c S'$ ($S \longrightarrow_i S'$) when $S \longrightarrow S'$, derived by Rule RINIT, RCOM, RDEL or RSEL of Fig. 1 (resp., any other rule); $S \Longrightarrow_c S'$ when $S \longrightarrow_i^* \longrightarrow_c \longrightarrow_i^* S'$.

Theorem 5.2 (Type Soundness). Let $C \Vdash S$ and $C \Vdash_{ws} S$. Then

1. $S \Longrightarrow_c S'$, or
2. $S \longrightarrow_i^* (\mathcal{F}, \mathcal{D}, \mathcal{W}, \mathcal{B})$ such that:

   Finished processes, $\mathcal{F}$: $\forall P \in \mathcal{F}.\ P = (\epsilon \vDash \tau,\ v)$, for some v;

   Diverging processes, $\mathcal{D}$: $\forall P \in \mathcal{D}.\ P \longrightarrow_i^{\infty}$;

   Waiting proc., $\mathcal{W}$: $\forall P \in \mathcal{W}.\ P = (\Delta \vDash b,\ E[e])$ and $e \in \{req\text{-}c^l, acc\text{-}c^l\}$;

   Blocked processes, $\mathcal{B}$: $\forall P \in \mathcal{B}.\ P = (\Delta \vDash b,\ E[e])$ and $e \in \{send\, v, recv\, v,$
   $deleg\, v, resume\, v, sel\text{-}L\, v, case\, v\, \{L_i \Rightarrow e_i\}_{i \in I}\}$ and P transitively depends
   on a process in $\mathcal{D} \cup \mathcal{W}$.

A well-typed and well-stacked ML_S system will either be able to perform a communication, or, after finite internal steps, it will reach a state where some processes are values ($\mathcal{F}$), some internally diverge ($\mathcal{D}$), some are waiting for a partner process to open a session ($\mathcal{W}$), and some are blocked on a session communication ($\mathcal{B}$). Crucially, in states where communication is not possible, $\mathcal{B}$ transitively depends on $\mathcal{D} \cup \mathcal{W}$. Thus, in the absence of divergence and in the presence of enough processes to start new sessions, no processes can be blocked; the system will either perform a communication or it will terminate (partial lock freedom).

Corollary 5.1 (Partial Lock Freedom). If $C \Vdash S$, $C \Vdash_{ws} S$, and $S \not\Longrightarrow_c$ and $S \longrightarrow_i^* (\mathcal{F}, \emptyset, \emptyset, \mathcal{B})$ then $\mathcal{B} = \emptyset$.

6 Inference Algorithm

We use three inference algorithms, $\mathcal{W}$, $\mathcal{SI}$ and $\mathcal{D}$. The first infers functional types and communication effects and corresponds to the first level of our type system. The other two infer session types from the abstract interpretation rules of Fig. 4 ($\mathcal{SI}$) and the duality requirement of Definition 5.3 ($\mathcal{D}$), corresponding to the second level of the type system.

Algorithm $\mathcal{W}$ is a straightforward adaptation of the homonymous algorithm from [1]: given an expression e, $\mathcal{W}$ calculates its type t, behaviour b and constraints set C; no session information is calculated. $\mathcal{W}$ generates pairs of fresh constraints $c \sim \psi$ and $\bar{c} \sim \psi'$ for each global channel c in the source program; ψ and ψ' are unique. Results of $\mathcal{W}$'s soundness and completeness follow from [1].

For all constraints $(c \sim \psi) \in C$, Algorithm $\mathcal{SI}$ infers a substitution σ and a refined set C' such that $\epsilon \vDash b\sigma \Downarrow_{C'} \epsilon$. The substitution only maps ψ variables to session types. The final C' is derived from C by applying σ and possibly adding more type constraints of the form $(T \subseteq T')$. The core of this algorithm is the abstract interpreter $\mathcal{MC}$, which explores all possible transitions from $\epsilon \vDash b$.

Algorithm $\mathcal{MC}$ is designed in a continuation-passing style, using a *continuation stack* $K :: = \epsilon \mid b \cdot K$.

As transition paths are explored, previously discovered branches of internal and external choices in session types may need to be expanded. For example, if Algorithm $\mathcal{MC}$ encounters a configuration $(l : \oplus\{L_i : \eta_i\}_{i \in I}) \vDash l!L_j$ where $j \notin I$, the inference algorithm needs to add the newly discovered label L_j to the internal choice on the stack.

To do this, internal and external choices are removed from the syntax of sessions, and replaced with special variables ψ_{in} and ψ_{ex}. These variables are bound by unique *choice constraints*, extending the syntax of constraints (Fig. 2):

$$C :: = \ldots \mid \oplus\{L_i : \eta_i\}_{i \in I} \sim \psi_{\text{in}} \mid \&\{L_i : \eta_i\}_{i \in (I_1, I_2)} \sim \psi_{\text{ex}}$$

$\mathcal{MC}$ updates ψ_{in} and ψ_{ex} constraints in C with newly discovered branches. For example it may add new labels to an internal choice, or move active labels to inactive in an external choice.

We now give more detail for some inference steps of Algorithm $\mathcal{MC}$. The full algorithm can be found in an online technical report[1]. Algorithm $\mathcal{MC}$ terminates successfully when all sessions on the stack have terminated, the input behaviour is τ and the continuation stack is empty:

$$\mathcal{MC}(\Delta \vDash \tau, C, \epsilon) = (\sigma, C\sigma)$$
$$\text{if } \sigma = \text{finalize } \Delta$$

When this clause succeeds, Δ may be empty or it may contain frames of the form $(l : \psi)$ or $(l : \text{end})$. The helper function finalise Δ returns a substitution σ that maps all such ψ's to end. If this is not possible (i.e., a session on Δ is not finished) finalise raises an error.

New frames are pushed on the stack when the behaviour is $\text{push}(l : \eta)$:

$$\mathcal{MC}(\Delta \vDash \text{push}(l : \eta), C, K) = (\sigma_2\sigma_1, C_2)$$
$$\text{if } (\sigma_1, \Delta_1) = \text{checkFresh}(l, \Delta)$$
$$\text{and } (\sigma_2, C_2) = \mathcal{MC}((l : \eta\sigma_1) \cdot \Delta_1 \vDash \tau, C\sigma_1, K\sigma_1)$$

where checkFresh checks that l has never been in Δ.

When the behaviour is an operation that pops a session from the stack, such as a send $(l!T)$, $\mathcal{MC}$ looks up the top frame on the stack, according to the stack principle. There are two cases to consider: either the top frame contains a fresh variable ψ, or some type has been already inferred. The algorithm here is:

$$\mathcal{MC}((l : \psi) \cdot \Delta \vDash \rho!T, C, K) = (\sigma_2\sigma_1, C_2)$$
$$\text{if } C \vdash l \sim \rho$$
$$\text{and } \sigma_1 = [\psi \mapsto !\alpha.\psi'] \text{ where } \alpha, \psi' \text{ fresh}$$
$$\text{and } (\sigma_2, C_2) = \mathcal{MC}((l : \psi') \cdot \Delta\sigma_1 \vDash \tau, C\sigma_1 \cup \{T \subseteq \alpha\}, K\sigma_1)$$

$$\mathcal{MC}((l : !\alpha.\eta) \cdot \Delta \vDash \rho!T, C, K) = \mathcal{MC}((l : \eta) \cdot \Delta \vDash \tau, C \cup \{T \subseteq \alpha\}, K)$$
$$\text{if } C \vdash l \sim \rho$$

[1] Spaccasassi, C., Koutavas, V.: Type-Based Analysis for Session Inference. ArXiv e-prints (Oct. 2015), http://arxiv.org/abs/1510.03929v3.

In the first case, $\mathcal{MC}$ checks that ρ in the behaviour corresponds to l at the top of the stack. It then produces the substitution $[\psi \mapsto !\alpha.\psi']$, where α and ψ' are fresh, and adds $(T \subseteq \alpha)$ to C. The second case produces no substitution.

The clauses for delegation are similar:

$$\mathcal{MC}((l:\psi) \cdot (l_d : \eta_d) \cdot \Delta \vDash \rho!\rho_d, \, C, \, K) = (\sigma_2\sigma_1, C_2)$$
$$\text{if } \; C \vdash l \sim \rho \text{ and } C \vdash l_d \sim \rho_d$$
$$\text{and } \sigma_1 = [\psi \mapsto !\eta_d.\psi'] \text{ where } \psi' \text{ fresh}$$
$$\text{and } (\sigma_2, C_2) = \mathcal{MC}((l:\psi') \cdot \Delta\sigma \vDash \tau, \, C\sigma_1, \, K\sigma_1)$$

$$\mathcal{MC}((l:!\eta_d.\eta) \cdot (l_d : \eta'_d) \cdot \Delta \vDash \rho!\rho_d, \, C, \, K) = (\sigma_2\sigma_1, C_2)$$
$$\text{if } \; C \vdash l \sim \rho \text{ and } C \vdash l_d \sim \rho_d$$
$$\text{and } (\sigma_1, C_1) = \mathsf{sub}(\eta'_d, \eta_d, C)$$
$$\text{and } (\sigma_2, C_2) = \mathcal{MC}((l:\eta) \cdot \Delta\sigma \vDash \tau, \, C_1, \, K\sigma_1)$$

The main difference here is that, in the second clause, the sub function checks that $C \vdash \eta'_d <: \eta_d$ and performs relevant inference. Moreover, the input Δ must contain at least two frames (the frame below the top one is delegated).

The cases for receive, label selection and offer, and resume are similar (see online report). In the cases for label selection and offering, the algorithm updates the ψ_{in} and ψ_{ex} variables, as discussed above. In the case of resume, the algorithm checks that the stack contains one frame.

In behaviour sequencing and branching, substitutions are applied eagerly and composed iteratively, and new constraints are accumulated in C:

$$\mathcal{MC}(\Delta \vDash b_1 ; b_2, \, C, \, K) = \mathcal{MC}(\Delta \vDash b_1, \, C, \, b_2 \cdot K)$$

$$\mathcal{MC}(\Delta \vDash b_1 \oplus b_2, \, C, \, K) = (\sigma_2\sigma_1, C_2)$$
$$\text{if } \; (\sigma_1, C_1) = \mathcal{MC}(\Delta \vDash b_1, \, C, \, K)$$
$$\text{and } (\sigma_2, C_2) = \mathcal{MC}(\Delta\sigma_1 \vDash b_2\sigma_1, \, C_1, \, K\sigma_1)$$

When a recursive behaviour $\mathsf{rec}_b \, \beta$ is encountered, Algorithm $\mathcal{MC}$ needs to properly setup the input constraints C according to Rule REC of Fig. 4:

$$\mathcal{MC}(\Delta \vDash \mathsf{rec}_\beta \, b, \, C) = (\sigma_2\sigma_1, C_2)$$
$$\text{if } \; C = C' \uplus \{b' \subseteq \beta\}$$
$$\text{and } (\sigma_1, C_1) = \mathcal{MC}(\epsilon \vDash b, \, C' \cup \{\tau \subseteq \beta\}, \, \epsilon)$$
$$\text{and } (\sigma_2, C_2) = \mathcal{MC}(\Delta\sigma_1 \vDash \tau, \, (C_1 \backslash \{\tau \subseteq \beta\}) \cup (\{b' \subseteq \beta\})\sigma_1, \, K\sigma_1)$$

Here the algorithm first calls $\mathcal{MC}$ on $\epsilon \vDash b$, checking that the recursion body b is self-contained under C', in which the recursion variable β is bound to τ. This update of C prevents the infinite unfolding of $\mathsf{rec}_b \, \beta$. It then restores back the constraint on β, applies the substitution σ_1, and continues inference.

The clause for $\mathsf{spawn} \, b$ is similar, except that C is unchanged. Variables β are treated as the internal choice of all behaviours b_i bound to β in C:

$$\mathcal{MC}(\Delta \vDash \beta, \, C, \, K) = \mathcal{MC}(\Delta \vDash b, \, C, \, K)$$
$$\text{where } \; b = \bigoplus\{b_i \mid \exists i. \, (b_i \subseteq \beta) \in C\}$$

Inference fails when $\mathcal{MC}$ reaches a stuck configuration $\Delta \vDash b$ other than $\epsilon \vDash \tau$, corresponding to an error in the session type discipline.

To prove termination of $\mathcal{SI}$, we first define the translation $[[b]]^g_C$, that replaces β variables in b with the internal choice $\bigoplus\{b_i \mid (\{b_i \subseteq \beta\}) \in C\}$. Due to behaviour-compactness (Definition 5.1), $[[b]]_C^g$ is a finite *ground* term, i.e. a finite term without β variables. Except for Rule BETA, transitions in Fig. 4 never expand b; they either consume Δ or b. Since $[[b]]_C^g$ is finite when C is well-formed, $\epsilon \vDash [[b]]_C^g$ generates a finite state space and Algorithm $\mathcal{MC}$ always terminates.

Similar to ML type inference, the worst-case complexity of $\mathcal{MC}$ is exponential to program size: $\mathcal{MC}$ runs in time linear to the size of $[[b]]_C^g$, which in the worst case is exponentially larger than b, which is linear to program size. The worst case appears in pathological programs where, e.g., each function calls all previously defined functions. We intend to explore whether this is an issue in practice, especially with an optimised dynamic programming implementation of $\mathcal{MC}$.

Soundness and completeness of $\mathcal{SI}$ follow from the these properties of $\mathcal{MC}$.

Lemma 6.1 (Soundness of $\mathcal{MC}$). *Let C be well-formed and $\mathcal{MC}(\Delta \vDash b, C) = (\sigma_1, C_1)$; then $\Delta\sigma_1 = \Delta'$ and $\Delta' \vDash b\sigma_1 \Downarrow_{C_1}$.*

Lemma 6.2 (Completeness of $\mathcal{MC}$). *Let C be well-formed and $(\Delta \vDash b)\sigma \Downarrow_C$; then $\mathcal{MC}(\Delta \vDash b, C_0) = (\sigma_1, C_1)$ and $\exists \sigma'$ such that $C \vdash C_1\sigma'$ and $\forall \psi \in dom(\sigma)$, $C \vdash \sigma(\psi) <: \sigma'(\sigma_1(\psi))$.*

Completeness states that $\mathcal{MC}$ computes the most general constraints C_1 and substitution σ_1, because, for any C and σ such that $(\Delta \vDash b)\sigma$ type checks, C specialises C_1 and σ is an instance of σ_1, after some extra substitution σ' of variables (immaterial for type checking).

Algorithm $\mathcal{D}$ collects all $c \sim \eta_1$ and $\bar{c} \sim \eta_2$ constraints in C', generates duality constraints $\eta_1 \bowtie \eta_2$ and iteratively checks them, possibly substituting ψ variables. It ultimately returns a C'' which is a valid type solution according to Definition 5.3. Soundness and completeness of Algorithm $\mathcal{D}$ is straightforward.

We now show how $\mathcal{SI}$ infers the correct session types for Example 2.1 from Sect. 2. We assume that Algorithm $\mathcal{W}$ has already produced a behaviour b and constraints C for this example. For clarity, we simplify b and C: we remove spurious τs from behaviour sequences, replace region variables ρ with labels (only one label flows to each ρ), and perform simple substitutions of β variables.

Example 6.1 (A Swap Service). There are three textual sources of endpoints in this example: the two occurrences of acc-swp in coord, and req-swp in swap. A preprocessing step automatically annotates them with three unique labels l_1, l_2 and l_3. Algorithm $\mathcal{W}$ infers b and C for Example 2.1; the behaviour b (simplified) is:

$$\text{spawn}\,(\beta_{coord}); \text{spawn}\,(\beta_{swap}); \text{spawn}\,(\beta_{swap})$$

In this behaviour three processes are spawned: one with a β_{coord} behaviour, and two with a β_{swap} behaviour. The behaviour associated to each of these variables is described in C, along with other constraints:

1. $\text{rec}_{\beta_{coord}}\,(\text{push}\,(l_1 : \psi_1); l_1?\alpha_1; \text{push}\,(l_2 : \psi_1); l_2?\alpha_2; l_2!\alpha_1; l_1!\alpha_2); \beta_{coord} \subseteq \beta_{coord}$
2. $\text{push}\,(l_3 : \psi_2); l_3!\text{Int}; l_3?\alpha_3 \subseteq \beta_{swap}$
3. $\overline{swap} \sim \psi_1$
4. $swap \sim \psi_2$

The above behaviour and environment are the inputs to Algorithm $\mathcal{SI}$, implementing session type inference according to the second level of our framework. The invocation $\mathcal{SI}(b, C)$ calls $\mathcal{MC}(\epsilon \vDash b,\ C,\ \epsilon)$, where the first ϵ is the empty endpoint stack Δ and the second ϵ is the empty continuation stack. Behaviour b is decomposed as $b = K[b']$, where $b' = \mathsf{spawn}\,(\beta_{coord})$ and K is the continuation $[\ ]; \mathsf{spawn}\,(\beta_{swap}); \mathsf{spawn}\,(\beta_{swap})$. The algorithm thus calls $\mathcal{MC}(\epsilon \vDash \mathsf{spawn}\,(\beta_{coord}),\ C,\ K)$, which, after replacing β_{coord} and unfolding its inner recursive behaviour becomes:

$$\mathcal{MC}\big(\epsilon \vDash \mathsf{push}\,(l_1 : \psi_1); l_1?\alpha_1; \mathsf{push}\,(l_2 : \psi_1); l_2?\alpha_2; l_2!\alpha_1; l_1!\alpha_2; \beta_{coord},\ C_1,\ \epsilon\big)$$

Here C_1 is equal to C above, with the exception of replacing Constraint 1 with the constraint $(\tau \subseteq \beta_{coord})$. Inference is now straightforward: the frame $(l_1 : \psi_1)$ is first pushed on the endpoint stack. From behaviour $l_1?\alpha_1$ the algorithm applies substitution $[\psi_1 \mapsto ?\alpha_4.\psi_4]$, where ψ_4 and α_4 are fresh, and generates constraint $(\alpha_4 \subseteq \alpha_1)$ obtaining C_2. We thus get:

$$\mathcal{MC}\big((l_1 : \psi_4) \vDash \mathsf{push}\,(l_2:?\alpha_4.\psi_4); l_2?\alpha_2; l_2!\alpha_1; l_1!\alpha_2; \beta_{coord},\ C_2,\ \epsilon\big)$$

After the next push, the endpoint stack becomes $(l_2 : ?\alpha_4.\psi_4) \cdot (l_1 : \psi_4)$. The next behaviour $l_2?\alpha_2$ causes $\mathcal{MC}$ to create constraint $(\alpha_4 \subseteq \alpha_2)$ obtaining C_3, and to consume session $?\alpha_4$ from the top frame of the endpoint stack.

$$\mathcal{MC}\big((l_2 : \psi_4) \cdot (l_1 : \psi_4) \vDash l_2!\alpha_1; l_1!\alpha_2; \beta_{coord},\ C_3,\ \epsilon\big)$$

Because of $l_2!\alpha_1$, $\mathcal{MC}$ generates $[\psi_3 \mapsto\ !\alpha_5.\psi_5]$ and $(\alpha_1 \subseteq \alpha_5)$ obtaining C_4.

$$\mathcal{MC}\big((l_2 : \psi_5) \cdot (l_1 :!\alpha_5.\psi_5) \vDash l_1!\alpha_2; \beta_{coord},\ C_4,\ \epsilon\big)$$

Since l_1 in the behaviour and l_2 at the top of the endpoint stack do not match, $\mathcal{MC}$ infers that ψ_5 must be the terminated session end. Therefore it substitutes $[\psi_5 \mapsto \mathsf{end}]$ obtaining C_5. Because of the substitutions, C_5 contains $\overline{swap} \sim\ ?\alpha_4.!\alpha_5.\mathsf{end}$. After analysing β_{swap}, $\mathcal{MC}$ produces C_6 where $swap \sim\ !\mathsf{Int}.!\alpha_6.\mathsf{end}$.

During the above execution $\mathcal{MC}$ verifies that the stack principle is respected and no endpoint label is pushed on the stack twice. Finally the algorithm calls $\mathcal{D}(C_6)$ which performs a duality check between the constraints of $\overline{swap}$ and $swap$, inferring substitution $[\alpha_4 \mapsto \mathsf{Int},\ \alpha_6 \mapsto \alpha_5]$. The accumulated constraints on type variables α give the resulting session types of the swap channel endpoints: $(\overline{swap} \sim ?\mathsf{Int}.!\mathsf{Int}.\mathsf{end})$ and $(swap \sim !\mathsf{Int}.?\mathsf{Int}.\mathsf{end})$.

7   A Proposal for Recursive Session Types

The system we have presented does not include recursive session types. Here we propose an extension to the type system with recursive types. The inference algorithm for this extension is non-trivial and we leave it to future work.

In this extension, a recursive behaviour may partially use a recursive session type and rely on the continuation behaviour to fully consume it. First we add *guarded* recursive session types: $\eta :: = \ldots \mid \mu X.\eta \mid X$. The first level of our type system remains unchanged, as it is parametric to session types, and already contains recursive functions and behaviours.

A recursive behaviour $\text{rec}_\beta \, b$ operating on an endpoint l with session type $\mu X.\eta$ may: (a) run in an infinite loop, always unfolding the session type; (b) terminate leaving l at type end; (c) terminate leaving l at type $\mu X.\eta$. Behaviour b may have multiple execution paths, some terminating, ending at τ, and some recursive, ending at a recursive call β. They all need to leave l at the same type, either end or $\mu X.\eta$; the terminating paths of b determine which of the two session types l will have after $\text{rec}_\beta \, b$. If b contains no terminating paths then we assume that l is fully consumed by $\text{rec}_\beta \, b$ and type the continuation with l at end.

To achieve this, we add a *stack environment* D in the rules of Fig. 4, which maps labels l to stacks Δ. If $\Delta_1 = (l : \mu X.\eta)$, we call an *l-path* from $\Delta_1 \vDash b_1$ any finite sequence of transitions such that $\Delta_1 \vDash b_1 \to_{C,D} \cdots \to_{C,D} \Delta_n \vDash b_n \nrightarrow_{C,D}$. A l-path is called *l-finitary* if there is no $b_i = \tau^l$ for any configuration i in the series; otherwise we say that the path is *l-recursive*. We write $(l : \mu X.\eta) \vDash b \Downarrow_{C,D}^{\text{fin}} \Delta'$ when the last configuration of all l-finitary paths from $(l : \mu X.\eta) \vDash b$ is $\Delta' \vDash \tau$. Similarly, we write $(l : \mu X.\eta) \vDash b \Downarrow_{C,D}^{\text{rec}} \Delta'$ when the last configuration of all l-recursive paths from $(l : \mu X.\eta) \vDash b$ is $\Delta' \vDash \tau^l$. When no $l-$ paths from $(l : \mu X.\eta) \vDash b$ is l-finitary, we stipulate $(l : \mu X.\eta) \vDash b \Downarrow_{C,D}^{\text{fin}} (l : \text{end})$ holds. We add the following rules to those of Fig. 4.

REC2

$$\frac{(l : \mu X.\eta) \vDash b \Downarrow_{C',D'}^{\text{fin}} \Delta' \qquad (l : \mu X.\eta) \vDash b \Downarrow_{C',D'}^{\text{rec}} \Delta'}{(l : \mu X.\eta) \cdot \Delta \vDash \text{rec}_\beta \, b \to_{C,D} \Delta' \cdot \Delta \vDash b'} \qquad \begin{array}{l} \Delta' \in \{(l : \text{end}), (l : \mu X.\eta)\} \\ C' = (C \backslash (\text{rec}_\beta \, b \subseteq \beta)) \cup (\tau^l \subseteq \beta) \\ D' = D[l \mapsto \Delta'] \end{array}$$

RCALL

$$\frac{}{(l : \mu X.\eta) \vDash \tau^l \to_{C,D} D(l) \vDash \tau}$$

UNF

$$\frac{(l : \eta[X \mapsto \mu X.\eta]) \cdot \Delta \vDash b \to_{C,D} \Delta' \vDash b'}{(l : \mu X.\eta) \cdot \Delta \vDash b \to_{C,D} \Delta' \vDash b'}$$

Rule REC2 requires that both l-finitary and l-recursive paths converge to the same stack Δ', either $(l : \text{end})$ or $(l : \mu X.\eta)$. In this rule, similarly to rule REC in Fig. 4, we replace the recursive constraint $(\text{rec}_\beta \, b \subseteq \beta)$ with $(\tau^l \subseteq \beta)$, representing a trivial recursive call of β. This guarantees that all l-paths have a finite number of states. The D environment is extended with $l \mapsto \Delta'$, used in Rule RCALL to obtain the session type of l after a recursive call. Rule UNF simply unfolds a recursive session type.

8   Related Work and Conclusions

We presented a new approach for adding binary session types to high-level programming languages, and applied it to a core of ML with session communication.

In the extended language our system checks the session protocols of interesting programs, including one where pure code calls library code with communication effects, without having to refactor the pure code (Example 2.3). Type soundness guarantees partial lock freedom, session fidelity and communication safety.

Our approach is modular, organised in two levels, the first focusing on the type system of the source language and second on typing sessions; the two levels communicate through *effects*. In the fist level we adapted and extended the work of Amtoft et al. [1] to session communication, and used it to extract the communication effect of programs. In the second level we developed a session typing discipline inspired by Castagna et al. [3]. This modular approach achieves a provably complete session inference for finite sessions without programmer annotations.

Another approach to checking session types in high-level languages is to use substructural type systems. For example, Vasconcelos et al. [18] develop such a system for a functional language with threads, and Wadler [19] presents a linear functional language with effects. Type soundness in the former guarantees session fidelity and communication safety, and in the latter also lock freedom and strong normalisation. Our system is in between these two extremes: lock freedom is guaranteed only when processes do not diverge and their requests for new sessions are met. Other systems give similar guarantees (e.g., [3,16]).

Toninho et al. [16] add session-typed communication to a functional language using a monad. Monads, similar to effects, cleanly separate session communication from the rest of the language features which, unlike effects, require parts of the program to be written in a monadic style. Pucella and Tov [13] use an indexed monad to embed session types in Haskell, however with limited endpoint delegation: delegation relies on moving capabilities, which cannot escape their static scope. Our Example 2.2 is not typable in that system because of this. In [13] session types are inferred by Haskell's type inference. However, the programmer must guide inference with expressions solely used to manipulate type structures.

Tov [17] has shown that session types can be encoded in a language with a general-purpose substructural type system. Type inference alleviates the need for typing annotations in the examples considered. Completeness of session inference relies on completeness of inference in the general language, which is not clear.

Igarashi et al. [9] propose a reconstruction algorithm for finite types in the linear π calculus. Inference is complete and requires no annotations. Padovani [11] extends this work to pairs, disjoint sums and regular recursive types.

Mezzina [10] gives an inference algorithm for session types in a calculus of services. The type system does not support recursive session types and endpoint delegation. It does allow, however to type replicated processes that only use finite session types, similar to our approach.

References

1. Amtoft, T., Nielson, H.R., Nielson, F.: Type and Effect Systems - Behaviours for Concurrency. Imperial College Press, London (1999)
2. Caires, L., Pfenning, F.: Session types as intuitionistic linear propositions. In: Gastin, P., Laroussinie, F. (eds.) CONCUR 2010. LNCS, vol. 6269, pp. 222–236. Springer, Heidelberg (2010)
3. Castagna, G., Dezani-Ciancaglini, M., Giachino, E., Padovani, L.: Foundations of session types. In: PPDP, pp. 219–230. ACM (2009)
4. Gay, S., Hole, M.: Subtyping for session types in the pi calculus. Acta Informatica **42**(2–3), 191–225 (2005)
5. Gay, S., Vasconcelos, V.: Linear type theory for asynchronous session types. J. Funct. Prog. **20**(01), 19–50 (2010)
6. Honda, K.: Types for dyadic interaction. In: Best, E. (ed.) CONCUR 1993. LNCS, vol. 715, pp. 509–523. Springer, Heidelberg (1993)
7. Honda, K., Vasconcelos, V.T., Kubo, M.: Language primitives and type discipline for structured communication-based programming. In: Hankin, C. (ed.) ESOP 1998. LNCS, vol. 1381, pp. 122–138. Springer, Heidelberg (1998)
8. Hüttel, H., Lanese, I., Vasconcelos, V., Caires, L., Carbone, M., Deniélou, P., Padovani, L., Ravara, A., Tuosto, E., Vieira, H., Zavattaro, G.: Foundations of session types and behavioural contracts. ACM Comp. Surv. (To appear)
9. Igarashi, A., Kobayashi, N.: Type reconstruction for linear π-calculus with I/O subtyping. Inf. Comput. **161**(1), 1–44 (2000)
10. Mezzina, L.G.: How to infer finite session types in a calculus of services and sessions. In: Lea, D., Zavattaro, G. (eds.) COORDINATION 2008. LNCS, vol. 5052, pp. 216–231. Springer, Heidelberg (2008)
11. Padovani, L.: Type reconstruction for the linear π-calculus with composite regular types. Logical Methods Comput. Sci. **11**(4) (2015)
12. Palsberg, J.: Type-based analysis and applications. In: PASTE, pp. 20–27. ACM (2001)
13. Pucella, R., Tov, J.A.: Haskell session types with (almost) no class. In: Haskell Symposium, pp. 25–36. ACM (2008)
14. Shivers, O.: Control-flow analysis of higher-order languages. Ph.D. thesis, CMU (1991)
15. Tofte, M., Talpin, J.: Implementation of the typed call-by-value lambda-calculus using a stack of regions. In: POPL, pp. 188–201. ACM (1994)
16. Toninho, B., Caires, L., Pfenning, F.: Higher-order processes, functions, and sessions: a monadic integration. In: Felleisen, M., Gardner, P. (eds.) ESOP 2013. LNCS, vol. 7792, pp. 350–369. Springer, Heidelberg (2013)
17. Tov, J.: Practical programming with substructural types. Ph.D. thesis, Northeastern University (2012)
18. Vasconcelos, V., Gay, S., Ravara, A.: Type checking a multithreaded functional language with session types. Theor. Computer Sci. **368**(1–2), 64–87 (2006)
19. Wadler, P.: Propositions as sessions. In: ICFP, pp. 273–286. ACM (2012)

SimAutoGen Tool: Test Vector Generation from Large Scale MATLAB/Simulink Models

Manel Tekaya[1]([✉]), Mohamed Taha Bennani[3],
Nedra Ebdelli[2], and Samir Ben Ahmed[3]

[1] TELNET Innovation Labs, University of Carthage, Tunis, Tunisia
manel.tekaya@gmail.com
[2] University of Mannouba, Manouba, Tunisia
Nedra1ebdelli@gmail.com
[3] University of Tunis El Manar, Tunis, Tunisia
Taha.Bennani@enit.rnu.tn,Samir.benahmed@fst.rnu.tn

Abstract. Safety-critical applications require complete high-coverage testing, which is not always guaranteed by model-based test generation techniques. Recently, automatic test generation by model checking has been reported to improve the efficiency of test suites over conventional test generation techniques. This study introduces our novel tool SimAutoGen, which employs the model checking technique (as a formal verification technique) to derive test vectors from Simulink models of automotive controllers according to structural coverage metrics. Model checking based on test generation is challenging for two reasons. First, the input model to the model checker requires conversion into a formal language. Second, standard tools have limited ability to generate test vectors for large-scale Simulink models because the state-space explodes with increasing model size. Our proposed SimAutoGen avoids the first problem by expressing the properties to be verified, which correspond to a structural coverage metric, in the Simulink language. To solve the state-space explosion problem, we developed a new algorithm that slices the Simulink model into hierarchical levels.

1 Motivation

Apart from providing formal verification, model checking efficiently and automatically derives test sequences from transition system models. Automatic test generation exploits the capabilities of model checkers, generating counter-examples with properties that violate the model [3]. As demonstrated by Gadhari et al. [4], the model checking technique generates test cases from models more efficiently than random generation and guided simulation. Motivated by this study, we began developing SimAutoGen three years ago. We limit our scope

This research and innovation work is conducted within a MOBIDOC thesis funded by the European Union under the PASRI project. This work is a collaboration between TELNET Innovation Labs and computer science and industrial systems laboratory.

© IFIP International Federation for Information Processing 2016
E. Albert and I. Lanese (Eds.): FORTE 2016, LNCS 9688, pp. 267–274, 2016.
DOI: 10.1007/978-3-319-39570-8_18

to Simulink models because Simulink is the most popular graphical modeling language for embedded automotive software. Several model checking approaches for test case generation from MATLAB/Simulink models have been already proposed, including AutomotGen [4], SmartTestGen [9], and SAL (which integrate the sal–atg tool for automatic test generation) [10] and the V&V Diversity platform [8]. In [5], we compared the performances of SimAutoGen, sal–atg and the SLDV test case generator. Model checkers are recognized for their flexibility and ease of use [3]. However, we identified three main problems with model checkers:

1. Test case generation with model checkers is feasible only when the available model can be handled by the model checker.
2. Model checkers are severely limited by the state-space explosion problem.
3. The properties of model checkers are usually expressed in Linear Temporal Logic or Computational Tree Logic, which differ from the language of the model.

Our tool SimAutoGen corrects these problems in the context of test vector generation from Simulink models. First, SimAutoGen does not transform the Simulink model. Second, we implement a new slicing algorithm inspired by the method described in [7], which solves the state-space explosion problem in large-scale Simulink models. Third, the properties to be verified are expressed in the Simulink language, and specified according to the criterion of the structural coverage model.

2 Structural Model Coverage Criteria

The structural coverage metric can be utilized in two ways, as a test adequacy criterion that decides whether a given test set completely or adequately complies with that criterion, or as an explicit specification for test vector selection. In the second case, the structural coverage metric behaves as a test selection criterion (a generator for white-box tests), because the model and the code generated from it are structurally similar. Thus, we can expect certain interrelations between the attained model and the code coverage. Kirner [11] discussed the preservation of code coverage at the model level. In our work, the structural coverage metrics are employed as the test selection criterion. The test vectors generated from the Simulink models by our model checking technique must conform to the structural coverage criterion. To accomplish this objective, we specify the Simulink properties for three criteria of the control flow coverage (Condition, Decision, and MC/DC), and the criterion of boundary value analysis. These four criteria are briefly described below.

1. **Condition coverage criterion**: This criterion is determined by ensuring the coverage of the Boolean inputs to the logical Simulink blocks.
2. **Branch/Decision coverage criterion**: According to this criterion, a block with conditional behavior is covered provided that all conditional behavior has been exercised at least once. For this purpose, SimAutoGen supports the following blocks: Logical Operators, Switch, MultiportSwitch, Relational Operator, and Saturation.

3. **MC/DC coverage criterion**: Chilenski [13] investigated three categories of MC/DC: Unique Cause MC/DC, Unique Cause + Masking MC/DC, and Masking MC/DC. Based on [13], we employ masking MC/DC. In masking MC/DC, a basic condition is masked if varying its value cannot affect the outcome of a decision due to structure of the decision and the value of other conditions. Masking MC/DC for logical operator blocks is described in [14]. Besides the properties, each block needs an assumption to ensure generation of the required test vector. In SimAutoGen, the masking MC/DC coverage criterion is applied to the following blocks: Logical Operators, Switch, MultiportSwitch, Relational Operator, and Saturation.

4. **Boundary value analysis**: This criterion ensures data coverage of the numeric type inputs to the mathematical Simulink blocks (Sum, Product, Division, and Subtraction).

3   Software Description

We present SimAutoGen, a tool that automatically generates test vectors from MATLAB/Simulink models [2]. Our methodology is based on model checking [6]. The main highlights of the tool, which is designed for automotive controller testing, are listed below:

1. Determines structural coverage metrics at the model level corresponding to the coverage metrics at the code level.
2. Generates test inputs by model checking, thus obtaining the model coverage criteria.
3. Does not convert the Simulink model to an intermediate formal language.
4. Specifies the test objectives (properties) as Simulink properties.
5. Avoids the state-space explosion problem during model checking by enhancing an existing solution.
6. Improves the reliability of testing, thus reducing the test phase cost of large-scale Simulink models.

The current implementation of SimAutoGen uses the model checker Prover Plug-In [12] integrated into the Simulink Design Verifier tool (SLDV) [1]. SimAutoGen is implemented in Java (Eclipse Environment) and extracts the relevant information from the Simulink models by a MATLAB script. This information is then used for test generation.

4   Software Architecture

SimAutoGen is developed in the Eclipse and MATLAB environments. The portability of SimAutoGen is ensured by the Java script. A structural overview of SimAutoGen is presented in Fig. 1.

User Interface. It is a Java Swing-based application that displays the inputs and outputs of SimAutoGen. The three inputs to SimAutoGen are (1) a Simulink

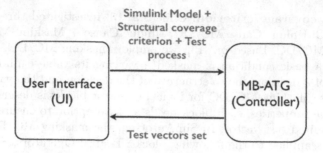

Fig. 1. SimAutoGen overview

model (a .mdl file), (2) a user-selected structural coverage criterion, and (3) a user-selected process. The three processes, Atomic testing, Unit testing, and Slicing, will be detailed in the appendix. The Atomic testing feature processes tiny Simulink models that require no slicing (i.e., single-output models). This feature is useful for a preliminary implementation testing. The Unit testing feature slices large Simulink models with two or more outputs, and is suitable for testing advanced implementations. The output of SimAutoGen is a set of test vectors or a set of slices. Slicing can be selected for purposes other than test vector generation.

Core Elements. SimAutoGen is a new approach called MB–ATG [5], whose structure is described in Fig. 2. MB–ATG is implemented in three steps. The first, second, and third steps handle large-scale Simulink models, automatic test vector generation from each slice (according to the structural coverage criterion), and integration of the test vectors generated from each slice, respectively. The second step uses the model checker Prover Plug-In and expresses the properties in the Simulink language. The property ψ and the assumption H as the model M are implemented with Simulink operators called Proof objective and Assumption, labeled P and A, respectively. Both operators are accessible through the SLDV library. In the third step, redundant test vectors are eliminated from the integration.

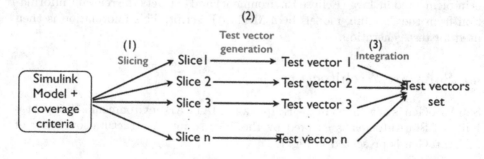

Fig. 2. Structure of MB–ATG

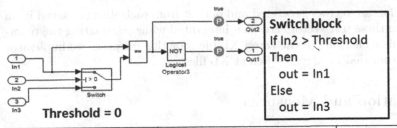

Properties	Test input specification	Test input
Test objective 1 (P1)	In2>Threshold (out = In1)	(In1,In2,In3)(0,1,0)
Test objective 2 (P2)	In2 <= Threshold (out = In3)	(In1,In2,In3)(0,0,0)

Fig. 3. Decision coverage for the Switch block

SimAutoGen implements two MB–ATG components: large-scale Simulink model slicing and test vector generation. Large-scale slicing is performed by a new slicing algorithm inspired by the static method described in [7], which constructs dependency graphs based on two dependence relations: Data Dependence and Control Dependence. The Simulink blocks Data-store/Data-read pairs and From/Goto pairs were not treated in the dependence analysis of [7] because they are not connected through explicit links; rather, they communicate remotely through implicit communication protocols (Data-store/Data-read pairs, for example). Our new algorithm models both types of links. The authors of [7] extracted the blocks corresponding to the specific slicing criterion. However, our objective is to slice the whole model into disjoint components (slices). To this end, we trialed two methods; forward slicing and backward slicing. The slicing criteria in forward slicing are the global inputs. This solution is problematic because most of the Simulink models contain Event input variables, which affect all blocks. Consequently, we adopted backward slicing, whose outputs are the slicing criteria. In particular, we compute the slices of the Simulink model by performing a backward reachability analysis and marking the relevant blocks for each output. We then remove the unmarked blocks and all empty subsystems from the model. A subsystem is a set of blocks that you replace with a single Subsystem block. The second MB–ATG component (test vector generation) has two elements: a model transformation protocol and test-vector integration. The model transformation protocol parses each slice and weaves the properties and assumptions according to the block type and the user-selected structural coverage criterion. Before the weaving of properties and assumptions, this protocol locates and calculates ψ and H insertion position. Next, it updates the location of the neighboring blocks. Finally, it weaves P and H over the Simulink model. The model transformation protocol is described in [5]. Figure 3 shows the coverage of the Switch block according to the model decision coverage, with the properties woven on it. The transformed slice is processed by the model checker Prover Plug-In. In this case, a counterexample (equivalent to a test vector) is generated. The test vectors generated and output from each slice are saved in an XL file. All of these test vectors are then integrated while eliminating the repetitive and useless elements in the saved XL file. For this purpose, we implement a new algorithm that compares different XL files.

5 Evaluation and Measures

5.1 Model Description

Our tool was evaluated on six automotive industrial models, classified as shown in Table 1. The FastCor and Detection models are large-scale models with 400–800 blocks. AirFlow and AirMPmp have two outputs and between 44 and 75 blocks. ThrAr and AirMnfld are smaller models with 40 blocks and a single output.

Table 1. Models description

Features \ Models	FastCor	Detection	AirFlow	AirMPmp	ThrAr	AirMnfld
Inputs	21	25	9	8	6	8
Blocks number	434	874	75	44	40	38
Implicit signal	12	17	0	0	0	0
Subsystems number	12	19	2	2	2	2

5.2 Output Description

Table 2 shows the slicing results of the four large-scale Simulink models described above. The two largest models, FastCor and Detection, are respectively partitioned into three and five slices, whereas both medium-sized models are divided into two slices. The model splitting decreases the average number of inputs, blocks, and subsystems per slice, thereby avoiding the state-space explosion. The number of implicit connections represents the number of hidden links between the blocks of a single slice.

Table 2. Slices description

Slices Features \ Models	Fastcor			Detection					AirFlow		AirMPmp	
Slices	S1	S2	S3	S1	S2	S3	S4	S5	S1	S2	S1	S2
Inputs number	11	20	11	8	13	13	6	13	7	6	8	8
Blocks	104	298	90	126	489	449	39	579	40	51	39	37
Implicit connections	3	5	4	3	4	4	2	4	0	0	0	0
Subsystems	7	10	10	7	9	9	2	9	2	2	2	2

Table 3. Measures related to the execution time of SimAutoGen

Measures \ Models	Fastcor	Detection	AirFlow	AirMPmp	ThrAr	AirMnfld
PST	1.247	4.070	1.073	1.015		
SST	12.892	14.983	11.383	11.003		
WT	3.354	10.14	2.467	2.279	10.661	9.543
IT	1.219	1.936	0.292	0.583		
GT	220.19	1295.009	17.952	20.514	22.134	
TV	5|13|5	8|9|10|4|8	2|2	1|1		
ITV	19	60	3	2	4	3

Table 3 shows various measures related to the execution time in milliseconds of the large- and atomic-scale models. Here, WT, IT, and GT denote the execution time of weaving, integration, and generation of all slices, respectively. The variables TV and ITV denote the number of test vectors generated per slice and the number of integrated vectors in the entire model (after removing the redundant input values), respectively. For the slicing action, we determined the parallel slicing time (PST) and sequential slicing time (SST). A comparison of the execution times of the slicing algorithm using sequential and parallel methods shows the improvement because of the use of Parallel Computing Toolbox of MATLAB. Therefore, we have used this toolbox in weaving and test vector generation processes. GT presents the execution time of counterexample generation. It shows that the model checker prover Plug-In consumes a large part of the total execution time.

References

1. Simullink Design Verifer 1: User' Guide. Mathworks, Inc (2012)
2. Getting Started Guide: R2014b. Mathworks, Inc (2014)
3. Fraser, G., Wotawa, F., Ammann, P.: Issues in using model checkers for test case generation. J. Syst. Softw. **82**(9), 1403–1418 (2009). Elsevier
4. Gadkari, A., Yeolekar, A., Suresh, J., Ramesh, S., Mohalik, S., Shashidhar, K.: Automatic test case generation from simulink/stateflow models using model checking. Softw. Test. Verification Reliab. **24**(2), 155–180 (2014). Wiley Online Library
5. Tekaya, M., Bennani, M.T., Alagui, M.A., Ben Ahmed, S.: Aspect-oriented test case generation from Matlab/Simulink models. In: Zamojski, W., Mazurkiewicz, J., Sugier, J., Walkowiak, T., Kacprzyk, J. (eds.) Theory and Engineering of Complex Systems and Dependability. AISC, vol. 365, pp. 495–504. Springer, Heidelberg (2015)
6. Clarke, E.M., Grumberg, O., Peled, D.: Model Checking. MIT Press, Cambridge (2000)
7. Reicherdt, R., Glesner, S.: Slicing MATLAB simulink models. In: 34th International conference on software engineering (ICSE), pp. 551–561. IEEE (2012)
8. Bahrami, D., Faivre, A., Lapitre, A.: DIVERSITY-TG : Automatic test case generation from Matlab/Simulink models. In: Embedded real time software and systems (2012)

9. Peranandam, P., Raviram, S., Satpathy, M., Yeolekar, A., Gadkari, A., Ramesh, S.: An integrated test generation tool for enhanced coverage of Simulink/Stateflow models. In: Design, Automation & Test in Europe Conference & Exhibition (DATE), pp. 308–311. IEEE (2012)
10. Hamon, G., De Moura, L., Rushby, J.: Automated test generation with SAL. In: CSL Technical Note, p. 15 (2005)
11. Kirner, R.: Towards preserving model coverage, structural code coverage. EURASIP J. Embedded Syst. **2006**(6), 1–15 (2009). Hindawi Publishing Corp
12. Sheeran, M.: Prover Technology - Prover plug-in documentation (2000)
13. Chilenski, J., Miller, S.P.: Applicability of modified condition/decision coverage to software testing. Softw. Eng. J. **9**(5), 193–200 (1994)
14. Rajan, A., Whalen, M., Heimdahl, M.: The effect of program and model structure on MC/DC test adequacy coverage. In: ACM/IEEE 30th International Conference on Software Engineering ICSE 2008, pp. 161–170. IEEE (2008)

Author Index

Printed in the United States
By Bookmasters